Development and Environment Studies Titles from Zed

Zed has been a leading publisher of an exceptionally innovative and wide-ranging variety of books in Development Studies. Our specific lists in this area include:

- Globalization;
- New Development Paradigms;
- Experiences of Grassroots Development;
- Studies in Structural Adjustment;
- Sustainable Development in the North;
- Environment and Development;
- Gender and Development;
- Urban Development;
- International Health Policy and Practice;
- Studies in Conflict and Violence in Society.

In addition, Zed has published a number of *key student texts* in Development Studies. Recent titles include:

John Martinussen, *Society, State and Market: A Guide to Competing Theories of Development*

Ronaldo Munck and Denis O'Hearn (eds), *Critical Development Theory: Contributions to a New Paradigm*

Majid Rahnema with Victoria Bawtree (compilers), *The Post-Development Reader*

Gilbert Rist, *The History of Development: From Western Origins to Global Faith*

Wolfgang Sachs (ed.), *The Development Dictionary*

Frans Schuurman (ed.), *Beyond the Impasse: New Directions in Development Theory*

Nalini Visvanathan, Lynn Duggan, Laurie Nisonoff and Nan Wiegersma (eds), *The Women, Gender and Development Reader*

For full details of these titles, our various Development Studies and Environment lists, as well as Zed's other subject and general catalogues, please write to: The Marketing Department, Zed Books, 7 Cynthia Street, London N1 9JF, UK or e-mail: sales@zedbooks.demon.co.uk

Visit our website at: http://www.zedbooks.demon.co.uk

Feminist Futures: Re-imagining Women, Culture and Development

edited by Kum-Kum Bhavnani, John Foran and Priya A. Kurian

Zed Books

LONDON · NEW YORK

Feminist Futures: Re-imagining Women, Culture and Development was first published by Zed Books Ltd, 7 Cynthia Street, London N1 9JF, UK and Room 400, 175 Fifth Avenue, New York, NY 10010, USA in 2003.

www.zedbooks.demon.co.uk

Cover designed by Lee Robinson/Ad Lib Designs
Set in Monotype Dante by Ewan Smith, London
Printed and bound in Malaysia

Distributed in the USA exclusively by Palgrave, a division of St Martin's Press, LLC, 175 Fifth Avenue, New York, NY 10010.

A catalogue record for this book is available from the British Library

ISBN 1 84277 028 4 cased
ISBN 1 84277 029 2 limp

Contents

Acknowledgements

We thank the Faculty of Arts and Social Sciences of the University of Waikato for the fellowship that brought Kum-Kum and John to Hamilton, New Zealand, to work with Priya on the project. The other 'home' institutions of the University of California, Santa Barbara and Smith College also have our thanks for their support of initiatives to do with women, culture and development that have informed and nurtured this volume.

Robert Molteno and Zed Books have been a pleasure to work with and we are delighted that this book appears with Zed, a publisher whose readership is best placed to engage with the ideas and arguments it generates.

Our greatest thanks are reserved for all the contributors, who bore with length constraints, endless editorial comments and repeated requests for revision (from three editors). Working so closely with this group was a pleasure as well as a privilege, and never a chore.

And a special thank you to Debashish Munshi, who generously provided inputs in the form of critical comments, editorial suggestions and more, time and again during the entire process of putting this book together.

Both Kum-Kum Bhavnani and Priya Kurian also want gratefully to acknowledge the work of John Foran. John made sure that we stayed with the publication time-line (almost), kept us on track with editing the manuscript and, most arduous of all, formated and printed the manuscript in readiness for publication. If the book took shape as quickly as it did, it is because of John's incredible organizational abilities. We have very much enjoyed working together on this project and look forward to more such projects together.

This book is dedicated:

By John, to his parents, Jack and Ramona, in one way or another strong supporters of women, of culture and of development.

By Kum-Kum, to her late mother, whose futures always included feminisms.

By John and Kum-Kum, to Cerina and Amal, already practising their reimaginings on both of us.

By Priya, to Akanksha and Alya, who remind her of our shared commitment to make the future livable, equitable and sustainable.

Notes on Contributors

Ifi Amadiume is a tenured full professor of religion and holds a joint appointment in the department of religion and the African and African American studies program at Dartmouth College, New Hampshire. Her books include *Male Daughters, Female Husbands: Gender and Sex in an African Society* (Zed, 1987) – a Choice outstanding academic award book, and on the list of Africa's 100 Best Books of the Twentieth Century; *Reinventing Africa: Matriarchy, Religion and Culture* (Zed, 1997); *Daughters of the Goddess, Daughters of Imperialism: African Women, Culture, Power and Democracy* (Zed, 2000); and with Abdullahi An-Na'im, *The Politics of Memory: Truth, Healing and Social Justice* (Zed, 2000).

Kum-Kum Bhavnani is professor of sociology, women's studies and global and international studies at the University of California, Santa Barbara. From July 2000 to July 2002 she served at Smith College, Massachusetts, as founding editor of *Meridians*, a recently established journal which focuses on feminism, 'race' and transnationalism. She has written books and articles on racism in feminist thinking, women, culture and development, feminist epistemology and critical social psychology.

Light Carruyo is in the department of sociology at Vassar College, New York. Her dissertation is titled 'Forest Politics, Gendered Subjects: Local Knowledge and the Negotiated Meanings of Development and Conservation in Rural Dominican Republic'.

Peter Chua teaches global issues in the department of sociology at San Jose State University, California, and is working on a book titled 'Condoms and Transparent Inequalities: Knowledges, Markets, and Social Change'. His broader research interests involve the interrelations of regional and global inequalities around race/ethnicity, gender, class and sexuality.

Dana Collins is assistant professor of women's studies at Georgetown University, Washington, DC. Her dissertation is titled 'Laboring Districts, Pleasuring Sites: Hospitality, "Gay" Life, and the Production of Urban Sexual Space in

Manila'. Her research interests include transnational cultural studies, sexualities, urban communities and the study of space and place.

Arturo Escobar is Kenan distinguished teaching professor of anthropology at the University of North Carolina, Chapel Hill. He is the author of *Encountering Development: The Making and Unmaking of the Third World* (Princeton, 1995), and co-editor, with Sonia E. Alvarez and Evelina Dagnino, of *Cultures of Politics/Politics of Cultures: Revisioning Latin American Social Movements* (Westview, 1998). His interests include political ecology, anthropology of development, social movements and science and technology, and he is working on a book on state, capital and social movements in the Pacific rainforest region of Colombia.

John Foran is professor of sociology at the University of California, Santa Barbara, and was visiting professor of sociology at Smith College, Massachusetts, from 2000 to 2002. His books include *Fragile Resistance: Social Transformation in Iran from 1500 to the Revolution* (Westview, 1993), *Theorizing Revolutions* (editor, Routledge, 1997), *The Future of Revolutions: Re-thinking Radical Change in an Age of Globalization* (Zed, forthcoming) and *The Origins of Revolutions in the Third World: Why a Few Succeed, Why Most Fail* (in progress). He has written on many aspects of revolutions, from race, class, gender and culture to agency, causes and outcomes.

Wendy Harcourt is director of programmes and editor of *Development* at the Society for International Development, Rome, Italy. Her books include *Feminist Perspectives on Sustainable Development* (Zed, 1994), *Power, Reproduction and Gender* (Zed, 1997), and *Women@internet: Creating New Cultures in Cyberspace* (Zed, 1999); her essays focus on gender and development, alternative economics, environment, sustainable livelihoods, reproductive health and rights, culture and globalization.

Linda Klouzal is in the department of sociology, University of California, Santa Barbara, where her dissertation in progress is titled 'Revolution First-hand: Women's Accounts of the Cuban Insurrection'. Her scholarly interests include revolutions, women and development, social psychology and emotions.

Rachel Simon Kumar teaches development studies at the University of Auckland, New Zealand. Her doctorate on reproductive health and development policy in India is being rewritten as a book manuscript. She has worked as consultant researcher and development trainer in India and South-east Asia, and is a part-time lecturer in women's studies. Her current research interests include issues in gender and development, reproductive health, policy analysis, and discourses of development and citizenship. She has published in international journals on issues in gender and development.

Priya Kurian teaches environmental politics, public policy and media and politics, in the department of political science and public policy at the University of Waikato, New Zealand. She is the author of *Engendering the Environment? Gender in the World Bank's Environmental Policies* (Ashgate, 2000) and the co-editor, with Robert Bartlett and Madhu Malik, of *International Organizations and Environmental Policy* (Greenwood, 1995). Her research interests lie in the intersections of gender, environmental policy, globalization and sustainability, within the larger matrix of development.

Ming-yan Lai has taught in the foreign languages and literatures department and women's studies at Purdue University, Indiana, and has published articles on gender and cultural studies in East Asia, which have appeared in *Genders, Cultural Critique, Peace and Change* and *NWSA Journal*. She is completing a book manuscript on nativist constructions of modernity and their gender politics in contemporary China and Taiwan.

Amy Lind is assistant professor of women's studies at Arizona State University. Her book-length manuscript, tentatively titled 'Development Engendered: Women's Movements and the Cultural Politics of Neoliberalism in the Andes', addresses the gendered, racialized and heteronormative dimensions of development theories, practices and politics in Ecuador, Bolivia and Peru. She has published articles on this topic in numerous anthologies and in such journals as *World Development, Latin American Perspectives* and the *Journal of Developing Societies*.

David McKie is professor of management communication at the University of Waikato, New Zealand, and in 2002 was visiting professor at Southern New Hampshire University in New England. He formerly taught in the UK and Australia. He has co-authored, with Tom Jagtenberg, *Eco-impacts and the Greening of Postmodernity: New Maps for Communication Studies, Cultural Studies, and Sociology* (Sage, 1997) and has published widely on communication, futures, media, policy and globalization, public relations and virtual reality. He is currently co-writing three books: one on business creativity, a second on diversity management and a third on management communication.

Minoo Moallem is an associate professor and chair of women's studies at San Francisco State University. She is co-editor, with Caren Kaplan and Norma Alarcon, of *Between Woman and Nation: Nationalisms, Transnational Feminisms and the State* (Duke University Press, 1999). She is currently working on a book entitled *Between Warrior Brother and Veiled Sister: Islamic Fundamentalism and the Cultural Politics of Patriarchy* (University of California, forthcoming). Trained as a sociologist, she writes on transnational feminist theory, gender and fundamentalism, globalization and Iranian cultural politics and diasporas.

Debashish Munshi teaches management communication at the University of Waikato, New Zealand. A journalist-turned-academic, his research projects lie in the intersections of media, management, politics and culture with a special emphasis on issues of gender and diversity. Apart from over 500 signed articles for newspapers and magazines, his scholarly work has been published in major academic journals in the USA and Australasia. He is currently working on two co-authored book projects, one on decolonizing diversity management, the other on management communication.

Maria Ofelia Navarrete is a former guerrilla combatant in El Salvador. Now active in Salvadoran politics, she was elected to the National Assembly in 1997 as a deputy for the left-wing FMLN party and is the subject of the documentary, *Maria's Story*.

Jan Nederveen Pieterse is professor of sociology at the University of Illinois, Urbana-Champaign. He is the author of *Development Theory: Deconstructions/Reconstructions* (Sage, 2001); *White on Black: Images of Africa and Blacks in Western Popular Culture* (Yale, 1992); *Empire and Emancipation* (Praeger, 1989 and Pluto, 1990); and editor or co-editor of *Christianity and Hegemony* (Berg, 1992); *Emancipations, Modern and Postmodern* (Sage, 1992); *The Decolonization of Imagination* (Zed, 1995 and Oxford, 1997); *World Orders in the Making: Humanitarian Intervention and Beyond* (Macmillan and St Martin's, 1998); *Global Futures: Shaping Globalization* (Zed, 2000); and *Globalization and Social Movements* (Palgrave, 2001).

Anjali Prabhu received her PhD from Duke University in 1999 and is currently assistant professor of French and Francophone studies at Wellesley College, Massachusetts. She is completing a book that is provisionally entitled 'Against Creolization? A Postcolonial Reading of Hybridity through Métissage and Critical History'. Recent publications include forthcoming articles in *Studies in Twentieth-Century Literature* and *Research in African Literatures*.

Raka Ray is associate professor of sociology and South and South-east Asian studies at the University of California, Berkeley. She is the author of *Fields of Protest: Women's Movements in India* (Minnesota, 1999; Kali for Women, 2000), and articles on topics from gender and feminist theory to Third World social movements and relations between dominant and subaltern groups in India in such journals as *Annual Review of Sociology* and *Feminist Studies*. Her current project explores changes in the meanings and relations of servitude in India.

Jessica Share is a graduate student in the department of women's studies at the University of Iowa. Her dissertation research is in the area of sexuality and activist communities.

Julia Shayne is an assistant professor of sociology and women's studies at Emory University. Her research interests include the gender of revolution, Latin American feminisms, development and resistance in the Third World. She is currently working on a book titled '"The Revolution Question": Feminism in Cuba, Chile, and El Salvador Compared (1952–1999)'.

Banu Subramaniam is an assistant professor in the women's studies programme at the University of Massachusetts, Amherst. She is co-editor with Moralee Mayberry and Lisa Weasal of *A New Generation of Feminist Science Studies: Adventures Across Natures and Cultures* (Routledge, 2001). She works on the intersections of gender, race, colonialism and science and is particularly interested in translating frameworks from the feminist and cultural studies of science into experimental practice in the sciences.

Anna Tsing is professor of anthropology at the University of California, Santa Cruz. She is the author of *In the Realm of the Diamond Queen: Marginality in an Out-of-the-Way Place* (Princeton, 1993) and co-editor, with Paul Greenough, of *Nature in the Global South: Environmental Projects in South and Southeast Asia* (Duke, forthcoming). Her current research focuses on environmental dilemmas and mobilizations in Indonesia.

Yvonne Underhill-Sem is a Pacific feminist population and development geographer whose PhD dissertation was a feminist post-structuralist analysis of maternities in population geography. She continues to publish in this area, recently contributing a chapter on childbearing in Wanigela, Oro Province, Papua New Guinea to a forthcoming book on *Geographies of Women's Health*. She has been a lecturer in Papua New Guinea and New Zealand as well as an independent scholar for several years. She is now working at the Africa, Caribbean, Pacific Group of States (ACP) in Brussels where she is part of a new team responsible for integrating humanitarian and social issues into economic agendas. She has been involved with DAWN (Development Alternatives for Women for a New Era) for several years as Pacific Regional Coordinator and more recently as Joint Coordinator (with Ewa Charkiewicz) for DAWN's Sustainable Livelihoods theme.

Luisa Valenzuela is an Argentine fiction writer who spent more than ten years in New York teaching in the writing division, first at Columbia University and then at New York University. She is the author of a number of novels and stories, including *Strange Things Happen Here* (1979), *The Lizard's Tail* (1983), *He Who Searches* (1987), *Bedside Manners* (1995) and *Black Novel with Argentines* (1992/2002). In 2001 she published a novel, *La Traviesa*, and a collection of essays on writing, language and women, *Peligrosas Palabras*. She currently lives in Buenos Aires where she is a columnist for *La Nación*.

Darcie Vandegrift is assistant professor of sociology at the University of Wisconsin at Whitewater. Her work examines cultural processes of development and community resistances to social inequality in Costa Rica. She is currently working on a book manuscript, tentatively titled 'Paradise Under Development: Social Inequality and Memory in a Costa Rican Caribbean Tourist Economy'.

Abbreviations

BJP	Bharatiya Janata Party
DAWN	Development Alternatives with Women for a New Era
EIA	Environmental Impact Assessment
FGM	Female genital mutilation
FMLN	Frente Farabundo Marti di Liberacion Nacional
GAD	Gender and Development
GALF	Grupo de Auto-Conciencia de Lesbianas Feministas
GE	Genetic engineering
GRB	Gendered Revolutionary Bridge
GoI	Government of India
ICPD	International Conference for Population and Development
ICT	Information and Communication Technology
ILGA	International Lesbian and Gay Association
IGLHRC	International Gay and Lesbian Human Rights Commission
IMF	International Monetary Fund
Kabalikat	*Kabalikat Ng Pamilyang Pilipino* (Working in Partnership with Filipino Families for Better Health)
LGBT	Lesbian/gay/bisexual/transgender
MCH	Mother and Child Health
NEP	New Economic Policies
NGO	Non-governmental organization
PCD	Christian Democratic Party
PCN	Party of National Reconciliation
PCP	Partido Comunista del Peru
PCS	Proyecto Contra el Sida
RCH	Reproductive and Child Health Policy
SEWA	Self-Employed Women's Association
SETI	Scientific Search for Extraterrestrial Intelligence
SSP	Sardar Sarovar Project
UNDP	United Nations Development Programme
USAID	United States Agency for International Development
UTC	Union of Peasant Workers

WAD	Women and Development
WCD	Women, Culture and Development
WCH	Women and Child Health
WID	Women in Development
WRPE	Women's Role in a Planned Economy
WTO	World Trade Organization

CHAPTER I

. . . .

An Introduction to Women, Culture and Development

Kum-Kum Bhavnani, John Foran
and Priya A. Kurian

§ AT the close of the twentieth century, there were clear indications that women in the Third World and the poor suffered the dire consequence of global (mal)development. This debilitating malaise continues into the new century. Its most recent symptoms include: the attack on the World Trade Center in New York on 11 September 2001; the US-initiated war on Afghanistan shortly thereafter; the use of the discourse of terrorism by the governments of India and Pakistan that threatens to spill over into a nuclear stand-off; the continued Israeli occupation of the West Bank that regularly escalates the cycle of violence; the US government's targeting of Iraq, Iran and North Korea as an 'axis of evil'; the Enron débâcle, in which a large US transnational corporation went bankrupt despite making millions of dollars for its chief officers through, among other things, the provision of expensive electricity for parts of India and investments in China. These examples continue to dominate public discussion, while the crises of HIV/AIDS, the impact of (and resistance to) IMF- and World Bank-directed structural adjustment policies, and the consequences of environmental destruction worldwide seem to have receded from public view. It is in this context that we feel an urgent need to reflect on development, culture and women.

In reading the outpouring of opinion from the left and among liberals urging progressives to think more deeply about the events of 11 September, often circulated on e-mail or posted on the internet,[1] it becomes quite clear that missing in these responses to the attacks on the World Trade Center is a recognition that there is torment and strife in many parts of the world – that the attacks on the US need to be seen in the root context of global (mal)-development, with particular implications for women and culture. Indeed, we believe that a misplaced emphasis on modernization strategies for the past half century is central to understanding why development has not led to a greater decrease in inequality between Third and First Worlds. In other words, development has failed the Third World.[2] Although many explanations have been advanced, this failure is exacerbated by the end of the Cold War and the rise of projects of globalization, bringing with them an increasingly feminized poverty, an alarming process of environmental degradation and extremely elusive conditions for peace and security. What is less often recognized (although sometimes acknowledged in a sub-clause, phrase or equivocal foot-note) is that women's contributions and a regard for culture are key elements in a meaningful development that aims to improve living conditions of all poor people in the South.[3]

Women in the Third World face multiple challenges, among them poverty, unemployment, limited access to land, legal and social discrimination in many forms, sexual abuse and other forms of violence. Though similar in form to those faced by women in the First World, there are specificities of history, political economy and culture that make these realities differentially oppressive and exploitative for Third World women (see Amadiume 2000). But the women of the Third World are not victims. As 'subaltern counterpublics' (see Fraser 1997a), women in the Third World meet these challenges and confront them actively, often in remarkably creative and effective ways. In other words, there is far more to their lives than a set of interlocking 'problems' – there are many deeply fulfilling experiences, powerful emotions, beautiful creations and enduring relationships, sometimes born through struggles waged against the terms of existence. As Light Carruyo puts it in this volume: for WCD, develop-ment is not 'something that is "done to" the Third World; instead, there is an acknowledgement that Third World actors, elite and non-elite, male and female, organized and not organized, contribute to the construction of the discourse and practice of development'.

The purpose of our book is therefore to assess the situation of women across many sites in the Third World in order to elaborate a fresh vantage point that relies on aspects of both earlier and more recent approaches (such as Sen and Grown 1987, Mohanty 1991, Tsing 1993, Braidotti et al. 1994, Marchand 1995, Snyder and Tadesse 1995, Ong 1997, Fagan, Munck and Nadasen 1997, Marchand and Runyan 2000, and Bergeron 2001, among many others) and at the same time suggest a new lens through which to look at women in the Third World and the ways women resist and celebrate the circumstances of their lives. We are certainly not proposing something no-one else has done before – we are merely trying to focus attention on and give a term and platform to an emerging approach that we think is a way forward out of the impasse in development studies. This volume represents an effort to suggest the shape of a new paradigm for development studies, one that puts women at its centre, culture on a par with political economy, and keeps a focus on critical practices, pedagogies and movements for social justice.

It has been argued that work within development studies has shifted from an emphasis on political economy to now include area studies and environmental studies, along with a greater interest in gender relations (Hoogvelt 1997). However, despite this shift, overly structural and economistic approaches to development predominate, as espoused by international aid agencies such as the World Bank. The 1992 World Bank Report argued that 'Women must not be regarded as mere recipients of public support. They are, first and foremost, economic agents' (World Bank 1992: 60). The Bank's stated commitment to women's participation in economic development is a fundamental part of its neoliberal strategy for improving economic productivity (see World Bank 1994), involving the embodiment of Third World poor women as able workers and entrepreneurs while ignoring their other roles as wives, partners, mothers, citizens and activists – roles that form the backbone of all societies, but which are difficult to discern, let alone comprehend, within conventional economic analyses. As such, the World Bank has not been able to engage with the actual realities of people's lives, including gendered realities. For example, women plantation workers in Sri Lanka not only pick tea leaves, but they also have to organize their paid work in relation to their daily domestic responsibilities such as feeding the household. This responsibility can mean, therefore, that it is the husbands who have to collect the daily wages for the women's work. These are paid at just the time when cooking tasks have to begin, with a consequent lack of control by the women over their wages. Patterns such as this demonstrate how the economic agency of women is layered by a complex set of realities.

Most recently, globalization, transnationalization and internationalization are posing important issues for scholarly debates as well as for activists' practices, yet these terms often ignore the ways in which interdisciplinary thinking – and here we explicitly include work in the humanities – can contribute to an understanding of the present social and cultural conjuncture. We note that the adjective 'global' usually centres on the First World (Western Europe, North America, Australia and New Zealand), thereby continuing to privilege the First World even as it analyses global relationships, which turns the analytic gaze away from the Third World and the agency of people living in it. Our book aims to rectify that bias by placing Third World women firmly at the centre of inquiry. Even as we do this, we are aware that the 'Third World' denotes a heterogeneous set of places, cultures and societies. Yet, in centring Third World women, we intend also to participate in debates over the desirability of bringing together many diverse experiences under one rubric, just as the categories 'woman' (Butler 1997a, Halberstam 1998) and 'Third World' do.

For some time now, there has been considerable discussion about the gendered dynamics of development (e.g. Boserup 1970, Benería and Sen 1981,

Tinker 1990, Kabeer 1994, Porter and Judd 1999). These discussions are essential to our argument. However, we offer this volume to demonstrate what could happen when Third World women are placed at the centre of development and global processes. This not only transforms the projects of development, along with their underlying discourses of modernization, but, in addition, starts to make culture(s) visible. For example, in her study of the migration of Filipinas as servants/labourers, Parreñas (2001) shows the centrality of community and family, alongside the nation-state and the labour market, for understanding the textures of the women's lives. That is, in order to engage with gender, as distinct from merely acknowledging its presence, it is necessary to discuss culture.

However, simply attending to gender in an explicit manner is not enough. It is here that Raymond Williams's famous notion of 'culture' as lived experience is helpful. Williams argues for an understanding of culture not simply as a set of habits or traditions, but as a way to comprehend how people actually live their lives – a 'structure of feelings'. In other words, culture as lived experience insists on an agentic notion of human beings and is thus understood as a dynamic set of relationships through which inequalities are created and challenged, rather than as a singular property that resides within an individual, group or nation (Williams 1960; see Hall et al. 1980 for a further development of this argument). We do this in counterpoint to the structuralism of much of the 'cultural turn' in social theory, which is often devoid of agency, subjectivity, consciousness or emotion. A 'structure of feeling' is meant to denote the blend of pattern and agency we feel should characterize cultural analysis.

WID, WAD, GAD ... WCD

There is a rich history of theoretical, applied and policy work on how best to tackle the relationship between women and development studies. This is now discussed almost canonically as the progression from WID to WAD to GAD (Rathgeber 1990, Moser 1993, Razavi and Miller 1995). Boserup's 1970 work – considered an early example of an academic, policy-oriented book that noted women's exclusion from development projects in the Third World – was taken seriously partly because the development community began to realize that the 'trickle down' approach to development had not been effective (Braidotti et al. 1994). Boserup's work is often taken as signalling the origins of the Women in Development (WID) approach by pointing to women's invisibility and exclusion from development (Moser 1993). WID was a way of 'mainstreaming' women (Martinussen 1997: 305) through arguing that they should be treated on equal terms with men – the 'equity approach' that gained ground in the 1970s. WID then shifted its underlying discourse from equity to anti-poverty to efficiency in the mid-1980s. The anti-poverty discourse *going on Rai's ideas?*

complemented the 1970s' 'basic needs' approach to development, whose solutions included income-generation strategies and skill development for women (Moser 1993). The discourse of efficiency, which developed in the 1980s, resting on WID assumptions, argued that development would become more efficient if women's resources were utilized to the full; in this way women's participation in the economy and gender equity were seen to be synonymous, a view which the World Bank and Eastern Bloc shared, with no small irony. While it stressed income generation and skills training, this way of viewing the relationship between development and women differed from the anti-poverty discourse: the former targeted women in order to increase their efficiency in the productive process, and thus promote economic growth through an efficient use of women's labour (Gardner and Lewis 1996, Braidotti et al. 1994).

WID / part = gender eq.

Meanwhile, by the second half of the 1970s, the Women and Development (WAD) approach, theoretically informed by Marxist-feminism (Rathgeber 1990), raised some critical questions about the WID paradigm. WAD argued that as women's contributions have always been central to any possibility of development, the question to be asked was why women were excluded from projects of development. Consequently, the WAD approach focused not only on the integration of women into development and the simultaneous transformation of mainstream development, but also on the dependence of Third World nations on the richer nations. As expressed in the work of Development Alternatives with Women for a New Era (DAWN), and developed by Sen and Grown (1987), the self-organization of women is a key facet of WAD analysis and practice.

always central – why ex clu

The Gender and Development (GAD) approach is presently the discourse used by most scholars, policy planners, the World Bank and the International Monetary Fund to discuss the relationship between development processes and women's inequality. GAD aims to 'not only integrate women into development, but [to] look for the potential in development initiatives to transform unequal social/gender relations and to empower women' (Canadian Council for International Co-Operation 1991: 5). However, aid agencies and development practitioners tend to use the concept of gender in reductionist ways, failing to grapple with issues of power, conflict, and the larger social, cultural and political contexts that frame women's ability to resist conditions of oppression. Indeed, the use of narrow, rigid understandings of gender, despite their seeming focus on the inequality generated within notions of masculinity and femininity, can lead to an over-emphasis on structures and institutions at the expense of seeing the agency of women, an agency that may not just perpetuate inequalities but also challenge them. To our minds, 'woman' is more able than 'gender' to connote agency while simultaneously implying the need for centring gendered analyses.

empower

All three approaches, we feel, fall short of a larger analysis of the ways in which capitalism, patriarchy and race/ethnicity shape and are shaped by women's subordination and oppression. For example, Rai argues that the WID and GAD literature 'largely continue to work within a liberal framework' (2002: 45), a framework that often homogenizes Third World women. It is also argued that WID and GAD make ethnocentric assumptions about the content of relations between women and men in different societies, 'seeing only exploitation, subordination and conflict, [rather than] co-operation and the importance of familial bonds' (Gardner and Lewis 1996: 124).

While we are sympathetic to these critiques of WID, WAD and GAD (as well as indebted to the many contributions of each), we also fault all three for not taking culture adequately into account. Even when they draw, to differing extents, upon culture as a means of discussing women's oppression, they also tend to see Third World women as victims in need of rescuing from their cultures, assumed to be static and unchanging. To approach culture as lived experience rather than as a static set of relationships permits an opening of new avenues for development, because a lived experience approach to culture centres the relationship between production and reproduction and ensures that women's agency is visible (see Chua, Bhavnani and Foran 2000). The work included in this book links women, culture and development in a new and innovative way.[4] Such a linkage is located at the intersection of three cutting-edge interdisciplinary areas in the academic world: feminist studies, cultural studies and critical development studies (or, more generally, Third World studies).

Feminist studies in both the humanities and social sciences has suggested that analytic/critical work and policies are impoverished if adequate attention is not paid to women. Feminist scholarship in the USA, along with analyses of gender and sexuality, has started to grapple with the implications of the widely accepted argument that 'woman' is not a unitary category. But such an engagement still implicitly foregrounds US and European feminist studies, has a modernizing impulse and thus bypasses the diverse writings, cultural products and other regional and global actions of women in the Third World.

Cultural studies has directed attention to the importance of analysing cultures within their context – both locally and globally. It follows Williams and others to argue that cultures may be conceptualized as more than the habits, customs and mores of particular societies. However, the approaches found in cultural studies, although drawn upon by feminist scholars in the USA, are rarely utilized to provide insights into specific aspects of societies in the Third World. The newer approach of a Third World cultural studies, encompassing as it does a broad range of perspectives including post-colonial studies, subaltern studies and Third World postmodernism, begins to move in the direction we have in mind (see Foran 2000). But it still needs to take on insights that integrate gender, sexuality and ethnicity in a biospheric context into analyses of culture, the economy and politics (Escobar 1995 is a landmark on this point).

Third World/development studies is an area of inquiry that resists being incorporated in a singular way into the projects of globalization. Although development studies has centred on the Third World, its analyses tend to be driven by economistic policy considerations, which generally locate women and culture as peripheral to a central project of increasing the gross domestic product of Third World nation-states. Third World studies typically draws on the insights of social science and historical schools such as dependency, world-system theory and modes of production analysis to argue that global and international processes need to be seen *in situ*, with a focus on the countries of the South. However, the labour, cultures and histories of women are rarely taken into account within either Third World or development studies, or, when they are addressed, most often treat women merely as victims in a system of cruel and unjust inequalities. In other words, these paradigms either deny women agency, or do not attend to the relationship between Third World women's participation in the private and public domains simultaneously.

Thus, both development and Third World studies have reached an impasse in their assessment of future prospects for the Third World, due to their failure to see the centrality of women and the significance of culture. Development and Third World studies have been further limited by their systematic marginalization of concerns of environmental sustainability that have far-reaching implications for poor rural Third World women (see Agarwal 1998, Kurian and Munshi 1999, Kurian 2000a and, in the practical sphere, Wangari Maathai, who started the Green Belt movement in Kenya in 1977).[5] The environment, in fact, has been marginalized in development discourse through the very techniques mobilized against women in androcentric theorizing (Jagtenberg and McKie 1997). This volume therefore argues for a shift in development theory and practice to envision a development project that is democratic, empowering of non-elites and environmentally sustainable.

Women, Culture, Development: Three Visions

Kum-Kum Bhavnani A WCD approach takes as central that production and reproduction cannot be separated in the lives of most women. I draw on a Marxist notion of production,[6] further developed by Juliet Mitchell (1971), to define productive activity as activity that creates surplus value. However, as is now often commented on but still not always grappled with, women's productive activity is intimately related to their reproductive activity, including social reproduction. That is, women all around the world are usually expected to be in jobs where the necessary skills (and limitations) for 'women's work' are derived from ideological notions of women's abilities as well as from the work of women that contributes to household needs, the raising of children, cooking food and so on – what many have referred to as the 'double shift'. Even when women work as builders and labourers, where the job is not evidently related to stereotypes of women's fragility and lack of strength, the paid work that is done outside the home is in intimate relationship with the work that is done inside the home. Despite the actual tangle of production and (social) reproduction in women's lives, in line with Eli Zaretsky's (1976) argument, it is evident that the rise of capitalism in the nineteenth century forced a sharp split between the spheres of the public and the private, or the domains of production and reproduction, a split that means that reproductive activity is less visible in most discussions of productive activity. The invisibility of social reproduction in such discussions may explain why so many dimensions of women's lives are missing from non-feminist discussions of production, or within development studies generally.

A WCD approach, to my mind, begins from a position that women's lives are a glorious tangle of production and reproduction, not only impossible, but also undesirable, to untangle totally. Undesirable, because such a disentangling would imply a neat separation between production and reproduction, which would imply that women's (and men's) lives are much tidier than they actually are. Given that it is harder to see the differing elements that configure women's lives, a WCD approach (in the sense that we are advocating) affords the possibility of a more complex view on the ingredients in this tangle.

In drawing on culture as lived experience, a WCD lens brings women's agency into the foreground (side by side with, and within, the cultural, social, political and economic domains) as a means for understanding how inequalities are challenged and reproduced. In integrating production with reproduction alongside women's agency, a WCD approach can interrogate issues of ethnicity, gender, religion, sexuality and livelihood simultaneously, thereby providing a nuanced examination of social processes. Through a WCD lens, ethnicity, religion, age and sexualities, in addition to class and gender, become aspects of women's lives that cannot be omitted from any analysis or practice. A WCD perspective argues that to speak of 'culture' simultaneously with development encompasses more poignantly the everyday experience, practice, ideology and politics of Third World women, and thus may provide clearer ideas for a transformative development, and a development that attends to aspects of people's lives beyond the economic.

Bina Agarwal's work demonstrates, for example, that in order to create a transformative approach to development, it is necessary to make land rights a central issue for rural women in the Third World, and not to focus only on skills training and related intervention strategies. She argues that rethinking rural women's land rights enhances their status *vis-à-vis* men, thus causing a shift in gender relations. Further, she 'illustrates how women's control over economic resources is crucially mediated by non-economic factors' (Agarwal 1995: 264). It is these non-economic factors that are particular to a WCD approach, for they are capable of retaining the economic as a key means of grappling with the subordination of poor women in the Third World, while not privileging the economic above other aspects of people's everyday lives. Culture is brought into the discussion because it provides a non-economistic, yet still partly material, way to produce knowledge and to present different strategies for making struggle and achieving social change.

To discuss the integration of production with reproduction and to foreground women's agency in achieving change can appear to be a rather abstract project. Let me therefore describe three organizations – the Self-Employed Women's Association (SEWA), the Women's Group of Xapuri, Brazil, and Tostan: Against Female Genital Mutilation in Senegal – that provide instances of such an integration.

SEWA was founded in 1971 as a trade union for women working in the informal sector in Ahmedabad, Gujarat, India. Once this was set up, the women were joined by vegetable sellers who were being harassed as they tried to sell their goods in the marketplace, by Muslim women who stitched quilts in the home and were agricultural workers, and by women who had been victimized when asking for legal wages in the tobacco-processing plants (Rose 1992). SEWA took the issue of the harassment of the vegetable sellers to the Indian Supreme Court, which ruled that the women had a right, as workers in the informal sector, to have a separate place to sell their goods. Since that success, SEWA has set up a bank for microcredit (with each of its members as a shareholder), provided child care and access to health care for its members as well as literacy and other skill development classes. The organization, considered by many to be a role model, also advises women on how best to create co-operatives (M. A. Singamma Sreenivasan Foundation 1993), and has over 220,000 members, 362 producer groups and 72 co-operatives (Srinivas 1997). The main theme uniting these activities is empowerment for poor women (Bhowmik and Jhabvala 1996).

Women's relationship to the environment has been widely discussed (see, *inter alia*, Dankelman and Davidson 1988, Shiva 1988, Jackson 1993, Mies and Shiva 1993, Agarwal 1998 and Kurian 2000a), although comparatively little has been written about women's role in defending forests in Brazil (Campbell 1995). While the tragically murdered rubber-tappers' union president, Chico Mendes, is well known for having mobilized local populations to prevent clearing of the forests in the state of Acre, very little scholarly work has attended to the women of Xapuri who were part of that union (Campbell 1995 is an exception), even though almost two-thirds of the women in Acre have tapped for rubber at least once (Kainer and Duryea 1992, cited in

Campbell 1995) and women rubber-tappers have been active in defence of the forest. As a result of working together on demonstrations (*empates*) to protect the forest, the women set up the Xapuri Women's Group in 1987. The group has been meeting since then to support women's rights, provide literacy and skills education, and to challenge domestic violence.

Female genital mutilation (FGM) affects between eight and ten million women and girls per year in Africa (Sarkis 1995). It is also an issue that leads to heated discussions about cultural practices and their role in the subordination of women, and calls to change such practices. The practice is protested by local and international women's organizations on the grounds of health concerns for women (the cutting is often conducted in unsanitary conditions and the women's sexual health is also at risk), as the violation of a woman's basic human right to enjoy sexual relations and as a form of institutionalized violence against women (Doorbenoo 1994, Kassindja and Bashir 1998). FGM was confirmed as being legally permissible in Egypt in June 1997 (*New York Times*, 26 June 1997). As a result of the protests of women across the world, by January 1999 the practice was banned in Burkina Faso, the Central African Republic, Djibouti, Guinea, Senegal and Togo and was being challenged by women in Kenya and the Sudan. Tostan is a non-governmental organization (NGO) in Senegal that has worked with rural peoples for some time in a basic education programme (Melching 2001). In 1996, some of the women who had come together through Tostan established the 'Malicounda Commitment', a series of pledges that FGM should cease (Mackie 1998). Tostan spearheaded a widespread grassroots opposition to FGM and the practice was declared illegal by the Senegalese government in January 1999 (*New York Times*, 18 January 1999).

Each of these organizations can be considered an example of development, for each works in a planned manner to achieve social, economic, political and cultural change. Yet none of the organizations privileges the economic above other domains and all, at least implicitly, work with a notion of culture as lived experience. I consider them examples of WCD because:

- they have been initiated by women for women (in contrast to, for example, the Grameen Bank which was set up by an academic male economist to help poor women obtain credit and thus may be seen more accurately as being part of a 'rescue' narrative for Third World women);
- they explicitly attend to the relationship between production and reproduction in women's lives;
- they represent diverse forms of meaningful agency for social change.

Each of the organizations integrates all three elements of WCD to create new ideas about development, focusing on one particular aspect of women's lives, and using this to fashion imaginative links to other dimensions of social life.

John Foran In trying to articulate a sense of what 'women, culture and development' can mean as an approach to *real* Third World development and positive social change, I think in terms that are both autobiographical and theoretical. As a graduate student in the late 1970s, new to sociology but immersed in such social theories as existential Marxism, I happily came to awareness of the rich and varied political struggles going on in Latin America, the Middle East and elsewhere in the Third World, and made these my field of study. After initially embarking on a master's thesis on the Allende years in Chile (from which I had to turn away as the depth of the tragedy worked its way into my soul), I found the project that would preoccupy me for the decade of the 1980s – a study of the causes of the Iranian revolution. This meant an encounter with theories about revolutions, most influentially Theda Skocpol's ambitious structural interpretation of the French, Russian and Chinese revolutions, where she famously intoned: 'Revolutions are not made; they come' (1979: 17). As this went against my own theoretical and political instincts, I set about trying to show how people had made the revolution in Iran. To do this, I had to think through how political economic structures – themselves greatly but not solely shaped by the West in a process of dependent development – were challenged by the actions of social groups. The key to this puzzle for me gradually crystallized into the notion of 'political cultures of resistance' – the various ways that people creatively draw on experience, emotions, subjectivity, sedimented traditions and ideological refashionings to make sense of political and economic exclusion and to mobilize themselves and others in revolutionary struggles (Foran 1993, 1997a).

I now had two legs of the triangle that would become WCD a decade later, at the end of the 1990s. In the intervening period, I spent a lot of time comparing the causes of revolution in Iran with other Third World cases – first Nicaragua and El Salvador, then Mexico and Cuba and eventually a set of almost two dozen cases (Foran 1997). In trying to understand better how coalitions formed and fragmented, I necessarily became aware of the contributions of feminists and scholars of race and ethnicity to the complex discussions then going on about the intersections of race, class and gender, eventually coming to replace the term 'intersection' with 'interconnection', since identity is not the mathematical addition of essentialized categories, but rather the social relationships among them, relationships that are subject to shifts and changes in various ways (Foran 2001; the insight here is taken from Bhavnani 1997).

What WCD can be rests on an assessment of the vast potential of creatively combining (in many possible ways, as this introduction and our book as a whole attest) the three fields of critical development studies, feminist studies and cultural studies. Each needs the others to see its own blind spots. Each can contribute an angle of vision that is indispensable for breaking out of the impasse of the crisis of development. From critical development studies I have learned that Third World development, in its many times and places, is inescapably shaped by the unequal encounter of national projects with powerful 'external' actors. The work where this insight originally touched me remains in my view one of the most nuanced treatments of the issue: Fernando Henrique Cardoso and Enzo Faletto's *Dependency and Development in Latin America* (1979, originally published in Spanish in 1969), to which I owe the concept of dependent development.

Out of the many variants of cultural studies that have influenced me – from the original English contributions of Raymond Williams, E. P. Thompson and later Stuart Hall, to subaltern studies, post-colonial studies and Latin American postmodernism – I have come to think of a distinctive (if broad) field called Third World cultural studies, where the woven threads of lived experience, subjectivity, agency, dreams and visions underline the centrality and embeddedness of culture in everyday life.[7] A specifically Third World cultural studies represents a political approach to culture, and a cultural approach to politics, focusing on how political cultures and discourses circulate and compete – features that are not *intrinsic* to Third World cultural studies, yet which seem in my view to happen here more often than in what we might term First World cultural studies, let alone the conventional 'sociology of culture' approaches in the USA.

From the long and evolving traditions of feminist interventions into development studies – the genealogy of WID, WAD and GAD that for us leads to WCD – come the strands that most appealed to me, most powerfully the work of DAWN and Gita Sen and Caren Grown's 1987 classic, *Development, Crises, and Alternative Visions*, with its brilliant demonstrations of the links that can be made when poor women are put at the centre of analysis, links that run from ecology and subsistence to patriarchal militarism and neoliberal structural adjustment.

My vision of WCD, then, is one where analysis can move flexibly between political economic macrostructures and local discourses and practices (see Freeman 2001 and Bergeron 2001 and the many works they cite for a similar approach). It would be one where scholars can centre the activities and struggles of Third World women, learning from their great variety and seeking to articulate paths to the dialogue that must precede any wider unity across lines of race, sex and world, and where Third World actors are neither victims nor heroes (see Jameson 2000), but play leading parts in the struggle against globalization from above. Indeed, development studies should confront and appropriate globalization – not the other way around – forging alliances with cultural and feminist studies. This kind of scholarship and analysis (for it is not carried out only in the academic world), to which many people are already contributing, is not new, as we have made plain already, but deserves a name, for which I see no better term at present than Women, Culture and Development.

Priya Kurian The chants of the women activists protesting against the damming of the mighty Narmada river in western India echo in my ears as I think about my understandings of women, culture and development. It was in mapping the environmental impact assessment processes of a gigantic, World Bank-funded power and irrigation development project, the Sardar Sarovar Project (SSP) in the Narmada Valley (Kurian 1995, 2000a), that I first started to seriously explore the interweavings of feminist studies, cultural studies and development studies.

In hearkening back briefly to the academic genealogy of my graduate studies in a US university, it is not entirely clear when my separate, parallel immersions in environmental policy, women's studies and Third World development studies started to come together. The tenuous connections I had begun to make theoretically between these three areas – environment–gender–development – became sharper and more focused when I started fieldwork in India. A fourth element came in with fieldwork: the significance of culture. How these elements interact, respond to one another, and shape our understandings and practices of development and environmental policy are explored in my book on the World Bank's environmental policies (Kurian 2000a). Yet the question of how we conceptualize and give meaning to the highly contested terms of 'women', 'culture' and 'development' remains. How do we theorize a WCD approach that takes as its political project the centrality of rural Third World women – themselves a diverse, heterogeneous group – in the process of development? The suggestions below draw on my ongoing research, and as such are offered as one small part of the larger puzzle that we can draw on to inform our desire for better development.

A first step in thinking of a WCD approach is to get away from the reductive understanding of culture that permeates much of the mainstream development literature. The assumptions of a linear development process of moving from the primitive to the modern characterizes much of the WID, WAD and GAD schools of thought (although there is much indeed that we have otherwise learned from them). The homogeneous Third World woman in this literature is best depicted as being in the grip of 'culture', defined narrowly as oppressive traditions. Yet, as I discovered in my study of the implementation of environmental impact assessment (EIA),[8] cultural values and practices need to be written into the EIA process to make the goal of environmental sustainability a possibility. Far from confining indigenous and rural communities to museums, as charged by development officials and elites, recognizing the centrality of culture – defined broadly as the lived experiences, and material and emotional contexts that form the fabric of people's lives – is a significant part of making EIA meaningful in the Third World context. In other words, EIA processes will necessarily have to respond and adapt to the cultural specificities of local contexts, including recognizing the significance of indigenous knowledges, in order to be effective and meaningful.

A second issue that a WCD approach needs to acknowledge is an understanding of culture as not merely an embodiment of the lived experiences of people, but as ideas, norms and values that also suffuse the concepts of environment, development and, more specifically, science and technology. Researching and writing about the SSP reinforced for me not only the centrality of environment in the study of development, but also the key insight that ideas about the environment are deeply contested cultural concepts. Both human and non-human nature are affected by global, market-based economic, political and cultural systems that help tie ecologically marginalized places to vulnerable and marginalized people (see Plumwood 1998). Development that is not tied to a notion of creating ecologically rational and socially just societies has material implications for women in the Third World and for the way they come to terms with culturally defined notions of sustainable livelihoods. It is clear that struggles over resources in the Third World are shaped not only by material forces and political power, but also by the ideologies and understandings of what is meant by the environment. Differing notions about environment between those supportive and those opposed to the SSP, for example, continue to drive the ongoing struggle in the Narmada Valley.

A third issue that a WCD approach needs to grapple with is ways of acknowledging the power and place of gendered values and ideologies in conjunction with the centrality given to women. Recognizing women as pivotal to sound development, in other words, is not to say that an analysis of gender can be done away with. Thus, if gender is understood as reflected in the worldviews and ideologies of individuals and institutions, in the distribution and control over knowledge and resources, and in the practices and control of bureaucracies, then my gender analysis of the World Bank revealed the deeply masculine bias that permeates EIA theory and practice, a bias that has profound implications for Third World women. This is not, however, to argue for an idea of gender as a coherent core – it is opening up such seemingly coherent categories of women and gender that will allow us to re-vision a development project that enables and affirms women's agency. Indeed, an equally critical element of WCD is that it makes explicit the need to theorize women's agency in a larger context of often, but not always, oppressive structures. It allows us to ask: What are the political, social, emotional and economic conditions that make resistances possible?

Finally, WCD makes explicit the urgency of addressing the imbalances in our accounting of economic and cultural conditions that frame Third World women's existence. If development studies and the social sciences have been characterized by an over-emphasis on economistic approaches, then, as Anjali Prabhu argues in this volume, literary studies have too often ignored the economic in their focus on the 'purely' cultural. This recognition of the interweaving of culture and economics comes into play when we examine the phenomenon of technolust that drives the proponents of information and communication technologies (ICTs) and biotechnologies.

The explosion of computer and Internet technologies, inextricably intertwined with the biotechnological revolution, has huge implications for the Third World and specifically for its women. In the new frontiers of exploitation, indigenous knowledges, as much as the biophysical environment (including especially the gene pool) of Third World nations, form the capital to be extracted and commodified for (primarily) First World consumption. A WCD approach would help to explore the ways in which Third World grassroots activists and peoples respond to these new forms of colonization and exploitation. How do we work for development that empowers local peoples, provides local access and control over technologies, and keeps the process of social transformation in local hands?

In studying development projects involving ICTs in India, Australia and New Zealand, similar tensions are evident between what cyberspace can and should do. But it seems clear that ICTs, used sensitively and appropriately, could be a tool for women's empowerment (see Visions essays by Munshi and Kurian and Escobar and Harcourt in this volume). Indeed, answering the questions I raise above calls for a nuanced approach of gendering and enculturating technologies, shaped to local contexts, that may well embody what I call a 'Women, Culture and Development' approach.

In this volume we map some of the links that exist among feminist studies, cultural studies and development studies as well as attempt to sketch in new ones. One goal of the Women, Culture and Development approach is to ensure that political economy is not privileged above culture, but, rather, that the two are seen as operating simultaneously and in synchrony. Thus, the contributors to the volume analyse the complex ways in which culture – in all its myriad forms – both shapes and is shaped by the term 'woman' and is created by women across the Third World. We also interrogate the way in which the use of culture(s) permits the expression of alternative, sustainable and empowering forms of development, a term whose purpose we define as 'well-being' and creativity in all domains of life. In this way, the chapters do not simply identify the theoretical and practical limitations of the three areas of study discussed above, but specify some of the links among women, culture and development to create a new, interdisciplinary framework that both alters the intellectual identities of each element and uncovers linkages across areas routinely defined as distant from each other.

While we have three sections in the book – sexuality and the gendered body, environment/technology/science, and cultural politics of representation, along with a series of Visions essays – we also see the chapters as approaches to the three interdisciplinary areas we discussed earlier in this introduction: critical development studies, Third World feminist studies and Third World cultural studies. The volume opens with three Visions essays – by Maria Navarrette, Luisa Valenzuela and Anna Tsing – which suggest particular possibilities for a WCD approach. Luisa Valenzuela's emphasis, as befits a writer of hauntingly lyrical fiction, is on language: 'a language made of the loudest silence. Made of courage. Made of memory.' This complements Anna Tsing's 'cautionary narrative' to 'consider the problem of privatization', and both harmonize well with 'Maria's Stories' of guerrilla warfare and revolution, democratic parliamentary struggle and vision of a feminist future. The themes and topics they address are echoed in the writings that follow.

Critical development studies Amy Lind and Jessica Share's chapter provides a glimpse of how to think about queering critical development studies through a WCD lens. That is, their focus on how heterosexuality is 'institutionalized, naturalized and regulated' within conventional ideas of development, and their critique of the link between sexual identity and national and financial well-being focuses on and enriches our understanding of both gender and women as well as of culture in development studies. Similarly, Ming-yan Lai and David McKie, working with fictional narratives, suggest possibilities for a critical development studies such that, as the latter puts it, 'space, time and even gender itself can be imagined very differently from contemporary physical and social constrictions'. David McKie's desire to present his argument through a discussion of speculative fiction and 'non-linear developments', by 'connecting seemingly unrelated developments through narratives to build more imaginative and integrated frameworks', tellingly exemplifies what the three of us see as fundamental for a WCD perspective, namely, that the imagining of non-linear futures ensures 'multiple, gendered topographies of tomorrow'.

Ming-yan Lai is especially effective in showing that culture, and representations of development dilemmas in literature, reveal much about the underlying social realities of development, and not always in a straightforward way where gender is concerned. The contradictions of Taiwan's masculinist, anti-imperialist nationalist literature are thus shown to be efforts to keep women in their marginal places even when centring women in a critique of Western/Japanese domination. The implication of the analysis is that anti-imperialist (and by extension anti-globalization) struggles must be feminist as well as anti-capitalist if they are to have a chance of success. Collectively, these three essays offer possibilities for reimagining a critical development studies that has gender and sexuality embedded within it, that is attentive to cultural productions from science fiction to nationalist discourses, and that makes the key links with the domains of the political and economic.

Alternative directions for a critical development studies are also present in the Visions essays by Raka Ray, Dana Collins, Linda Klouzal and Darcie Vandegrift. Ray's critique of 'basic needs', forcing questions about what type of society is being imagined, pairs well with Dana Collins's desire that the WCD paradigm actively engage with the contradictory linkages between resistance, pleasure and possibility in imagining future societies. Linda Klouzal's proposal that any analysis of development and, thus, any possibility for a critical development studies would work better with greater insights into suffering and trauma is also echoed in Darcie Vandegrift's aptly titled 'Seeing the Complexity', which calls for a new politics, a dreaming for the future out of what she calls the 'psychic legacies' (Vandegrift 2001) of the past.

Critical feminist studies Earlier in this discussion we argued for a critical feminist studies alongside a critical development studies. Anjali Prabhu's essay on *So Long a Letter*, in which she reads a literary text in the context of her own view of WCD, asks 'Can we then assume that a woman writing automatically remedies the masculinist tendencies of nationalist discourse?' While Prabhu is sceptical of any automatic ascription of 'radical' to women's writings, she points out that 'the feminist nationalist rhetoric concerning development and modernity … is destabilized through the uprooting procedure by which the female narrator appropriates it'. In this way she provides an opening for a critical feminist studies where she asks readers to consider the implications of gender as performative for the 'women' in WCD. What, she asks provocatively, can 'agency' mean in this context?

Critical feminist studies is also a key theme in the chapters by Ifi Amadiume, Priya Kurian and Debashish Munshi, and Minoo Moallem. Ifi Amadiume, in looking at African matriarchitarianism and Mammy Water, questions the modernizing impulse that underlies much feminist scholarship – 'feminism and these traditions of organized women's empowering cultures' are not mutually exclusive, she argues – by asking readers to reflect on the wide array of 'sexist policies of the patriarchal colonial state' that shape and are shaped by 'the place of the isolated individual female in a collective women's world', and by reflecting on the heritage of Igbo women, which 'includes solidarity and resistance strategies that have enabled mass mobilization by African women'.

The call for a critical feminist studies to engage with colonialism, as well as the relation between tradition and modernity and individualistic subjectivities in the contemporary capitalist world, is taken in an innovative direction by Priya Kurian and Debashish Munshi in their essay on 'Negotiating Human–Nature Boundaries'. Starting from an overdue recognition of the interdependence of the non-human and human worlds, they explore 'the need for more fluid and more porous boundaries – within the constraints of ecological and social rationality – through an examination of the place of science and knowledge in development'. Travelling through narratives of anthropocentrism in development, how these hinder ecological and social rationality, and the relationship between these and genetic engineering, Kurian and Munshi show that the tension between activism and their own argument 'underscores the urgency of feminist interventions'. Thus, they suggest questions for considering how a WCD approach could transform development studies while simultaneously transforming projects of development.

Minoo Moallem's essay may be thought of as a reflection on critical feminist studies, for she argues that feminist transnational and post-colonial studies, as well as gender and sexuality studies, have offered central contributions 'in understanding revolution both as a social event and as a discourse'. In her investigation of the *mostaz'af* (the disempowered), Moallem demonstrates how the power of the *mostaz'af* lies 'in its capacity to bring together ... the local and the global into the same frame of reference'. She shows how culture is mobilized in revolutions, not always for progressive purposes, and how it can undermine authoritarian regimes, especially when filtered through gendered images of the daily lives of women and children in the contexts of poverty and survival. Thus, her essay demonstrates how the nation can be 'done' and 'undone' at the same time.

The Visions essays by Peter Chua and Julia Shayne also capture a spirit present in our optimism about critical feminist studies. Shayne draws inspiration for WCD-informed revolutionary development projects from Latin American feminists who are revolutionaries, for they remind us 'that women have been organizing, shaping and redirecting projects as national in scope as revolutions for decades'. Chua, in focusing on education, intriguingly suggests that the links among condoms, democratic education practices and current knowledge institutions could 'provide genuine democratic resources for a journey of hope for many women living in the Third World'.

Cultural studies The essays by Banu Subramaniam, Yvonne Underhill-Sem and Rachel Simon Kumar provide examples of how cultural studies could be further developed through an engagement with events and issues specific to the Third World. In her discussion of science and religion, Banu Subramaniam focuses on the 'nature of their intersection within the landscapes of contemporary Indian politics'. By exploring how ancient traditions have come to be repackaged as modern, material science in a period of 'archaic modernity', illustrated in naming India's nuclear bomb 'Shakti', Subramaniam exposes the ruling Bharatiya Janata Party's (BJP) eager embrace of a Western science which 'extends its hegemonic hand to stabilize the Hindu nation' and how

Vaastushastra, the ancient science of architecture, has shaped public space as an amalgam of science, technology, religion and capitalism. She closes with the challenge of linking pedagogy and practice: 'How do we intervene in our theories and practices to incorporate this new reality, these seemingly contradictory and conflicting realities across the world? How do we find new ways of thinking about these issues and teaching them? We must find alternatives to the theories we currently have, alternatives that wrestle with the oxymoronic imagery of this archaic modernity.'

Space is also key to Yvonne Underhill-Sem's look at what she terms the smaller-scale tragedies that occur in out-of-the-way places to illuminate new ways of thinking about bodies in development studies. In a conflict centred on the claims of two women to a share of the royalties stemming from a logging operation in the close-knit community of Wanigela, Papua New Guinea, she skilfully shows how the women's bodies became the focus of discontent, thereby contributing to the sexual embodiment of development studies by directing closer attention to the bodies closest in, 'so that the collective "bodies" out there cannot be so easily overlooked'.

Rachel Simon Kumar's study of the role of the state in directing the rationales of development with respect to women's reproductive identities reminds readers of how important an analysis of the state remains in cultural studies. In reviewing the ambivalence of the Indian state's nationalist (and simultaneously neoliberal) discourse that 'constructed women as emblems of national culture and tradition', she elegantly shows the mechanisms by which the state defines its obligation to women's health, thus laying open the particularities of the 'intimacy between politics, cultural ideologies and development'.

Both the Visions essays by Jan Nederveen Pieterse and Light Carruyo discuss empowerment in the context of development studies by drawing on methods derived from cultural studies. Nederveen Pieterse discusses how empowerment – as a word, concept and discourse – might be reclaimed for an alternative development, while Carruyo's work on tourism, development and forestry in the Dominican Republic does the same for the term 'development' itself, critiquing its genealogy but also recasting it in a positive call for an 'alliance model' among many actors engaged in a grassroots pedagogy of development, as well as suggesting the alternative term 'sustainable well-being'. These political resemantizations are continued in the conversation by Arturo Escobar and Wendy Harcourt and the essay by Debashish Munshi and Priya Kurian reflecting on ICTs and utopias. The former makes links among utopias, development and ICTs and the latter write about the possibility of creating a network of empowered women 'netizens' who could knit a community-oriented net of knowledge.

Nets and webs, utopias, representation, sexuality, the state, political economy: these are all specific examples of areas that a WCD perspective might include and they all come together in John Foran's Visions essay, 'Alternatives to Development: Of Love, Dreams and Revolution', closing the volume on the note of hope we wish WCD might provide for feminist futures.

In conclusion, we see the WCD project as one of support for scholarship that breaks out of the impasse of development studies, and as a ground for resistance to globalization-from-above development and organizing for social transformation. We envision feminist futures worthy of real development and vibrant cultural diversity. In the words of the global justice movement, we believe that another world is possible. And we would like to see scholars engaged in development, feminist and cultural studies crossing the boundaries that separate them from each other and from activists, especially those located in the Third World – both women and men.

Notes

1. The US-based Social Science Research Council has constructed a large archive of valuable analyses at its web site: www.ssrc.org. Other important websites include: http://www.pitt.edu/~ttwiss/irtf/Alternative.html; http://www.commondreams.org; http://AlterNet.org; and http://www.indymedia.org

2. In the knowledge that the concept is controversial, we still prefer the term 'Third World' to refer to the geographical areas we would like to include in this volume – Africa, Asia (excluding Japan), Latin America and the Middle East. We see a need for careful genealogical work on the best available terms – Third World and global South – as a basis for further creative thinking on alternatives to both. One striking term for discussion, coined by one of our contributors, Anna Tsing, and adopted here by Yvonne Underhill-Sem, is 'out-of-the-way places'.

3. See Escobar (1995) for a historical discussion of the notion of development.

4. Our approach in this work, it should be noted, is highly distinct from the 1995 book *Women, Culture and Development*, edited by Martha Nussbaum and Jonathan Glover, where the editors focus on lending credence to a 'critical universal[ist]' position on the question of 'women's functioning'. While sympathetic to and supportive of Amartya Sen's 'capabilities approach' that seeks to redefine development in terms of the quality of life, we believe that it is fruitless to establish a universalist position on women's lives that is somehow outside culture. Our volume also differs radically from Nussbaum and Glover in that we reject the assumed equation of culture with tradition, with traditions, themselves, being cast as oppressive (Nussbaum and Glover 1995: 4). For two other works with titles suggestive of our own, see Marchand and Parpart (1995) and Perry and Schenck (2001).

5. See, however, Braidotti et al.'s (1994) discussion of the theme of 'Women, Environment and Sustainable Development' (WED) as a part of their overview of the evolution of development studies.

6. 'Whatever the social form of the production process, it has to be continuous, it must periodically repeat the same phases. A society can no more cease to produce than it can cease to consume. When viewed, therefore, as a connected whole, and in the constant flux of its incessant renewal, every social process of production is at the same time a process of reproduction' (Marx, *Capital*, volume I, chapter 23, cited in Bottomore et al. 1983: 417).

7. Peter Chua has characterized the perspective in the following terms: 'Third World cultural studies explores what culture is in all aspects of life, what we mean by it, what we do with it, and its unique political and historical relations with the "Third World." It analyses and politicizes the ways in which making sense of all parts of the world and of our place as individuals, groups, communities, and nations within it are cultural processes. It examines how cultural meanings are transmitted and considers how the selection and interpretation of cultural messages are essential to the process through which our identities are constructed' (cited in Foran 2000).

8. EIA, first introduced as a practice for government in the United States in 1969 and now used by many governments and international aid agencies, seeks to analyse predictable impacts of projects, programmes or plans on the environment.

VISIONS I

· · · · · · · · · · ·

Maria's Stories

Maria Ofelia Navarrete

Editor's Preface

The following is the result of an interview with, and a remarkable film about, Maria Ofelia Navarrete, a Salvadoran activist. The interview was conducted by John Foran, who also edited it, in Northampton, Massachusetts in March 2001, on the occasion of the 'At the Meridians' conference organized by Kum-Kum Bhavnani, where Maria was a keynote speaker. Senait Kassahun and Danielle-Simone Vacarr translated at the interview, and the resulting text was transcribed and translated by Danielle-Simone Vacarr. It was translated into Spanish by Jose Oscar Garcia of the Centro de Intercambio y Solidaridad in El Salvador for Maria to finalize; Leslie Schuld at CIS facilitated communication with Maria. My warmest thanks to all four.

The film *Maria's Story* was produced in 1990 by Pamela Cohen and Catherine M. Ryan, and directed by Monona Wali and Pamela Cohen, who have generously allowed the editor to quote extensively from it. He has interwoven passages from the film with the interview to tell Maria's story in two different periods. Co-produced with Channel 4 in Britain, the film was shown nationally on public television in the United States. All extracts spoken by Maria and dating from 1988 are italicized. They therefore applied to specific scenes and contexts that may not be the same as presented here.

With the permission of the filmmakers and Maria, the editor has taken the liberty of arranging the materials into sections. The reader can therefore identify what was said by Maria in 1988 and in 2001. Together, the extracts provide insight into the history and vision of a revolutionary activist in two distinct periods, one in the midst of a revolution and one afterwards. The editors feel that the author's life and work eloquently embody the themes of Women, Culture and Development in the context of revolutionary struggles under diverse and difficult conditions.

Early Years: 'I was a peasant, born of a widow … '

I was a peasant, born of a widow on 31 March 1950, the ninth of ten children. *My mother did laundry. And she grew corn, sorghum and beans just to get by. You can't imagine how hungry we were. When I went to school, all the parents bought desks for the kids. But how could my mother afford this when it cost ten pesos? All the way through sixth grade I had to ask permission to stand beside those who had desks. And when there were exams, I took them sitting on the floor.* As you can imagine, my life had many limitations; we had very few economic resources, which obliged me at nine years old to start working as a servant in a house – that was how time ran until I was about 15 years old when I married a peasant from my village. *Jose came to me, said he wanted me to marry him, that he would put me through school. Look how bad he was, he knew that school was the most important thing to me. He told me, 'If you marry me, I'll put you through school.' 'You're lying,' I told him. I was a peasant, wife of a peasant farmer. I did housework, grind, iron, wash, sew … go to mass! But this life allowed me to see many unjust things. The poor are always forgotten, and all their possibilities limited, some people with absolutely nothing. So this inequality and poverty is what made me decide to lead this life.*

I want to bring you back a little and tell you about the house that I worked in at age nine. The son of my boss was politically active and every day he would listen to a programme on Radio Havana called 'Voices of the Revolution' – all about the Cuban revolution. That was really my introduction to politics, the first time I really heard about it. I was just a servant; he put the radio on and I just had to listen while I worked.

So that is where I heard my first political ideas: taking care of the poor, and other idealistic intentions, it makes you feel good. I became a youth activist in the Christian Democratic Party (PCD) for which my boss was the mayoral candidate. At night we'd go out and paint slogans and put up propaganda, it was a great thing. In 1972 we won the presidential elections with the engineer José Napoleon Duarte, but with the help of the North American ambassador the military decided to give power to the PCN (the right-wing/army Party of National Conciliation) candidate, Colonel Arturo Molina. It was a shameless fraud, and everyone knew it was fraud, but what could one do, as it was legitimized by the United States?

So around that time a number of popular organizations started sprouting up and in 1977 I enrolled in one of them, the UTC, the Union of Peasant Workers. We were well organized throughout the country and had formed an alliance with other Christian peasant organizations. *The demands of the UTC were that they give us food on the plantations during the coffee and sugar harvests, and that they raise our wages. But just to stop and say, 'Please give us a spoonful of beans and a tortilla', they threw the National Guard on us. The government kept increasing the repression. First they beat us. Then they selectively captured and killed*

*people. Some were involved in politics, but others weren't. The army went after
everyone. In the invasions, the military operations, the civilian population was always
a target. They pursued us to the death, and those they caught they killed. It was an
indiscriminate massacre.*

In 1979 there was a *coup d'état* staged by the militia. It was a time of
unbearable repression. There were some progressive elements present in the
new cabinet, but they disappeared under the military repression. After the
coup we were left with an unstable country. The United States saw this and
decided it would be good to put Duarte in power. They took him out of exile
in Venezuela and put him in office. The Americans saw Duarte as the perfect
candidate to lead a counter-insurgency. In 1982 they created some false elections
to make it look real and of course he won. The right wing managed to
recompose itself and give birth to a new political party, ARENA (Republican
National Alliance), offspring of the PCN, to fight Communism. They had a
large army of death squads to enforce and impose repression.

By the time of the 1979 coup I was an activist in a powerful popular
movement of workers, teachers, students, Christians and others called the
Popular Revolutionary Bloc (BPR). Also to be remembered was our archbishop
– Oscar Arnulfo Romero – who accompanied us in our struggle, he was our
voice. He was the only one to publicly denounce the repression of the
dominant classes over the people. First they offered him money to live like a
king if he would keep his mouth shut. He refused. Then they threatened to
kill him and still he showed no fear. I'm sure he must have been scared, but
his conscience proved stronger than his fear and he kept on denouncing them
until his assassination by a death squad while celebrating mass in March 1980.
By then there was an entire social movement of Christians under the guiding
ideas of liberation theology.

In 1979, two military operations took place in my village of Arcatao. One
came on the second of February when we were celebrating the day of the
Virgen de la Candelaria. We were all gathered for the celebration when about
400 soldiers stormed the village. *We couldn't leave the house or they'd kill us. We
started to sing in our hammocks and open the doors so as not to let on that we were
afraid.* They took some people, tortured others. In August, another military
operation occurred. And on the ninth of September I finally had to leave my
house like so many others before me. *All of us – Minita was only three years old,
Morena nine, Ceci a bit older.*[1] *We carried Minita on our backs – I never lived in a
house again. I fled from my house escaping from the military and I never returned.*

The War Years: 'I fled from my house and I never returned ...'

I never returned. First I went to a little village in Honduras. My village
shares a border with Honduras. After 15 days I received notice from a Hon-

duran official that I must leave the country immediately because someone had told them that a number of Salvadorans had taken refuge there. Some of us went to another village high atop a mountain range. The territory belonged to El Salvador, and was actually in my municipality, but we thought that it was so high up we could remain there relatively guarded and safe.

I lived in the hills with my family for over a decade. The hardest thing was just learning to survive. No food, no shelter, nothing. Sometimes just eating roots and berries. We were always on the run. I don't remember the exact date but it was somewhere in November of 1979. *The guerrillas, the FMLN, were living in the hills, too. We helped and protected each other.* We didn't really know much about them, we only heard of their activities. In the mountains arrived a guerrilla fighter or a number of them to incorporate us to help the guerrilla movement. And that's where we became guerrillas. *When they say you're converted to the side of the guerrillas, it's not true that you're forced to sign up. No, it was the daily necessities of our lives that made us work together.* The principal reason was because we had an enemy that wouldn't allow us to go to our own homes and whose punishment was death. This offered us the possibility to fight back and not allow ourselves to be killed. If they were to kill us, we needed to learn to defend ourselves. We took this step with the mentality of self-defence. Along with the need to defend ourselves, was the ideal of constructing a society of brotherhood where we loved one another, where there was justice. Others had kept running, but we were determined to persevere, we had the inspiration of creating an equal society, a new society.

But every time we got a little something together, the army came in and destroyed everything. Finally I thought, 'Well, if this is war, let's really fight back.' So in 1980 I joined the FMLN. If someone would have told me [in 1979] that one day I would be sitting and planning military strategy, or even carrying a gun, I would never have believed it. But just to survive I've learned to do so many things I never imagined I could do. Look, if you adopt the armed struggle it's because you have no other choice. It's not because it's the most wonderful thing in the world. It's that love of life is instinctive, even animals have it. So, when you see the possibility of saving your life, you save it. And if that means picking up a gun, you pick it up! The government accused us of being Communists, terrorists and subversives, but look at the people who were fighting – young boys, young girls, old women like me! This war was a problem of people who didn't get enough to eat. It was a problem of not having a roof over your head, and not having justice.

In 1981 the guerrilla leaders proposed the possibility of a military offensive. We didn't even have arms, only a strong morale. I participated as a combatant in the attack of Chalatenango on 10–11 January and they didn't kill us. They [were] full of weapons, and also fear. And us, without arms, but full of valour. After this military offensive, which was at a national level, the battle lines were drawn. There was a large civilian population that was unhappy.

Some were discontented with the regime, but the large majority lived in constant fear of the repression on and near the front lines. We discussed the need to organize their activities. I was put in charge of the organization of the civil population.

That's when we started to get really organized. The previous year practically no one even had enough to eat, so we began to teach the people that despite the fact that we were at war we needed to plant and grow food. Small groups were formed to begin the production of the most elemental necessities. The first were the secretariats of production and security: we had to produce food to stay alive and to protect ourselves so that we wouldn't be killed. We organized so we would have schools, health care and farming.

With the passage of time new necessities began to surface, for example the need to organize a secretariat of health. We also realized that we could no longer permit so many children to join because being at war they weren't learning to read, so we created both the secretariat of health and of education. They were in their early fundamental stages. They were born of pure necessity. So we pushed forth with our literacy programme, enlisting those who knew how to read to teach those who didn't. We did all this with the clear awareness that we were forging a battle in which armed struggle played the principal role.

So that is how we went along developing these tiny organisms. But we began to realize the need for a larger organization to unite and oversee all of the smaller organizations. In September of 1983 I was elected president of all these smaller organizations. The first president of the cabinet of the entire region, the region of Chalatenango. Here in this office [at the 2001 interview] we are conducting a little conversation, but our work back then was an enormous undertaking. We had to direct the entire civil population. We had to make warriors of everyday citizens. And as I was elected president of this new movement, they decided to incorporate me into the leadership of the overall revolutionary movement. So I joined the general revolutionary leadership.

There was a Jesuit priest, Rafael Moreno, now he lives in Mexico because he's Mexican, but he was with us for 25 years. We informed him of what we needed and he took care of it. He was like our ambassador at the United Nations and at one point he even denounced the government for their actions against us. Thanks to the struggle of everyone, and his commitment, in May of 1985 we succeeded in getting the UN to sign an accord which read: 'The civil population, even though it offers food and support to the guerrilla fighters of the FMLN, as long as they refrain from taking up arms, maintains its character of civil population. As such their lives and welfare should be respected.' It was two lines, that's all the text said.

With these two lines we finally had something to work with. We worked to make it a reality. The civilian population in the battle lines were the target of our enemies. They were sought out with the intention of killing them, children, horses, women, everyone. We did win something at the UN, but it was one thing to win it at the table, in theory, another to win it in the battlefields. If we had left well enough alone, we would have lost all we had gained. So we organized an entire movement around protecting this accord and making it reality. First of all we ensured that the organizations would accompany and support the civil population. We began to explain to the citizens that they needed to stay in their homes and fight for their land and their rights and we sought out support for them in the churches and NGOs. When the army arrived they captured some and murdered others, but finally the people started fighting back and the army came under international ridicule. We managed to help many stay legally in their homes of origin.

The Peace: 'It's been quite a job to readjust our way of thinking ...'

During the war, it filled me with joy to know that these communities so poor and suffering, now protected by the FMLN, had great harvests and they didn't have to pay rent for the land. It made me so happy to see how humble peasants who never used to raise their heads except to see the next row they're going to plough, now sat and discussed, who's going to teach class next year, and that they had to build a clinic. It was a wonderful thing: we were building a new society where the poor would have, basically, food, schools and health care. Those are the three most basic needs that a government can provide.

After the war, we had quite a job to readjust our thinking and strategies for struggle, and I don't think that we have succeeded yet, even eight or nine years after the signing of the peace accords. I have an idea to propose in some of these communities that we have organized. I'm going to see if it works next month in the general assembly, because what used to be called the social movement, the directors of the movement have turned into almost little NGOs and we all know that NGOs have one function and social movements have another. If we allow our social movement to turn into an NGO it will tame the activists – 'I receive a salary and this work permits me this salary so I hope everything works out, but if not, I'm still going to get paid.' A social movement cannot think like that; if it does, we are lost. This 'well, if it works, it works, and if it doesn't, too bad' – NO, we have to distinguish between the two. Social movements are what give life to development because they are rooted in everyday sentiments about basic needs and the ingenuity to obtain them as we move along: 'I'm not content with such and such a thing, I propose that we do such and such a thing' and everyone gets to speak and together we change things. This is the function of a social movement, while the function of NGOs is more to do technical things. Social movements can't be NGOs.

I didn't know too much then, I still don't know all that much, but at the

Problems of Development

time I knew nothing of the inner workings of the state economy. I knew about human beings. Then I knew nothing of the World Bank or other institutions like it. I'm going to tell you what I think now after all this time; in our country the government's economic model is trying to take us to the same level as the developed nations. This will never happen, we are not a developed country. But as long as this is the desire of the four richest families in the country, those in charge, this is the direction our government will take. But in doing so, in trying so hard to leap ahead, they are committing horrible atrocities upon the majority of the population. We're struggling to make cutting-edge advances in technology when a large part of the population still can't read. There exists a great inequality when men can still hit their wives, when women still don't have access to a decent job, or to a dignified life. Our government is failing us. It has an exclusive vision that only serves the richest four families and excludes millions and millions.

I only know what I've lived and experienced. In serving in the national assembly [from 1997 to 2000] I grew to learn a lot about public politics at a national level. I think that the left, or better said, the revolutionary movement, needs to participate in a current analysis of the world situation, because I think that the methods, or some of the methods – these ideas we have stuck in our heads – need to be changed. We must break with them if we intend to achieve any real change. I can be on the left, spend 30 years in parliament and not see any changes for the people, so I think we need to raise people's consciousness and together we must put pressure on the political parties to make real changes. For instance, we can't have the people believing in a movement that in all reality never intends to take power, one who once they get there say, 'Oh no, we're not prepared, no, no we can't do this.' If we're going to tell them to fight they better be fighting for something real, we better be prepared to take power and have the abilities and capacity to do so. I say all this because just recently during the latest earthquake, an economist friend of mine, a member of the FMLN, went on TV and proposed a plan of national reconstruction. His plan proposed to instal a socialist model at the national level. As I see it, this isn't okay. First of all because it's not rational or objective: I can't call this glass of water I'm holding milk – it's not milk, it's water. We can't go telling the people that we're going to build a socialist model if we don't have the proper conditions to do so. That's just a lie to get them hooked, to inspire them. Don't misunderstand me, there's nothing wrong with socialism, socialism is great, but we've got to be realistic here. We must fight, we must fight to have our voices heard over those four rich families. We need to have a plan of reconstruction that takes into account that we are a deforested nation, a nation with earthquakes and volcanoes, a nation in which the majority of the people are illiterate, a nation in need of schools and means of production. There needs to be a different conception of reconstruction, but to begin speaking about what we're going to have for dinner when we can't even manage to get breakfast yet, that's not okay.

For now, I believe that the government needs to turn its attention to the rest of us, to those of us not served by this exclusive vision. In a country as poor and small as ours they've made extraordinary strides in technology and the like, but we still have no schools, an earthquake can come and tear down entire villages because there was no architectural planning. No-one ever bothered to say, 'No you can't build here, it's unstable.' For instance, there's been a great exodus of rural people to the cities in search of food and shelter and better educational opportunities for their children. Families live in card-board boxes and just scrape by selling fruit or ice cream so long as their children can attend school. There is no decentralization of resources, in fact there is far too much centralization in the urban centres. There was no urban/rural planning to say, 'Okay we're going to develop the northern zone', for example, the zone where I live where there is plenty of space and the terrain is a little harder so it holds up better under earthquakes. But no, they don't want to develop the northern zone. There is a very narrow vision of what will be developed, and in this vision, human development is the least im-portant, the only thing of importance is economic development.

The Future: 'As long as the soul is free … one can be happy …'

Now I'm going to tell you what I see for the future. It's a poor vision, based only on what I have seen and lived. I never studied politics.

We women need to be the principal agents of change. First of all, we constitute the majority of the population and it is on our shoulders that falls the brunt of economic activity. Upon our backs also falls the responsibility of education. We have an integral role to play in terms of educating the next generation because we raise them. Yet we cannot forget that we women are the most effective reproducers of this model that we don't want, the model that marginalizes women. Paradoxically we are the ones reproducing this model because we teach with it.

I'm referring to my country, to the underdeveloped countries. I don't know how things are in the US, but in our countries, the women suffer. The man marginalizes her, he deems her as the lesser, he hits her, but then she teaches her son that he is superior to her daughter and when he marries, he will also be superior to his wife. It cannot be this way. In our countries that's how the woman is, she reproduces the model of marginalization, she reproduces the social distribution of labour. Such and such jobs are for my daughters, such and such jobs are for my sons. We women are seen as noble mothers, martyrs, bearers of pain, but we're not seen as women with rights, as equals. So, there has to be a struggle against this in our thinking.

This worries me because it's cultural, and you know how much culture weighs! It's as much in our veins as in our heads. It weighs on me. I see this generation of youth growing up like this – it can't continue because the youth represent the only hope that in the future this way of thinking will no longer exist. Therefore, we must teach them differently. It causes me great anguish, but we must set ourselves to do this work, to change things one by one, this is what we must do. Create a new culture. A culture of equality, of equity, not continue with this culture of marginalization that we have now. We know that culture reflects our values and the creations that society makes and that these are transmitted by each of our histories.

Yes, yes, I have faith. I do a little something every day, I'm not going to change the whole world, no, I'm certainly not going to change it, but the journey of a thousand miles begins with the first step and so we must take that first step because of the happiness that humans bring us. A child's smile is enough to refresh my sentiments and this is what allows me to continue. The great triumph of the revolution was to resolve the basic needs of everyone. *I'm not going to ask that mango trees grow mangoes eight days after planting, because I know that's not possible, but please, building schools and teaching children to read, that's possible, and let's do it if we can!*

We have to spread the word of the need to organize, and how together you are capable of achieving things that you can't do alone. I'm going to make a proposal when I return home so that in these communities we'll be able to do something. When there's a theft we leave it to the state to resolve, but why can't we resolve it ourselves? We have to be responsible for our communities and this would teach us how. One can be happy and still poor, the two are not mutually exclusive. As long as the soul is free of ambition and greed, as long as it is free without measure or limits, one can be happy. I envision a just society, a brother- and sisterhood, one with love and solidarity between peoples. I'm going to write you later and tell you all that I've learned here.

I have things up here (pointing to her head and smiling).

Note

1. Minita, Jose and Maria's youngest daughter, was a radio operator during the war and is now studying medicine; their middle daughter, Morena, six years older than Minita, was a medic during the war, starting at age 13, and is now a schoolteacher in Arcatao, their home town. Their eldest daughter, Ceci, was killed in an army ambush in March 1987. Maria also lost brothers, nieces and nephews in the war. Arcatao's population of 10,000 eventually fell to 1,000 due to army murders and flight.

The Woof and the Warp

Luisa Valenzuela

§ AS a fiction writer, I am convinced that a shift of paradigm will take place when we reach some kind of critical mass on the subject of women's language – when it is completely mapped, erasing double standards and invisibilities. Also when the incorporation of symbolic languages is accepted in the common discourse. The reappropriation of language gradually exerted by women is opening us to a new perception of the world, and the recognition of woman as a social construction may well counterbalance the implacable progress of the so-called New World Order. The time seems ripe, at least calendar-wise, since the number 'one' has finally lost its thousand-year-old precedence.

Time was phallic in the past millennium.

Our point of view will change now that we prioritize duality, now that the date faces us with the two, a much milder and conciliatory digit than the erect one, reminder of monotheism, of dogma, of the univocal. The number one left no room for the other. In the two all oppositions fit equally, the yin and the yang, the dark and the light. According to Chevalier and Gheerbrant's *Dictionary of Symbols*, in ancient times the number two was an attribute of the Mother and designated the feminine principle. We can acknowledge this wisdom even today, surmising that in the year 2000 we have crossed a threshold towards a much more open time when woman will be able to complete the development of all the abilities she kept discovering and for which she fought so hard throughout the magnanimous, magical, monstrous twentieth century.

As if this weren't enough, the new millennium put us in touch – logically – with the proliferation of the zero, honouring the circle. We should make the most of this new starting point and bring all aspects of women's language to the forefront. We might start thinking in virtuous circles, concentric and unending. Like the circles of the Mothers of the Plaza de Mayo in Buenos Aires every Thursday. The circle is an expansion from a centre, knowledge of self, much as it is said feminine energy moves: in eddies. The protest of the Mothers continues, the circles expand or contract but will never end; every Thursday at three in the afternoon, until the destiny of each victim of the military dictatorship of 1976–82 in Argentina is known.

A language made of the loudest silence. Made of courage. And memory.

When history becomes cyclical, forgetting can be dangerous. These Argentine women refuse to forget. They look forward but continue going round and round in front of the Presidential Palace, soliciting a complete report as to the whereabouts of each of their *desaparecidos* and demanding just punishment for the guilty parties.

> There have been many massacres throughout Argentine history, but this is the first time the victims have names and are individualized. We struggle to keep it that way, so that each one without exception will be remembered as they were, with all their joys, ideals and sorrows. For this reason we also need to know how they ended their days. They are not simply one more number in a computer somewhere. They are beings who were very much alive and whose memory will continue to live while we are still living.

Laura Bonaparte often makes this statement, speaking as a representative of all the Mothers who wear the white kerchief on their heads.

Another language, the white kerchiefs. They are the opposite of the black ink stains with which the men in power attempted to erase the terrifying past. They first began to be used in the Plaza de Mayo out of necessity so that these brave women could recognize each other. And what would every mother have in her wardrobe? A nappy, was the answer. One can write on the white kerchiefs that the Mothers wear on their heads. And in fact this has happened, because little by little the women began incorporating the names of their disappeared children, embroidered or painted on the white cloth, thus inscribing the terrible history of their country's darkest moments.

Mothers of the Plaza who are proliferating throughout the world, wherever there were or are children or grandchildren lost to repression or dictatorships. Women who propose holding fast to a name. In the tapestry of life – who better than a woman to know it – each knot is unique and irreplaceable. Faced with the death of their loved ones, they have learned to sing louder than ever a song of life, and this song in all its pain and magnificence has crossed all boundaries.

When passing through Buenos Aires, Richard Schechner noted that protests that march in a straight line have authoritarian resonance, while demonstrations that develop in a circular manner are basically anti-authoritarian. One more recognition of women's forms of expression.

If I mention only the Mothers it is simply because they are the most emblematic. Equally important in my country is the Association of Grandmothers, HIJOS, or the Families of the Disappeared. They all respond to the same language that these women inaugurated, configured mainly by silence, by the colour white, by empty silhouettes. A basically feminine language that has managed to resound stridently throughout the whole world.

Pain and censorship (oh so feminine curses!) have taught women to express themselves using different, unusual forms. The protests, the distress and fury, are no longer made known with blows but with white kerchiefs and circles that are reminiscent of eternity. Women throughout history have learned to move beyond words so as to express the inexpressible. With completely feminine weapons that are the opposite of weapons but act as such, with everyday elements re-semanticized, turned around like a glove. A soft kid glove transformed into a boxing glove that strikes with the persistent gentleness and precision of a drop of water.

As such, it is important to remember the Chilean *arpilleras*, those *art naïf* works the women of Neruda's Isla Negra first created during the Pinochet dictatorship. These burlap creations were collages of embroidery, materials, little rag dolls stitched on the coarse cloth of potato sacks. They narrated, in a form that could be called charming, candid, the dramas that the people of Chile went through during the ill-fated years. Tourists bought them perhaps as one more piece of local folklore, took them home and, with luck, at some moment, their eyes opened and they understood. A perfect way of telling that which goes beyond words.

Like the white silhouettes the Mothers imposed upon the entire downtown Buenos Aires (what is locally known as *el centro*) in the final times of the military dictatorship. One morning, suddenly, the city awoke plagued with ghosts. Thirty thousand, to be exact. The 30,000 *desaparecidos* had their presence stamped on the walls: enormous sheets of butcher paper, white like the white kerchiefs, where the empty silhouettes of men, women and children were imprinted, with their names and dates, so that never again could anyone ignore their ever-present absence.

A few years later, a new stroke of genius in the same direction. During the annual demonstration against the coup, there appeared marching alongside the Mothers a countless number of youths with their faces hidden behind completely white, neutral masks, upon which every observer could project the features of a *desaparecido* or a *desaparecida*. White masks, inoffensive only in appearance, peaceful, as the opposite of war. There they were, the masks worn by members of the association HIJOS, bringing back to our memory all those of whom the military had attempted to erase even the trace of their tomb.

These are the closest examples I have at hand to show woman's work from the dark side of language, her lateral and efficient way of expressing that which is suffused, suppressed, banned, painful, dangerous. Women are today historically the most apt to trick the censors, simply because they have acquired full consciousness of censorship, being as they were the favourite victims throughout the centuries. Woman, the silenced one, has managed to reappropriate a language that was alien to her, with which she was degraded and rendered invisible.

Woman is mythically the one who can manage to say what cannot be said.

We know that the price to pay is high, we don't forget the sad story of Eve and the famous tree, but now more than ever we are willing to pay it, to run the necessary risks in order to open up new possibilities in a male world that seems to be heading for disaster.

I believe that the hope for a better future is in the hands of women. Or at least in the hands of the feminine, of Shakti, of the social construction called woman. She who won't struggle to occupy the places until now reserved for men. She who questions them thanks to her ability to operate in the margins and crevices. Those who learned to make glorious use of what years ago was called interstitial liberty some day not too far off will make global use of these old abilities. And of many new abilities – why limit ourselves?

Acknowledgements

This essay was translated from the Spanish by Nancy Gates. The editors wish to thank Light Carruyo for providing them with an initial draft.

. . . .

Consider the Problem of Privatization

Anna Tsing

§ IF there is a new buzzword in the international development community, it is 'privatization'. As international law and policy promote 'private' corporations and 'private' families, what will this mean for women? If 'public' alternatives are systematically undermined, how might this transform women's ability to mobilize as women?

The neoliberal vision of privatization that has become so powerful these days encourages particular, peculiar notions of agency – for women, as well as men. The more powerful these notions, the easier it is for us to step into them without thinking, even as we spin rather different dreams. This is not an alliance, I believe, that feminists should endorse. And so I offer this series of thoughts as a warning, a cautionary narrative that might inform our hopes and plans. My 'vision' here is of the care feminists must take as we work towards more equitable and livable worlds.

To consider the problem of privatization in even a speculative manner, I must first pick my way through a number of conceptual and practical thickets. To find a starting point from which questions about women, development and privatization are worth asking, I begin with 'development'.

Development, and More Development

Development proliferates. It likes to imagine itself as everywhere and unstoppable. It spreads because it always has a plan. In the service of proliferation, it is always ahead of itself, pulling the present behind it: it builds futures; it destroys pasts. It purposefully overwhelms us in its insistence that we not be left behind. Yet, for all its imagined power, it is as malleable – and as unruly – as a child.

'Development' has been a set of *projects*, that is, bundles of ideas and practices that fit together in some ways. Development projects, while shaped by international mandates, are yet varied in their inception as well as their effects because they form their coherence in relation to historically specific conjunctions and collaborations. Particular political actors come together to make development projects that are internationally recognizable and fundable at the same time that the projects articulate their socially and culturally specific dreams and schemes. To establish a place from which to ask my questions, I offer not development in the abstract, but in one concrete instance.

I first knew development in one of its most aggressive forms: the authoritarian rule of Suharto's New Order regime in Indonesia, particularly as it worked to normalize and dispossess rural minorities. *Pembangunan*, 'development', was the term for the expansion of the state. For forest-dwelling minorities, it referred to resettlement programmes aimed at clearing the forest for timber companies, mines and plantations – the state's corporate clients. It referred, too, to cultural programmes in which the so-called backward customs of minorities were showcased as national blights that the regime could change. Through them, the regime endorsed a theory in which rural people caused their own poverty through backwardness. Yet the targeted minorities had to be taught to be poor; before development, many were rich in both culture and resources. Through development, minorities were asked to give up their livelihoods, religious commitments and ways of life to endorse a position at the bottom of the social hierarchy in exchange for only a possible attenuation of state harassment. Given this history, it is hard for me to think about 'development' in Indonesia – whether for women or for men or gender-undifferentiated communities – with a positive vision. Perhaps that's why this statement highlights dangers even in a hopeful moment.

In the 1970s and 1980s, New Order rural development at its bottom level usually targeted communities, public space, culture and technology as its demonstration objects: the promotion of individual profit hid behind a rhetoric of the public good. By the 1990s, however, privatization-oriented models of development had begun to influence state planning and rhetoric. The stated goal of all development began to shift towards the funding of private entrepreneurship, even in the countryside. In the mid-1990s the state offered its own interpretation of the internationally acclaimed Grameen Bank model of funding the poor, and small loans were offered to individual residents of 'backward villages'. The Grameen Bank had offered loans to poor, credit-less rural women in Bangladesh to start small enterprises. In Indonesia, the recipients of state funds in the Kalimantan villages I knew were almost always those male household heads who were clients of the state-appointed village leaders. Meanwhile, the land grabs of plantations threatened to finish off village lands. Loans to 'backward villages' served to teach villagers how to be grateful but poor, just as their poverty was being firmly established through dispossession. The loans tightened the circle of masculine patronage, establishing the ability of some individuals to benefit from state discipline. In this way, a positive-seeming 'women and development' innovation, proliferating without feminist architects and in a terrain of coercion, led only to a more entrepreneurial patriarchy.[1]

In 1998, the Suharto regime fell. The transition has been an exciting time in Indonesia. New visions open up everywhere, even as new threats and challenges abound. Much that was not possible before seems now possible, even public criticism of that once-so-sacred term, development. Yet the possibilities are constrained, too, by the collaboration that overthrew the New Order. In Suharto's last days, the democratic opposition came into alliance with international agencies and transnational business enough to argue that Suharto was thwarting globalization; therefore he must go. It was a winning combination. But it put in place an equation: democracy equals globalization equals privatization. Some groups argue against this equation, but it is hard now to dislodge. A new hegemony has tentatively emerged. What will it mean for development, and women?

The Feminine, the Private

Feminists have had a lot to say about the private, but we have not yet turned our analysis to the contemporary cultural current called privatization. What are the connections between the private sphere of women's feminine containment and the privatization of public goods and spaces?

Let me begin in the North. As I have been arguing, Southern development projects are never just copies of Northern desires and plans, coming into being as they do as particular social interventions. Still, it is worth looking at Northern development packages to see what the South will at least have to address. Development packages are always cultural: they argue for particular ways of seeing and doing things according to a set of meaning-bound standards. They are often quite culturally exotic. (Imagine telling people they should work harder to earn less, just because they'll be considered 'modern'.) To dress their packages up as worthwhile, package designers strive to naturalize the cultural standards of their packages, that is, to make us accept them as universal 'human' wants while we exoticize the standards they are trying to replace. So it is up to critical analysts to take a more distanced look at what is being sold as the latest fashion in internationally appropriate cultural standards.

Privatization is never merely an economic strategy. It is suffused with political culture. In the United States, privatization developed in the 1970s and 1980s as part of a neoconservative social agenda. This agenda recognizes only two kinds of legitimate social bodies: private corporations and private families. It has called for the destruction of other public goods, practices and institutions, from welfare to public education, environmental regulation, equal opportunity hiring and social services. If there is discrimination, this should be overcome, neoconservatives argue, by redoubled individual efforts; it is not a public matter. Government spending is fine as long as it promotes families, corporations and their economic or security interests; other forms of spending are said to be unnecessary to society. Yet the slippages that allow public funding of the private, as well as private funding of the public, have facilitated the compromises and collaborations that have made privatization into such an important public agenda in the United States. Spokespeople for schools, minority cultures and the environment can appeal to corporate sponsorship. Lesbians and gays can press for more flexible definitions of family. Federal bureaucratic labyrinths can be dismantled in favour of local solutions. There is still room for progressive concerns – but in a newly privatized form.

Thus, business and professional women in the United States, including feminists and progressives, have not seen privatization as a disaster. The rhetoric of the promotion of families, in an economic boom period, has allowed elite working women to negotiate for desirable lifestyle changes. Through their collaboration with family values enthusiasts, they have gained the right to negotiate for model families in which spouses and children are important as well as careers. 'Mommy tracks' and 'flextime' have been created in business. Non-enforcement of laws about working conditions has allowed nannies to enhance the lives of working mothers. In the academic world, women bargain for spouse appointments. Each of these is possible because of the public promotion of the private family, understood as a legitimate item of elite consumption.

The problem with this cultural politics is that it promotes only individual benefits. Inside it, it is difficult to cross boundaries of class, ethnicity and even marital status to identify with others. Ideals of equality and access give way to negotiations of individual privilege. Ironically, women negotiating for life-style benefits use a rhetoric of gender equity to obtain their goals. But, in the context of privatization, their achievements deepen status differences rather than mobilizing women as a group. Spouse appointments in the academic world, for example, work directly against the goals of equal opportunity hiring that feminists worked for only a few decades ago. If we consider the fact that no one has even dared to propose that academic departments might hire clusters of friends or intellectual collaborators, we can see how far this initiative lies from utopian feminist dreams: only spouses are acceptable in the regime of family values.

What might this cultural politics mean for the South? The power of Northern models is very much felt in the South, from structural adjustment packages to the selective funding of non-governmental organizations. Yet development packages are always transformed as they emerge in the projects of Southern collaborators. The one thing that I can say about the impact of expectations about privatization in post-Suharto Indonesia is that it is surely unpredictable, and just as surely caught up in Indonesian struggles for public culture. Yet the question of privatization is worth asking and re-asking as Indonesian agendas for development, and gender, are reformulated.

The stakes are high because one enormously promising change has already occurred. After years of repression, Indonesian feminism has re-emerged with a new vigour. Suharto's New Order criminalized feminism. The concocted story of the Communist women's movement sexually abusing and torturing military martyrs formed part of the founding myth of the regime. The fall of Suharto was similarly marked by a shocking story: the mass rape of Indonesian Chinese women during the 1998 uprising. Yet this story did not stop protest, as military instigators might have hoped; instead, it sparked an invigorated feminist mobilization of the sort that has not been seen in the North since the 1980s.

What will feminists be able to accomplish in the current global climate? Many international observers assume that because Indonesia is predominantly Muslim, the main issue will be women's rights to speak in public. However, elite women have long played an important role in national politics in Indonesia, and this continues in the post-Suharto era. Women have emerged as strong spokespersons in non-governmental organizations and opposition parties as well as in the current leadership. Women's ability to speak with authority – so difficult to establish in the United States – is more straightforward in Indonesian national fora. The big issues, I believe, will lie elsewhere.

One suggestive anecdote speaks to the indirect ways the agenda of privatization may make itself felt: young women in Indonesia, my friends say, are turning against birth control. The New Order had a coercive mass birth control programme that almost everyone resented. Progressive young women, in a gesture of defiance of that policy, have now jumped to have babies early and often. How often desire emerges in such reversals! And how easily this plan sits in the new international thinking about the wonder of families. Is this a privatized feminism?

I have tried to make two points. First, development visions take form as context-specific interventions. They make futures in relation to particular pasts. They mobilize collaborators and gain their form in relation to the links they forge. They take the charismatic, powerful packages of development designers and transform them to become something new, for better or for worse. Second, privatization shifts the possibilities for mobilizing women as women. If feminists want to hold on to the possibility that women are a force for social justice, we will have to play this game very carefully, if at all.

Note

1. Grameen Bank lending has come under increasing critical scrutiny, even in its home setting in Bangladesh. Feminists have begun to argue, indeed, that Grameen's women creditors become more rather than less vulnerable because of these loans.

. . . .

PART ONE

Sexuality and the Gendered Body

CHAPTER 2

'Tragedies' in Out-of-the-way Places: Oceanic Interpretations of Another Scale

Yvonne Underhill-Sem

Story of an Accident

I had just walked about 100 metres to the river to look for the bush knife left by my seven-year-old nephew, when I heard the sound of something heavy crashing through the trees. This was followed immediately by the agonizing scream now indelibly fixed in my memory. I sprinted back to the area where we had just finished chopping and loading firewood to find my 65-year-old mother-in-law, Sia, sprawled in the small stream with her lower right leg dangling by a finger-length thread of skin. A huge branch lay alongside her and she looked alternatively at her leg and then at me with a combination of terror and disbelief. My aunt, who was also in our firewood-gathering group, had already returned to the village with one load of wood and my nephew stood watching in frozen confusion. I pulled Sia gently out of the stream, her leg dragging behind her, and covered her lower body so we did not have to keep looking at her bloodless but almost detached lower limb. There was mixture of disbelief and inevitability in her eyes and her cries and the best I could do was to utter reassuring words about getting help soon.

We were in a garden area accessible only by foot and some 30 minutes' walk from the nearest houses. It was another 20 minutes' walk to the nearest health centre with a radio-telephone, but some 500 kilometres away from the nearest emergency health care. In spite of the otherwise logistical impossibility of this situation, four years later Sia is still with us, although not entirely unscarred, thanks to the fortunate combination of local action and relative economic privilege. The swift and careful work of local women and men ensured Sia was carried out of the garden on a stretcher hastily made of bush materials, and taken to the health clinic before she lost consciousness. This effort was matched by that of Sia's son, who lived in Port Moresby, the capital of Papua New Guinea in the Western Pacific. From his relatively privileged position, as a telephone owner and regular and credible employee of a large organization, he was able to mobilize financial resources quickly enough for a daylight emergency air evacuation from Wanigela's grassy airstrip.

The Tragedy of Tragedies: Where is Culture?

Too many other people have died and continue to die in similar or more tragic incidents in 'out-of-the-way' places. For Tsing (1993: 27) 'an out-of-the-way place is, by definition, a place where the instability of political meanings is easy to see'. By this, Tsing suggests that for communities that are located within the geographical boundaries of specific nation-states, but are considered by urban majorities to be isolated and/or living primitive lives, the discursive constructions of the nation-state are easily contestable. She uses this concept to argue for understanding marginality as formed by dialogues between the relatively isolated Meratus Dyaks in south Kalimantan and urban, cosmopolitan Indonesians. By exploring the particularities of the Meratus arguments, Tsing effectively shows the intertwined and contestable links between small, relatively isolated communities, the nation-state and global entities. I build on this concept of 'out-of-the-way places' to make more explicit the potency of grappling with the slippery linkages that constitute, and are constituted by, the use of the more ubiquitous terms 'developing countries', 'the Third World' and 'the economic South'.

My use of 'out-of-the-way' purposely signals my dissatisfaction with these terms and the economic constructs on which they rest. Although all the terms enjoy wide circulation in scholarly, institutional and activist discourses, their meanings are politically sensitive and are as often strategically specific as they are naïvely nonsensical. While all concepts share the risk of eventually becoming engrained with unintended meanings, my use of 'out-of-the-way places' is in keeping with Escobar's (1995: 14) plea for the 'liberation of the discursive field so that the task of imagining alternatives can be commenced'. As a less politically loaded term, 'out-of-the-way places' also provides for the possibilities of thinking about 'marginal' places differently. Local places are important even within the complex compressions of space and time that characterize the globalizing tendencies of contemporary political economies (McDowell 1999). However, they are also more than fixed, bounded entities. Local places are known and defined in relation to other places. Marginality is not just geographical distancing, but also political, economic and cultural distancing. The importance of the concept of marginality is its imagined centre, which, by definition, can be anywhere. An 'out-of-the-way place', then, is also a relational concept that requires an examination of what and where the centre is. Equally important, this examination includes attention to the dynamics of local historical and cultural understandings. To engage with these insights requires working with complex constellations of culture and power at various scales of analysis. Tragedies can often cross these scales, but in doing so, too often local places are overlooked.

Almost daily, tragedies involving the loss of human life capture the imagination of the world's media, which effectively relay them to the collective imagination of those with access to newspapers, radios, televisions and increasingly the Internet. Often it is the sheer number of lost lives that catapults events from different parts of the world into distant homes. Other times it is the peculiar circumstances of human death and misery that turn them into tragedies for a myriad spectators. Tragic though all these events are for the individuals involved, I am not concerned so much with the tragedies that make the headlines. Rather, my focus here is on the 'smaller-scale' tragedies that occur in out-of-the-way places, such as the one we avoided in Wanigela. I am thinking about the tragedy of 18 Tuvalu schoolgirls who were burned to death in their locked dormitory. The doors and windows were locked to stop the girls and boys meeting secretly in the night. The boys were not locked into their dormitories. I am also thinking about the daily death of women during childbirth, as the result of domestic and other bodily violence and from both curable and incurable diseases.

Despite evidence from many reports and pithy rhetoric from the various authorities who have some responsibility for avoiding such tragedies, it seems that these tragedies may be a 'true' and enduring universal for humankind. For those bodies involved, the resounding response to this view is deadly silence. While there may well be some truly 'natural' tragedies, most human tragedies are preventable. For many people, the easiest way of preventing them is to consider the structural deficiencies that contribute, for instance, to inadequate rural health and education services. My argument is that greater attention needs to be given to the complex and place-specific constellations of power relations within which particular 'tragedies' occur. In this chapter I examine the complex power relations that constitute, and are constituted by, the small closely knit community of Wanigela. Because the power dimensions in this community are cast in idioms and understandings from this particular place and time, solutions to the problems of such tragedies as I have described are not couched in calls for better health or transport services. These solutions belong to the discourses of policy-makers and planners in national government offices who are situated in different places and times. Instead, this is a story about how women, as a group and as individuals, are deeply embedded in the masculinist discourses that constitute the conflicts over the distribution of royalties flowing from a logging operation in Wanigela.

My intention is not that this particular narrative is transformative in itself, but, as political philosopher Iris Young (1997) points out, when linked with similar narratives, the effect is a subversion of those mainstream and malestream understandings of women that view development from a predominantly economic perspective. Instead, this story emphasizes how working from the everyday experiences of women in out-of-the-way places provides for different ways of thinking about 'development' and 'politics'. This is the cultural dimension that has too long been 'black-boxed' in preference to globalizing economic analysis (Chua, Bhavnani and Foran 2000).

Furthermore, I hope to show that by examining the ways in which tragedies beset women in out-of-the-way places, new ways of thinking about human bodies in development studies are exposed. By beginning with the body of a particular woman in a particular time and place, I am arguing here for more sexual embodiment in the practice of thinking about women and development. I argue that this is one highly effective way of identifying the major dimensions of power that constitute all social relations. Sia was not just an old woman going about her daily chores. She was intimately connected to a raft of highly contested land debates in the villages and for many people this 'accident' was related directly to her involvement in these debates, not just to her misfortune of being hit by a falling branch in a remote garden area. This formulation of culture as lived experience shows how it is possible to ensure that material and discursive constructions of development issues are mutually constituted.

Of Site and Situations

I write this study after a 14-year connection to Wanigela, Oro Province, Papua New Guinea, first as a relative by marriage and then as a graduate student. My contingent connections with this place have provided me with special, often privileged, access to language, kinship relationships and knowledge that I draw on for my analysis. I have visited Wanigela numerous times since 1986 and lived there for a number of months in 1995–96. Since then I have continued to visit, although my current residence outside Papua New Guinea has limited my ability to remain closely in touch with one of the places I call 'home'. My formal research in Wanigela, which argued for a feminist post-structuralist approach to population geography and specifically fertility analysis (Underhill-Sem 2000), involved collecting demographic data, kinship information and detailed narratives of the maternity experiences of about 30 women in Wanigela. In addition to these more formal data-gathering exercises, as a resident of Wanigela I was also involved in discussions about many current events in the area. The major one was the commencement of a relatively small-scale logging operation on a block of traditionally owned land that had been officially leased to the government some 50 years earlier. There were other issues of community concern that I was party to – the sudden death of young mothers in one part of the village, plans for a new high school and ceremonial activities like bridewealth exchanges. Although relatively small, like many out-of-the-way-places, this community was big on issues to discuss. I draw on these informal discussions for this chapter.

The Everyday Culture of Resource Politics in Wanigela

Since the mid-1980s, the logging industry in Papua New Guinea has been under close scrutiny because of the relative ease with which corrupt practices by national politicians and bureaucrats have been able to siphon huge financial benefits away from the people who 'owned' the resources (Barnett 1992). A number of legislative and procedural attempts have been made by various national governments to establish a sustainable, non-corrupt forest industry. However, in the multi-ethnic and politically diverse country of Papua New Guinea, this is not an easy task and continues to be subject to political wavering among resource owners, elected politicians, forestry officials and foreign companies. Filer's (1997) work contains many detailed examples of how these tensions play themselves out at the local and national level throughout Papua New Guinea. I am working from yet another perspective that further complicates these tensions, because I want to get closer to the culture of politics embedded in the everyday lived experiences of women.

To return to the story that began this article. A year before Sia's accident in the garden, discussions had begun between a relatively small logging company based in another province in Papua New Guinea and some self-appointed representatives of the major clans in Wanigela. Although there had been interests in logging this area before, projects had never materialized because land in Wanigela, like most land in Papua New Guinea, remains in customary tenure and is therefore subject to customary non-written 'law'. Clans are the basic landholding unit, but rarely do clan lands in Wanigela form large contiguous blocks. Rather, clan lands can be found at widely scattered locations. Boundaries to these lands are recognized verbally in relation to well-known landmarks like rivers, large trees, mountains and depressions, many of which change gradually over time. For the purposes of large-scale logging or mining, this system makes 'economically viable' blocks of land hard to identify unless there is a workable collaboration with the relevant landowners. This difficulty had prevented any previous logging projects.

In Wanigela, however, there was a 12,000-hectare block of land for which, in 1954, the government had managed to negotiate a lease for 99 years. The lease was subsequently awarded to Utan Plantations for copra, coffee and cocoa production. In the early 1990s Utan was facing financial difficulties because of low agricultural prices compounded by an increasingly unreliable transportation system. Forced to find alternative ways to boost its low returns, it initiated discussions with various logging companies about the possibility of logging some of the hardwoods within its leasehold area. Only about 100 hectares of the 12,000 hectares leased were planted, so a large part of the leaseholding was still covered in hardwood timber with 58 years to run. Utan management finally contracted a relatively small logging company which opted to selectively log the hardwood and replant with fast-growing balsa. As a leasor, this was within Utan's right; however, Section 2(a) of the lease agreement states that standing timber can be removed from the land for the 'purpose only of improvement of the land' (Lease Document). This provision clearly prohibits the lessee from cutting timber for sale, so close attention had to be paid to how much would be paid to 'traditional' landowners and the local community, how this would be paid and, more importantly, to whom it would be paid. Furthermore, the government road did not run the entire way from the coast to the logging area; the use rights of parts of the road therefore also had to be purchased, as did the land adjacent to the temporary landing jetty.

I am not going to detail the considerable debate that followed over how much was to be paid and how this was done. Instead, I want to focus on how 'real' landowners are identified and especially how women are incorporated into this process. This is never an easy question in Papua New Guinea, where over 90 per cent of land is still held in non-written customary tenure. Every piece of land has its own history of ownership, which is recalled in different ways by different people at different times. There is rarely a single correct interpretation. Rather, the greatest degree of acceptance is achieved when claims are no longer hotly challenged, and contesting parties signal their agreement to disagree by retreating from public debates. Those bold enough to go ahead in this situation are taking a risk, and it is more likely that the project or activity that led to the disagreements in the first place evaporates.

Women are closely involved in these debates, because in Wanigela it is widely understood that they are also resource owners. Despite differences in the day-to-day life of men and women, there is always time for family groups to talk about these issues, especially as couples and family groups walk to their often distant gardens on a regular basis. Women and men in different groupings are involved in a variety of activities, ranging from laundry to house building and sports training to card playing, when there is often time for both fun and laughter as well as serious discussions. Moreover, when evening meals are eaten and it is time to drink tea or chew betel nut, the talk inevitably turns to these contentious issues.

In the case of the Utan leasehold property, the widely acknowledged owners were three major clans whose forebears had been members of a surveying party that accompanied a government surveyor into the bush in 1946. Together they agreed where the boundaries were and a map was drawn up and subsequently gazetted. The relative extent of the land belonging to each clan was reflected in the relative proportion of recompense each clan was given in return for its land. In the 1990s there were oral records of this survey and a collective memory of the proportionate share each clan was due. Each of the men originally involved had descendants currently resident in Wanigela, although some groups had more representatives than others. My mother-in-law, Sia, was however the only resident descendant of one member of that group of three. As a woman this caused problems, but these were not problems of invisibility.

In this predominantly patriarchal place, where on marriage women become members of their husband's clans, the clans that the women originally came from are not, nevertheless, forgotten. So when it comes to sharing resources of one sort or another, these clans are only overlooked at the risk of later retribution. Women are not visible in various public hearings in which the sharing of resources, such as bridewealth distribution, was debated. However, they are actively involved in the daily discussions that form part of the often many months of build-up leading to the more public event.

During 1995 and 1996, numerous meetings were held by various groupings of people – clans who were the direct descendants of the three men who surveyed the land, neighbouring clan groups, distantly related clan groups and family groups. Women were part of all these groups. However, when it came to the large public meetings few women participated in the forum discussions, although their presence was welcome for preparing and serving refreshments.

At first, Sia was not too concerned with the discussions because her husband and son were attending the meeting as members of their own clan (Yeyeu) and, among other things, they were tracking events as they related to Sia's clan as well because it was well known throughout the area that she was a member of one of the major clans (Kwakwabu). Despite Kwakwabu not having a male representative in these meetings, Sia was confident her interests would be respected. However, as time went on Sia realized that other clans were claiming more than their share of the royalties. Sia then tried to generate the interest of a close cousin brother (male cousin), who was also part of her original clan but who had lived in the city for many years. She visited other clan members and sent letters to him. After a particularly urgent request from Sia, he eventually came back to Wanigela to attend a critical meeting. However, his lack of experience in the village discussions and his sidelining of Sia's advice saw him go off on a tangent. For Sia, he had failed to pursue the proper justice for their clan that she had hoped, as a man, he could.

Instead of letting the issue go, and despite active intervention by her husband and younger son on her behalf, Sia increased her correspondence with her first-born son who lived in Port Moresby. As a member of his father's clan, Sia's son was not directly involved in the land under dispute although every clan had important information to contribute in providing the context for which clans owned which land. However Sia was asking him to help her gain the recognition that she felt was owing to her father's clan. There was a financial interest involved, but the more pressing concern for Sia was to ensure that her father's clan was not covertly overlooked. Helping his mother with these issues meant her son would be transgressing longstanding norms about respecting one's mother's brothers. Instead, he would be directly challenging their interpretations of historical events. With little hesitation, Sia's son responded actively to his mother's request. He investigated the company and the lease. He studied the relevant documents, followed the legal requirements for royalty payments and confronted the leasors over the interpretation of the lease and the people they had identified as beneficiaries. Throughout these weeks he was relaying information back to his parents in the village, who in turn kept him informed of developments in the village.

Over the several months that this story unfolded, Sia was moving around the village more than usual. In addition to other tasks such as gardening, marketing and attending to church activities, she was visiting the houses of related clan members. Over time, Sia also became a familiar face at the public discussions. If she did not make it because of conflicting responsibilities, like caring for sick family members or being unwell herself, then her husband or village-resident son would attend the meetings and relay news back to her. It was clear that she was being kept informed of discussions and had an opinion about them. Quite often her opinion differed from that of the expressed consensus of the meeting. But she was not the only woman raising alternative views. Nie, the widow of another clan cousin, fully supported Sia. Her position was slightly different, however; Nie was defending her husband's clan because her son, though currently resident in the village, was not confident about talking about custom matters in public forums.

Accidents Do Happen

As discussions were getting more heated and various people were travelling to and from Port Moresby in attempts to influence the distribution of royalty payments, the first accident occurred. An integral space in all housing areas in Wanigela is a platform or veranda, the *kema*, sometimes attached to the main house and sometimes a separate structure. It is the place where people meet, talk, eat and often sleep. Because it is so well used, it is solidly constructed and well maintained. Rarely does it collapse. However, one evening the *kema* belonging to Nie's family collapsed under Nie, leaving her with a badly bruised leg. Although not a life-threatening accident, she left for care in the city a few days later. The next incident, involving Sia, occurred about three months later and was life-threatening.

Few people made the connection between these incidents publicly, yet for most the message was clear. These two women were overstepping the bounds by their engagement in contentious land issues and should keep away. Along with many others, I never learned how these 'accidents' were thought to have happened. This knowledge was not shared and talked about – it was not discursively constructed. However, after Sia's accident the family decided to stay further away from land discussions, even though they felt they were getting closer to reaching that state of agreeing to disagree. This was Sia's explicit advice, because she feared the next incident would be fatal. We all concurred with her wishes and did not engage any further in the discussions. Members of our family held particular documents, so we were still approached for advice from other related clans.

The logging continued for about 18 months before all the machinery was shipped out. Shortly after, logging trucks were no longer tearing down the road raising dust and scattering those who were walking. The road quickly reverted to the footpath it used to be, complete with patches of mud and grass growing in the middle. The balsa continues to grow, but there are no plans for harvesting it. Royalty money was distributed and Sia's clan got some, but the final pool for distribution was never known. People were no longer flying between Port Moresby and Wanigela every week or so. Some trade stores closed up. Fewer baked products were sold at the market. There were no more public meetings about land issues. Sia was back in the village after almost a year in Port Moresby, including several months in hospital. Now she sometimes walks with the aid of a stick. She and her family still talk about land issues in their private spaces. The story is still told of Sia's accident and numerous interpretations are made of it. I have presented just one version of this story to provide an insight into how embedded the various layers of politics and culture are with each other.

How the branch fell on her I cannot say – perhaps someone had been in the garden area earlier. Perhaps someone was in the garden area, although we did not see any traces of him or her. Why did the branch fall on Sia? Perhaps she was pushing the boundaries. Perhaps her son was pushing his boundaries. Perhaps it really was just a kind of warning. Perhaps a more powerful sorcery would have successfully caused Sia's death and a greater disability. Perhaps there were other people involved. Whatever the answers to these and other questions, this incident will never simply be put down to being in the wrong place at the wrong time. This incident was shaped by resource conflicts in Wanigela, just as similar disputes in Wanigela are now constituted by this incident. The answers to the many questions raised by this very incident and indented on Sia's body are part of a wider localized understanding of how the world works. They are part of the materially and discursively constructed culture of Wanigela that needs to be taken into consideration in any discussions of development.

Tragedies in Out-of-the-way Places: Matters of Scale

What does this story tell us about tragedies on an oceanic scale? And where do women come into this picture? Although women in Papua New Guinea as a group are widely known to be the backbone of the community, they simultaneously continue to suffer a far lower status than men. In many ways the daily lived experience of many women in Papua New Guinea is characterized by hardship, abuse and often death. Campaigning for the rights of women in Papua New Guinea is one critical way to develop a context for women to be heard in local and national democratic places. Yet the potency of women's involvement in local politics, as the above discussion illustrates, cannot be overlooked. Women do have power, but not the sort of power that is vested in specific institutions. The power women have is situated in specific places and times, because it is simultaneously constitutive and constituting of the societies and polities they belong to. That is, this power is not only woven into the very fabric of society, but also emerges from the general fabric to constitute the many ways in which women express themselves either as a group or individually. One cannot therefore damage women without damaging critical warps and wefts in the fabric that is the society. One cannot either predict or suppose a precise way in which women, as a group or individually, will exercise the power they hold. One can be sure, though, that it will happen.

The two women in Wanigela drew on more power than other members of the society were comfortable with. They were involved in discussions, but because both Sia and Nie were unconvinced that their concerns were being genuinely addressed they continued talking. Unable to convince Sia and Nie otherwise, members of the community chose other ways to express their opinion more forcefully and the bodies of these women thus became the focus of discontent. And with this bodily restraint, their opponents won. In other places, women are routinely raped, impregnated or physically tortured as a form of overpowering or disempowering them. My analysis seeks to show that while women and young people are very vulnerable to such despicable and uninvited incidents, their assailants inadvertently acknowledge the tremendous power they also hold.

The matter of scale that arises in this discussion draws on new thinking about working with a concept of scale 'not as size (census tract, province, continent) or level (local, regional, national), but as a relational element in a complex mix that also includes space, place and environment' (Howitt 1998: 49, cited in Marston 2000: 220–21). This is useful for understanding the apparent contradiction of the grandness of the concept of Oceania viewed against the localized understandings of place in Wanigela. In this way the matter of scale becomes one of an analysis of the embodiment of power in social relations and the places in which they operate. Understanding 'scale' only as how the 'local' dovetails into the 'regional', which dovetails into increasing levels of geographical size ending with the 'global', is part of an economic and biological imagination that fails to account for fluid cultural understandings and imaginations.

A Woman's Body Scarred

I have purposely used a particular experience in which a sexually distinct body is scarred. The sexuality of this body is not obviously relevant. Yet on the other hand it is highly relevant. I want to take women's bodies as being more than childbearing bodies. They are also hard-working bodies capable of considerable effort and strain in their daily lives. But the strength that eventually comes from this hard work, like men's bodies, is not invincible. Like men's bodies, women's bodies can be broken. And when this happens it is a tragedy.

In this chapter I have shown that by focusing on the bodies closest in, their flesh and blood and pain, collective 'bodies' 'out there' – that is, how women are discursively constructed – cannot so easily be denuded of their materiality, and therefore so easily overlooked. Rather than the many examples I could draw on about the untimely and often unfair death of women in childbirth, or as the result of domestic, civil or national violence, I want to discuss the politics entwined in masculinist activities. By doing this my analysis is intended to bring women's bodies into the centre of masculinist discourses about politics and land in the Pacific.

With reference to approaches that polarize political economy from cultural politics, Young (1997: 149) argues that 'specifying political struggles and issues in more fine-tuned and potentially compatible terms better identifies possible conflict and alliance'. Here I have examined the political nuances that surround one particular tragedy in one out-of-the-way place, by focusing on the lived experiences of women in out-of-the-way places. Taking this example of an accident that could happen to anyone in many places where large trees still stand, my intention is to widen the argument surrounding the bodily position of women in the day-to-day politics of life. In doing this I call attention to the ways in which women are actively shaping their lives by drawing on Young's (1994) concept of seriality, which explains how sometimes women come together as a veritable force to be reckoned with, but that at other times women as a group and individual women are not able to come together.

A sub-theme in this chapter is the concept of scale in terms of collectivities. Being situated in Oceania, where the 'problem of smallness and remoteness' is a familiar leitmotif embedded in many discussions of development (Hau'ofa 1993), I work with the concept of 'out-of-the-way places' to force a rethinking of the power relationships between places, regardless of geographic scale.

This is not to say that large-scale human slaughter is unimportant, since the protection of all human rights is an ongoing challenge. Nor do I wish to silence the call for greater action on the part of larger industrialized countries to take responsibility for their contributions to environmental degradation on a global scale. But my aim here is to contribute to the sexual embodiment of development studies by forcing closer attention to the bodies closest in, so that the collective 'bodies' out there cannot be so easily overlooked.

CHAPTER 3

Queering Development: Institutionalized Heterosexuality in Development Theory, Practice and Politics in Latin America

Amy Lind and Jessica Share

> When I speak of my right to my own culture and language as an indigenous
> woman, everyone agrees to my self-determination. But when I speak of my
> other identity, my lesbian identity, my right to love, to determine my own
> sexuality, no one wants to listen. (A Peruvian feminist, quoted in Reinfelder
> 1996: 1)

§ ONE of the first public meetings on issues of homosexuality in the growing, vibrant, Peruvian feminist movement was held in Lima, Peru in 1985. This meeting, organized and facilitated by the Grupo de Auto-Conciencia de Lesbianas Feministas (GALF),[1] was meant to provide a forum for discussion about the myths, stereotypes and realities of being a lesbian or bisexual woman in Limeñan society. Although it was a small meeting, it marked a historical turning point in relations between heterosexual and queer women in the feminist movement.

Since then, many such meetings have taken place in Latin American countries, as elsewhere, in which heterosexual feminists have learned from, and sometimes rejected, their lesbian colleagues and friends. The historical relationship between heterosexual and queer feminists has been laden with conflict and distrust, although this has changed in some national contexts. In Bolivia, for example, Mujeres Creando (Women Creating), a grassroots feminist organization established by two of the most publicly 'out' lesbians in the country, has played an important role in creating a public space for discussing lesbian rights in relation to feminist, anti-racist, leftist and anti-colonialist struggles. One of their strategies has been to 'out' other lesbians and bisexuals in the La Paz-based women's movement and elsewhere in the country.[2] The fact that Mujeres Creando is familiar with outing strategies illustrates the transnational nature of lesbian/gay/bisexual/transgender (LGBT) organizing in Latin America, where ideas about 'gayness' circulate across borders among First World and Third World communities (Howe 2000).[3]

Historically, the transnational circulation of knowledge about LGBT issues has been institutionalized in part through the globalization of consumer cultures and economies, as well as through social movement networks which have responded politically to globalization, consumerism and neoliberalism. Significantly, one way in which knowledge and resources have been introduced in Latin American countries has been through development aid and policies (Fernández-Alemany 2000, Wright 2000). Beginning primarily in the mid-1980s, funding for LGBT organizations/networks in Latin America was provided by development agencies to address issues of HIV/AIDS among gay men and other populations considered 'at risk' (Wright 2000). An irony of the development field is that while sexuality has rarely been discussed other than in terms of women's reproductive rights and health, or in terms of social 'problems' such as prostitution or the AIDS epidemic, funding from agencies such as the United States Agency for International Development (USAID) has helped to institutionalize and make visible Latin American LGBT movements. In the 1980s and 1990s in virtually every Latin American country, small groups transformed into well-established non-governmental organizations (NGOs), thanks to support for HIV/AIDS outreach and support provided by international agencies, ministries of health and private foundations. Because of the focus on AIDS, a virus contracted by men more often than women, lesbians and other queer women received little funding for their political and organizational efforts, whereas queer men's organizing efforts received much attention and were relatively well funded (Fernández-Alemany 2000, Wright 2000). While this lack of attention to women's issues is not uncommon (Reinfelder 1996), it has been through this type of development practice that LGBT groups have been brought into the visible fold of national development.

Because of heterosexist biases in practice and theory, lesbians and other queer women who struggle for political visibility and rights must address both heterosexism within the women's movement as well as sexism in male-dominated 'gay' struggles in Latin America. In each of these arenas – women's movements and LGBT movements – activists must contend with Western biases in development frameworks and, generally speaking, with the contradictory effects of Westernization on/within Third World political movements.

We cannot address all of these issues in this chapter; however, we provide a precursory analysis of two important aspects of this discussion. First, we propose to 'queer' the development field, through conducting an analysis of institutionalized heterosexuality (or heteronormativity) in development theory and practice and its effects on lesbians, bisexual and heterosexual women. Second, we discuss Latin American LGBT political responses to institutionalized heterosexuality in the development field and elsewhere. We approach the topic of development from an interdisciplinary perspective. Rather than providing an economistic explanation of development and of LGBT political responses to it, we examine the economic as well as the political, cultural, social and ideological dimensions of development theory, practice and politics (see introduction to this book; also see Alvarez, Dagnino and Escobar 1998).

We would like to be explicit about our usage of the terms 'queer', 'queering development', 'institutionalized heterosexuality' and 'heteronormativity'. We recognize that the term 'queer' is not used regularly in Latin America, except perhaps among people who can travel to English-speaking countries, read and/or communicate in English, or work among LGBT activists familiar with the term. Just as the term 'gay' was introduced in the region in the 1970s (see below), the term 'queer' has been introduced in the late 1980s and 1990s. We choose to use it to connote the multiple forms of sexual and gender identities that exist, although with the understanding that this term, too, needs to be problematized. Drawing from queer theory, we suggest that this framework of sexuality is more appropriate than a dualistic framework of homosexuality/ heterosexuality (see Sedgwick 1993). As opposed to definitions of homosexual and bisexual, the notion of 'queerness' helps us to rethink dualisms in Western thought about 'good' versus 'bad', and 'normal' versus 'abnormal' genders and sexualities.

By 'queering development' we are referring to how sexuality and gender can be rethought and reorganized in development practices, theories and politics. In our queer analysis of development, we examine how hetero-sexuality is institutionalized, naturalized and regulated both explicitly (by excluding LGBT people from the analysis) and implicitly (by assuming that all people are heterosexual, marriage is a given and all men and women fit more or less into traditional gender roles). We draw from Adrienne Rich's (1986) original research on compulsory heterosexuality,[4] as well as from more recent scholarship on the institutionalization and regulation of heterosexuality in distinct cultural, legal and national contexts (e.g. MacKinnon 1987, Sedgwick 1993, Balderston and Guy 1997, Ingraham 1999). Similarly, we use the term 'heteronormativity' to illustrate how heterosexuality is normalized, naturalized and reproduced in Latin American (and other) societies and in the international development field, among others (Butler 1990, Bornstein 1998).

In this chapter, we argue that institutionalized heterosexuality has re-percussions for heterosexual women as well as queer women. We provide some examples of how queer women in Latin America negotiate their own positions, find meaningful spaces from which to organize politically and to construct alternative representations of family, sexuality and agency. We frame our discussion within the transnational context of international development discourses, global economic shifts, Third World political movements, the historical institutionalization of the gender and development field, and the ways in which local women's movements have articulated their identities and political struggles.

Next, we address the historical regulation of sexuality and the politics of sexual identity in Latin America. In the third section, we discuss institutionalized heterosexuality in development theory and practice and its effects on LGBT communities and women. We then draw from our research in Latin America to exemplify some of the negative effects of institutionalized heterosexuality on LGBT communities and political movements, highlighting the contradictions of queer organizing in an era of development and globalization. Finally, we address some concrete ways in which scholars and activists can think about women's and LGBT people's lives differently, in part by denaturalizing and delinking gender, (hetero)sexuality and the family in development theory and practice.

The Historical Regulation of Sexuality and Gender in Latin America

The historical regulation of sexuality in Latin America has been documented and examined from multiple perspectives (Balderston and Guy 1997, Mogrovejo 2000, Green 2000, Ungar 2000). In most Latin American countries homosexuality is currently criminalized,[5] and police repression as well as both right-wing and leftist paramilitary groups have served to discipline and destroy the life of queer communities (Ordoñez 1995, Lind 1997). In Colombia, so-called social cleansing practices of paramilitary groups have included the torture and murder of gay men, transvestites and sex workers, along with homeless adults and children. All are considered 'disposable' (*desechable*) and marked as undesirable in Colombian society (Ordoñez 1995). The practice of social cleansing has been well documented in Ecuador, Colombia, Brazil, Argentina and Peru (Mott 1996, Ordoñez 1995, Lind 1997). Often, lesbians remain invisible in homophobic discourses of paramilitary groups. This is one irony of women's experiences as sexual others: sometimes they escape physical violence because of their invisibility, yet are subject none the less to the violence of representations, cultural stigmas and the traumatic effects of political repression among people they know. At other times, lesbians too have been subjected to torture, arrest and/or imprisonment. In Lima, Peru, for example, sporadic yet systematic raids of lesbian and gay working-class bars occurred throughout the 1980s and 1990s, leading to the arrest of hundreds of lesbians and queer women and sometimes to their exposure on national public television (IGLHRC 1996). In the mid to late 1980s, in the midst of Peru's civil war and military state of emergency, arrested women were often released during the night curfew, only to face their second arrest by military patrols on the streets of Lima. In Mexico, the Independent Civil Commission on Homophobic Hate Crimes has recorded 199 murders of homosexuals as of August 2000, almost all of them unsolved. In rural areas in Mexico, the toll of dead gay men and women (21 listed victims have been women) may actually be closer to 500 over the course of the past five years (Ross 2000). Apart from systematic murders and physical violence, one of the most effective and widespread forms of repression of LGBT communities has been through police edicts and other local laws that legislate public behaviour in bars, dress codes and sexual practices. The Argentine police force and government, in particular, has utilized edicts to arrest and harass gay men and transgendered people, including transvestites (Ungar 2000). In Monterrey, Nuevo Leon, Mexico, transvestites are arrested on a daily basis. Upon their arrest, many are subjected to 'bribes; physical, psychological and sexual abuse; inhuman conditions of detention; deprivation of property' (IGLHRC 2001).

Despite this history of human rights violations in LGBT communities, in many countries (among them Peru, Chile, Brazil, Nicaragua, Costa Rica, Argentina, Uruguay, Colombia, Venezuela, Cuba and Mexico), large LGBT communities exist and have contributed in multiple ways to the queering of public space and politics (Green 2000, Thayer 1997, Lind 1997, Rosenbloom 1995a, Leiner 1994). LGBT activists have addressed homophobia and in-stitutionalized heterosexuality at various levels, including through activism surrounding human rights violations, the HIV/AIDS epidemic, mental health issues, poverty and familial displacement, both in formally democratic and military authoritarian contexts. In addition, LGBT activists and policy-makers have challenged heterosexist assumptions in development plans and practices, politics, the economy, the state and the criminal justice system. Through these historical and political experiences, LGBT activists have revealed how heteronormativity in societal institutions and public discourse affects the most intimate aspects of women's and men's daily lives, sense of security and of family, expressions of identity and identifications with politics and the public sphere.

In Latin America, interesting discussions have taken place about the politics of sexual identity and self-definition. As in other identity-based social movements (e.g. Afro-Latin American, women's, indigenous), cultural struggles over self-definition among LGBT people are an important part of their broader struggles to end US and other forms of imperialism, military authoritarianism, structures of racism and classism and the historical repression of queer people. Debates flourish, for example, as to how to define oneself in terms of sexuality and gender (e.g. *chito*, femme, *feminista*, homosexual, *lesbiana*, *tortillera*, gay, *maricon*, etc.) and how self-definitions reinforce Western categories of sexuality, reappropriate or provide alternatives to them. LGBT people have struggled for positive self-definitions in light of the historically derogatory ways they have been treated and labelled (e.g. verbal abuse as well as abuse by practitioners of psychology and medicine, the criminal justice system, religious and educational institutions and popular culture) and *vis-à-vis* US cultural imperialism. In this context, some queer people embrace the 'American' way of being 'gay', while others reject it. In the contemporary neoliberal context, some also blame neoliberal approaches to development (including integration into the global economy, privatization, economic liberalization and decentralization, coupled with an ideology of individualism and competition) for increased cultural tensions and class differences within LGBT communities (Fernández-Alemany 2000, Babb 2001).

The term 'gay' started to be used in Latin America in the 1970s. Drawing from earlier, original research on the topic of 'gayness' in the region (Murray and Arboleda 1995), Honduran researcher Manuel Fernández-Alemany examined the origins and local meanings of 'gay' in Honduras. For Fernández-Alemany, 'gay' is an imagined identity: 'The "American" way of being gay was largely a construct made of imagined and romanticised images of gay freedom and happiness in an equally imagined paradise of personal achievement – America' (Fernández-Alemany 2000: 2).[6] Stephen Murray and Manuel Arboleda (1995) argue that the term 'gay' in Latin America often represents 'foreign values, US imperialism and elitism'. However, some people have also reclaimed the term 'gay' and given it local meaning. Others have chosen to reappropriate historically pejorative terms such as *maricon* to describe themselves or their LGBT friends, much like the use of 'queer' in the United States, Canada and Britain (see Sedgwick 1990, 1993, Smith 1996).

LGBT activists have raised important issues about (hetero-)sexuality and gender as defined in the fields of human rights and development. Indeed, in Latin America these two fields are intimately connected, given that so many human rights groups receive foreign funding and rely on lending agencies and international solidarity groups for financial and ideological support. While historically the international development field has not addressed LGBT issues, with some minor exceptions (see below), LGBT activism has raised awareness around issues of sexual rights in development theory and practice.

Institutionalized Heterosexuality and the Disciplining of Women's Lives

Heterosexist assumptions in development frameworks, including paradigms of family structure, gender and sexuality, often contribute to the homogenization and stereotyping of 'Third World women' in development discourses and practices. This has very real effects on women's lives in Third World contexts – particularly women whose needs are not addressed or who are left out of community organizations and projects because they do not fit into the traditional norms of sexuality and gender. Institutionalized heterosexuality also contributes to homophobia and the violent repression of LGBT communities in Latin America and indeed throughout the world.

We have become aware of the heteronormalizing tendencies of development frameworks through our own research experiences. For example, my (Amy's) graduate research training speaks to how traditional, heterosexist ideologies of the family are reproduced as the norm in development theories and policy frameworks. As a graduate student, I conducted master's level research on the collective survival strategies of women in the context of economic crisis in Ecuador (Lind 1990). In my fieldwork I examined why women chose to create their own community-based organizations to address their gender-specific needs (a term I problematize), family roles and identities. I argued that women from diverse cultural, regional and class backgrounds were among the first to organize collectively, as women, to address the foreign debt crisis and the role of development institutions in perpetuating poverty and neocolonial relations in Ecuador. At the doctoral level, I took this research a step further and examined how Ecuadorian women's organizations reinforce and challenge dominant notions of 'women's roles in development', gender needs, economy, citizenship and political participation. Increasingly, what struck me about conducting interviews with members of various women's organizations was not who was participating, but rather who was not. I found that women's organizations served to discipline women as much as the state, the military, political parties or other male-based institutions did.

Most women in these particular organizations were married with children; some were single mothers or unmarried and still living with their parents. While perhaps their cultural (e.g. indigenous, mestiza) and regional (e.g. from the oriente, the coast or the sierra) backgrounds may have been diverse, how they conceptualized their gender identities was not, in the sense that they naturalized heterosexual norms in their self-definitions. This was so, despite the fact that there were clearly other perspectives on gender, sexuality and the family held by women in their communities. When I began to see both who was present and who was not, and what issues were being discussed and what ones were not, it became clear that community-based women's organizations, along with larger societal institutions, serve as disciplining mechanisms by reinforcing and reproducing norms of gender, family, sexuality, ethnicity and nation (Lind in progress). 'Hidden histories' of gender, the family, the state and development were present in these women's organizations (Dore and Molyneux 2000). Women's organizations are not always transgressive or transformative; far from it, they also serve to discipline women's lives. Thinking about it from this perspective, it is not surprising that sex workers, lesbians, Afro-Ecuadorian women and indigenous women have all chosen to develop their own movements, autonomous from the more visible 'women's movement' in Ecuador (see for example Abad et al. 1998). Ethnic nationalism, regional biases, homophobia and traditional forms of morality all contribute to how women (in this case) are seen as either normal or deviant, acceptable or unacceptable, in their home communities as well as in the context of national politics and development.

Although we recognize that the gender and development field is a product of women's activism throughout the world and acknowledge its importance, we believe that it is time to think about gender differently, since notions of gender and the family also serve as disciplining mechanisms. In many recent meetings we have attended, feminist scholars have addressed how gender has become a widely accepted, even status quo category of analysis in the international development field, whereas (for example) sexuality or race has not (Baden and Goetz 1997).[7] This is not a coincidence, since 'gender' as it is defined in many development frameworks and operationalized in practice normalizes the traditional family and does not challenge the broader social structure. In research conducted in Bolivia in the spring of 1999, I (Amy) found that dozens and perhaps hundreds of municipalities in Bolivia now include a 'gender focus' in their constitutions or in some other aspect of a community development plan (IFFI, personal interview, April 1999). In this scenario, women's integration into decentralization initiatives and local planning is seen as positive, yet what remains naturalized is a heteronormative understanding of women's roles in development, including how women are linked to their family positions and are devoid of sexual agency.

In Bolivia, this heteronormative understanding of women's roles in development was reproduced through the late President Hugo Banzer's restructuring of state ministries after 1998. Gender issues are now housed in the Vice-Ministry of Gender, Generational Affairs and the Family. Previously, gender concerns were housed in the Vice-Ministry of Gender, Ethnic and Generational Affairs (1994–97). During that period women's and indigenous people's concerns were awkwardly placed within and addressed by one state agency (a problematic approach in and of itself – see, for example, Paulson and Calla 2000). President Banzer reinvoked a traditional notion of 'the family' as a state concern and linked it directly to gender. In the context of what cultural critic Jean Franco (1996) refers to as the 'gender wars' in Latin America, where governments and the Catholic Church have launched attacks on the usage of 'gender' in state constitutions and political processes,[8] Banzer's new ministry was an attempt to re-establish a traditional definition of the family and link it directly to his goals of modernizing the country. In this case and many others, maternalist ideologies of gender and nationhood (Taylor 1997, Bunster-Burroto 1986) tend to naturalize sexuality as heteronormative and regulate it along with family structure. What is 'natural' becomes conflated with heteronormative values of sexuality, gender, modernization and modernity (see also Balderston and Guy 1997a: 4–5). Meanwhile, homosexuality continues to be criminalized in Bolivia, gay bars are almost entirely underground, gay men and transvestites have suffered from police repression and violence, and many lesbians live entirely in the 'closet' for fear of public and family backlash.

Another example of heteronormativity in the development field concerns the practices of organizations that focus on 'integrating women into development'. As has been well documented, many self-defined feminist NGOs have benefited historically from international solidarity and development aid (Jaquette 1994, Vargas 1992, Alvarez 1999). This is so despite the fact that many feminist groups oppose development practices, in particular neoliberal economic policies, structural adjustment measures and the region's explosive foreign debt crisis that began in the early 1980s (Benería 1996). While development aid may have helped to institutionalize women's grassroots political struggles, the drawback of this historical institutionalization is that many feminists must now frame their struggles in terms of development in order to receive the funding, often creating further class divisions among middle-class feminists and the working-class/peasant/indigenous women who typically are the constituents of state and NGO development projects (Schild 1998).

Although discourses and practices of development are rarely explicitly marked in terms of gender and sexuality, they are inherently gendered and sexed: one need only view the numerous visual representations of 'Third World women' in the literature of the United Nations, the World Bank, religious organizations such as Catholic Relief Services (CRS), etc., to see how women are marked as mothers, wives and heterosexual. While we recognize that many women are, in fact, mothers, wives and/or heterosexual, the systematic effect of this representation is the normalization of Third World women's lives as heterosexual and family-bound, in addition to being poor, illiterate, lacking formal education, traditional and non-white (Mohanty 1991).

Despite important advances made by feminist practitioners since the inception of the gender and development field (Rathgeber 1990, Tinker 1990, Kabeer 1994, Jackson and Pearson 1998), 'sexuality and development' is rarely discussed except in terms of reproductive health, and sexual identity is linked to national and financial well-being in apolitical, heteronormative ways. Because of this, as we have argued, queer identities and alternative family paradigms are 'invisible' in daily economic transactions and household life. They become obscured and constructed as academic abstractions, irrelevant to 'real' women's lives and therefore not influential in policy-making or development theories (Barroso and Bruschini 1991, Gilliam 1991, Thadani 1996).

One way this occurs is through the usage of standard social and economic indicators in development practices. For example, through presumably objective, often quantifiable indicators of women's status, including life expectancy, literacy, sex ratio, birth rates, nutrition and income-generating activities, women are determined to be in need or poor and 'underdeveloped', or conversely, well-off and 'developed'. In many development publications, the lives of Third World women are collapsed into a few frozen 'indicators' of their well-being (see Mohanty 1991). Furthermore, some feminist scholars and policy-makers argue that sexuality is not an important issue, especially for poor women.[9] But the institutionalized regulation of sexuality does influence survival, channelling development funds and efforts into arenas where acceptable sexuality is defined, reproduced and monitored.

For example, the state, non-governmental organizations and lending institutions normalize, sexualize and regulate men's and women's lives, often using the rubric of modernization, in tourism development (Alexander 1991), family planning practices (Hartmann 1995) and the global sex industry (Enloe 1990, 2000, Kempadoo and Doezema 1998), as well as in traditional development practices that attempt to integrate women into local development initiatives. Chandra Mohanty (1997) suggests that women's homosocial networks, often rooted in traditional kinship structures and community ties, give married women job and security advantages that non-married women do not have. This is largely invisible and ignored in many studies of women's roles in local development initiatives. Women, who are often excluded from formalized production networks, sometimes establish informal and communal ties with other women in their communities. These connections are typically based on institutionalized heterosexuality – a privilege that queer women do not always have access to, depending on their relations with their families and communities. In this sense, merely celebrating women's increased visibility in politics and development does little to challenge the systemic binarism that relegates women to the reproductive sphere in the first place, nor the inescapable economic dependence on fathers and husbands that it engenders. 'Family' and 'heterosexuality' merge, tightening any space for kinship to broaden its meaning and welcome LGBT people, same-sex desire and homosocial relationships into the community. The performance of gender in these contexts and its Western interpretations in development theory and practice is a considerable part of the legal and social code that locks queer people out.

LGBT Movements and the Politics of Development

LGBT groups have been among the first to challenge institutionalized heterosexuality in Latin American societies. The 'NGO-ization' of LGBT groups has brought with it a strong, growing network of local, regional and international organizations, many of which are connected to the international development field in one way or another. For example, many local groups have received foreign aid[10] and, generally speaking, homosexuality is more widely visible in popular culture (telenovelas, films, magazines, books) and more commonly discussed among people in their daily lives (on this point see

Foster 1997 and Rodríguez Pereyra 2001). As elsewhere, part of the reason for this heightened awareness is that LGBT people are fighting back more than ever. The 'queering' of Latin American societies is occurring in many places and spaces, including at Gay Pride marches which have been held in major cities such as Buenos Aires, Rio de Janeiro, Mexico City and Managua.[11]

The International Lesbian and Gay Association (ILGA), although originally Europe-based, was probably the first international organization to fund Third World LGBT groups. Beginning in the early to mid-1980s, ILGA funded representatives of several grassroots gay and lesbian organizations to attend their international meetings, then commonly held in Europe. Peru's GALF, Brazil's GALF, Mexico's El Closet de Sor Juana, Costa Rica's Las Entendidas, among many other lesbian groups in Latin America, Africa and Asia, were able to send representatives to the meetings and establish regional networks. Now, ILGA has transformed itself into an international, rather than a European, umbrella organization with over 350 member groups in approximately 80 countries. ILGA was also the first international organization to be granted official status by the United Nations, following much scrutiny by UN representatives and US politicians (e.g. Jesse Helms) who fought to withhold UN funding from ILGA because (among other reasons) the North American Man-Boy Loving Association (NAMBLA) was a member of ILGA. In 1994, ILGA voted to oust NAMBLA from its membership in order to maintain its status with the UN – a political negotiation that was highly controversial and contested within ILGA meetings.

In a sense, ILGA represents the globalized nature of Latin American (and more generally, Third World) LGBT struggles. In his research on gay organizations in Santa Cruz, Bolivia, Timothy Wright argues that, while in 1985 the Bolivian government claimed to 'launch itself in the global age … by 1992, for better or for worse, globalisation was reaching into the quiet, personal and taboo corners of human sexuality' (Wright 2000: 91). Wright is referring to how the AIDS epidemic has contributed to an 'explosion' of public debate on sexuality, and especially homosexuality, in Bolivia when USAID began to fund gay organizations as part of its strategy to address public health concerns, including the AIDS epidemic. He argues:

> AIDS became a new justification for international development assistance in 1988 when USAID awarded the [Ministry of Health] a three year, $500,000 assistance grant to begin HIV/AIDS surveillance work and to provide some basic training for preventative education … rumblings from overseas arriving via mass media, together with development dollars … began the process by which the traditional silence on homosexuality unraveled. (Wright 2000: 97)

Wright acknowledges the multiple ways in which LGBT people in Bolivia have survived and struggled, yet he also points out that 'The AIDS epidemic has fostered the sudden foundation of gay organizations in unlikely places', including through development practices, which leads him to frame his study as a case of the 'globalization of sexual identity' (2000: 107). According to Wright, another aspect of the politics of sexuality in Bolivia concerns how USAID, the Ministry of Health, local health care professionals and LGBT activists have different perspectives on who is considered 'gay' (such as men who define themselves as gay or *marica* versus men who define themselves as heterosexual yet have sexual relations with other men) and how and where gay communities are found (whether in 'gay neighbourhoods' as one might find in US cities such as San Francisco or New York, or through other networks which are not place-based). As a paid employee in this project (Wright worked for Proyecto Contra el Sida, or PCS, the Bolivian organization that managed the project based on a traditional development model of expert–client relations), Wright wrote a report in which he argued that service delivery would be most likely to reach the target population through a team of outreach workers and a telephone hotline rather than through a geographically fixed service centre (which is based on a notion of a geographically fixed gay community – see Wright 2000: 99). Despite his policy recommendations, officials from PCS argued for and won the geographically fixed service centre. Thus practitioners in the project struggled over how community and sexual identity are defined. The policy outcome reflected a US- and international development-based understanding of gay community and identity more than any of several local understandings of community and identity. This study exemplifies the contradictions that exist among and within local LGBT organizations as they negotiate on the one hand with lenders and administrators and on the other with their clients – in this case men who have sexual relations with men, some of whom do not identify as homosexual in any form and/or are afraid to participate because of social stigmas.

Wright's research demonstrates the need to 'queer' the development field; that is, to make institutionalized heterosexuality visible in development policies and projects, as well as in development practitioners' own heteronormative ways of thinking about sexuality in men's and women's lives. Unfortunately we are not familiar with any in-depth studies of lesbian (or other queer women's) experiences in the development field; this research has yet to be conducted, although clearly there are many stories to be told. We can say with certainty, however, that in many development frameworks, lesbians and other 'unacceptable' women are hardly, if at all, perceived as a subset of households or families and rarely made visible as women. The women who are included in development frameworks (e.g. frameworks of household survival, rural development, subsistence agriculture, informal sector employment) are generally viewed as family-bound. Framing women's lives in this way contributes to the heterosexist structuring of national social orders and prevents many LGBT people from envisioning and/or organizing their lives in alternative ways (Borren 1988). Heteronormativity in development discourse (and in other discourses) disallows any construction of queer identity or existence to flourish, except when defined in terms of a social problem or health hazard.[12] Ironically, this has given gay male organizations more significant power (especially through funding for AIDS projects) than their lesbian counterparts.

The silence surrounding issues of sexual orientation and identity stems from and is reproduced by stereotypes which claim that homosexuality is derived from the West and is therefore irrelevant to the lives and experiences of people in Third World countries (Reinfelder 1996). Such a bias has contributed to the fact that, until very recently, sexual orientation has been omitted from international human rights agendas and LGBT people have been disregarded as active participants in community and national decision-making processes (Rosenbloom 1995).[13] It was not until ILGA, the International Gay and Lesbian Human Rights Commission (IGLHRC) and hundreds of LGBT groups pressured human rights communities around the world that international groups such as Human Rights Watch and Amnesty International decided to include sexual orientation on their agendas. The increased visibility of lesbian rights – in human rights agendas and through placing pressure on the UN to officially approve a lesbian rights agenda – has also made visible institutionalized heterosexuality at an international level. This visibility has helped to situate the heterosexual experiences of women as a relative one and not as the universal norm. With this awareness, we can begin to examine and understand how, for example, lesbians experience rape, murder, forced marriage, imprisonment, social and familial oppression, psychiatric treatment, inadequate and discriminatory health care, pension, inheritance, international partnerships and custody issues from very different standpoints than those of socially accepted, heterosexual women (Reinfelder 1996).

As the opening quote by a Peruvian feminist illustrates, the stereotype that homosexuality is a Western import denies lesbians and other queer women their identities and rights to full citizenship. Seen as traitors to nationalist movements and/or as too Westernized, queer women in Third World contexts have been oppressed by both the political right and left. For example, one Peruvian lesbian activist was expelled from the Communist Party (Partido Comunista del Peru, or PCP), in the late 1970s,[14] on the basis that her lesbian identity was a product of capitalism, thus rendering her a potential traitor in the eyes of the party. Approximately seven years later, she was persecuted by the military and sought (informal) political refuge in the United States. Ironically, her persecution by the military was most likely due to her past involvement in PCP but also perhaps to the fact that she was a published lesbian writer. This story and many more like it remain untold to the general public and largely invisible.

Despite the silencing, queer women have addressed their invisibility in numerous ways, including challenging heterosexism in national and regional women's movements (as at the GALF meeting in Lima), establishing their own groups and publications, and by creating more inclusive political agendas that speak to a broader spectrum of women and take into consideration sexual agency and self-determination. In Bolivia, for example, the founding members of Mujeres Creando have published a book on sexism and racism in Bolivian society, in which the authors make connections among the racialization of Bolivian women and their sexualization – in development discourse, national political discourse and in various other intellectual, activist and cultural arenas (see Paredes and Galinda, n.d.). In Mexico, Norma Mogrovejo (2000) has published an important and controversial book about the relationship among lesbians, the women's movement and the homosexual movement in Mexico. It is controversial in part because Mogrovejo 'outs' several women who had not chosen to come out publicly for one reason or another. Each of these publications raises many issues that LGBT activists and individuals think about in their daily lives and political struggles. Each could serve to help practitioners, policy-makers and activists rethink institutionalized heterosexuality in Latin American cultural contexts and 'encounters with development' (Escobar 1995).

Queering Development: LGBT Activism and Research in Latin America

As we have shown, while the insights made by LGBT groups about in-stitutionalized heterosexuality have until recently rarely been taken seriously by development theorists and practitioners, we are calling for a merging of LGBT scholarship with gender and development scholarship. Perhaps it would not be a marriage, but at least a negotiated partnership, in which development theorists and practitioners unpack the ways in which gender and sexuality have been conflated and naturalized in women's lives. As with other scholarship on development in Latin America and the WCD perspective generally, we agree that an integrated approach that combines economic as well as political, cultural and social factors, rather than one that prioritizes the economic over other factors, is more effective for understanding women's and LGBT people's lives in the region (see introduction to this book; also Chua, Bhavnani and Foran 2000 and Alvarez, Dagnino and Escobar 1998).

To our knowledge, little research has been conducted to examine how development itself is marked in terms of sexuality; how this reinforces hetero-sexual norms in studies of women's lives in Third World contexts; how this plays out in practice and how LGBT groups have responded to institutionalized heterosexuality in the development field (and elsewhere). In closing, we wish to offer some suggestions for future research on women, sexuality and development, with the aim of denaturalizing institutionalized heterosexuality and of queering development.

Rethinking the family In many traditional studies of 'women's roles in development', families or households are the units of analysis. When it is assumed that all families are structured on the basis of traditional kinship systems (including the institution of marriage), queer women and non-traditional heterosexual women remain invisible. Researchers could do more to understand how women and men perform certain gender roles and functions in their communities, in relation to how they do or do not fit within the institutionalized norms of heterosexuality. This has repercussions for queer women as well as for heterosexual women who are considered social outsiders. Examining how women discipline themselves, as well as how institutions serve to discipline us as citizens, mothers, labourers, etc., would also allow us to see both who gains from institutionalized heterosexuality and who loses out.

Researching LGBT lives More research could be done to examine queer lives, experiences and perspectives in Third World contexts. Even some queer-positive research has tended to dichotomize queerness in terms of 'indigenous' versus 'Western' forms of homosexuality (Thadani 1996, see also Howe 2000): we support a research agenda which complicates rather than reproduces this historical dichotomy.

Denaturalizing institutionalized heterosexuality To the extent that socially acceptable heterosexual women benefit more from development policies and projects than do queer women, development frameworks are heterosexist. One way to think differently about concrete development policies and practices would be to denaturalize heterosexuality in conceptual frameworks of household survival strategies and economic crisis, time-use studies of women's reproductive work, women's labour force participation, gender and international trade, the effects of foreign investment on local communities and women's community roles, to name but a few.[15]

Sexual rights as a development issue Women's sexual rights must be seen as a development issue, as they concern the survival, autonomy and rights of many women and men throughout the world. Increasingly, women's rights have been seen as human rights (to draw from the political slogan, 'Women's Rights are Human Rights', circulated widely at the United Nations Decade for Women in Beijing in 1995), but lesbian rights are only beginning to be incorporated into human rights agendas and are rarely if ever considered an issue of development. While LGBT organizations have received funding for some projects (especially projects related to HIV / AIDS education, counselling and prevention), much needs to be done to address the economic, social, political and cultural rights of LGBT people, including the right to housing, employment, access to basic resources and self-determination.

LGBT forms of resistance Research could be conducted to examine how LGBT individuals, groups and social movements have contributed to rethinking development, democracy, political participation, citizenship and the so-called public and private spheres of everyday life. In this chapter we have barely touched on the diversity of LGBT experiences in Latin America; much could be done to examine the complex ways in which people subjectively interpret their identities, work choices, living situations, families and political desires in neocolonial contexts. Some important studies of sexuality and performativity include those of Lancaster (1994), Balderston and Guy (1997), Green (2000) and Babb (2001). Norma Mogrovejo's (2000) study of lesbian struggles and their relationships with broader homosexual and feminist movements in Latin America is also an important source. More could be done, however, to document LGBT forms of resistance to homophobia, heterosexism and social control.

The queering of development is a much-needed project. Fortunately, in June 2001 the Office of the United Nations High Commissioner for Human Rights moved to increase its work on sexual orientation and gender identity (IGLHRC 2001a). This will have significant effects on UN policy frameworks, research and project implementation. It may also push national governments to pay attention to LGBT issues. Considerable pressure continues to be placed on the international community to address human rights violations and to consider sexuality a survival (and development) issue. For a lesbian who is beaten up outside her home in São Paulo, a Limeñan lesbian picked up by the military simply for appearing 'masculine', and a heterosexual single mother who is employed as a sex worker or whose sexual relationships are perceived as 'deviant' by her neighbours in Mexico City, sexuality is most definitely a survival issue. Even 'acceptable' women who fit within traditional norms of gender and sexuality face multiple issues such as sexual abuse and lack of knowledge about their bodies and women's health, along with related factors including poor body image, eating disorders,[16] depression and mental illness. It is our hope that these issues will be taken seriously by development organizations concerned with the survival of women in Latin American countries and elsewhere. Likewise, we hope that institutionalized heterosexuality will one day be seen as but one sexual/gender identity among many others.

Notes

We would like to thank Stephanie Brzuzy for her helpful comments on earlier drafts of this paper.

1. The Grupo de Auto-Conciencia de Lesbianas Feministas (GALF) was initiated in the mid-1970s in Lima. It was the first organization of its kind in Peru to address lesbian-feminist issues and served as an important space for self-reflection and political organizing in the lesbian community. Due to personal reasons as well as the effects of Peru's civil war in the 1980s, some members of GALF left the country and the organization ceased to exist. It has now re-emerged and redefined its membership to include Peruvians living outside Peru as well. GALF has its own electronic newsletter, *Labia*.

2. 'Outing' is a particularly controversial political strategy in Bolivia. In a context where homosexuality is heavily stigmatized and there are very few visible lesbian public figures to serve as role models, many lesbians do not want to come out publicly for fear of losing their jobs, their families or, in some cases, their lives.

3. In this chapter we use the terms 'First World' and 'Third World', as have many scholars and activists, to acknowledge the immense power (and neocolonial) relations among rich and poor countries. We also use these terms in the political sense, as we believe it is necessary to rethink the entire historical project of development because it helps to shape unequal relations between First World and Third World regions – and also the ideological notions of progress and modernity that help support the economic, political and cultural hegemony of development and modernization (for a review of this literature, see Escobar 1995).

4. Rich was perhaps the first feminist scholar to argue for an analysis of hetero-sexuality as a social institution that structures societal institutions, processes, cultural practices, everyday life and our most intimate feelings. Rich points out that it is compulsory heterosexuality and not just gender oppression (the oppression of women, in her definition), that contributes to the historical demonization of lesbians and other sexual others (including heterosexual women deemed 'unacceptable' for one reason or another), sexual slavery and the naturalization of domestic violence and rape within marriage.

5. Most Latin American countries have repealed laws that criminalize homosexu-ality itself. However, most if not all countries continue to criminalize homosexual practices through various laws (e.g. anti-sodomy laws), policies (e.g. operations to 'clean the streets' of male prostitutes and/or transgendered people) and legal edicts, among other means. In his study of constitutionalism and LGBT movements in Latin America, Mark Ungar found that 'Homosexuality itself is illegal in 85 countries around the world. It is punished with death in eight of them (each of which practices a strict interpretation of Islamic *shari'a* law) and draws a prison term of ten years to life in seven, 3–10 years in eleven and up to three years in ten others. In most of the remaining 49 countries, it carries variable and arbitrarily enforced punishments' (Ungar 2000: 2).

6. In this case, 'America' refers to the United States. Fernández-Alemany (2000: 2–3) points out that, like the term 'gay,' in the USA 'America' does not represent a homogeneous and uniform identity, nor can it be reduced to a single and monolithic identity. Some gay men he interviewed in Honduras tend to essentialize and roman-ticize the meaning of 'America', due of course to the cultural and economic hegemony of the USA in the Americas.

7. For example, at the conference 'The Future of Women's Studies', held at the University of Arizona, 20–21 October 2000, Norma Alarcón argued that gender has become a status quo category of analysis, allowing many (often white) women to receive funding for their research, whereas women of colour who conduct research on race are unable to receive funding for their projects. At the conference 'Gender Policies in Latin America', held at the University of Miami in March 2000, we discussed the historical shift from the 1970s and 1980s, when many women's organizations were considered radical or oppositional, to the present, when second-wave feminisms in Latin America have become institutionalized and status quo, versus others (particularly so-called autonomous feminists) who oppose working within what they call the 'gender technocracy'.

8. In fact, a group of politicians in Chile has attempted to eliminate the term 'gender' from the Chilean constitution and the educational system on the basis that 'gender' implies a war against men (see Oyarzún 2000).

9. For example, Angela Gilliam argues that 'Most of the world's working women – including many poor women in the United States – identify survival issues to be food, housing, health care and employment, not sexuality' (1991: 218). Gilliam shows how women themselves position these concerns as separate and independent categories in which sexual autonomy does not have an integral or reciprocal connection. In this view, food and jobs become 'immediate' needs and sexuality becomes trivialized as a political project outside the boundaries of everyday life (Miller and Razavi 1998).

10. The American Friends Service Committee (AFSC), for example, has funded regional conferences and networks of gay and lesbian activists. In some cases, international lending agencies have influenced national governments to launch HIV/AIDS awareness and outreach programmes, often by subcontracting NGOs, establishing a project competition that NGOs apply to, or delegating a project to a particular NGO. As state ministries (e.g. health, social welfare) turn over the management of AIDS/HIV programmes to NGOs, this helps to strengthen local LGBT movements.

11. In some cases, such as in Buenos Aires, activists sometimes cover their faces while they march, indicating that they are willing to 'come out' in public, yet fearful that they may be politically repressed. Gay Pride marches in Latin America take place on the anniversary of the 1969 Stonewall riots in New York City. LGBT movements have taken advantage of the transnational flow of knowledge, including memories of Stonewall, in order to construct their own local struggle. While perhaps someday marches in Latin America will mark a regional event or memory, rather than a US-based one, activists have none the less reclaimed Stonewall for their own political purposes, including the local repression of LGBT people as well as the politics of international development and globalization. During Gay Pride marches in Buenos Aires in the 1990s, activists often held signs protesting about municipal edicts and police repression – local forms of violence – while also commemorating those who died at Stonewall.

12. As some scholars have pointed out (Farmer 1992, Patton 1996), the HIV/AIDS crisis has been sexualized and racialized, making 'Africans' as well as 'homosexuals' an object of development – of interest to development practitioners – only when they are perceived as a public health hazard and a threat to national security.

13. Until the 1990s, even the international human rights community was reluctant to address human rights violations on the basis of sexual orientation. Amnesty International, for example, only began to address issues of persecution on the basis of sexual orientation in the mid-1990s. International organizations such as the Interna-

tional Lesbian and Gay Association (ILGA) and the International Gay and Lesbian Human Rights Commission (IGLHRC) have played important roles in addressing these issues and getting them on national and international agendas (such as the United Nations, Amnesty International, Human Rights Watch).

14. Her involvement in the Partido Comunista del Peru (PCP) was prior to the PCP's split into three factions, including PCP-Sendero Luminoso (Shining Path). Just following the party split, Sendero Luminoso went underground in the late 1970s after being rejected by the legal left and repressed by the government.

15. One informal study by members of Peru-based GALF examined economic survival strategies among butch and femme lesbians in Lima. In this never-funded, unpublished study of Lima's large butch-femme lesbian community, researchers found that femme lesbians supported their butch partners at times when butch women could not 'pass' as acceptable women – nor as men.

16. Argentina, for example, has the second highest rate of eating disorders in the world, next only to the United States. Throughout Latin America, women who experience poor body image and/or eating disorders are typically survivors of incest or another form of sexual abuse and/or have experienced extreme poverty, racial or class oppression (unlike the United States, where notions of body image are quite distinct).

CHAPTER 4

. . . .

Claiming the State: Women's Reproductive Identity and Indian Development

Rachel Simon Kumar

§ CONVENTIONAL approaches to development view market institutions as pivotal to the organization of the social, economic and political lives of people. As Evans (1996: 1033) points out: 'Too often development theory has operated, *de facto*, on the premise that the only institutions that mattered were those directly facilitating market transactions.' This narrow conceptualization obscures the reality that individual relationships with the market are, in fact, derived from the wider social, cultural, juridical and political fabric of particular contexts. Far from being independent, economic relationships are defined by individual and collective identities informed by institutions and networks in the social sphere, foremost among them those structures that shape power relations in society. This chapter focuses on the role of the state in directing the rationales of development, an area that has been relatively unexplored in development literature. Inherent to the arguments made here is the premise that the state is not merely a neutral administrative institution, but is rather a bearer of ideologies and values that actively give particular interpretations to the way development is strategized. These interpretations, in turn, define the relationships that individuals have with the markets and institutions of production.[1]

The lacuna in the scholarship on the state and its ideologies is especially significant in women and development research and practice. This literature, by and large, is premised on the primacy of the market in defining women's political and social identities (see, for instance, Sen 1990). At a macro level, women's political fortunes are implicitly tied in with their productive capacities – integration into mainstream development processes is a precursory step to emancipation and recognition within society and polity (Bandarage 1984). What we might call 'development identities', therefore, both facilitate and forestall political status.

This view underplays the idea that women's political and economic identities are mutually constitutive; just as institutions of the market define sociopolitical status, the construction of women as a development constituency is influenced by the wider political structures in society. In this essay, I argue that the state and the market are linked inextricably in locating women within the discourse of development. Developmental discourses reflect, among others, the discourses of the state (e.g. nationalist discourses) and society (e.g. cultural representations). The state's discourses circumscribe the parameters of women's status in development – from the kind of activities they can participate in to the notions of emancipation and rights. The role of the state in constructing women's developmental identities in the state has taken on a particular relevance since the 1990s, when, under the doctrine of market development, economic and political discourses converged to define notions of citizenship and development, and the rights and obligations of individuals and the state (Lister 1997).

The arguments in this chapter are grounded in the literature on and empirical analysis of gender policy in India.[2] I focus on the Government of India's (GoI) recently instituted Reproductive and Child Health Policy (RCH).[3] The RCH, as a population policy, is an important instrument for engendering development. Its formulation in the wake of the 1994 International Conference for Population and Development (ICPD) at Cairo has had significant impact for the construction of a gender-sensitive reproductive policy. More provision, for instance, has been made for women's needs at the level of strategy (Anita 1996, Chatterjee 1996). But what is relevant in the context of this chapter is that reproductive policy in the last decade is being institutionalized against a wider expectation of women's political claims (see among others, Cook 1993, 1995, Correa 1994, Correa and Petchesky 1994, Petchesky 1995). The RCH has been designed against a background of discussion on the claims to rights that all citizens are entitled to and what the state is obliged to provide. Yet the RCH is also an instrument of development – it functions to stabilize population growth against the objective of economic development of the state. As such, a feminist evaluation of the policy will enable us to examine how political and developmental identities of women intersect, and how their construction defines political possibilities for women in Indian development.

Gender Identity and the Indian State

Feminist scholars are divided in their opinions regarding the role of the modern Indian state in the lives of its millions of women. Some point out that the state responds in ambivalent ways to the vulnerable conditions in which women live in Indian society (Misra 1997, John 1996, Rai 1996, 1996a), while others present the Indian state as monolithic in nature (Agarwal 1988, Kasturi 1996). Those who characterize the state as ambivalent point to its ineffective action in individual cases of women's welfare, inadequate resources for women's social programmes and the general inaccessibility of the state for the average woman despite constitutional statutes that recognize women's equality in Indian society. With respect to what it offers women, Rai (1996) refers to India as a 'weak' state. On the other hand, others assert that the Indian state is unequivocally patriarchal. Agarwal (1988) points out that India, like other South Asian states, perpetuates patriarchal relations with two express intents – to domesticate women and control their sexuality. Similarly, Kasturi (1996: 100) contends that the process of development in India 'has actually strengthened patriarchal structures in India'. In the 1990s, the upsurge of communal identities and religious traditions made women a prime site around which political claims are contested, a politics in which the state is a complicit actor (see Hasan 1994). It is along these lines that Rai (1996, 1996a) and Basu (1998) argue that the state is an inconsistent actor: on many occasions, the state and traditional patriarchy are in binary opposition, while in other circumstances, the state *is* the patriarchy that oppresses women.

The Indian state's ambivalence to women's interests can be demonstrated through a review of its responses to legal and political issues in recent history. The Shah Bano case of the 1980s is a classic and oft-cited example, where the state placed partisan and electoral interests above the welfare of Muslim women in the country. In order to appease conservative Muslims, the government overturned a Supreme Court ruling and withdrew legal provisions that entitled divorced Muslim women to claim maintenance from their husbands (Engineer 1987, Kumar 1993). The state has also been criticized for its ineffective handling of the 1987 case of *sati*, when a young widow was burnt to death on the funeral pyre of her husband. Although the government passed a Commission of Sati (Prevention) Act in 1987, it is a legal provision fraught with problems. While prohibiting the glorification of *sati*, the bill treats the act as suicide, placing the onus of responsibility on the victim (Kasturi 1996). In cases of rape, despite the existence of harsh penalties for the aggressors, the state has likewise tended to place the onus of proof on the women victims (John 1996, Swarup et al. 1994). Similarly, where laws protecting women exist, their enforcement is weak. Dowry was officially made illegal with the passing of the Dowry Prohibition Act in 1961, but the practice still continues widely. In response to the widespread abortion of female foetuses, the Pre-Natal Diagnostic Techniques (Regulation and Prevention of Misuses) Act of 1994 was passed, prohibiting all genetic counselling facilities, genetic clinics and laboratories from divulging information about the sex of a foetus. Its efficacy is, by and large, seen as inadequate (*The Hindu*, 25 December 2000).

On the other hand, the Indian Constitution recognizes the equality of the sexes and acknowledges in its Directive Principles that women are a vulnerable group requiring special rights. The state encourages the political participation of women in the electoral process. The Parliament recently passed the 73rd and 74th amendments to the Constitution of India, whereby one-third of all seats in the third tier of elected local government bodies (*panchayats*) in the country were reserved for women. A similar legislation is being pursued for national bodies as well (the Women's Bill), but this is still under debate in Parliament following opposition to the bill from several political parties. In the case of community-based laws, the rights of Christian women in Kerala were strengthened by the Supreme Court's judgment in the Mary Roy case in the 1980s, which conferred equal rights to property for daughters and sons in the Kerala Christian community (Panikulangara 1986). In late 1999, the Kerala government set out stringent regulations regarding sexual harassment at work.[4] More recently, it also came out with a proposal to ensure maternity benefits for women labourers who are daily wage earners in the informal sector of the economy (*The Hindu*, 9 March 2000).

Alongside their community-based identities, women's political identity in the state is also defined by their role in development and nation building (Agnihotri and Mazumdar 1995, Chaudhuri 1995, Desai 1986, John 1996, Kasturi 1996). Post-independence India, with its colonial legacy, was essentially an agglomeration of multiple ethnic, religious and communal identities bound together under a common nationalist umbrella. The nationalist agenda emerged from a common enemy – the colonial rulers – and a common goal, namely, nation building through economic development. The nationalist movement, from even before independence, advocated freedom, dignity, justice and equality as essential attributes for all citizens, and this enabled women to participate as partners in nation building (Agnihotri and Mazumdar 1995). In 1938, the Congress Party produced 'Women's Role in a Planned Economy' (WRPE), a document that shaped the post-independence foundations of women in nation building. Chaudhuri's (1995) analysis of the document reveals that there are strong references to women playing equal roles with men in nation building – their citizenship is affirmed in their capacity as producers and labourers: 'the only social status to be recognised in planned society will be that of the individual worker ... neither motherhood, nor wifehood, nor, *a fortiori*, widowhood matter at all' (cited in Chaudhuri 1995: 219).

Yet, contradictorily, these nationalist discourses also constructed women as emblems of national culture and tradition. The official channels of the state promoted the image of a self-sacrificing wife and mother assuming her 'natural' place in the home for the upbringing of India's greatest asset – her children. This image of woman is, in fact, far from secular – it hearkens back to a lost Vedic time and is a portrayal of a Hindu Brahminical ideal of woman (Chaudhuri 1995, Uberoi 1996).[5] In the 1930s, the ideology of women's purity influenced the foundations of policy-making in modern India. Chaudhuri points out that the WRPE notes that women's responsibility in independent

India, alongside the role of socialist worker, would equally be to 'create a cultural environment in the home for the proper nurture of the children' and '[not become] a cheap imitation of man or render her useless for the great tasks of motherhood and nation-building' (cited in Chaudhuri 1995: 233, 224).

In contemporary India these two images of women – as socialized mother and abstract worker – still co-exist and are in tension. Scholars argue that these constructions are reproduced in the state's developmental policies related to women. Agarwal (1988: 14) notes that this is the ideology of gender – the assumption that women are (or should be) primarily housewives and mothers and, secondarily, workers – that permeates the policies of modern developing states like India. Women, in most policies related to productive and reproductive functions, land/property holding and technology control, are located within the context of the family, thereby assigning primacy to (*de facto*) male heads of households (Kelkar 1987). Swaminathan (1991) argues further that the tendency to demarcate certain provisions in the state's Plan Documents as 'women's issues' (especially those related to reproduction and child care) reinforces gendered assumptions about women's roles in society. The World Bank's (1991) study of Indian women found that the major cause for women's subordinate status was their predominance in the 'inside' (domestic) spaces of society. Development policy, the Bank argues, should emphasize women's productivity as an economic actor in the 'outside' (public) sphere.

Thus, the dominant state discourses polarize women's identity along a 'mother–worker' continuum. As this binary is reproduced alongside developmental discourses, the notion of mother is associated with 'traditional-private-politically ineffective' while that of worker is associated with 'modern-public-politically effective'. Official political discourses in India seem to advocate a movement from a reproductive role to a productive one. Contrary to the state's official propaganda, the equally pervasive discourses of communal groups (sometimes implicitly supported by political parties) appear to restrain women in their reproductive roles.

Women's Economic Identity and Rights in the 1990s

If political identity has an effect on women's representation in economic policy, the reverse is also true: economic constructions of women have implications for their claims to political rights. The significance of political gains through developmental interventions of the state should first be clarified. Jayal (1994) argues that the enhancement of political 'rights' is not directly a consequence, or even a factor, of developmental change in India. She points out that the history of developmental intervention in welfare activities in India cannot be seen as akin to the social programmes of a welfare state. The welfare state is motivated by a conceptualization of rights (both a liberal and social rights conceptualization) which is absent in the case of India. The aim of development intervention in India was not to maximize welfare, or enhance the rights of a collective, but to provide a foundation for the project of modernization and growth. There are implications that follow because development welfare is not expressed in a language of rights. There is no obligation for the state to provide for citizens' welfare and, likewise, citizens have no foundation, other than moral grounds, to make claims for development interventions from the state. The state, in a sense, becomes a paternal benefactor, and casts the relationship between the citizen and state as one of 'giver and receiver, benefactor and beneficiary' (1994: 23). Issues of political rewards are, therefore, outside the debate of development; gaining access to the state, say, through visibility of a specific group, is incidental to the intent of state intervention in development.

The debate surrounding access to rights through development has been gaining momentum since the 1990s, when there were perceptible shifts in the developmental state's attitudes to its obligations to the citizenry. With the adoption of the New Economic Policies (NEP), India has moved towards becoming a neoliberal state (Byres 1998). The fundamental philosophy of neoliberal discourse is that it extols the citizen as a rational, self-interested, competitive and productive individual. The state's role is primarily to provide conditions for unfettered economic interaction; it aims to be non-interventionist. 'Rights' of the individual are represented in terms of non-interference, as s/he makes choices. In India, the period of economic reform has set into motion a period of deregulation in trade practices, greater efforts to link up with the international economy, increased emphasis on export-oriented growth and attempts to provide an efficient administration. In terms of its welfare activities, the state has not reneged on its obligation of providing state-subsidized[6] health and education, despite criticism that expenditure in these sectors has fallen in the 1990s (Alternative Survey Group 1997) and that poverty levels have risen (Byres 1998). However, what the state has instead begun to focus on in its welfare interventions has been to increase 'efficiency' by reducing 'the "menu" of subsidized services and standardi[zing] their quality' (Jayal 1994: 23) rather than expanding intervention in wider arenas of social and economic life. One consequence of such rethinking is that welfare will increasingly assume a competitive dimension and resources will be distributed among various groups either on the basis of identity politics or by how the state defines its development imperatives. How women and their various activities are constituted within the priorities of market development will have implications for their credibility as 'citizens'; this, in turn, will influence their access to the state's financial and political resources.

The neoliberal discourse on individual rights must be examined against representations of women's economic productivity. For women in India, the adoption of neoliberal discourses of development has come at a critical juncture. Internationally, in the last couple of decades development agencies have been reconsidering the nature of women's contributions to development. When the discipline of women and development evolved in the 1970s, there was a shift from seeing women as 'beneficiaries' and welfare recipients of development to an acknowledgement of their productive capabilities. Since the 1980s, there has been a move to adopt the 'efficiency approach', that is, a recognition that women are efficient producers and managers of the household and community (Kabeer 1994, Moser 1993, Razavi and Miller 1995). What is advocated is that development in general is more likely to be successful if the various bodies of the public space – the state, market and local community – draw on women's contributions to society. Thus, women's productive role is not just recognized under neoliberal discourses, it is actively prioritized. The recognition of women as 'economic actors' has greatly enhanced interest in them as a target group through which to foster development initiatives locally and nationally. The World Bank (1991: iii) notes that '[w]omen [in India] must be seen as economic actors – actors with a particularly important role to play in efforts to reduce poverty'. John (1996: 3076) argues that poor women are increasingly being represented by the Indian state and international development agencies as 'good subjects' who make 'sound economic sense'. The sum effect has been that whereas much early Women and Development research grounded its assertions for women's participation in mainstream development on grounds of *justice*, contemporary discourses of women's development are focused on *efficiency*. In other words, investment in women's development has shifted from grounds of *needs* to *merit* (Jaquette 1990, cited in Kabeer 1994: 25).

This section aimed to highlight some of the ways in which development and other social discourses simultaneously counteract and contradict, and formalize certain representations of women as participants in the Indian economy and policy. Thus, there are two discursive axes that frame women's identity in the Indian state. On the one hand, there is the mother–worker binary, drawn from nationalistic representations of women's roles, and on the other, the shift in development contexts has brought a focus on women's identity as economic actors. These constructions are neither independent nor isolated. The one is implied in the other; they are mutually reinforcing. Given that these constructions frame the context in which policy for women is strategized, my objective is to examine if gender policy is a site for political gain. The evaluation of the RCH which follows provides a case study of a specific developmental policy. It allows for an exploration of the implications, when identities from developmental and political discourses merge in reproductive policy.

Reproduction and Developmental Identity

The RCH policy mirrors perceptible shifts in the discourses around population policy in India and globally in the 1990s. In India, the RCH's emphasis on decentralized planning, enhanced quality of care in the provision of reproductive services and non-coercive family planning makes it unlike other population programmes that have preceded it. The RCH, *prima facie*, appears to be grounded in a valid concern about the reproductive well-being of women and the social circumstances under which they are able to exercise reproductive decisions (Chatterjee 1996). The RCH documents list a range of efforts to ensure gender-sensitivity in the population programme: the state will provide medical and counselling intervention for a variety of reproductive health needs (such as pregnancy, reproductive tract infections, sexually transmitted diseases, contraception and so on). There is also a strong component of the programme that focuses on issues around women's emancipation, for instance, educational training programmes for the community and the health providers (Government of India 1997).

My evaluation here does not question the state's attempts to provide for a gender-sensitive policy. Certainly, on paper at least, some material provision for programme changes has been approved. Instead, my analysis seeks to focus on the state's motives for implementing the policy, in particular what it sees as end objectives for women from the policy. These goals are, I argue, tied to the representations of women and their roles as citizens.

The RCH in India is founded on modest objectives. It defines reproductive health as

> people [having] the ability to reproduce and regulate their fertility, women [being] able to go through pregnancy and child birth safely, and the outcome of pregnancies [being] successful in terms of maternal and child survival and well being, and couples [being] able to have sexual relations free of pregnancy and of contracting diseases. (Government of India 1997)

There are three categories of people that, according to this definition, the RCH policy is intended to benefit: 'people', 'women' and 'couples', and three key objectives for the state's intervention: population control, disease control and child survival and health. At first glance, these objectives are disparate and aimed at diverse groups of people. For instance, *people* require contraceptives, *women* are guaranteed childbirth support, and *couples* ensured disease-free sexual relations. On closer reading, however, it will be seen that there is one point where this discursive disparateness converges. The site where a majority of these interventions are operationalized is a woman's body. It is usually women who are targeted by the state for contraceptive use and women are the beneficiaries of the state's pre-natal programmes. Recently, the state has begun to focus attention on issues of reproductive tract and sexual tract infection – here too, the programmes are offered almost exclusively for women. Because all these interventions have critical development significance, it is essential for the state to construct a female citizen who accepts the state's interests as her own. My contention is that the state imbues the female citizen with an identity that is grounded in the concerns around reproduction that interest the state. The state's reconstruction is, therefore, not of an abstract 'person', 'couple' or 'woman'. Instead, the dominant identity deployed by the state is that of mother.

Certainly at the level of implementation, the idea that 'mothers' were the key recipient group was unmistakable. Most of the policy-makers I talked to could not conceptualize the personhood of women without grounding this in a social frame. While to a lesser degree they referred to 'adolescent girls' as women who were sexually inactive, for the most part women were associated with the idea of motherhood. The remarks of the following policy-maker, a middle-level official in the health system, reflect this tendency for the imagery of mother to represent and even be substituted for the idea of women. For instance, he says: 'Mainly [the programme is meant] for *women's health* ... that is, there should be a *healthy mother*' (Interview #11).

Women's health, as the policy-maker notes, on implementation is translated into a *healthy mother*. The rephrasing is significant: in the former, women's health is a goal. In the latter – *there should be a healthy mother* – women are instrumentalized. A healthy mother is a prerequisite to a goal, namely, that of having healthy children. The official seems to suggest that women are important because they are able to fulfil another need or objective. This official's comment is not an isolated remark. Among the recurrent themes that arose in my analysis of policy documents and interviews was that of instrumentalization of the construct 'mother'. Some of the following comments were made by policy-makers (from senior-level bureaucrats to local health providers):

> the emphasis is always on *the mother and child*. There may be some reason for the planners for deciding or taking such a decision considering this mother and child as a unit. So the role played by the *mother in the family, in the society and probably in the nation* [is the focus of policy-makers]. (Interview #1)

> Only a *strong mother can have a strong child*. That way, a strong child when brought up like that [healthily] when it has its own child or is married, can have healthy children. (Interview #12)

> Mainly women will benefit more from it. All these programmes will *first benefit women, then from that children will get it*. (Interview #11)

> Health [services] should be more concentrated upon the care of maternal and child health care ... [so that] *the population that is born should be healthier*. (Interview #9)

In each of these excerpts, the dominant imagery of mother is not a static referent to women's position in society but depicts an active role that mother-hood embraces, which is to nurture healthy children. Each of the policy-makers associates the importance of mothers with the advantages that they hold for children. Thus, the use of the idea of mother assumes significance only in relation to what children and the future population is likely to gain. The following comment by interviewee #1 supports my earlier argument that a mother is the site where the three key objectives of the state's policy converge – fertility control, child/infant health and disease control. In this policy-maker's view, all reproductive obstacles, from infertility to sexually transmitted diseases – *anything – any diseases or disorder or any problem* – are to be treated so as not to 'prevent the *mother* or *child* from surviving [and] gaining good health':

> *Anything which is an impediment to child survival, or for safe motherhood or for the health of the mother* ... Remove those obstacles. It may be RTIs (reproductive tract infections), STDs (sexually transmitted diseases), AIDS, [or] infertility, for example. So anything – any diseases or disorder or any problem which prevents the mother or child from surviving [and] gaining good health. (Interview #1)

The emphasis on mothers is not limited to ensuring the good health of children alone. The RCH documents also instrumentalize women's repro-ductive activities in relation to the developmental efforts of the state. The following two excerpts from the documents exemplify this connection:

> *Deficiencies in the arrangements for mother and child health care* lead to higher incidence of maternal mortality and child/infant mortality and these also lead to low health status of women and children, and in the long run is *a costly burden on the national system*. (Government of India 1997a)

> The RCH Programme intends to integrate fertility regulation, maternal and child health with reproductive health services ... with the aim *to reduce infant and maternal mortality eventually contributing to the stabilization of population* and improve the health status of women and children. (Government of India 1997b)

These excerpts extend the significance of motherhood, particularly healthy motherhood, from within the intimacy of the mother–child dyad to the broader context of development. Women's/mothers' health, as the excerpts note, has a bearing on the 'national system'. Women's reproductive health has been cast into the public domain of state–citizen relationships, where the state defines its obligations to women's health (here, to reduce infant and maternal mortality) and women's responsibilities to the state (that is, to contribute to the stabilization of population).

There has been considerable criticism of government programmes that focus on maternal and child health. Beall (1997) points out that most MCH (Mother and Child Health) programmes ignore the 'M' component and focus on the 'CH'. Bang and Bang (1989) debate instead the idea of a WCH (Women and Child Health) approach. Scholars see the popularization of the ideology of the mother as a state-sponsored means to economize on social programmes by assuming that women have a 'natural' willingness to undertake health responsibilities and work in the interests of family and community (Beall 1997, Kabeer 1994).

My objective here is not to critique the ideology of MCH programmes. Instead, I would like to examine what the neoliberal context and the construction of women as mothers in reproductive policy indicate about political access to rights in the state. Let us review what the analysis of the RCH reveals. First, the context of efficiency is unmistakably inscribed in the text of the RCH documents and in the constructions of women made by policy-makers. The instrumentalization of motherhood positions reproduction as an economic activity with developmental value. Women as mothers are also economic and developmental agents – actors in the population drama. Second, it is interesting that the imagery of both 'worker' and 'mother' are blended in the reproductive policy. Unlike conventional nationalistic discourse, where mothers and workers were polarized identities in women's economic relationships with the state, in reproductive health policy to be a mother *is* to be a productive worker in nation building. In constituting women as mothers in reproductive health policy, the state converts women's social role / reproductive identity (within the 'personal' domain of home and family) into an economic / productive (and public, developmental) identity. Against a backdrop of the neoliberal discourses that have dominated developmental thinking since the 1990s, the merging of the identities of reproduction and production has a special significance. The neoliberal discourses, particularly in Western polities, are accompanied by a valorization of the individual's responsibility to be a productive, economic actor if s/he is to be a good citizen. As the RCH is embedded within a strong discourse of obligations that women are to discharge, for them to be 'responsible mothers' (i.e. to comply with the state's population stabilization programme) in development policy is also to define their political identity.

Third, as women's reproductive identity evolves into a developmental currency, it is also worth examining whether this translates into an increased political claim to the state. Is the aim of developmental intervention, as Jayal (1994) charges, likely to be associated with meeting practical needs rather than with enhancing strategic interests?[7] Some insight may be drawn from a discussion of rights that was part of my interviews with policy-makers. I asked them whether the issue of women's reproductive rights was significant in the RCH policy. Some of their responses are given below:

Now, every human being has certain rights – international rights, some reproductive rights. But at the present stage of economic level in India we will not be able to provide all those rights to people. (Interview #7)

... but the way, once women have been made aware of their rights – their legal rights, their property rights, right to health – the way they have come up and the way that they are mobilizing other women ... it is fantastic ... *that kind of thing is not there in the RCH project.* (Interview #3)

So these [goals] that we have set for ourselves do not need ... – yes, to ensure safe pregnancy – if power equations could be changed ... but other than that – most of the goals that we have set for ourselves will be achieved even independently of trying to work on power equations [in society]. (Interview #4)

In these reproductions, the enhancement of women's political and social bargaining positions is not construed as related to the purpose of instituting the present reproductive policy. While interviewee #3, a consultant to the government, conceded that a broader sense of women's rights was not part of the RCH, for the most part the officials assert that rights are incompatible with the purposes of the policy. The most important point evident in these excerpts is that the grounds for rejection of rights are that they contradict the purposes of development. Official #7 points out that at '*the present stage of economic level in India*', rights cannot be made a core issue. Official #4, on the other hand, contends that the objectives of development can be accomplished *independently* of trying to alter women's strategic positions. The final excerpt indicates that the gains to be made from this gender-sensitive policy are solely at a fundamental material level. As the bureaucrat goes on to argue – *but other than that* – there is likely to be little strategic gain for women.

The narrow interpretation of rights, as alluded to by these state officials, reveals the multiple levels at which political and economic identities are seen as defining women's representation in the state. The state frames women's political identities against the context of development: their 'rights' are interpreted within the larger framework of their obligations as citizens interested in the state's welfare. This conditionality almost places a constraint on women's collective political claims. The norms used to construct women's identities within the developmental state influence the kind of emancipatory processes open to them. And, contrary to conventional Women and Development postulates, women's political agency does not directly follow a mere positioning as productive agents within development.

As revealed in this case, development (both as a discipline and as practice of the state) focuses on the economic value of women's activities – only those identities that express this capacity are valorized. Women's reproductive identity of motherhood has come under the state's gaze because of its economic significance. And because emancipation is defined within the limits of what constitutes good development, women's claims on the state for greater bargaining capabilities or 'rights' are not recognized as valid. Development, even 'gendered' development – with its implicit emphasis on market growth – appears, in this instance, to offer only limited opportunities for challenging power relations that constrain women's experiences of well-being. Women's representations in the state, defined by their construction as agents of development, actually limit their possibilities for empowerment. Therefore, to break out of this, women must also deliberately stake political claims independent of their participation in development.

The possibility of political gains for women is particularly pertinent with regard to the issue at hand here – women's reproductive identity. Feminists have always sought to destabilize the 'production–reproduction/public–private' dichotomy that has confined women to specific roles, attributes and positions in society. Bringing women's reproductive activities into the public sphere has, in particular, been central to Women and Development writings from early on (Benería and Sen 1981, 1982). Yet, in the 1990s, feminists have been zealous about guarding women's privacy because they are mindful of the state's power to regulate individuals' bodies (Landes 1998). As exemplified in the RCH, in crossing the boundary between 'mother' and 'worker', women do not necessarily experience personal freedoms; if anything, women's claims to the state are limited by the expectations that the state has attached to the conceptualization of mothers as productive beings. The important lesson to be drawn is that if development is a key arena where women in India strive to make political gains, the role of the state in defining the context of development cannot be underestimated. This understanding is critical to any efforts to employ development interventions and strategies to empower women.

Conclusion

I began with the assertion that women's developmental identity should be framed within a broader perspective that encompasses the role of the state and wider social networks. As the analysis of the RCH in India revealed, it would be naïve to adjudge all gender-sensitive development policy as transformative, unless its objectives and rationales are weighed against the political leverage that women are likely to gain as a collective. It is important to recognize the discourses that frame women's rights to development. If women's economic and political identities are constructed solely against discourses that stress their instrumentality, women's role within a market-oriented development agenda is tenuous indeed. The caution here is not against market or neoliberal discourses *per se*, but rather, the representation of women within this form of development in India.

For researchers, a WCD approach offers important lessons to consider.

Scholars must recognize the political subtext of state policies and programmes, and the way women are constituted within the political agenda of the developmental state. The intimacy between politics, cultural ideologies and development is particularly important in the lives of women. The paradigms that frame women and development scholarship must open up to incorporate non-economic influences (including, *inter alia*, the political and cultural identities of women, and competing state discourses) in evaluating the possibilities and outcomes of women's developmental experiences. Critical approaches to gender such as Women, Culture and Development can offer a theoretical and methodological foundation to make development praxis accountable to the goals of women's development.

In sum, the road to charting solutions for women's emancipation in developing contexts is made no less difficult by recognizing this complexity. It does, however, provide a viable critique of programmes and policies that look for simple solutions to complex situations. The way that ideologies permeate the workings of political and developmental policy must be deconstructed at multiple levels before such categoric solutions to women's emancipation can be universalized.

Notes

1. This position reflects a body of recent post-structuralist analyses of the nature of the state, as argued, for instance by Franzway et al. (1989), and Connell (1990), among others.

2. I use the term gender policy to refer to policy that is, by design, intended to be beneficial primarily to women.

3. The empirical evaluation presented here is based on data that were collected in India between August 1997 and March 1998. The data set comprises primarily two kinds of information: a collection of documents published by the GoI relating to the Reproductive and Child Health Programme, and interviews with policy-makers and health-providers who were involved in the implementation of the programme. The bulk of this latter data is located in the context of Kerala, a state in southern India.

4. Kerala's commitment to action against sexual harassment has been evident in two high-profile cases in 1999 and 2000, where the courts and law enforcement agencies have acted to ensure strict punishment for male perpetrators of sexual violence. In one of these cases, a cabinet minister charged with making sexual advances to a female bureaucrat was forced to resign from his post and was subsequently charged by the Kerala Crime Branch (*The Hindu*, 29 December 2000).

5. The dominant image of women in the national psyche is drawn from ancient Hindu texts (for instance, the mythical characters Sita from the Ramayana and Savitri from the Upanishads epitomize absolute devotion towards one's husband). Of course, the basic attributes of passivity, gentleness and submissiveness resonate with the notion of ideal womanhood in most religions.

6. It must be noted that food and agricultural subsidies have been reduced considerably since the start of the NEP.

7. The distinction between practical and strategic interests/needs is drawn from Moser (1993). Moser points out that developmental intervention may provide much-needed goods and services to people, but may not address larger issues of emancipation, rights, etc. or challenge existing power relations. In the case of the RCH, as I pointed out above, there is undeniably a move towards improving health services according to the practical needs of women. But, given the ideologies underlying the policy, it is questionable if women's political well-being will be altered in any significant way.

· ·

CHAPTER 5

Bodies and Choices: African Matriarchs and Mammy Water

Ifi Amadiume

§ IN this chapter I will examine collectivist notions of women's solidarity in relation to women's power in traditional cultures and societies in Africa. My ultimate goal is to highlight growing tensions in the realm of agency and culture between what I describe as traditional African matriarchitarianism and new counter-forces, such as Mammy Water. Using examples of traditional organizations of women's cultures that embody matriarchitarianism, I argue that feminism and these traditions of organized women's empowering cultures are not mutually exclusive. Yet, with globalization, traditional African matriarchs are increasingly marginalized and face serious competition for the control and shaping of women's bodies. There is thus a need to revisit old grounds to raise new questions about the place of increasingly assertive individual subjectivity and choice for women and girls in new globalizing conditions of social change.

Globalization and Matriarchitarianism

As intellectual discourse seems rapidly to be shifting to globalization, there is a renewed interest in rethinking feminism and proposing new feminist agendas, of which the Women, Culture and Development (WCD) perspective is a promising one. For African women,[1] it is important that we enter this discussion from a critical perspective that is informed by our experiences in social history. African women had to struggle even to get a voice in feminism; they were not considered equal partners in the making of feminist agendas or policies. Without equality of voice and access, globalization in African experiences is no more than advanced neocolonialism informed by advanced capitalism, in which Africans are simply consumers of imported cultures. The current expression of the new globalization is in finance capitalism in the form of loan management and trade intervention. But from the point of view of many Africans who live from hand to mouth day by day, all this is seen as recolonization, and the place-based knowledge of local lives is once again a site to raise questions about recolonization and imperialism. As feminists committed to the discourse of social justice we are forced to deal with issues of reflexivity, cultural context, values and local intersection. Thus, the local reasserts itself and plays a role in reshaping the global conversation and the critique of the assumptions of the concept of globalization.

If concern about social inequality is an essential, progressive, feminist perspective to counter the assumptions of capitalism, a focus on the local equally challenges the assumptions of the universal benefits of globalization. In generalizing about globalization from a supposed progressive perspective, there are several romantic assumptions about a loss of control by states, and a universal equal movement of people and equal access to new technologies, goods and markets. It is thought that these forces are transforming our relationship to the world in the same way. This is the illusion of a shrinking world. Yet, if we think of slavery, colonialism and apartheid, globalization is not really new, but rather only a matter of scale and speed – old hegemonies in new forms. Globalization can be seen as an agent of imperialism and an updated version of the modernization which was directed through colonial conquest. Concerns about enslavement, colonialism, apartheid and modernization in terms of equity and social justice are as relevant as ever in the encounter between African communities and the forces of globalization. Place-specific knowledges counter generalizations and can provide us with the tools to challenge imperialist agendas and sexist development. By the same token, gender knowledges counter patriarchy and sexism in our concern with criticism and empowerment. In each of these emphases – on social justice in the face of neocolonial exploitation, on the potential of the local, on women's knowledges as sites of resistance, on the multiple complexities of subjectivity and its interpretation in the context of globalization – my work resonates well with the WCD perspective of this volume.

As globalization from above gathers force, African women will suffer more abuses and more exploitation than ever before. Just as major historical contacts with Euro-Western cultures involved attacks on the humanity and cultures of African peoples, we equally expect that there will be an intensification of the erosion of the indigenous languages of Africans and of specific cultures of African women. Girls also face modern violence, in addition to the older traditional violence of early marriage, early childbirth and patriarchal oppression. It is, however, equally important not to lose sight of the traditional connections between mothers, daughters, girls and women in pre-colonial societies and many traditional contemporary societies in Africa today.

I will use case studies to argue that colonialism created the dichotomous opposition of tradition versus modernity. The European colonial presence was defined as a civilizing mission that brought modernity to 'savages' and 'barbaric' African 'tribes'. European-invented modernity in comparison to pre-colonial gender structures can be seen as a sexist, conservative tradition that is driven by a rigid patriarchal ideology of power. It insists on defining power as male to the continued exclusion of women, even highly educated and professional women (Amadiume 2000: 22). Sadly, the lasting legacy of this experience is that modernity is conceived as the opposite of tradition, yet this claim is false, as there is a critical dialectic in which supposed modernity also presents problems for women.

In traditional societies, girls had the possibility of inclusive membership in a protective women's culture that was headed by matriarchs. Women in traditional society in Nnobi, other Igbo societies and African societies in general made and had space for themselves and were therefore involved in cultural production. I shall call this 'the matriarchal umbrella' which embraced all women, and I argue that all women benefited from this umbrella which created a solidarity among women.

From this point of view, traditional pre-colonial Nnobi (Igbo) matriarchy was an ideological superstructure, whose ideas showed a connection between the matricentric production unit and the relations of production. All those who ate out of one pot were bound together in the spirit of common motherhood. The political culture borrowed an idea first applied to biology and production, and applied it to the basic ideological superstructure that was reproduced at wider levels of social organization in the political structure. The result was a matriarchal system in which all Nnobi people were children of one mother, the goddess Idemili, who was worshipped by all the people of Nnobi (Amadiume 1987, 1997). What was the place of girls in this type of society?

In the past few years, much of the focus on the study of women and girls in traditional societies in Africa has been concentrated on concerns about the abuse of girls and practices of circumcision (Amadiume 2000: 122–61). Women's bodies historically have been a signifier of culture in very fundamental and significant ways. Chris Knight (1991) argues for an ancient revolution made by human females, who used menstrual, ovarian synchrony and external environmental cues such as the moon and tides to originate a symbolic human culture. As a precondition for and guarantor of women's total solidarity, Knight's model leaves no room for counter-normative classifications and tensions inside the female camp. I have used terms such as matriarchy to conceptualize this female power camp, which constitutes a female-oriented side of the sociocultural system. It is this growing tension between normative matriarchal orientation (matriarchitarianism) and counter-normative individualist female body signs which presents itself as a conflict between tradition and modernity in the African context. Generally, in traditional African societies, girls' initiation schools and traditional women's associations headed by matriarchs teach moral virtues and aesthetic ideals for responsible citizenship. Under the leadership of older women, girls' social transitions are achieved without the sort of patriarchal violence idealizing war-blood and killing valour, even in contexts where the girls are tested and trained in ordeals of courage and endurance, sometimes involving circumcision. Yet this is not all that traditional cultures did and not all traditional cultures circumcised women.

In the traditional, pre-colonial Igbo dual-sex political system, the titled women were central to consensual decision-making and controlled the market-places. In Nnobi, it was Ekwe-titled women, the earthly representatives of the goddess Idemili, who controlled the village women's council. They held overall veto rights in village assemblies. The Ekwe system can therefore be seen as a political matriarchal system, which was, however, in a dialectical or structural relationship to the *umunna* (patrilineage)-based patriarchal system, each in dialogue with the other. A third classificatory system, the non-gendered collective humanity, *Nmadu*, a genderless word meaning person/human, was again based on non-discriminatory matriarchal collectivism, as a unifying moral code and culture. The cultural appropriation of the ideology of children of one mother, the goddess Idemili, generated affective relationships as opposed to the androcentric political culture of patriarchy, imperialism and violence. The indigenous religions were also pluralistic, as earth goddess religion was combined with ancestral religion and the religions of various gods and goddesses. In other words, traditional pre-colonial societies were pluralistic (Amadiume 1997) and not merely a consequence of European modernity.

Culturing Girls – Zambia and Nigeria

Like many colonized African scholars, I have found myself working with the methodology of intellectual archaeological digging to recover disqualified, submerged, subordinated or appropriated African knowledges, more especially women's knowledges. I also find that I need to recover an African knowledge history as I draw my illustration from an old anthropology classic, Audrey Richards's *Chisungu* (1992 [1956]). To recover our culture, we often swallow our pride to read offensive works.[2]

Richards, a colonial white woman anthropologist, observed the Chisungu ceremony of the Bemba people, who are now located in Zambia, in 1931. Her ethnography showed how girls passed from socialization by their mothers to ritual initiation by the *nacimbusa* (I shall call this woman the ritual matriarch) into 'the community of married women' through the Chisungu ritual, where no man could enter the house when this ceremony took place. The knowledge taught is ritual knowledge, since belief in supernatural forces is involved. This is what Richards called the magic aspect of the rite; the ritual was transformative because it shows that women also understood the politics of religion.

The Chisungu inculcated Bemba concepts of male and female, the authority of age, female solidarity and women's power over reproduction.[3]

Bemba women were very much involved in wealth production.[3] They also generated a women's culture, the world of women. Ideal expectations of women were industriousness and loyalty to one's own sex. As a transformative ritual, the Chisungu ceremony opened a gate of knowledge into this women's world. The ceremony was done after the puberty rite of the first menses. It was a nubility rite preliminary to the marriage ceremony. Richards witnessed over 18 separate ceremonies in the initiation house and the surrounding bush. Her ethnographic record is thus rich in narratives, symbols, signs and meaning in indigenous women's culture.

The *nacimbusa*, the ritual matriarch, must have knowledge of ritual, industry, organizational skill, tact and personality and unusual intellectual ability. She was usually an elderly woman and successful midwife, generally of royal clan, and the office tended to be hereditary. A *nacimbusa* wore a feather headdress (also worn by certain chiefs), was given respect at a chief's court and addressed with chiefly praise songs, and it is not surprising that *nacimbusa* women were wealthier than other people.

Although Richards does not notice it, the data suggest that the political system is dual-gendered and presents a matriarchal umbrella. Here you have an interesting concept of gender-bending that is pervasive in matriarchies. In the Chisungu ceremony the bridegroom, *shibwinga*, is an example of gender flexibility, for this term was also used for the sister or cross-cousin who may replace the bridegroom in aspects of the ceremony. Not only is there ritual gender-inversion, we also have the important role of aunts. Richards writes, 'A nacimbusa will teach the secrets of the chisungu to her brother's daughter, to whom she owes special obligations, and from whom she can demand service, and she may also teach them to her own daughter' (1992: 57). A *nacimbusa* had a special relationship with the *nacisungu* girl she had initiated and practically saw her through life. In addition to their biological mother, this women's culture thus provided women with a social mother to support them throughout their adult lives. The ritual was a periodic restatement of the structure of women's society and the seniority and authority of older women. Older women were confident leaders and teachers, and girls behaved towards them with respect and humility. This was before mission Christianity, colonial schools and post-colonial culture took over the education of girls and women as well.

What is missing in Richards's account is the anti-colonial struggle by African peoples, a struggle for liberation and independence and thus also for cultural independence in colonial and post-colonial discourse. In 1931 Audrey Richards had thought that indigenous cultures of Africa would 'die out' under enforced colonial modernity. Against this, the argument for the right to culture in colonial and post-colonial discourse posits the resilience of traditional cultures in Africa. Support can be drawn from Ngozi Onwurah's 1993 documentary film, *Monday's Girls*, whose dominant narrative centres on a ritual for the culturing of girls' bodies by matriarchs. Through this we see two young women, Florence and Asikiye, make choices and decisions in relation to their future through the film's dominant narrative, which centres on a ritual for the culturing of girls' bodies by matriarchs. The location of the film is among the Wakirike people in the island town of Ugoloma, a fishing and trading people with a population of 20,000 in the Rivers district in southern Nigeria. Wakirike people perform Iria, a ceremony that is a puberty rite and also a girls' rite of passage – a coming-of-age ceremony – in which the girls are called Iriabo(s). The matriarchs constitute the important ruling council of women called the Egbereremi.

In the Iria ceremony, the ritual matriarch acts as a social mother and teacher. The girls are taught about men and motherhood, grace and self-discipline. When the parents take their daughters to the priestess Monday Moses, she says of a girl, 'then I am in charge of her. I make her beautiful' (Onwurah 1993). While in confinement, the girls listen and dance to mixed music that includes Caribbean reggae, African American soul and Nigerian high-life. Archaic elements are also present, as when Monday Moses says that the end of the confinement depends on the moon and the tide. As ritual matriarch, Monday Moses proclaims that if a girl fails to perform the ceremony, the goddess will be angry; such a failure will bring disgrace to the family. The girls are loved and pampered like princesses and they equally have to display their decorated bodies to their community in a public ceremony, a test to which each girl reacts differently. Some feel shy and embarrassed, while some are defiant and face the challenges without fear.

There is no totalizing ritual in Ngozi Onwurah's documentary. The two girls represent diverging perspectives, the traditional, happy and obedient Florence and the rebellious city girl Asikiye, a music student who has spent ten years in the city. These two girls present contrasting arguments and make different choices in relation to tradition in a changing culture. While Asikiye thinks that some traditions should be forgotten, Florence, Monday's granddaughter, sees the benefit of tradition. Monday Moses, the matriarch in this film, says that she makes the girls look beautiful, not with clothes, but with the traditional body paint. The ceremony involves body display and, from a modernist perspective, the girls could be perceived as abused and the matriarchs as wicked old women punishing young girls.

Notions of freedom in Western feminism and European thought might reject the idea that Florence, who supports tradition and respects the ritual matriarch, is at all subversive. From a Eurocentric perspective there would be no doubt that Asikiye is the real feminist rebel, simply because she opposes

African village traditions and ideals. She is following her own individual will. Yet, Florence is actually bending cultures, practising her native cultural ritual and Christianity and still wanting to finish her basically Western education before getting married. She does not feel any conflict of culture, unlike Asikiye, who rejects the body rules of the ritual that require her to bare her 'virgin' breast in public for inspection to confirm that she is still a girl, and not a woman who has already suckled a baby but wants to pass as a girl. Asikiye also rejects the authority and knowledge of the matriarchs and considers the women ignorant and their tutoring stupid. She is not allowed by the matriarchs to compromise the regulations of the Iria.

Here again in Wakirike society, as with Nnobi Igbo society, there are two ruling camps. One is the patriarchal ruling council of men in which Asikiye's father sits. In this men's gathering, Asikiye's father says of his daughter: 'She cannot impose her will on the community' (Onwurah 1993). The other is the matriarchal camp of the women's council, the Egbereremi, which uses gentle persuasion and prays for the girls. The cosmopolitan and individualist Asikiye is unmoved by threats or gentle persuasion and leaves for the city without completing the ritual. With city clothes, straightened hair and curls, she hides her eyes behind dark sunglasses and prefers the anonymity of the city and its night clubs.

I want to stretch this comparison of the two girls and the two locations a little further. One important site in this context of rapid globalization is the city, where violence against women – including state violence – is extremely frightening and vicious (Amadiume 2000). Under these circumstances, we could say that Asikiye escapes one form of violence to expose herself to another in the hazardous life of the city and its threat to women. Violence in this sense is external to the women's rituals and cultures. Under these circumstances, one might ask which of these girls would more easily find support and protection if confronted with any of these new patterns of violence against women? The one under the matriarchal umbrella, or the one who lives anonymously in the city? Is there a feminist imperative that the rule of law must supersede ritual? Is the rule of law more empowering to women than ritual?

Gender, Sexuality and Power Ambiguity

Even though Florence and Asikiye are considered daughters by their Wakirike people, their different choices of destiny change the way they are perceived and represented. The presence of a structural women's system can create co-operation and balance, or it can result in tensions in dichotomous conceptual systems and a related gender polarity. Florence will obviously graduate into the women's system and enjoy the protection of matriarchs. Asikiye will, in contrast, experience a negative representation and possibly name-calling. It might be said that Asikiye's 'head is not correct' because she is possessed by a bad spirit, or that she is a 'stubborn girl' who is bent on having her own ways, and that could only lead to destructive choices or a bad marriage. She might marry someone who in appearance looks like a handsome stranger, but would turn out to be an ugly monster in disguise! I argue that this sort of name-calling and perhaps gossip from within the women's group sanctions individuals who are subverting the group. This sort of punishment is different from popular, negative perceptions and representations of women who are seen as transgressing against the wider social system where cultures contend for dominance. Popular negative representations of women are invariably about body parts, sex and wickedness, as women are called prostitutes, insatiable whores, husband snatchers, witches and Mammy Water.

In the popular imagination, there is fear of unmarried women because their sexuality is unregulated. There is equally fear of isolated old women as victims of failed kinship; they are supposedly witches. Successful older and wealthy women are either revered as matriarchs, or they are feared enemies subverting patriarchy by controlling men, thus reversing gender. Also feared are beautiful isolated young women, as a prototype of the enchanting water goddess, Mammy Water, whom some consider a postcolonial temptress goddess. Henry Drewal writes of Mammy Water: 'She personifies unattainable, exquisite beauty, vanity, jealousy, sexuality, romantic not maternal love, limitless good fortune – not health, long life or progeny, but riches, material and monetary. She is thus very much part of international trading system between Africa and Europe commencing in the late fifteenth century and now including other regions of the world as well' (Drewal 1996: 311). Like Asikiye, Mammy Water likes the city and wears dark sunglasses! Asikiye might be seen as a modernist, but Mammy Water, it seems, is a mirage of modernity.

Scholars disagree about the identity and origin of Mammy Water (Drewal 1988, 1988a, 1996, Gore and Nevadomsky 1997, Jell-Bahlsen 1997). There is, however, an area of convergence in both the physical descriptions and character attributes of the Mammy Water of popular culture, and the identification of symptoms of possession. In West Africa, it is generally claimed that these spirits have luxurious homes at the bottom of the waters, are usually very beautiful, assuming various human shapes, but manifest particularly as half-woman and half-fish, like mermaids. Mammy Water is represented as an enchanting, naked, beautiful woman who can be seen combing her long hair sitting on a rock in the sea or on the shore. It is also believed that this beautiful woman can cause tragic accidents. She can give her followers riches, but will deny them children.

Henry Drewal has done by far the most extensive and sophisticated work on Mammy Water and in his description, Mammy Water is a 'free' nature spirit, European and not African. She is without family or children and is totally outside any social system. She attracts those with sexual problems such as impotence and barrenness. She relates to her followers as a jealous lover (Drewal 1996). Although men can be possessed by a Mammy Water spirit, the associated religion of possession sickness is dominated by women. Mammy Water is matrilineally inherited. Possessed women become priestesses and healers, as they are educated in the knowledge taught by this water goddess (Jell-Bahlsen 1997, Nwapa 1997). Mammy Water is therefore a goddess of affliction, which is conditional to the calling of her followers and priestesses. Others might argue for some duality, since her priestesses are also healers, but their healing power comes from affliction-possession and trance.

The problem of Asikiye, like the problem of Mammy Water and the embodying of modernity, is not simply a question of the recognition and acceptance of hybridity, a mix of European and African. All cultures hybridize thought, incorporating what is useful. When hybridity is simply the mixing of local elements with European, Western or global cultural motifs through local agency, one can of course recognize a natural tendency to exchange cultures or associate with other cultures. This is not the case in a situation where Christian conversion and education teach white ideals of beauty to the detriment of local values and ideals. Some may see embodying the Other as inversions and ways of subverting local control. But subverting to whose benefit? Is it to the benefit of a racist ideal or to self? To be 'local' becomes a derogatory term, almost like calling someone 'a villager'. Straight wigs, especially blonde ones, are again being widely used by African women, including women of African descent. Dreaming of blue eyes or white skin and straight hair becomes a problem of self-negation or abusing others.

We can see that Asikiye's life is defined by Western ideas of beauty – light skin, tinted, permed hair and sunglasses. As such, she is a prototype of Mammy Water. Florence is a contrast to this imported ideal of modern womanhood. Yet, Florence is traditionally modern, that is, using and enhancing her natural beauty – roundly cropped hair and body painted in familiar motifs and women's designs with natural vegetable dyes from plants picked from her local stream. Imported Western ideals of beauty are here questioned simply because they are used to render the local as 'bush' and ugly and therefore inferior.

Mission Christianity and colonialism imported women's inferiority in body and status. Sexist policies of the patriarchal colonial state gave boys a head start in education in terms of numbers and in professional subjects geared to work in government, trade, industry, church ministry and education services (Amadiume 1987: 135). Girls were educated in domestic services, cooking, cleaning, child care and sewing. There was a historical Christocentric bombardment of messages that ordained women to serve their husbands, look white and follow Christ. This came with the creation of the new-nation state known as Nigeria. Under these circumstances, the empowering education that would balance this inferior, perceived feminine perspective of the colonial education came from cultural education by the matriarchs in their own ways of doing things.

We indeed see Asikiye who said no to her father and disrupted ritual, expressing body freedom as she danced in a night club; the same body that she had enclosed and refused to the gaze of her village people may be available to a stranger. Her body belongs to her privately, just as the bodies of Florence and the other girls become a collective body of Wakirike womanhood and political matriarchy. This is a different situating of body culture and power. Florence acts collectively, Asikiye acts individually. What should be our concerns about these girls in the context of post-colonialism, globalizing capitalism, mounting violence against women and the staggering statistics of the onslaught of HIV/AIDS extermination?

Mammy Water, Sex and Capitalism

Postcolonial globalization, identities, locations and places are again steadily being transformed by the forces of capital. City anonymity can indeed be as isolating as the private sphere of the nuclear family. When discussing the culturing of girls in the Iria fattening room ceremony of the Wakirike of Nigeria, I had asked questions about the choices and futures of the two girls – Florence and the rebellious Asikiye. By rejecting the matriarchal umbrella is Asikiye walking into the oppression of isolation, or into freedom?

Big as the city is, class and race can turn it into a circumscribed space with only brief illusions of escape, a mirage of power just like the enchanting Mammy Water. There are, of course, other views, which see empowerment in transgression and in the ability of individual women to take charge of their bodies against all odds. Carole Boyce Davies (1998) argues, for example, that in spite of the misrepresentation and commodification of the black female body in carnival (under slavery and after, this body enters the New World as commodified), no matter what their condition, Caribbean women in the New World 'make space' and take charge of their bodies to express freedom. The transgressive female body is both voice and resistance; there is therefore a distinction between women who are staged and women in action (Davies 1998).

The phenomena of Asikiye and Mammy Water raise the problem of the place of the isolated individual female in a collective women's world, and equally in the individualistic modern capitalist world. Mammy Water, a major theme in the work of the African woman pioneer writer, Flora Nwapa, provides some clues as to how to read these phenomena. Nwapa's novels are focused on her icon, a water goddess. Time and time again, she turns to a

persistent 'feminist' question of female deviation from convention in traditional and modern settings, and the search for alternative means of women's
'empowerment' and personal happiness (see Ogunyemi and Umeh 1995, Umeh
1998, Ogunyemi 1996). I have argued that the focus on this water goddess
with a fixed stereotypical sexuality enabled Nwapa to expand the boundaries
of discourse on women's sexuality in a radical fashion that is rare in the
writing of women in Africa (Amadiume 1998).

Mammy Water spirit, a water goddess called Uhammiri or Ogbuide, is the
major spiritual and symbolic form in Nwapa's novels. Nwapa explores women's
experiences of possession by this spirit. Belief in this spirit, who is called by
different names, is widespread in Africa and the African diaspora. This is
especially so in communities near rivers, creeks, lagoons, oceans and lakes. In
these same communities, there also exist several other female water deities
who are not Mammy Water. This is not surprising, since Africans generally
deify rivers as goddesses. But what is interesting is again the motif of women's
historical habitation on shorelines, the original ecosystem of Chris Knight's
theory of menstrual synchrony and symbolic culture. This time we have a
spirit of individual self-embodiment, and not the making divine of the spirit
of women's collective solidarity.

Imagining Choice or Isolation?

Nwapa's concern about women's bodies is grounded in the conflicts arising
from domestic practices within the confining spaces and patriarchal ideologies
of the European-imposed family structure. These conflicts derive either from
expectations imposed on women, or the reality of this type of family as a
prison. The issue and context are all about modernity. In other words, it is not
quite correct to read these stories as an attack on African traditional cultures
and saving African womanhood from African traditions. Nwapa's Mammy
Water is a hybrid, a mulatto, stemming from colonially derived desire for
'whiteness' by colonized African natives, as Nwapa herself confirms in an
essay on the origin of Mammy Water (Nwapa 1997). The tensions in Nwapa's
stories are post-colonial, characterized by afflictions such as isolation, unhappiness and disconnection, as the women's needs become more personal and
individualistic.

In *The Lake Goddess*, a forthcoming woman-centred novel,[4] Nwapa introduces a women's network of widows, but distinguishes between women's
culture and men's by attacking certain patriarchal Igbo social rules and
etiquette. In Nwapa's narrative women own kolanut trees, break kolanuts,
initiate marriage and cheat on the circumcision ritual. The mothers bribe the
midwife to pretend that Ona has been circumcised when they perform all the
necessary ceremonies. I had previously read this action as a clever proposal by

Nwapa on how to preserve and 'respect' custom in a modern context. I also think that Nwapa might be saying much more than that, as the women's action suggests a struggle for woman's body, whereby the matriarchs rethink their bodies and drop the required circumcision ritual.

Women may have reconfigured their bodies in that one instance, but in other post-colonial situations women still find themselves struggling against fragmentation. For example, in the modern African context, religion that had earlier sealed women's solidarity begins to divide women. In *The Lake Goddess*, Christianity divides mother and daughter. Ona is unable to find a balance between Christianity and the call of Uhammiri. When all attempts at normative behaviour have failed, including schooling and marriage, she ends up outside society and squarely in the domain of Mammy Water. With the intensification of Ona's mental illness, the goddess becomes increasingly her only source of contentment. She says to her father: 'I love to see her. I have a sense of well-being when I dream my dreams.' As 'a woman possessed', the call of the goddess of the lake compels Ona to leave her husband and their three children. The context in which the final rupture takes place is further proof of Nwapa's concern with the individual woman's needs. Ona tries to tolerate sex to please her husband, but finds it strange and alien.

Nwapa thus succeeds in writing a radical discourse on women and sexuality into African women's heritage – a venture that she had already alluded to in *One is Enough* (1995 [1981]) where the protagonist, Amaka, weighs her options. One of these options is to consider, stereotypically, lesbian sex as in Europe and America. African women are thus challenged to take this on board and not to shy away from this controversy, which opens possibilities for various feminist interests and different women's needs in a fast-changing world. Pursuing this cause, Nwapa eroticizes the image of the Woman of the Lake and disengages Ona from her husband.

In Nwapa's concern to highlight individual women's quest for sexual freedom, she fails to exploit the full possibilities in Igbo gender flexibility, which she had knowledge of but had her main characters dismiss in her novels. Yet, Igbo women have and share with other women a heritage of solidarity and resistance strategies that have enabled mass mobilization by African women in historical social movements (Amadiume 1997). Under the forces of capitalist-driven globalization, we need to contrast individual choice with women's solidarity, in the context of the matriarchal umbrella with its traditional African women's knowledge and power network systems.

The problem of motherhood and the stigmatization of female infertility have led critics to emphasize Nwapa's disaffection with traditional Igbo culture. Nwapa engages in this criticism through her implied condemnation of church and boarding school education. We can read this in her stereotypical characterization of both Ona's mother, Akpe, and grandmother, Mama Theresa, as fanatical Christians who totally reject traditional religious belief and do not have a good relationship with Ona. Similarly, Madam Margaret, the head of the convent school that Ona attended, is called 'a religious fanatic' and a 'mean, hard, and evil woman'. Yet, in preparing Ona for the call to priesthood, Nwapa begins to unnecessarily disengage Ona from normal domestic and economic life. Ona is not interested in motherhood, children or husband. In her determination to reciprocate her husband's kindness she tries initiating love-making once in a while, which pleases her husband, but at the end of it all this leaves her sleepless while her husband snores with contentment. It is on one such occasion that Ona 'saw a naked woman standing in front of her. She had very long hair dripping with water' (Nwapa forthcoming: 172). As Ona recounts, she journeys to the abode of the lake goddess, who tells her, 'I have waited for a long time for you to be my priestess, I have chosen you. I want you but I don't want to force you or hurry you. Don't wait too long. Give this message to the man who lives with you. Tell him that you belong to me' (184). This is a new individualistic possessiveness and belonging; a new religiosity that will disengage a woman from society.

Nwapa contrasts a men's conversation, in which god is masculinized, with that between two women fish-sellers. The two women seem crucial to the completion of the story, because through them Nwapa recovers the traditional woman-centredness of her narrative, raising feminist issues and giving voice to women in Ona's words: 'Ogbuide wants all women to have voices. Women should not be voiceless. Ogbuide hates voiceless women.' It is not surprising that it is to these women that the beautiful and ageless lake goddess, who is partial to women, gives her message to them through her gifted priestess Ona; the essence of the message is that women should submit themselves to Ogbuide and return to goddess worship!

Nwapa, it seems, has come full circle, from individualistic concern with personal freedom and happiness to the collective project. What is achieved in Ona, however, is a dislocated priestess – no domestic duties, no marketing and trading, no women's organizations. She is only a priestess living in a temple, keeping the ritual rules and taboos of the Woman of the Lake. Ona is, of course, a creation of Nwapa's imagination.

Because part of Nwapa's argument includes a critique of Christian mission imperialism, the failure to rehabilitate Ona as priestess, as well as a full member of society doing women's daily chores, indicates to me that Nwapa has not completely escaped her Catholic upbringing and its teaching about the ideal life of a priest. I have a problem with new conceptualizations of a celibate and isolated priestess living in a shrine, because priestesses of traditional Igbo religions were fully integrated into society and the women's system, in very much the same way as the Nnobi, Bemba and Wakirike ritual matriarchs.

Fragments and the Matriarchal Umbrella

Symbols do not speak for themselves; they are dependent on translation and interpretation. So also is Mammy Water not complete in herself. She needs to be placed in relation to other women-embodying goddesses and wider women's struggles. These two types of discourse are dichotomized, because Mammy Water is represented as an anti-motherhood, anti-kinship goddess: she is the temptress spirit. This is not the case with the more normative fertility mother goddesses such as earth, birth and river goddesses who were seen as central to Igbo religions and social structure.

The Nnobi goddess Idemili was a subversive phenomenon in terms of gender–power relations. This matriarchy was tolerant of gender flexibility. The grounding of the goddess Idemili in economic, political and religious dialectics truly made her an embodiment of female solidarity with an ideological message of a collectivist humanism and humane empowerment. The kinship morality of *umunne* (children of one mother) bound siblings in love and alliance. There are no terms for brother and sister or sisters or brothers. They are children of one mother. There is therefore no need for an Oedipal complex, the bane of Western feminist thought, in the matricentric unit. There is no casted blood sisterhood in the familial, but an inclusive eating out of one pot. Since there is no term for sister that is not relational to mother or brother, one could not conceive of a social paradigm based on an exclusive set of sisters. There is a further distinction between the goddess Idemili and Mammy Water, as Mammy Water is seen as a goddess of wealth, but not children. If we look at Igbo traditional conceptual systems, we see that there is a concern about individual women's isolation.

Some tend to think that the choices for feminist roles without the rejection of traditional culture are very limited. This would suggest an assumption that feminism and traditional culture are mutually exclusive, or that African traditions and modernity are dichotomous. Let us look at the options that Flora Nwapa's Amaka in *One is Enough* considers open to a married and barren wife. The options are adoption of a stranger, asking for the children of her brothers and sisters, marrying a young girl to have her husband impregnate her, or claiming her pregnant maid's baby (Nwapa 1995: 20–21). They include the traditional institution of woman and woman marriage that was widely practised in many societies in Africa until the Christian church and colonial administrators banned it.

Native cultures were disqualified and marginalized in official policy and discourse. Yet, these cultures in their authentic, hybridic, reinvented forms remain sources of renewal and enrichment in the modern context of culture wars. The traditional cultures of the matriarchs that I narrate are different from male-invented tradition responses to the colonial encounter (Ranger

1997). We need to understand that these matriarchs, who embody the collective wisdom and power of women and in many ways the society, have a highly evolved understanding of culture and politics, for they use culture to continually redefine biology. They go beyond making a statement about the importance of giving birth and the natural duties of mothers in socializing girls, since they also teach ethics of kinship and social relations.

Might we call the relationship between the matriarchs and girl initiates a second giving-birth, thus thinking of them as important players in a whole set of reconfigurations in a rite of passage involving symbolic statements and actions? The rituals achieve fundamental transformations that direct girls into new gendered consciousness as women in the world of women who are situated in the social world and universe of their various societies.[5] The relationship of the girls with their mothers might change, because even though there is a continuity of ordinary home life and daily chores, there is a separation, since the new teachers and companions are no longer the biological mothers. They are now a community of women, as young women begin to build their own network of women through the life course. Thus, much more than lessons of wifehood and motherhood are inscribed in the initiation of girls' rituals. What is achieved is a shared universe, in which signs and objects come to represent a collective memory that is passed on from generation to generation.

Women in these systems have agency and a subjective relationship to the processes of construction and regulation of meaning and experience. My point is that matriarchy is not an invention only of the past. Tradition and modernity are not dichotomous. I have used the contemporary Wakirike case study to dispel that supposition. It is a modernist, post-colonial thinking that sees matriarchy as a thing of the past, when the tradition is quite alive, sometimes in old forms, and sometimes in new hybrid forms in church women's organizations, national women's organizations and national women's development mobilization structures set up by wives of politicians and first ladies (Amadiume 1987: 166–71; Amadiume 2000: 43–61, 247).

Modern women, it seems, are appropriating and adapting traditional practices to their needs. What is different is the nature of leadership and legitimate authority over women and girls. This was indeed the case in Nigeria, when different national women's organizations got involved in the case of the murder of the child bride Hauwa in 1987 (Amadiume 2000: 125–31). Hauwa was a nine-year-old girl who was betrothed to a husband and at the age of twelve was forced to live with him. Hauwa resisted this by running away and by hunger strikes, while her supposed husband meted out several punishments by cutting off her limbs. She eventually died from infection to her wounds. One of the national women's organizations, Women In Nigeria (WIN), went so far as to take Hauwa's husband to court. The involvement of women's organizations had come too late to save Hauwa. However, that case inspired a heated national debate and renewed interest in issues of early marriage, sexuality and the abuse of girls, revealing new problems facing girls in modern society.

All the same, one must admit that in changing conditions in traditional societies as well, girls are no longer so perfect! There probably are more pre-initiation pregnancies, and few girls are able to muster the bravery required to pass some of the ordeals of initiation rites. More importantly, many girls like Florence do not get married after initiation and many do not even get initiated before marriage. However, matriarchitarian structures are present both in traditional societies and in cosmopolitan cities. Though I think that there are no easy answers, I venture to suggest that city girls like Asikiye can be encouraged to join organizations of women's cultures that continue to demonstrate the power of women's solidarity, albeit with a dimension of class contradictions (Amadiume 2000).

Conclusion

In focusing on the dialectic of the collective and the individual woman, I have tried to avoid taking the side of a discourse that makes small gains for women, situating women in small crevices of power and not in the wider contexts of organized forces. I have discussed Mammy Water enchantment in the traditional setting, against the wider organized power of women. When we shift from these women's worlds, Mammy Water assumes a different significance in the lives of individual women under colonialism and neocolonial capitalism. White women, capitalist goods and Western power become unattainable objects of desire, which are represented in the enchanting goddess, Mammy Water, whose images efface that of indigenous African matriarchs.

In closing, it is clear that the disagreements about the meanings of Mammy Water are many, with profound implications for how we read culture and women in the context of African development. For Gore and Nevadomsky, Mammy Water relationships are 'framed as a sexual attraction' (1997: 60). For Henry Drewal (1996), Mammy Water is about local conceptualizations of the Other. For Jell-Bahlsen (1997), Mammy Water beliefs are similarly local, but the image is foreign. Thus, the discourse on desire and sexuality completely moves away from women's histories and women's systems to a world of patriarchy and capital, in which post-colonial African women, posited purely as individuals, are isolated in their desires and afflictions, consuming imports from Europe and India and in turn dreaming of Whiteness. As the world is being redefined daily by a globalization that centres neoliberalism, it is time for the local to redefine our communities. This can be done through resistance and struggles that create demands for the right of all peoples to decide the bases of a just economic, political and cultural exchange on this planet we share.

Notes

A version of this chapter has appeared as 'Bodies, Choices, Globalizing Neocolonial Enchantments: African Matriarchs and Mammy Water', in *Meridians: Feminism, Race, Transnationalism*, 2 (2) 2002: 41–66.

1. I know that there are problems of generalization posed by the usage of terms such as 'African women', 'Third World women', 'women of the South', 'Western women'. In this essay the usage is purely strategic, and I feel justified because my analysis and theory are based on a comparison of specific case studies from which I derive general cultural patterns. I therefore operate here at two levels of discourse, the particular and the general, to engage in a *global* discourse. It is in the context of this global discourse, as it affects responses from Africa, that I also use the general terms Western and Euro-Western culture to refer to African experiences with European and American hegemony. I am of course fully aware of differences of history, culture, class, race, gender, etc. in all of these societies and feel confident that progressive thinkers will accept my usage of these terms and the general criticism that I make. I have, sadly, observed increasingly in Europe and America a certain robust confidence in challenging and silencing African women and diaspora African women when we dare call attention to the crimes of racism, slavery or colonization. Then we are accused of dichotomization or generalization or living in the past!

Africa or African obviously refers to the continent itself as a geographical space and to cultures associated with the continent. It is well understood that within the African continent there are regional, national, ethnic, cultural and language differences. There is also a race question in East, Central and Southern Africa and in North Africa. North Africa is sometimes considered to belong to the Middle East and therefore distinct from so-called sub-Saharan Africa or Black Africa, showing that we do indeed have a race issue in Africa. In Afrocentric perspective, Black Africa includes North Africa, especially Egypt and the huge African diaspora of the world. This is, however, not my concern in this chapter in which the use of generalized terms are purely strategic, employed for dismissing assumptions that Africa's collective experience of colonialism resulted in the disappearance or a total erasure of all pre-existing cultures.

Under globalization, we have seen the power of capitalism and bureaucracy in the shaping and forming of new global identities. We have also had to engage discourses on huge topical issues such as debt, structural adjustment programmes, the environment, HIV/AIDS, etc. The use of generalized categories thus becomes purely strategic, and quite effective when necessary for a solidarity front against persistent and transforming Euro-Western, global economic, cultural and political forces. This is the argument of pan-Africanism.

2. Here I am reading a work by a woman who described Africans as savages in her 1932 book *Hunger and Work in a Savage Tribe: A Functional Study of Nutrition Among the Southern Bantu*. The preface to this book is written by one of the founding patriarchs of British anthropology, Bronislaw Malinowski. He too also called his supposed 'non-western' people savages in his books *The Sexual Life of Savages* (1929) and *Sex and Repression in Savage Society* (1927).

3. In their traditional setting, the Bemba of Zambia practised slash-and-burn shift-

ing cultivation. There was a gender division of labour, with women in charge of most food provision. Women must know food in the bush, such as wild vegetables, mushrooms, honey and caterpillars. A small girl of ten or eleven knew up to 40 different mushrooms and could distinguish edible ones from poisonous ones (Richards 1992: 26). They were dependent on trees for fertility and had good knowledge of them for economic and medicinal purposes. They had knowledge of at least 40 to 50 different trees and their magical properties. Their understanding of their environment was immense. Like most traditional African cultures, Bemba considered wealth to be in labour and not in goods: labour makes wealth, as the Igbo of Nigeria would say.

4. Unfortunately, *The Lake Goddess* is still forthcoming. My page numbers are to a MS of *The Lake Goddess* that was sent to me by Africa World Press, who later also sent me galleys. I was invited to contribute an article to *Emerging Perspectives on Flora Nwapa: Critical and Theoretical Essays*, edited by Marie Umeh and published by Africa World Press in 1998. The book has quite a few essays on *The Lake Goddess*. As I understood it then, the novel was supposed to have been published with the book of critical essays.

5. Oyèrónké Oyewùmí (1997) hardly acknowledges the degree of her indebtedness to my work, *Male Daughters, Female Husbands: Gender and Sex in an African Society* (Amadiume 1987), in which I distinguished biological sex from sociocultural gender, and contrasted rigid Western gender construction with flexible Igbo gender system in language, roles and statuses. I argued that this flexibility in gender construction enabled women's economic and political power, especially since women and men could play certain key roles and occupy certain statuses, terms for which were gender neutral. At the same time, I argued that gender played a strong role in the social structure, the culture and social relations. Women organized on the basis of gender and defended women's rights by the same logic. I also argued that colonialism disrupted Igbo women's traditional systems and imposed European notions of womanhood, but that aspects of traditional women's systems carried over into the present.

Oyewùmí applies the same ideas to her study of the Yoruba, but arrives at a different conclusion. In her view it was colonialism that invented the category women in Yoruba society. In the preface to her book, *The Invention of Women: Making an African Sense of Western Gender Discourses*, Oyewùmí states: 'In fact, my central argument is that there were no *women* – defined in strictly gendered terms – in that society' (1999: xiii, italics in the original). Thus, Oyewùmí denies gender as a principle of social relations and social organization in pre-nineteenth-century, pre-colonial Yoruba society. There is no doubt that a women's culture and women's knowledge system existed and still exist in Yoruba societies. Body did matter as gendered, since Yoruba women were circumcised. There were elaborate life-cycle rituals involving women's bodies as females through the life course of women from birth to death that are in fact absent in the lives of Western women, who are supposedly body-focused. Oyewùmí seems smitten by fear of body. Stuck in exactly the same thing that she is critiquing, she succeeds in imposing a Western fear of being women on Yoruba women.

In reality, Yoruba women, like other women in African societies, engage in issues of body and are comfortable with being women, as they use body symbolism to construct and reconstruct alternative cultural systems that favour women, as, for example, matriarchy. Thus, these women have a pragmatic relationship with many social systems that also include ideal notions of human equality. An ideal notion of the equality of persons or human beings is present in the Yoruba non-gendered concept of *Enyo* and similarly in Igbo *Nmadu*, but we still have to face the contradictions of gender that are based on a material reality.

. . . .

On Engendering a Better Life

Raka Ray

§ I HAVE spent the last ten years thinking about women's collective action in the Third World. How does it occur, what shape does it take, under what circumstances is it successful? I have spent less time thinking about how women as individuals conceive of their well-being and how they envision a better life. How do ordinary women, many with little contact with organizations and movements, reflect on and contemplate the politics of the possible? In this essay I reflect on the thoughts and life story of Lakshmi, a domestic worker in Calcutta, India. I do not write about Lakshmi as a representative of domestic workers. Rather, she is a thoughtful member of civil society, who thinks about a better world for herself, her children, and those who might be even less fortunate than her. I turn to Lakshmi because, as a member of one of the lowest castes, as a worker in one of the worst-paid and least-esteemed jobs, and as a woman, she clearly belongs to a category of persons on whose behalf we might ask: whom is development for?

I will look at the requirements of a 'good society' through Lakshmi's eyes, and consider what development might look like were we to take her seriously.[1] In what follows, I offer my reading of Lakshmi's life based on extended conversations with her – with the following caveats. First, Lakshmi's words were uttered in a context in which it was clear that she was a domestic and I belonged to the employer class. Second, I recognize that this is my reading of Lakshmi's life. Finally, I understand Lakshmi's words as generated from within a specific 'habitus', yet respect her desire to be treated as an agent who exercises choice within drastically limited circumstances. That is, I accept the contradictory position of subjects being both 'rational actors and unable to think beyond the "naturalized" givens of their communities' (Kandiyoti 1998: 147).

Lakshmi's Life

As a scheduled caste woman, Lakshmi, aged 40, is inserted into the cultural and political landscape of Calcutta in that domestic work is the work most readily available to her. It is, after all, the largest source of employment for women in urban Bengal. Lakshmi works a twelve-hour day, cooking and cleaning for her elderly employer. It takes her an hour to get to work and she earns barely enough to meet her most basic needs.

Although Lakshmi knew that I was interested in her life as a domestic worker, she was more interested in telling me about her marriage. 'I married by choice despite resistance from my family. My uncles and aunts asked me repeatedly, "Lakshmi, are you sure, are you absolutely sure?" but I said I was.' However, her life was not easy after marriage. Her husband sold goods out of a roadside stall, and they could not make ends meet. Once she became pregnant, she tried her hand at several jobs – piece-rate sewing, making and selling cow dung patties for fuel, and so on. That was still not enough to sustain her *sansar* ('family'; also, 'world'). As babies were born, she continued to try various ways to make ends meet, until she finally became a domestic.

The reason for her unhappiness, however, is not the hard work she does. Rather, even as she talks with pride about her new confidence and abilities, she returns continually to her relationship with her husband and to her realization that he never loved her as she thought he did. He always wants her to be subordinated (*parajito*, 'defeated') to him. Her sociable nature makes him jealous. She speaks with great sorrow about her husband's failure to love and appreciate her, his jealousy and possessiveness, and his will to dominate. When I ask her what she wants from her future, she says, 'Just some love. One can't live without love. Just like a plant or a tree, one withers and dies. There is a man who loves me now and does a lot for me, but he is not my husband.' She looks away, and then turns to me again. 'But tell me this, am I wrong to accept love from someone else when my husband has refused it to me for so long? If a thief steals, are you going to beat him up or find out what the circumstances were that led him to commit this act?'

She has no desire to give up working outside the home. It was going out of the house and working that opened her eyes to the world and made her realize that her husband's behaviour towards her was not appropriate: 'I now see that women can have independence and I don't have it and my husband doesn't want me to have it.' Further, she believes that both men and women should work outside the home: 'I believe one should work, earn and then eat. And I pray that I am always fit enough to do so. For the sake of fairness, I think both husband and wife should do work around the house.'

But not everyone can get a job. Those who have the ability to do so must have a sense of responsibility towards those who cannot: 'I will never give money to a temple but I will to a beggar. I believe you should help those who do not have the *kshamata* ('capability') to work. Sometimes, when I am badly treated, I think, am I not a human being? But then the man sleeping on the pavement, is he not a human being too? In that case, I must tell myself, I am so very fortunate.'

Yet working outside the home comes with costs. She has five daughters, three of whom are still at home. Because she is not at home, she cannot protect them from predatory men. She must constantly think of ways to keep her daughters safe. This has stopped her from physically leaving her husband, but she says she will do so as soon as the youngest child is married, even if it means moving into the home of her employer to become a full-time, live-in maid. While she recognizes her responsibilities towards her daughters, she no longer acknowledges her duty towards the man who is her husband.

Lakshmi's Vision

What does Lakshmi's story tell us about how this 'ordinary' woman conceives of a developed culture or just society? A gender-just society in particular would be one in which women were given dignity, respect and recognition, no matter what work they did; where gender-unequal norms were challenged; where women would have rights over their own bodies; and where compassion for those less fortunate must always guide one's actions.

It is her husband's failure to give her recognition that leaves Lakshmi feeling unfulfilled. It is the absence of his acknowledgement that she is important to him, or affects him, that Lakshmi finds unbearable. Because he has never shown her that she matters to him, because he does not respect the person that she is, he has lost the right to keep her. While Lakshmi's bitterness about lack of respect is directed against her husband, the larger point to be made is that we cannot underestimate the importance of the social need for respect and recognition. When she asked me whether I thought she was wrong to accept love from a man who was not her husband, she was asking me to understand that she had come to a moral position based on her husband's failure to give her the respect and recognition which should have been her right.

Lakshmi points to the importance of the ability to exercise choice, not just in the sphere of work, but also in the most intimate matters of life. She believes that her sexuality should be her own, that it should not be something solely associated with the status of marriage. Rather, she should own it and have the ability to judge who is deserving and not deserving of her. She sees her rights over her body as fundamental. She is grateful that her body has the capacity for work and also the capacity for enjoyment. In a context where women's sexual agency of any kind is threatening, Lakshmi's quiet insistence on her rights, and her use of the metaphor of the hungry thief, is radical indeed. Her fears about her daughters' safety further reflect the importance she gives to bodily integrity. Her daughters' rights over their own bodies are curtailed by the threat of predatory men.

In clearly stating that both husband and wife should work so that they can eat, and that both should do housework, Lakshmi expresses her dissent from legally backed hegemonic cultural norms that argue for a separation between men's and women's spheres and for women's particular roles within families. This is a protest that is articulated outside of the realm of organized politics, a dissent which originates in her lived experiences.

Finally, Lakshmi believes that one must live one's life as a social being, recognizing one's responsibility towards other members of society. Thus she believes that she must look out for those less fortunate than she, which implies that others more fortunate than Lakshmi should look out for her. She distinguishes between contributing to institutions such as temples, and contributing towards the maintenance of those who simply don't have the ability to maintain themselves. Indeed, manifesting what Gramsci (1971: 333) would call a certain 'good sense', a critical ethic that goes beyond the common sense of the 'real' world, Lakshmi articulates her belief in a society built on cultural ideals of collective responsibility, acknowledgement and care.

But we must also listen for the things Lakshmi did not say. Most notably, Lakshmi did not speak of the desire for more money either in and of itself, or for material things that more money could purchase. Without a doubt, Lakshmi's life would be better off if she had more money, and of course the Lakshmis of this world would be far better off with a decent wage and a union that would get it for them. But when asked about her desires for the future, or when discussing her philosophy towards her children or her own life, recognition, respect and compassion take centre stage. What, then, do we make of the disputes between Women in Development (WID) programmes and feminist scholars over the content of 'basic needs' which must be met before one can articulate a non-economic vision of a better life? The level at which Lakshmi lives might be thought by some to meet the standard of minimal basic needs, but it does not meet those standards for *her*. Her construction of basic needs includes human and social elements without which she does not believe she – or indeed anyone – can live.

Thinking about Development

Beneath all the rhetoric about development, the policies and counter-policies, the innumerable agencies and NGOs, the planners and economists, the allocations and misallocations of resources, lies a basic question. What sort of society do we want to live in? While 'development' is often used in its restricted sense, referring to the allocation of scarce resources for growth and (material) distribution, at the heart of even those questions lies a cultural vision of a better society and a better life. Recent UN guidelines have expanded the scope of the definition of development to include human rights and fundamental freedoms (see Howard 1995, Youssef 1995). Lakshmi's vision forces us to put substance into those rights and freedoms, and adds a sense of responsibility to community. It underscores the point made by recent feminist analysts of development that while access to food, water and shelter are undeniably core development goals, rural and urban development schemes must focus on reaching those goals in ways that integrally foster respect, community and bodily autonomy (see Kabeer 1994, Kabeer and Subramanian 1999). These needs are experienced as fundamental in the imagination of those who may perform the most menial tasks of society.

Finally, Lakshmi's words call scholars of development to focus on the cultures of families. Scholars and activists in the WID and GAD (Gender and Development) tradition have tended to emphasize women's economic marginalization and exploitation. Contemporary Indian feminists, reacting against orientalist and Mayo-esque criticisms of 'Indian culture', have also highlighted the complicity of the state and world economy, rather than the family, in women's oppression (see Mayo 1936 and the critique of Mayo in Sinha 2000). While we are wise to underscore the embeddedness of families and households in the more macro institutions of society, Lakshmi makes evident that, for her, it is in the family that daily hurts, neglect and violence are inflicted. She experiences the culturally sanctioned patriarchal relations of authority and ownership as directly oppressive. It is, after all, because she is his wife that her husband can afford not to value her humanity. We learn from Lakshmi and other 'ordinary' women that life within patrilocal and patrilineal families is difficult and often sorrowful. While their songs and folk stories often invoke the pain of daily living within these families, the documentation of these laments has remained outside the purview of those who study development (see, for example, Raheja and Gold 1994, Dev Sen 1999). Development may not be able to procure affection for women like Lakshmi. But it will be infinitely more meaningful if it enables women's familial lives to be graced with more dignity, humanity and autonomy.

Note

1. Conversations with Lakshmi took place in the context of my ongoing research on the social history of domestic servitude in India. I interviewed her in 1998 and again in 1999.

. . . .

Empowerment: Snakes and Ladders

Jan Nederveen Pieterse

§ IT is not entirely clear when 'empowerment' entered the vocabulary. Among feminists in the 1970s, 'emancipation' came be to be regarded as too large and ambitious an agenda, while 'empowerment' was seen as more practical and enabling immediate action. Over the past decades the term has been working overtime. It has become a totem word in development populism and is widely used in feminism, public interest campaigning, social movements and management. Empowerment, then, is used in both political and non-political contexts; the common denominator is that, at the very least, it refers to individual skills development.

Originally, empowerment meant delegation; since the seventeenth century, according to the Oxford English Dictionary, it has meant 'to invest legally or formally with power or authority; to authorize, license'; or 'to impart or bestow power to an end or for a purpose; to enable, permit' (James 1999: 14). In feminism, empowerment has gradually taken on the reverse of the original meaning: now it is self-empowerment and comes not from above, but from below. Its meaning ranges from having a voice, particularly in decision-making, to having control of resources. Rowlands notes that 'empowerment as a concept has arisen alongside the strengthening of focus on individualism, consumerism and personal achievement as cultural and economic goals' (1998: 11). In business-speak, empowerment has several meanings: organizations eliminate middle management and empower employees to supervise them-selves and junior staff; it refers to self-management as a corollary of corporate downsizing or as part of corporate identity politics.

According to Wendy James, empowerment is 'an ambivalent word. It is the kind of word that the social sciences should use with extreme care, if at all' (1999: 26). Is it possible to penetrate the aura of vagueness surrounding 'empowerment' to arrive at a critical core? One option is to try to establish a more or less rigorous definition, but given the wide variety of uses this is a difficult option. Another option is to view empowerment as an umbrella term for a wide array of 'progressive' politics. Then we would still want to know what is distinctive about empowerment, for faced with different forms of collective action, how would we know what is empowering and what is not?

That the term empowerment is now so widely used can be taken as a sign of the times itself. That is, empowerment should not offhand be approached as a lesser form of emancipation – emancipation-minus – but as a theme in its own right. As such, since empowerment contains 'power', it implies a particular angle on power and politics, and capturing this involves exploring the relationship between power and empowerment.

Power and Empowerment

Power has multiple connotations of energy (as in 'Power and Light'), capacity (as in horsepower) and 'power over' (domination, rule, authority, etc.). If we consider how power has changed meaning over time we come across pairs of terms such as domination and emancipation, capital and labour, imperialism and liberation, rule and resistance. The relationship between these terms is typically one of contradiction, opposition, with one logic trying to control or displace the other. Key concepts of power that are currently in use – hegemony (Gramsci) and discourse (Foucault) – do not function in this way. That is, to refer to progressive change we would use the *same* terms. The point of 'counter-hegemony' is to achieve hegemony and an alternative discourse is still discourse. Obviously, this implies a changed take on the nature of power. Empowerment, likewise, does not stand to power in a relationship of contradiction, but we are on a single terrain, presumably dealing with variations of power. These changing understandings may be correlated with other contemporary trends, such as capacitation in economics, enablement in development and governance and the concern with learning.

Empowerment is itself a form of power, emergent power. It follows that empowerment can be merely mimesis of power: as Paulo Freire said, the greatest risk for the oppressed is to imitate the oppressor. Similar problems apply to terms such as 'participation'. Empowerment can obscure conflicts of interest among different categories of women; forward movement is not inevitable and one person's empowerment may be another's disempowerment (see Rowlands 1998). To address this problem, we would need to problematize power. In feminist literature, 'power' is disaggregated into 'power over' (domination), 'power to' (capacity), 'power within' (inner strength) and 'power with' (achieved through co-operation and alliance). In feminist uses of empowerment the emphasis is clearly on 'power to' and capabilities, and not on 'power over'.

Capacitation has become a keynote in several fields. In Amartya Sen's capabilities approach (1985), capability refers both to the 'freedom to choose' and to control of a 'set of commodity bundles', a conceptualization that shows the imprint of liberal philosophy. Sen developed this theme in relation to 'functioning': 'Capability is primarily a reflection of the freedom to achieve valuable functionings ... a set of vectors of functioning' (Sen 1992: 49, 40). This parallels Martha Nussbaum's idea of translating *rights* to *capabilities*: 'The right to political participation ... the right to free speech – these and others are best thought of as "capacities to function". In other words, to secure a right for citizens in one of these areas is to put them in a position of capability to function in that area' (2000: 11).

The capabilities approach is the theoretical backbone of the human development approach that defines development as 'the enlargement of people's choices'. This is operationalized in capacity building in development projects, which refers to institutional as well as individual capabilities. *Capacity building* is the mainstream language of the World Bank and donors, while *empowerment* is associated with bottom-up, alternative approaches. Also frequently used nowadays is the terminology of 'enabling', 'disabling' and disempowerment. Government has become *governance*, a shift that refers to an enabling and facilitator role of government.

The starting point in progressive politics is usually *consciousness*: of class (Marx), the subconscious (psychoanalysis), gender (feminism), identity (recognition). Conscientization is the keynote of Paulo Freire's critical pedagogy. Consciousness-raising and 'awareness training' function in relation to gender, race and human rights. In political contexts, awareness is usually step one and collective action step two. Another angle is to view *learning* as the link between consciousness and capacity: capacitation essentially takes place through learning. Nowadays learning is a keynote in fields such as management (the learning organization), local economic development and governance. Development can also be redefined as a collective learning process (see Nederveen Pieterse 2001).

The Rhizome of Empowerment

One way of approaching the relationship between empowerment and other notions of progressive action is to conceptualize a 'ladder of empowerment'. A ladder, however, implies a linear progression, suggesting a step-like, cumulative forward movement in modes of collective awareness and action. In reality, collective action and the relations between different modes of collective action are probably much more complex, and more like a rhizome – the metaphor is of a tubular root sprouting in many irregular directions – than a staircase. Key terms such as resistance and empowerment are typically used in many different meanings across a wide register. Attempts to use them in a narrow register with tight definitions easily become artificial. Using loose definitions and understandings, and viewing interrelations between different modes of collective action like a rhizome (à la Deleuze and Guattari), gives us a more complex and realistic depiction, in which consciousness and praxis give rise to many options, as resistance grows in many directions, matching the loose use of language in actual politics and action.

Below is a schematic overview of various forms of collective action. The ordering criterion is the degree of social transformation achieved in different forms and conceptions of praxis. The table is structured as a continuum that runs from no social transformation (coping) to maximum transformation (hegemony).

Rhizome of collective action

Mode	Methods	Social transformation
Coping	Awareness of oppression; improvisation	No
Consciousness-raising	Class, ego consciousness, etc.; conscientization; change in discourse, gaze	Not necessarily
Resistance	Sabotage, gossip, pilfering; change in discourse	Not structural
Quiet encroachment	Niche opportunism	Better individual or group niches
Participation	In design, decision, implementation, beliefs	Depends on context and mode of participation
Empowerment	More voice, capacity, skill, power to	Better individual and/or group chances; not structural
Emancipation	Group rise in status, position or power	Social structure and values become more inclusive
Hegemony	Change in political, social, cultural, economic discourse and practices	A more inclusive power structure (e.g. social or cultural revolution)

This raises several questions. Is it justified to take social transformation as a yardstick of empowerment? In effect this follows a double logic: a *rhizome* of collective action and a *ladder* of social transformation. This may help to distinguish the contours of 'empowerment'. To which unit does this apply: to social groups, societies or the world? If it applies to social groups, then the logical end of empowerment – hegemony – may not apply. For example, for indigenous peoples such as Aboriginals in Australia the maximum achievement is emancipation, not hegemony. As a sequence, would this apply regardless of variety across time and place? In outline, presumably yes, but filled in differently in each situation. To each social formation there are different nodes that are key to refixing power. For example, in the belt of patriarchy, questions such as family law are crucial levers of change; in other contexts, questions of ethnicity, patronage, etc. may be crucial power points.

How does empowerment compare to emancipation? While emancipation targets 'power over', empowerment is concerned with 'power to'. Like emancipation, empowerment differs from protest because it is proactive; it differs from resistance because it is concerned with transformation. But while emancipation seeks the transformation of social and political hierarchy, empowerment seeks capacitation. This, too, is a matter of social equality but is to be achieved through a levelling of capacities, rather than through a levelling of entitlements or political change. In phase two, the levelling of capacities may translate into claims for economic and political equality, but this is not explicitly given in empowerment. Emancipation has a collective dimension, which is not necessarily the case in empowerment. Unlike emancipation, empowerment is ethically neutral, except that since it refers to the capacitation of those who were disabled it has an inherently egalitarian bias.

The advantage of 'empowerment' is that the terrain is widened ('liberation' has political overtones) and unburdened of ideological luggage ('emancipation' recalls the Enlightenment legacy); besides, the notion can be used flexibly (empowerment can be personal and collective, etc.), so it is 'a word of the times'. In contrast to notions such as class struggle, where typically the idea has been that there is one right way of going about it, empowerment does not suggest a single or straightforward logic. In empowerment, as in the Snakes and Ladders game, there are different ways of getting to a 'higher' place and several ways up involve falling down and starting over from a different point in the game. To empowerment, there is no single forward 'line of march'.

This enables us to situate empowerment. Since empowerment is used in political and non-political contexts, it straddles a minimum and normative meaning. Rowlands, for example, infuses it with normative content when she speaks of 'generative rather than controlling power' (1998: 15); however, what some view as generative others may view as controlling. The point of this reflection is that the minimum meaning of empowerment is interesting in itself. 'Empowerment' parallels the language of capabilities, capacitation and enablement in economics, development and governance. The significance of empowerment is that it indicates a shift in thinking about power, which is both subtle and profound: from 'power over' to 'power to'; from power derived from position in an institutional hierarchy to power based on skills, capacities. Institutions themselves matter to the extent that they are capable: this is the point of institutional analysis. Thus, empowerment denotes a turn to *capabilities* in social action and politics. Therein lies its significance and in this sense it is a welcome notion.

· ·

Gendered Sexualities and Lived Experience: The Case of Gay Sexuality in Women, Culture and Development

Dana Collins

> The evil that confronts us in Manila is not the face of the harlot but the face of hunger. Babylon is not a casino or cinema or brothel on the Pasig. It's that handwriting on the wall. (Quijano de Manila, from *Manila: Sin City? and Other Chronicles*: 271)

§ STUDIES of development in the Third World project two drastically different images of everyday reality. On the one hand, development, which is supposed to alleviate the ills of rapid modernization, instead facilitates the movement of labourers into the ever more exploitative processes of globalization. For example, studies of tourism and its informal partner, sex tourism, demonstrate considerable passive victimization whereby labourers are gendered, deskilled and exoticized in an industry that is supposed to serve as a quick fix to poverty in developing nations. On the other hand, researchers sifting through the lived experience of workers struggling with development are confronted by their equally significant expressions of pleasure and possibility. These expressions are often analysed as resistance to the local sex/gender systems and the global labour relations that work together to create the double bind for workers in global capitalism. However, the images of passive victimization encourage the loss of the Third World subject as a changing actor who struggles alongside the forces of globalization. In this case sexuality becomes simply a commodity exchanged in the sex and tourist industries, rather than a site where sexual Others may contest commodified exchanges and through which they struggle to define alternative sexual identities and lifestyles.

This chapter will grapple with the question of 'Whose development?' from a different vantage point. If development has been blind to women's lived experience, and a Women, Culture and Development approach[1] tries to imagine a development for women by integrating the analytical insights of lived experience, then where do gay men fit in? Third World gay men also struggle against normative sex/gender systems and global capitalism; they too become gendered Others through these historical relations. Rather than pitting the lived experience of gay men against that of women, Women, Culture and Development could address the intersection of gender, sexuality and development across *gendered sexualities*. This vantage point provides an alternative: it begins an investigation of sexuality as lived experience (as gendered, classed, racialized and historical), it grapples with the question of desire in exploitative relations, it pushes to the fore gender as a relational category (not just between men and women but between First and Third World men and, importantly, between gay men and women) and it raises the question of whether non-normative sexualities can serve as a subject location to resist gendered Othering.

I want to elaborate this vantage point by considering the case of one Filipino gay man living in Manila as a gendered Other who grapples with his sexuality and sexualized labour. This case is drawn from ethnographic research carried out in Manila from January 2000 to February 2001, during which I explored the local and global dimensions of a gay expression historically rooted and transformed in the urban neighbourhood of Malate. A focus on one Filipino gay man's lived experience of sexuality highlights its negotiation, naturalization, commodification and social transformation in the face of what some may characterize as the exploitative relations of sexualized tourism. Third World men who consciously embrace same-sex desire, irrespective of whether they take on the Western identity of 'gay', engage in an everyday active confrontation with normative sex/gender systems in the Third World that, needless to say, are systems very much imbricated in globalization. This confrontation results in their varied expressions of gender and sexuality at the same time that these men are interpolated as gendered Others who function as 'gay hosts' to foreigners.

I met José in a coffee shop located in one of the many urban malls in metro Manila. This particular mall is situated on the border of the Ermita and Malate districts. Ermita is known as the primary tourist district of Manila, although several prominent hotels and tourist sites are also located in Malate. Ermita housed the primary sex district in Manila until the early 1990s, when city government closures of sex establishments and any other establishments deemed 'immoral' by then mayor Alfredo Lim turned Ermita into what some of my interviewees describe as a ghost town. The sex strip of Mabini and M. H. del Pilar extended down into Malate, indicating again that the borders between these two districts were and remain porous; these two districts share the industries of tourism, entertainment and sex work and their proximity encourages the movement of tourists and business travellers between the two neighbourhoods. Malate is known locally as a bohemian and entertainment district which historically manifests a strong gay expression. The turn of the millennium saw an explosion in entertainment and dining establishments in Malate as well as the re-emergence of sex work, albeit in the more informal form of street prostitution.

The city's closure of Ermita's sex strip, as well as other state-sponsored attempts to deter sex tourism, has resulted in a shift in the official state position on tourism and its relationship to economic development in the Philippines. Although the state continues to prioritize tourism as a promising means for economic development, there are now efforts at planning sustainable tourist development by harnessing the support of the communities servicing the industry and aiming for development that does not negatively impact such communities. Despite these efforts, the Philippines remains one of the primary sex tourist destinations in South-east Asia. Decades of such tourism has established a social and economic infrastructure whose tentacles run deep into the sex trade. The informal structure of the social and economic relations in sexualized tourism is doubly unique for gay tourism, because it is an unrecorded sector of tourism in the Philippines. Hence, the social and sexual relations which develop out of the contact of gay tourism and gay life in Manila are less formally institutionalized by way of organized sex tours or sex clubs. In contrast to heterosexual sexualized tourism, it is more likely that gay tourists and Filipinos foster social and sexual exchanges at the level of chance encounters, gay space and informal communities in Malate. Here, notions of 'gay' and 'space' get reworked through the relationships among gay Filipinos, expatriates, tourists and entertainment business developers. The coffee shop, for example, with its tables placed on the mall walkway, serves as a strategic cruising location for Filipino gay men who seek relationships with foreigners.

José first started frequenting Ermita and Malate in 1989 when he ran away from his home province of Cavité, a poorer region to the south of metro Manila. José explained that he left home at 15 because of an abusive stepfather who could not accept José's gender (his sexuality). Initially, he worked as a call boy along Mabini Street in Ermita and stopped when he began work for an NGO that organized outreach programmes for street children. José was awarded this position because of his knowledge of the streets, as well as his extensive contact with communities of street children. He left this position when the NGO closed, and returned to live with his family.[2] Today José continues to frequent Malate approximately six days a week to meet foreigners, hang out with friends, drink and dance.

José describes his discovery of Ermita/Malate as a delightfully confusing urban environment, where for the first time he saw openly gay men and bars with a noticeable gay presence. He explains being drawn to the difference foreigners lent to the neighbouring sex strip. Ermita/Malate, in fact, felt like a different country when compared to his less developed province of Cavité. Like many of my interviewees, José saw Malate as the first 'free' space where gay men could both accept and develop their alternative gendered and sexual identities. And this development was in part facilitated by the presence of foreigners who lead Western gay lifestyles.

Although José now identifies as 'gay', he never saw himself as *bakla*.[3] He felt compelled to limit his gay expression while living in Cavité, because one is often assumed to be *bakla* if one acknowledges desire for men. José could not abide by the gendered and work restrictions that framed the life of the *bakla*. In Malate, José met Filipino gay men who engaged in a range of gendered identities and practices. They did not necessarily dress or act like women and none held *parlorista*[4] or seamstress positions. Neither did they have to play the role of the straight identifying hustler[5] to meet clients and boyfriends. Almost all hoped to meet a gay lover who also did not follow the conventions of *bakla*/heterosexual male relationships; they hoped to meet someone 'different'.

The presence of gay tourists and expatriates who frequent the district assert such a difference; they also serve as sources for income, travel, exposure and romance. José, like a core group of gay Filipinos who frequent Malate, prefers establishing paid companionship relationships with such foreigners. These relationships range from casual encounters to long-term relationships. Paid companions work as escorts for travel, romance, sex and intellectual engagement for gay tourists, businessmen and expatriates travelling and living in the Philippines. But when I asked 'Why foreigners?', quite often paid companions expressed a genuine desire for these men, highlighting the open and challenging relationships they have with them. Only in passing do they refer to the economic support that they receive from their 'boyfriends' and sometimes this support is joked about. But the stories escorts chose to tell about their foreign boyfriends were stories about love, loss and desirable encounters. Although José no longer considers himself a call boy, preferring to call his work paid escort, guide, or companion work that sometimes involves sexual exchanges, José will talk at length about the desirable nature of his sexual exchanges. The matter of his not mentioning that these exchanges also involve the indirect transfer of money for sexual companionship allows José to frame these exchanges as desirable and loving, rather than relations determined through commodification. And, when such relations are viewed as less directly commodified, they become less alienating.

José has one primary ongoing paid companionship relationship from which he receives monthly deposits in his bank account for approximately 10,000 pesos ($200). From this relationship, as well as other temporary paid companionship encounters, José earns enough money to economically support himself and his mother in Cavité. He shares this financial responsibility with his sister, to whom he is very close. Both his mother and sister know about and accept his sexuality. José opened a Sari-Sari store[6] in Cavité, from which he earned a small profit before being forced to close it after the store was damaged from the rainy season's flooding. Jose explains that it is from the influence of this boyfriend that he learned about business and began to direct his life towards work in the business field. He selectively referred to this boyfriend as boss, boyfriend, friend and ex-boyfriend, at varying times throughout the year I knew him. José sees this boyfriend once a year, arranges for his hotel room, books their travel to beach resorts, collects him at the airport and escorts him around Manila. In reference to this arrangement, José refers to himself as lucky because he can afford now to be choosy when selecting boyfriends. He recognizes that not all the working gays in Malate can afford this luxury.

José considers himself an intelligent man who provides challenging companionship to his clients. He sees his intelligence and ability to move between different classes and cultural circles as a benefit in his services. He explained that foreigners seem to prefer him to the others at the local gay bar precisely because he offers such intellectual companionship. Although José performed well in his classes at school, he felt bored with high school studies. He believes, rather, that the streets and travels with his companion taught him more about the Philippines and life than the detached study offered by official schooling. He explains that he has some regrets about the path he's chosen, because he recognizes that his escort work, and not having a degree, limit other work opportunities. José also believes that he cannot live this lifestyle for many more years. 'They (employers) always want the certification. It's a shame because I have knowledge and experience that is much better than that.' At the same time he feels that he has actively chosen his path and that gives him a sense of satisfaction. He explains that his wants are simple: 'I don't want to be rich or to have new and expensive clothes. I want a job that I like and an income that allows me to buy for my lover some of the time. I'd really like that because it's hard always being the one who has to be bought for. I want a place to live that I share with my lover, a place we can both come home to after working hard, where we will eat together, talk about our day and hold one another' (interview, 2001).

This picture of José's life appears cohesive and ideal because I have tried to remain true to José's expression of his lived experience of sexuality and work. Yet José and other working gays carve their lives out in an urban environment that they also recognize as harsh and limiting in terms of their access to economic rewards. Neither is Manila a safe city for those who become increasingly reliant on the streets for establishing their contacts with customers. José is part of an invisible labour force that facilitates tourism in the Philippines, and it is through these informal channels of playing gay host and through José's love, desire and sexual and intellectual labour that gay tourists are cared for in the Philippines. Yet the informal arrangement of these paid companionship relationships may disadvantage José. The economic compensation is often a less than equal exchange for the labour José puts forward while serving as a host, sexual companion and/or boyfriend. Further, José's employment opportunity (both in and out of the sex trade) decreases the longer he works as a gay companion. Foreigners enter and leave José's life due to their easy movement across national boundaries, a movement denied to José. This movement also allows travellers global access to men like José in Thailand, Hong Kong, Malaysia and Vietnam. A far too common statement expressed in the local gay bar where José and his friends spend much of their time is: 'They all grow restless. And there's always someone in Thailand.' There is also a question concerning to what class of gays does Malate really belong, given its more recent gentrification and the fact that none of these working gays can afford to live there. Yet Malate is a lively neighbourhood precisely because of their presence, labour and expression. Consumption and travel are encouraged because of these carefully constructed host relationships. Malate may feel like another country, and a dream country at that, yet the development of metropolitan Manila happens at the direct expense of development in the more rural areas much like José's home province of Cavité.

The change that matters to José involves his imagining and crafting a life that uses urban space and alternative gendered sexualities that at the same time are key to his resisting a normative (and confining) sex/gender system. This system is also economically limiting, and it is one José finds homophobic and degrading in its own right. Moving to and experiencing the pleasures of gay community where Filipino men come together and construct alternative lives is central to José's experience of social change. It is in this urban centre where gay life takes hold and flourishes, with the capital of gay business owners, through the labour of gay hosts and with the consumption practices of gay tourists. Making a living from tourism is part of producing a practice, identity and alternative life and also a way to claim space in this community. José does not characterize his relationships with tourists as degrading or exploitative; rather, he emphasizes his desire for sexual exchanges between men, the expression of his gender and sexuality, his love of travel and his search for satisfying intellectual engagements and business opportunities.

The difficulty for a Women, Culture and Development approach, then, is that resistance, pleasure and possibility are often practised and expressed through the relations that link labourers to normative sex/gender systems and processes of globalization. It is precisely through the commodified exchange of sex, love and desire with tourists that gay escorts sometimes imagine and practise non-normative relations that are socially meaningful and transformative. And, flirting with the boundaries of normative sex/gender systems often translates into one's being on the outside – a liberating space to be, if temporarily so. This is a far from passive picture of women and gay men in development. Hence a WCD approach must grapple with the contradictory nature of the links between resistance, work, gender and sexuality within normative sex/gender systems and global capitalism, because these relations are simultaneously confining and transformative. This approach can demonstrate that lived experience need not be hidden by macro approaches that focus on exploitation; rather, such an approach can elaborate lived experience as a struggle within boundaries.

Notes

1. At its core, a Women, Culture and Development approach asserts the importance of lived experience as a framework for understanding the integration of development in Third World women's lives. Women are centred in this approach because of their status as 'gendered Other' in development and their triple oppression as women, as workers on the lowest rung of the global economy and as racial and ethnic others. The focus on daily life is strategic, because development studies has not successfully integrated the everyday thoughts, practices and knowledges of women when assessing the impact of development on their lives. Development studies have overlooked lived experience precisely because it demonstrates the contested relations of gendered, cultural, sexual, racial and economic realities that constrain and enable women in developing nations. Hence, the stuff of daily life presents contradictions for the implementation of development projects that seek to overcome exploitation and improve quality of life, particularly if such experiences detail how development, in fact, disadvantages women. On the other hand, Women, Culture and Development demonstrates how a focus on lived experience provides insight into the various strategies women use to struggle against the constraints of sex/gender and global economic systems, as well as a way to reconsider the social structures that impinge upon these forms of resistance without framing them as simply exploitative.

2. José indicated that his mother and stepfather eventually separated, and it was after this separation that he considered moving home again. José expressed a lot of discomfort discussing this topic, hence I am uncertain as to the form of contact his stepfather maintains with the family given that divorce is illegal in the Philippines.

3. *Bakla* is the traditional Filipino 'gay' man who dresses and acts according to the dictates of normative femininity. *Baklas* are marginally accepted in Filipino society, yet their gendered, social and economic practices are narrowly defined. Employment positions are limited to feminized professions like hairdresser, garment maker or designer. Some *baklas* pass as women and work in prostitution. If a *bakla* takes on a lover, it is expected that he will monetarily support this lover (who identifies as heterosexual) without interfering with his lover's family life (girlfriend, wife and/or children).

4. *Parlorista* is a term used to describe a working-class 'gay' who either owns and/ or works for a local beauty parlour.

5. Many of the self-identified call boys are straight-identified and, for the most part, lead heterosexual lives when they are not with male customers.

6. A Sari-Sari store is a small one-room neighbourhood store or stand that sells basic foods and household items.

VISIONS 2

. . . .

Condoms and Pedagogy: Changing Global Knowledge Practices

Peter Chua

§ CONDOMS present a resource for hope. For many, especially certain groups of Third World women, the increased availability of male condoms opens new and improved health opportunities and makes empowerment possible in their lives. Yet the present institutional route to the increased availability of male condoms presents real challenges to the hopes of actualizing a better future in these women's lives (see Chua 2001).

In metro Manila (Philippines), for instance, the US government funds condom education programmes through local AIDS organizations such as the *Kabalikat Ng Pamilyang Pilipino* (Working in Partnership with Filipino Families for Better Health) Foundation. *Kabalikat* works to promote reproductive health education among women sex workers by operating drop-in centres that offer services, referrals and modern health products. Since 1993, *Kabalikat* has conducted a US-supported communication-based programme to change sex workers' individual behaviour. The programme aims to educate sex workers about so-called risky sex behaviours, better sexual practices through condom use and worker–client negotiation skills, using targeted media campaigns and outreach by *Kabilikat*'s staff and peer educators.

The programme assumes sex workers need the 'correct and proper' information and beliefs to improve their behaviour. To make behavioural change, it draws on a specific communication strategy – that of one-way transmission, as distinct from a dialogic approach. The strategy incorrectly essentializes sex workers' behaviour, thereby concealing their varied voices and resistances to condom education. Its unidirectionality masks the unequal relations of power and knowledge, for instance, between *Kabalikat* and its target client. Rather than focusing on false deficiencies in individual women's personalities, motivations and communication skills, a different health education strategy needs to be considered. An alternative and more participatory strategy needs to be developed and implemented that would focus principally on the social workings of power, culture and inequalities.

To transform prevailing condom pedagogy, there are two related challenges: democratic education and the practice of social change. The first, democratic education, arises from how organizations and governments instruct certain Third World women on the need to use condoms. Health education activities supported by leading international public health donors use positivistic persuasion models in health psychology, aiming to modify Third World women's individual behaviour. The models assume that through seemingly appropriate educational campaigns, Third World women and other targeted groups will improve their health behaviour. So governments, for-profit firms and many non-profit organizations rely on this social science assumption in order to promote condom use.

The most significant problem with these pedagogical models is their persistent reliance on a unidirectional approach to education, resulting in the paternalistic and non-egalitarian activities of public health campaigns. In these activities, genuine democratic possibilities are undermined by an institutional reliance on the scientific truths of health psychology and the possibility of modifying women's behaviour through educational transmission. Such behaviour modification works under the pretence of genuine democratic communication.

The one-way transmitting of messages supposes that the uncomplicated thinking of Third World women can be easily replaced with messages about healthier sexual practices. It views Third World women as victims of traditional beliefs and practices, who think incorrectly and behave improperly due to their ignorance about sexual hygiene and risky behaviour. This one-way approach prevents Third World women from communicating their reservations about personally intrusive and behaviour-modifying educational activities, because it pursues a process of transmission rather than an open-ended dialogue aimed at changing the value-systems of each side. It also supposes that health educators and social scientists are modern, well-informed humanitarians, offering their superior solutions to deserving Third World women. In contrast, to have genuine democratic forms of communication that go beyond simply transmitting a message, education campaigns would need to foster a genuine multi-directional dialogue with an explicit focus on the complicated relations of power between educators and sex workers. My objection to present activities is not the telling of anyone anything; rather, it is a question of how one tells them and how one would expect to be told oneself.

The second challenge arises from the problem of how knowledge institutions participate in making social change practices and depend on market and non-egalitarian approaches. The combination of one-way transmission of sexual health education and a paternalistic belief in its superiority comes to be intrinsically connected with an institutional desire to create economic markets for condoms. In part, this connection follows from the rhetoric and practice of Third World poverty reduction and social development through improved sexual and reproductive health of Third World women. This rhetoric suggests that by making these women have drastically fewer children through the use (and purchase) of condoms, their lives will improve as full economic, political and social participants. Poverty will end if only they use more condoms, which, by no coincidence, would result in expanded regulated markets and the international flow of commodities! The non-democratic and instructional transmission of condom use therefore represents an institutional consensus on how to deepen capitalistic social relations and what Third World social change is desirable.

For condoms to be an avenue for hope and a genuine resource for a far larger group of people other than social scientists, policy technicians and corporate elites, the two problems involving democratic education and the practice of social change would need to be addressed in many open forums and include more diverse participants. I can only begin to offer two modest visions for a broader dialogue on condom pedagogy. First, knowledge institutions would need to work from a more egalitarian model of social communication and knowledge expansion. Second, civic organizations and political institutions would need to take democratic decision-making practices more seriously in their work. From these different visions for condom pedagogy, the possibility for real social change might open.

Changing Knowledge Institutions

To overcome the problems with contemporary condom pedagogy, I propose that knowledge institutions need to work from a more egalitarian model of social communication and knowledge expansion. This work could be accomplished by delinking the neoliberal economic agenda of market expansion from knowledge institutions. In particular, institutions would actively resist the tendency to produce knowledge for the expansion of a condom consumer base. Academic research on condom consumption for the purpose of group marketing, for example, should be considered unethical and socially irresponsible as long as it fails to consider fully its social and political consequences. That is, applied positivist health psychology would work to distance itself from the internationalization of neoliberal trade policies and market-oriented ways of life, by altering how it conceives of condom education. Instead, these institutional practices would explore further the possibility for more egalitarian models of social communication.

The second strategy entails that knowledge institutions reconsider the practice of social science for the purpose of behaviour modification. This suggests a different institutional agenda and social science paradigm that involve anti-elitism, populism and humanism. In other words, knowledge production should not be about reformulating public policy, constructing market studies, and finding out more about targeted, often marginalized, groups in order to regulate their activities. Rather, it would be about letting marginalized groups seize the tools of knowledge and construct truth-claims by assessing their own social problems and formulating possible solutions to such problems without the assistance of elitist teachers and knowledge gate-keepers. Female sex workers could, for instance, take the lead in constructing their own particular occupational agenda, which might not necessarily be directly about reproductive health in the workplace. That is, genuine improvement in sex workers' lives and condom education would suggest the abolition of the teaching, scientific and knowledge-expert professions as outmoded relics of modernity's priests.

Instead of aiming to make zombie-like consumers, the changes would retool institutions to foster democratic revolutionaries. What would knowledge institutions be if they truly provided all the tools to turn the world upside down and create sex-positive, anti-racist and feminist institutional relations, rather than, at present, serving as tools for social control? This transformation of scientific institutions would move from corporate governance, as in higher education, to global accountability and cross-local governance. The transmission form of education relies on elite scientific knowledge; once the pedagogical form and educational content aim to create revolutionaries, a true democracy might become more possible.

Making a Progressive Process of a Way of Life and Struggle

Extending the knowledge institutional changes, I propose that civic organizations and political institutions need to take democratic decision-making practices more seriously in their everyday activities. These changes could be accomplished by expanding the participation of disempowered groups and by incorporating these processes within a *framework for transition* from prior systematic flaws to a better global future for many more people.

Significantly, these changes would focus more on the process of decision-making and less on pragmatic measurable outcomes. This focus requires a different institutional practice in how decisions are made and what sorts of evidence are used to make decisions. The evaluation of condom education programmes ought not to be based on performance and other measurable outcome indicators such as the number of condoms given out or the number of people who receive a given message. In contrast, for instance, evaluation of Filipina sex workers' condom education would be based on the actual activities and processes by which health and social wellness are achieved. Implicitly, this turn away from pragmatic decision-making would delegitimize scientific rationalization as the main criterion of condom education effectiveness.

The framework for transition provides a necessary yet cautious route to change civic organizations and political institutions, and fosters a progressive process and increased genuine participation. Replacing current institutional arrangements, such new unending revolutionary processes would allow for an ongoing and revitalizing journey towards genuine democracy.

An Open Epilogue

The emergence of an egalitarian condom pedagogy could provide genuine democratic resources for a journey of hope for many women living in the Third World. Instead of remaining in the present nihilistic impasse – a world of multi-coloured, multi-flavoured condoms – there is a need for a different way of life and struggle. The two visions I offer might begin to make central the experiences, lives and politics of Third World women in their fullest capacity and, simultaneously, to address reproductive health and many other substantive concerns. A sustained cross-local campaign of multiple alliances needs to wrestle interventionist and authoritarian forms of education away from policy-makers to realize the necessary emergent progressive process, politics and culture of a better future, particularly among different women across the Third World. The struggle for the journey for hope must continue to make such a different world possible.

. . . .

PART TWO

Environment, Technology, Science

CHAPTER 6

· ·

Managing Future(s): Culture, Development, Gender and the Dystopic Continuum

David McKie

§ MUCH traditional writing on development tends to cluster around linear projections, foreseeing a future singular rather than futures plural, favouring the factual over the fictional and ignoring contemporary popular culture's multiple, gendered topographies of tomorrow. In the spirit of the editors' expressed desire to consider the possibilities of new ways of imagining all women and men, this chapter reverses these tendencies. It focuses on future scenarios, mainly through science fiction film and novels, as a way to open an array of futures plural. In these speculative realms, space, time and even gender itself can be imagined very differently from contemporary physical and social constrictions.

Yet, in dividing these tendencies into the two broad camps of factual and fictional, I stress that overlaps exist between them and both have use value. Science fiction also creates multifaceted future scenarios, including the dangers of recurring eugenic, and genetic, engineering cutting across deeply held religious and secular beliefs (see Mathews 2000). Moreover, even in factually absurd film form, masculinist science fiction is usefully shocking in how freely it imagines worst case scenarios in speculative detail. If the optimistic grand narrative of Western progress is underwritten by science, then science fiction consistently reworks that utopic tall tale with pessimistic and/or catastrophic outcomes. Accordingly, as with much literature on development and gender, my starting point is the (in)visibility of gender. One valid reason for WCD writings to avoid certain genres of popular speculation has been the virtual absence of women and the visible absurdities of the masculine presence. Mainstream science fiction film from the 1990s, for example, has been largely colonized by macho men strutting across the future,[1] with a focus on problems largely irrelevant to development issues, and has dealt in simplistic, implausible solutions. In sharp contrast, certain written science fiction from the same period, especially when authored by women and/or influenced by feminism, projects very different perspectives.[2]

Science fiction aimed at adults in books and film tends to direct attention onto dystopic personal, political and social possibilities. In that role it implicitly and explicitly generates predictions which incorporate assumptions of development outcomes and target selected sources of potential disaster for the whole globe (or specific parts of it). In visions of the future, as in the present, the Earth is clearly a culturally, economically and environmentally divided planet (see Athanasiou 1996). As a result, many of the disasters and divisions commonly foreseen by science fiction occupy a continuum (hereafter called 'the dystopic continuum') with more 'real world'-based scenarios, science writing and corporate projections.

Warping Futures (1): Missing Matter(s) and the New Screen Paranoia of the 1990s

Kurian (2000a: 4) has identified how, paradoxically, 'despite increasing knowledge of the complex environmental problems that grip modern society, our social and political institutions remain to a large degree incapable of coming to terms with the environmental problematique'.[3] To an extent this is equally true of our popular imaginative institutions. Mainstream Hollywood film, for example, consistently inhabits the low likelihood areas of the dystopic continuum. The genre's relative irrelevance, in terms of probable outcomes, correlates to its neglect of stories of women, just as, 'in most writings about global and international development ... the labour, cultures and histories of women are rarely taken into account, or, when they have been, women are most often seen as lacking agency – as merely victims' (Bhavnani, Foran and Kurian 2000: 3).

It is an axiom of critical and feminist writing that science is too important to be left to scientists. Similarly, in terms of their reach in public awareness, their interaction with scientific thinking and their power to shape perceptions about futures, the ideas promulgated by science fiction are too important to be left to science fiction *aficionados*. In her recent anthology of a century of fantasy, science fiction and speculative fiction from the African diaspora, Sheree Thomas intelligently redeploys the concept of 'dark matter' from scientists who 'believe that the amount of "visible" matter in the universe is not enough to account for the tremendous gravitational forces around us'. Significantly, she also notes that contemporary 'astronomers and astrophysicists prefer to call the missing mass "dark matter," because it is the light, not the matter, that is missing' (2000: x). Thomas's insightful redeployment of the concept to writings from the African diaspora can also usefully encompass much mainstream science fiction film since the 1990s. That genre's attention to the highly visible matters of masculinity effectively obscures the larger, darker matter of other, more urgent, dystopic possibilities inherent in existing development.

Instead of engaging with such complex issues, science fiction films deal with largely irrelevant problems and offer simplistic, implausible, masculine solutions to them.

Heralded appropriately by a huge cardboard cut-out of city people fleeing an alien attack, *Independence Day* (Emmerich 1996) typifies megabudget films which bombard multiscreen cinemas across the globe. As science fiction it offers nothing fresh, except an alien spacecraft that looks the size of a substantial town. With marketing machinery, which costs as many million dollars as the movie's special effects, these images are able to saturate screens internationally. This location of the products of this genre along a continuum of possible dystopias raises three key questions. How does its topography reflect or refract the conceptual and material landscapes of the present? How does it use its potential to warp conceptions of gender identities and structures? And do its representations fracture or undergird the long-established nexus between development and colonization?

The answers to all three questions revolve around a return to traditional masculinity. *Independence Day* re-creates the 1950s worldview of fathers knowing best and mothers waiting, suffering and weeping. In the film's key speech, the United States president hails the possible victory over alien creatures as the day when Independence Day for the USA will become Independence Day for the Earth, as the celebration of planetary freedom (from alien colonization). Despite obvious parallels with previous unachieved visions of Western development and freedom being the future for the rest of the world (especially in the rhetoric of the 1950s), the film-makers ignore that past. Similarly, they ignore how the cultural context that sustained earlier visions has changed irrevocably. Back in the 1950s, gays had to stay in the celluloid closet, Soviet Communism was a potent force, and committees hounded un-American reds from under American beds. At that time, fear of the Communist threat served to authorize equivalent invasions by various kinds of science fiction bodysnatchers and mind controllers from outer space. US politicians and film-makers alike continue to remain comfortable with the binary divide of 'us' and 'them', but in the post-Cold War New World Order ruled by globalization, identifiable villains have been in short supply (at least before 11 September 2001).

So who or what can be fought in current celluloid space, and to what end? Since the success of television's *X-Files*, one threat that has been transmitted to a wider popular consciousness is a new viral paranoia. This strongly anti-government strain fosters a belief that, by secretly funding huge laboratories, upper echelons of government engage in systematic cover-ups of UFO contact-inspired research. Such labs reputedly cater for everything from biological experiments with captured alien DNA, including alien–human hybridity, to tests with extraterrestrial technology. The increasing credibility all this has attained in the popular imagination has reached the level of a new paranoia. More and more of the general public holds that people high up in the US government or military are responsible for hiding the 'real' risks of extra-terrestrial activity from the people.

While not incredulous about CIA and White House concealment, I remain unconvinced that substantial danger resides in ETs as the major non-human threat to humanity. Interestingly, Frank Drake, the scientist behind SETI, or the scientific search for extraterrestrial intelligence, agrees. He won a $100 million commitment from NASA that guaranteed coveted space telescope time would be devoted to SETI's search during the 1990s. Underpinning Drake's work is a belief that 'interstellar contact will enrich our lives immeasurably' and a desire 'to quell the misleading myths about extraterrestrials', which he sees as arising 'from the mistaken belief that they have visited us in the past, to the terrifying idea that they will wrest the future from our hands' (Drake and Sobel 1994: xiii). He argues further against fear, 'for unlike the primitive civilisations [*sic*] on Earth that were overpowered by more advanced techno-logical societies, we cannot be exploited or enslaved. The extraterrestrials aren't going to come and eat us; they are too far away to pose a threat' (p. xiii). Despite the simplistic slippage from ourselves as part of advanced technological societies distinct from 'primitive civilisations' into us as human beings on Earth, Drake does therefore accept the existing world order as arising from exploitation and slavery, as well as dismissing as groundless fears of alien takeovers.

Warping Futures (2): Popular Science and False Worlds

Lacking any scientific warrant, the question remains of the function served by *Independence Day* and this mainstreamed UFOlogist paranoia. At one level, for example, in fostering fears of alien kidnaps, it causes distractions from pressing questions of diversity relations in neocolonial globalization. At an-other level, the new paranoia can be seen as diverting attention from the environmental problematique that people, because their survival may depend upon it, have good reason to be paranoid about: medical dangers posed by non-computer viruses, risks to sustainable nutrition from transgenetic ex-perimentation and the continuing difficulties of sustaining decent air, food, housing, health and water for much of the planet.

Instead of addressing these threats, Hollywood offers in *Independence Day* a lantern-jawed president open-mouthed in astonishment when he discovers his own government has been secretly researching extraterrestrials and their equipment. For those who haven't seen the movie, the fruits of that research, allied with an updated JFK heroic pilot president, an alcoholic cowboy flyer with suicidal tendencies, a computer virus and masses of mindless male heroism, save the planet. By thus launching Ramboism into space, *Independence Day* only updates Stallone's 'me Rambo, you Communist, therefore you die' into 'me human, you alien, therefore you die', as Will Smith's heroic airman character punches out a technologically superior alien in a spacecraft. Despite its hugely First World orientation, one positive feature of *Independence Day* – since a large number of science fiction visions project an exclusively white population – is that its imagined development at least includes African Americans among the survival of macho genes and, in more minor roles, women of colour.

Another big-budget science fiction film, *Armageddon* (Bay 1998), has as its imagined catastrophe a meteor striking Earth. This risk has some scientific basis (see Verschuur 1996), and, because the danger is geological rather than human, the violence is displaced onto fights, involving a nuclear bomb, between the members of the team sent from Earth to save the planet. While the likelihood of human disagreements leading to nuclear disaster still cannot be ruled out, the chances of a large meteorite colliding with Earth remain remote. Nevertheless, its feasibility earns *Armageddon* a ranking above *Independence Day* towards the likelier end of the dystopic continuum.

In using science as one of the benchmarking measures of possible disaster, I run the risk of treating it as a singular monolith and further buttressing its already high economic and social status as a regime of truth. This does not mean that I accept science as objective knowledge (see Jagtenberg and McKie 1997), but that I position it as a field that can frequently make better truth claims in relation to certain kinds of risk than non-scientific disciplines. That said, science remains an imaginative field that is interwoven with other imaginative fields. In her study fusing NASA with *Star Trek*, Constance Penley expresses it well: 'Popular science envisions a science that boldly goes where no one has gone before but remains answerable to human needs and social desires' (1997: 11).

Alongside potential apocalypses and Armageddons, one other recurring late-1990s theme featured aliens already ruling the planet unbeknown to the original human inhabitants. In this theme earthlings discover that their belief in human autonomy on a liveable material planet is an illusion along the lines of Rusnak's *The Thirteenth Floor* (1999) with its tag line: 'Question reality. You can go there even though it doesn't exist' and *Dark City* (Proyas 1998), where aliens also rule the earth. At one point in *The Matrix* (Wachowski and Wachowski 1999), which is set in what resembles a post-nuclear wasteland (in a clear physical representation of a planet beyond development), the rebel leader Morpheus looks around and says: 'Welcome to the desert of the real.' In this reality machines have overtaken the world and humans lie inert in a pod with all sorts of wires pumping lies into their brains. They are used as batteries to sustain the artificial intelligence ruling the world of the late twenty-second century, while nearly the whole of humanity believes they are still living in 1999.

Inside *The Matrix*, and others in that thematic vein, promising metaphors and a potentially interesting ontology open the way to project a Chomsky-style vision of manufactured consent to support an unjust world (although on an alien–human, rather than North–South or First World–Third World scale). Moreover, in its conclusion, the film resolves all problems with Keanu Reeves as Neo, a male Alice in Wonderland, who plays a computer hacker recruited as the chosen one to save humankind. And his tools are, of course, guns, lots of them, to blaze his way to the familiar salvation of wasted aliens, and physical hand-to-hand fighting. In short, whatever the problem, the answer is violence. Despite the ending, this subgenre of life-as-usual as a perceptual illusion has considerable potential for questioning linear development and dramatizing an ethnically divisive environmental problematique where existing development becomes a literal dead end.

Warping Futures (3): First Contacts, Futures Brokers and Predator Populations

Cinema, with its primary audience of teenage males, differs from science fiction books by women and by authors influenced by feminism. Most strikingly, the latter align more closely with a range of contemporary issues connected to future consequences at higher probability areas of the dystopic continuum. These fictions can also be seen to address, albeit differently, similar issues to those of literature on development and gender. Pearson and Jackson's edited collection, *Feminist Visions of Development: Gender Analysis and Policy* (1998), for example, has an introduction with the following eight subheadings: 'Feminist Analysis Versus Women and Development', 'Commonalities and Differences', 'Historical Change and Gender Relations', 'Gender Interests and Emancipatory Projects', 'Domestic Groups: Cooperation, Conflict and Struggle', 'Feminisms and Green Fundamentalism' and 'Feminism as Deconstruction'. Equivalent content to each subheading can be found in Mary Doria Russell's two recent novels – the 1997 bestseller, *The Sparrow*, and its sequel, *Children of God* (1998). Both novels also offer good examples of the contrast with 1990s cinema.

Published prior to the Kosovo crisis, and in line with Pearson and Jackson's 'Historical Change and Gender Relations' (1998), Russell's first novel constructs the early fictional biography of Sephardic Jew, Sofia Mendes, as part of a longer history. Unlike recent NATO strategists, Russell displays a breadth of temporal vision that stretches back before 'the expulsion of the Jews from Spain in 1442' to the time 'the ancient Mendes were bankers, financiers to royalty hounded out of Iberia' and 'welcomed into the Ottoman Empire' (1997: 81–2). Projecting forwards into the twenty-first century, Russell then describes Istanbul 'tearing itself to rubble in the insanity that grew out of the Second Kurdish War'. All too credibly (with the hindsight of various Balkan conflicts), her novel also depicts 'the city, sealed off by UN troops, left to devour itself in isolation', and how Sofia at 13, 'alone and destitute in a world of pointless carnage', turned to prostitution to survive. Sofia's fictional fate has an interesting real-life overlap with *The Daughters of Development: Women and the Changing Environment*, in which the Thai writer S. Sittirak's autobiographical account refers to her 'hundred thousand younger and older sisters', who are 'prostitutes' (1998: xix).

While relevant to Pearson and Jackson's 'Feminist Analysis Versus Women and Development', Sofia's history, with some geographical licence, would be predictable by journalists or political analysts. That is, until the introduction of one of Sophia's tricks, a Frenchman called Jean-Claude Jaubert. This Frenchman introduces himself as 'a futures broker' representing 'a group of investors who sponsor promising young people in difficult circumstances' (Russell 1997: 83), and Russell continues with impeccable economic rationality:

> He had made his fortune in the Americas, where he'd mined slums and orphanages for bright, determined children … A lively secondary market had developed, a bourse where one could invest in an eight-year-old who'd tested extraordinarily high in mathematical ability, where one could trade rights to the earnings of a medical student for those of a talented young bioengineer. (Russell 1997: 83–4)

Russell's rational extrapolation of the main economic logic of late capitalism into a future intellectual prostitution system augments in fiction Pearson and Jackson's 'Feminism as Deconstruction'. It may currently appear an unthinkable scenario, but its exaggeration foregrounds a long history of brain draining and the transfer of exploited female labour from undeveloped to developed nations. Moreover, it carries a charge vested in a character who, in Russell's narrative, invites identification (and is associated with rural land reform in the planetary equivalent of the Third World). Russell does not simply provoke thought through microhistories, but tackles macro possibilities in novels that extend three of the major development concerns of recent quality science fiction writers: ecological possibilities (including indigenous–settler interactions), relationships between the human and the non-human, and population control.

Transgressive Boundaries: Planetary Post-colonialism, Kinship and Triage

Although Russell is perhaps the most outstanding recent representative of this style of science fiction authorship she has predecessors. Terry Dowling's trio of interlinked novels (*Rynosseros*, 1990, *Blue Tyson*, 1992, *Twilight Beach*, 1993) on a future Australia, for example, tackles two of these issues. In the wake of the Australian Commonwealth Government's Mabo legislation, which recognized Aboriginal land rights and initiated a substantial reshaping of Aboriginal–settler relations, and therefore development (especially in relation to mining in general and uranium mining in particular), the novels invert the existing balance of media, legal and technological power. Dowling's fiction creates a world approximating to a right-wing nightmare where only seven 'Nationals', for which read white European settler Australians, are allowed to cross the tribal territories of 'the Ab'O [a term provocatively echoing the common racist abbreviation of Aboriginal people to Abos] descendants whose Dreamtime/haldane augmented minds had given them power to control the air as it had the rule of Australia' (Dowling 1992: 43). Ironically, in the light of consistent analyses of anti-Aboriginal racist representations (see Langton 1993, Mickler 1992), Dowling's future Australia is 'a dangerous land' where 'memories were often short, especially given the media biasing of the tribes' (1992: 60).

An idea of the riskiness and potential for liberation in Dowling's future-world can be conveyed through a story called 'Going to the Angels', which addresses one of the most frightening features of the best Australian science fiction. That feature is triage, which Janet Turner Hospital defines as 'a system of priorities designed to maximise the number of survivors in times of crisis and natural disaster', as a way of controlling excess population. Hospital's future Australian politicians call such population culls a 'burning off of dead wood', which they see as 'a moral imperative' necessary for 'the greater good' (1992: 90). With equal bleakness, George Turner's *The Sea and Summer* extrapolates from existing trends to speculate why 'two-thirds of the world starves although it is easily possible with global planning to feed everybody' (1987: 216). He also takes the concerns down to street level, as a viciously stratified society of 'haves' called 'sweet' and 'have-nots' called 'swill' battle for survival in an overpopulated and flooded post-greenhouse Melbourne where the government secretly experiments with chemical sterilization for the poor. In attaching blame to the powerful and foregrounding issues of justice, Turner and Hospital apportion responsibility intelligently rather than propagate a mindless Malthusianism.

That approach contrasts with a multinational corporation, such as Monsanto's corporate vision on their web page in a paper entitled 'Guess who's coming to dinner? 10 billion by 2030':

> One of the future's few certainties is that the world's population will nearly double, reaching almost 10 billion inhabitants by the year 2030. Humanity must respond to the growing pressures on the Earth's natural resources to feed more people. Current population growth already is straining the Earth's

resources ... the number of undernourished people still is rising in most developing countries. Many economists and agricultural experts agree that simply continuing past technological innovation and investment in agricultural infrastructure – basic facilities such as roads, power plants, transportation and communication systems – will not produce sufficient crop yield increases and improvements to feed the world's burgeoning population. (http://www. monsanto.com/monsanto)

Monsanto answers this narrowly defined question of how to feed the Third World through further, seemingly humanitarian, development of its own genetically modified food. The corporation's dubious morality and hypocrisy are highlighted in the nearby (in most search engines) site 'Monsanto: A Legacy of Fraud', which cites a Monsanto official telling the *New York Times* that the corporation should not have to take responsibility for the safety of its food products:

> 'Monsanto should not have to vouchsafe the safety of biotech food,' said Phil Angell, Monsanto's director of corporate communications. 'Our interest is in selling as much of it as possible. Assuring its safety is the FDA's job,' Angell said. (http://www.purefood.org)

Angell's statement clearly throws doubt on Monsanto's ethical position. Even when the bottom line is not the key determining factor, however, present-day population control poses contentious ethnic, religious and ideological questions. Nevertheless, mainstream science fiction differs from WCD in focusing solely on masculinist solutions. Rarely are they attuned to key organizational switches in the field such as the move by many at the 1994 UN Cairo conference from discourses of population control to discourses of reproductive rights. Nevertheless, in their imagined futures science fiction novels pose the question of who should live and who should die, and, critically, which group should decide, in stark fashion with a consistent emphasis on technology, an equally consistent neglect of gender and a total lack of respect for the pieties of Western democracy and Christian traditions.

Dowling's take on the problem in 'Going to the Angels' (1992: 68) has the nerve to construct a kind of final solution whereby an Ab'O tribe performs secret cullings of the Nationals disguised as an off-world space programme. I read this as a satire on the genocidal and linked eugenic (see Leslie 1993) practices settler Australia perpetuated on the Aboriginal people, which is similar to Bessie Head's oblique attack on South African racism in *A Question of Power* (1974). Head's critique made its points by abstracting the apartheid system to a non-white southern African context; Dowling's futuristic reversal reminds current 'nationals' that they are not the ones to have actually suffered loss of land rights, nor present-day injustice. By dramatizing an inverted future, he highlights how they are also the least likely group to continue to suffer disproportionately in national, and international, population control measures.

As Michael Dibdin has remarked: 'Every era has an emblematic transgression which addresses its intimate fears and fantasies ... the cult crime in recent years has been serial killing – a death which says a lot about the lives we think we lead' (1993: 9). Versions of population cullings in science fiction may yet become the emblematic transgression of the twenty-first century. Yet, while urging a rethink of the unthinkable, in terms of immoral population measures, I also favour the positive possibilities of 'transgressive boundaries' such as Donna Haraway's famous call for the collapse of binary categories between nature and humans, where 'people are not afraid of their joint kinship with animals and machines, not afraid of permanent partial identities and contradictory standpoints' (1991: 154).

Reframing Evolution: Political Economies of Population Control on Another Planet

In advocating that people interested in Women, Culture and Development should read Russell, I find myself caught in some contradictions in promoting a novel underpinned by a Christianity that for me is part of the problem rather than a solution. Russell's novels are based on the heroic interplanetary adventures of a Jesuit priest engaged in missionary work. As such, they offer some very partial identities. The head of the futuristic Jesuit order, for instance, debates birth control with a black African pope, Gelasius III:

> 'We ourselves have experienced the death of a sister, sacrificed on Malthus's altar,' Gelasius III pointed out. 'Unlike Our learned and saintly predecessors, We are unable to discern evidence of God's most holy will in population control carried out by the forces of war, starvation and disease ...
>
> 'There is good to be achieved! The question is how ... It will be a matter, We think, of redefining the domains of natural and artificial birth control. Sahlins – you have read Sahlins? Sahlins wrote that "nature" is culturally defined, so what is artificial is also culturally defined'. (Russell 1998: 53–4)

Relevant as such debates are, they pale into insignificance alongside Russell's description of the systems of population control on the novel's other main setting, the planet Rakhat. As befits her background as a palaeoanthropologist and author of scientific papers on bone biology and cannibalism, Russell offers evolution-influenced speculations on imaginary social relations between the two classes who inhabit Rakhat. Just as on Earth, class, ethnicity and food are strongly associated. In the second book, *Children of God*, Russell's unusual thoughts on the area might fall under Pearson and Jackson's heading, 'Domestic Groups: Cooperation, Conflict and Struggle' (1998), as Sofia Mendes, now a one-eyed Jewish widow, sides with the lower stratum, the Runa, and urges them to change the inegalitarian structure of the planet: 'the Jana'ata have no right to breed you, no right to say who has babies, who lives and who dies. They have no right to slaughter you and eat your bodies!' (Russell 1998: 56). Her instigation of the Runa chanting, 'We are many. They are few', leads eventually to an armed revolt which threatens the very survival of the Jana'ata as a species. The most powerful population point for Earth, however, emerges near the end of *The Sparrow*. First, one of the book's main characters, Father Emilio Sandoz, offers a justification for Rakhat's cannibalism as 'the Jana'ata also strictly limit their numbers to those that can be sustained by this system of breeding', so that their 'population structure is almost exactly that of a predator species in the wild, about four percent of the prey population' (Russell 1997: 470).

Sandoz claims not to be defending them, but makes telling contrasts with an Earth estimated to hold sixteen billion:

> There are no beggars on Rakhat. There is no unemployment. There is no overcrowding. No starvation. No environmental degradation. There is no genetic disease. The elderly do not suffer decline. Those with terminal illness do not linger. They pay a terrible price for this system, but we too pay … and the coin we use is the suffering of children. How many kids starved to death this afternoon, while we sat here? Just because the corpses aren't eaten doesn't make our species any more moral. (Russell 1997: 471)

For me, the novel's Christian underpinning – the title and narratives conclude that there is providence in the fall of a sparrow – lacks conviction. Nevertheless, as the population issues extend the brutality of triage to cannibalism in a way that equates these horrors with large-scale death by starvation through unequal resources, Russell connects us firmly to present-day injustice rather than compassion fatigue. In its sophisticated inclusion of the religious dimension, Russell reflects the struggle within WCD internationally to accommodate faith and secularity into a vision of environmental and population sustainability. Science fiction also dramatizes the potentialities of bioengineering and cloning in ways that can alert society to risks that might otherwise be considered too late. Their depictions of the possible topographies of tomorrow engage emotion as well as intellect, and they both complement and challenge current academic approaches to development.

Corporate and Institutional Scenarios: Telling Other Tales of Non-linear Developments

If they were to scan futuristic fiction for ideas and possibilities, development theorists would not be alone. In *Blueprint for Space: Science Fiction to Science*

Fact, Ordway and Liebermann (1992: 9) explore how ideas 'for the human exploration of space are found in both fictional and non-fictional writings' and interweave contributions from scientists and science fiction authors. Undoubtedly, the particular genre has a strong impact on the social meaning. For example, in tracing the hybrid of crime and science fiction historically, Bekic and Forté suggest that: 'When crime is the theme science fiction writers have tended to be slightly more liberal than crime writers; more willing to assign part of the blame for crime to society.' Indeed, in what could be a direct reference to science fiction writing on population control, they comment that 'what is and what isn't illegal is decided by the state' and 'often for reasons other than a concern for justice' (1993: 33).

Those remarks reverberated as I read World Bank pronouncements on middle-of-the-road development 'business-as-usual' uninformed by the possibility of impending catastrophe:

> As the world enters the twenty-first century, there is room for neither gloom nor complacency. ... Emerging economies' success will depend in part on economic developments in Japan, the United States, and Europe; equally important will be the strengthening of domestic policies and reforms to lay the basis for strong growth. Worldwide, those countries will prosper that are best able to capitalize on the opportunities of globalization while effectively managing its risks. (World Bank 2000: 21)

The underpinning assumptions of 'not much change', and the corollary of no real need to change institutionally, run against the grain of contemporary business literature. That literature forecasts radical and rapid transformation, neatly summed up in Abrahamson, Meehan and Samuel's colloquial book title, *The Future ain't What It Used to Be* (1998), and confirmed in other areas such as Rost's *Leadership for the Twenty-First Century* (1993) and the new economy visions of Levine, Locke, Searis and Weinberger's *The Cluetrain Manifesto: The End of Business as Usual* (2000).

Amid these contested futures, the World Bank's view of the twenty-first century foregrounds three questions as urgent:

1. 'How to mobilize donors to increase assistance'?
2. 'How to help the poor in nonreforming countries'? and
3. 'How to make progress on several fronts simultaneously so that every little girl can eat well and drink clean water to be healthy enough to receive quality education in a school that is accessible year round?' (World Bank 2000: 21)

Questions one and two depend totally on capitalist business as usual and perpetuate, without making any provision for major catastrophic change, the First World framing of Third World actions. In fact, they follow almost exactly what Rost (1993: 94) identifies as the key characteristics of the outmoded, linear twentieth-century paradigm: 'rational, management oriented, male, technocratic ... hierarchic, short term, pragmatic, and materialist'. The third urgent question is exactly the kind ignored by science fiction film's new paranoia. The World Bank's sudden injection of the female – the use of girls is welcome, and entirely justifiable on account of the bias against educating females – sticks out in an otherwise gender-blind discourse. One of the strengths of Russell's science fiction topographies of tomorrow is how she embodies her fictional planet's key development decisions in Sophia Mendes's work with people on the land.

In parallel fashion, consciously fictional scenarios of a different sort have been taken up more by some corporations than by the World Bank and international development agencies. Davis-Floyd's 'Storying Corporate Futures: The Shell Scenarios' (1998) provides a fascinating account of how Shell brought in an English literature professor and expert on myth to help construct their blueprints of the future. The Shell scenarios have consistently extended short-termism – see Peter Schwartz's *The Art of the Long View* (1996) – and make allowances for the possibility of catastrophic future events. The book of another former Shell worker, Kees Van der Heijden, *Scenarios: The Art of Strategic Conversation* (1996), partly inspired this attempt to engage development studies in strategic conversations with ideas and representations from films and novels. In concert, these two theorists outline how scenarios can help us abandon the restrictive features identified in Rost's (1993) outmoded twentieth-century paradigm:

* By abandoning narrow, linear thinking in favour of adopting wider perspectives.
* By developing alternative ways of interpreting the present to see beyond the current range of vision.
* By connecting seemingly unrelated developments through narratives to build more imaginative and integrated frameworks.
* By engaging, while acknowledging existing emotional investments, with uncertainty in a practical and systematic fashion.

Already Imagined Futures and the End of the Official Version

The Global Business Network (see Hammond 1998) and others (see *Wired* magazine at http://www.wired.com/wired/scenarios/build.html), have contributed to public debates on diverse possibilities. Each set of scenarios provides a sense of how informed business, government and independent thinkers are using scenarios to conceive of plural futures and are preparing, emotionally as well as practically, for widely divergent courses of events. They offer optional routes incorporating differences, ranging from the World Bank's path of linear hope, versions of science fiction's different degrees of dystopia and something in-between. One book in the Women, Culture and Development area that has been based on the scenario approach is equally sceptical of institutional ideas of linear business as usual. This is clear, right from the futures plural of its title, *The Futures of Women: Scenarios for the 21st Century* (McCorduck and Ramsey 1996) and its first-page assertion: 'The Official Future Will Not Take Place'. McCorduck and Ramsey also astutely observe the need to consider the novelistic territory of feelings as well as intellect, since 'unfinished emotional business will play a much larger role in how the future shapes itself than anyone now believes' (1996: xi).

In conclusion, therefore, I hope that this detour round cultural territory not common in discussions of women and development stimulates discussion and research into scenarios, science fiction and their interplay. Practically, such territory can provide a useful source of ideas:

- For projecting the dystopic continuum, and thereby urging us to take action to avoid it.
- For opening diverse pathways during times of rapid change and uncertainty.
- For considering how future scenarios are split into gender/genre groupings which affect their popular cultural reach and audiences and thus their wider public purchase.

Workers in WCD could usefully make connections with popular Western representations as a way of contesting those ideas in popular media.

I for one would like to be part of something akin to Haraway's Livermore Action Group 'committed to building a political form that actually manages to hold together witches, engineers, elders, perverts, Christians, mothers and Leninists long enough to disarm the state' (1991: 155). Ideally, such an affinity coalition would encourage the adoption of non-linear approaches to the future as well as providing fora in which to synthesize the emotional force and imaginative verve of scenarioists, science fiction creators and genre *aficionados* with the grounded experiences and ideas of activists, academics and policymakers.

Notes

1. Typical muscle-bound males range from Arnold Schwarzenegger in both *Terminator* movies (see Kuhn 1990 for a pre-1990s history), through Sylvester Stallone in *Judge Dred* to Bruce Willis in the more recent *Armageddon* (Bay, 1998). The last one is typical in that the lead character, played by Bruce Willis, takes his male oil drilling crew, but not his knowledgeable, intelligent and tough daughter, into space.

2. As well as acknowledged science fiction writers Joanna Russ and Ursula Le Guin, other mainstream women and feminist writers tackling science fiction include

Margaret Atwood, Angela Carter, Doris Lessing and Marge Piercy (see the essays in Armitt 1991 for a useful survey of themes and perspectives).

3. Kurian (2000a: 15) then footnotes two useful definitions of problematique as 'an interrelated group of problems that cannot be effectively addressed apart from one another' and 'an ensemble of problems and their interactions'.

. . . .

CHAPTER 7

Negotiating Human–Nature Boundaries, Cultural Hierarchies and Masculinist Paradigms of Development Studies

Priya A. Kurian and Debashish Munshi

If the world exists for us as 'nature', this designates a kind of relationship, an achievement among many actors, not all of them human, not all of them organic, not all of them technological. In its scientific embodiment as well as in other forms, nature is made, but not entirely by humans; it is a co-construction among humans and non-humans. (Haraway 1992: 297)

§ THE overwhelming emphasis on ensuring industrialization, economic growth and participation in the globalized capitalist world order by Third World nation-states is such that non-human nature is rarely considered as anything but marginal, an inferiorized Other. Quite like the modern administrative state, which has been the main driver of economic growth, the development project has traditionally ignored the imperatives of environmental concerns and politics, resulting in a 'crisis of development' that is yet to be resolved. Indeed, the very success of the environmental movements of the late twentieth century may be seen as a reflection of the failure of the administrative state (see Paehlke and Torgerson 1990) and, by extension, of traditional development. Even critiques of development from the perspective of feminists/Third World poor women ignore the extent to which humans and non-humans are fundamentally dependent on one another – a recognition critical if we wish to create some kind of a socially and ecologically rational society (Kurian 2000). The biospheric context that frames, intertwines with and brings meaning to human existence is too often rendered invisible by development practitioners and theorists. In contrast, environmentalists, more so in the West than elsewhere, tend often to ignore the centrality of humans, their modes of production, cultural contexts and so on, in their quest for ensuring environmental protection. Neither is a viable stance. As Raymond Williams has argued, 'no society is too poor to afford a right order of life. And no society is so rich that it can afford to dispense with a right order, or hope to get it merely by becoming rich' (1989a: 222). In attempting to define a particular vision of a 'right order', this chapter interrogates the ways in which boundaries between humans and non-humans are created, maintained and policed in the context of the modern development project. Such boundaries will inevitably shape the emancipatory potential of the Women, Culture and Development paradigm that this volume seeks to sketch.

We begin with an exploration of anthropocentrism in development theory and practice, arguing for the need for an ecologically and socially rational society encompassing the human and non-human world. Our focus is on challenging the artificiality of boundaries that represents a neocolonial, totalizing vision of development. We explore the need for fluid and more porous boundaries – within the constraints of ecological and social rationality – through an examination of the place of science and knowledge in development (focusing specifically on aspects of the current debate on genetic engineering of foods). What do women, culture and development as both discrete and related concepts mean in a world marked by technoscience, grassroots activism and particular visions of, and relationships with, the non-human world?

Anthropocentric Development: Defining the Term

When we first started work on this essay, what struck us was how deeply mired development studies has been in masculinist, anthropocentric thought. Yet what is anthropocentrism? Is it just another term for what can be called 'human centred'? As a colleague pointed out, 'any approach to ecosystems will be anthropocentric exactly because the decision [on the use of ecosystems] is ultimately made by (and usually for) human beings' (Rixecker 2000). In this sense, no human action can really be non-anthropocentric. And yet, we think it is a term that does serve a purpose in describing constitutive practices and processes of cultural/political/economic systems that retard the possibilities of an ecologically rational vision. Eckersley defines anthropocentrism as 'the belief that there is a clear and morally relevant dividing line between humankind and the rest of nature, that humankind is the only or principal source of value and meaning in the world, and that nonhuman nature is there for no other purpose but to serve humankind' (1992: 51). In other words, it is not that decisions, policies and actions emanate from human actors but rather the *nature* of those decisions, policies and actions that warrant the label of anthropocentrism. So is this merely a quibble over semantics? Does it matter what we term it if really what we should be concentrating on is a better way of 'doing development'?

We would argue that the abstract, masculinist discourse of development that is a manifestation of anthropocentrism has very real consequences, both for how we see ourselves in this world and for the possibilities of creating a better world. For, in essence, anthropocentrism is about the creation of a particular kind of boundary, a rigid one that reinforces a division between *us* and *them*, where *they* are the non-human world. And boundaries, not always and perhaps not necessarily, limit us, divide us and ultimately make possible destructive practices that create a less ecologically and socially rational world. Anthropocentrism as an attempt at boundary setting demands to be challenged and transgressed if we are to reclaim the development project. As Fuss (1996: 3) points out, it is 'sameness, not difference, [that] provokes our greatest anxiety (and our greatest fascination) with the "almost human"'. For most development scholars, 'sameness' with nature remains an idea too alien to be considered. Even for those who work in the field broadly known as Women and Development (and thus active in challenging masculinist development theory and practice), nature and the environment remain merely the fuzzy background against which development practices play themselves out. Maintaining clearly demarcated boundaries between humans and nature thus allows both justification of anthropocentric development practices and reassurance of the dominant position of humans.

At heart, then, anthropocentrism is reflective of a particular set of cultural values that sanctions domination over the non-human world and an instrumental understanding of nature as resource. It involves an oppressive structure that Otherizes nature, denying it agency or value (Plumwood 1996); it denies human dependence on, and embeddedness in nature, resulting thereby in a refusal to shape human desires for development in accordance with the limits of nature. Ecofeminists in particular argue that the domination of nature in the West is closely related to the domination of women. But the parallels go further than just androcentrism, as Plumwood points out. Plumwood argues that all oppressive 'centrisms' – eurocentrism, ethnocentrism, androcentrism and anthropocentrism, for instance – have a similar structure that involves justifying and naturalizing oppressive practices, whereby 'the experiences of the dominant "centre" are represented as universal, and the experiences of those subordinated in the structure are rendered secondary or are not visible at all'. At work is an 'otherisation process' that involves 'radical exclusion' of the subordinate object as inferior and separate; homogenization and stereotyping; denial of the significance of the Other's contribution to any aspect of life; assimilation of the Other into the dominant structure; and denial or downgrading of the Other's independent agency and value (Plumwood 1996: 134–7). Such cultural values of domination and instrumentalism are manifested in the ubiquitous discourses of globalization – perhaps most prominently in the dystopic possibilities of the 'biotech century' (Rifkin 1998) – and are inherently masculinist with specific implications and consequences for women and subordinated others (see Kurian 2000a, Munshi forthcoming).

As feminist economists have pointed out, globalization processes are 'embedded in, and refracted through, power structures grounded in ethnicity, race, gender, class, and age' (Marchand 1996: 586). In fact, according to Kimberly Chang and Lily Ling (1996, cited in Marchand 1996: 586), there exist two distinct, and often polarized, versions of the globalized world: One is the 'masculinised high-tech world of global finance, production and technology'; and the other is the 'feminised menial economy of sexualised, racialised service'. Feminist analyses of neoclassical economics show how the male point of view invariably guides seemingly gender-neutral notions of market relationships. Workers or entrepreneurs, for example, are overtly gender-neutral terms, but women and men (as indeed members of different cultural groups) have very different experiences as workers or entrepreneurs (Bakker 1994). In fact, as Diane Elson (1992: 2, cited in Bakker 1994: 5) points out, a worker or an entrepreneur 'is most often taken to be a man – creating male bias in both economic analysis and economic policy'.

If androcentric economic paradigms promote the uneven nature of participation in the market by women (see, e.g., Brodie 1994, Bakker 1994), the anthropocentric approach to development reinforces this imbalance at a larger level because of its masculinist character. One example of masculinist anthropocentrism at work is evident in the notion of 'mastery over nature', which underpins much of development practice; it is a triumphalist process of appropriation and transformation of the non-human world that has led to some of the devastating environmental consequences the planet faces today.[1] Nowhere is this hyper-anthropocentrism more evident than in the developments of recent times, such as the patenting of life forms with ownership of thousands of transgenic organisms, plants and animals vested in a few multinational corporations, and the cloning of animals and humans already underway that will fundamentally transform existing ways of reproduction.

It is in *naming* anthropocentrism as one of the causes of the environmental crisis that we can begin to deal with it. We cannot, of course, just stop with naming. But recognizing the practices and values made possible by anthropocentrism is a necessary first step. It forces us to recognize that the modern development project has resulted in a crisis of the environment and of modernity itself; it is a crisis that Beck has argued requires a 'reflexive modernisation' – a wholesale reconstruction of society whereby the old order, the old categories dissolve and blur to result in new forms of global configurations (see Beck 1992, Beck, Giddens and Lash 1994). Far from suggesting that we need to get away from transforming nature – an impossible task – we seek to explore how ecological and social transformations can be geared towards a sustainable society.

Although much of the discussion, analysis and critical evaluation of the notion of anthropocentrism has taken place within ecophilosophy, our fundamental concern with this concept is not primarily at the level of ideas and values. The debate within ecophilosophy is robust and vigorous, but less developed are the material consequences of such a masculinist value system for the biospheric context in which we live. As is well documented in the gender and environment literature, anthropocentric development has survival implications for rural, poor, Third World women. Destruction of communally held lands, removal of access to forests, water, herbs and plants, and the promotion of 'terminator seeds' genetically engineered to ensure that their offspring will not germinate, all have a direct impact on women (see Agarwal 1992, 1998, Shiva 1988, 1998). Anthropocentrism, in conjunction with other systems of domination (of gender and class, for example), brings multiple oppressive structures into women's lives that are rarely recognized as significant to the development project. Challenging anthropocentrism, therefore, is a process of ensuring that the boundaries we seek to establish are always unstable, rewritten even in the moment of their making.

Such a challenge to anthropocentric development theory and practice would allow us to ask in what ways we can rework these definitions and practices to allow for ecological and social rationality. Beck, Giddens and Lash (1994), among others, have argued that self-critical rationality and institutional, as well as cultural / aesthetic reflexivity, are critical for dealing with ecological crises. Equally significant, however, is the need for an ecological democracy that allows for 'meaningful participation, supportive internal environments, and [institutionalization of] explicit and overt attention to gender, race, class and culture' (Bartlett and Kurian 1999: 428). An ecologically rational development project would need to seek social justice as one of its major objectives; it would indeed require a transformation of social values to ensure recognition of the reality that 'there *will be* no nature without justice. Nature and justice … will become extinct or survive together' (Haraway 1992: 311).

Ecological Rationality and the Development Project

Ecological rationality, a form of practical reason, is a rationality of 'living systems, an order of relationships among living systems, and their environments' (Bartlett 1986: 229; see also Dryzek 1987). It is the capacity of a system to maintain or increase the life-supporting capabilities of ecosystems consistently (Bartlett 1986, Dryzek 1987). Furthermore, Plumwood (1998: 561–2) argues that in the context of modern societies capable of inflicting significant environmental damage very rapidly, what is needed is 'the capacity to correct tendencies to damage or reduce life-support systems', thus allowing it to make 'consistently good ecological decisions that maintain its ecological relationships'. How does the ecologically rational society deal with the demands of development? Or perhaps, how do we embark on the development project in light of the requirements of ecological rationality?

Dryzek (1987: 58–9) points out that ecological rationality is a fundamental kind of reason that ought to have 'lexical priority' over other forms of reason. He argues that 'the preservation and promotion of the integrity of the ecological and material underpinning of society – ecological rationality – should take priority over competing forms of reason in collective choices with an impact upon that integrity'. And, at one level, this is indeed indisputable – the state of the biosphere will ultimately shape the viability of the development project. Yet this is not to argue that social concerns – such as gender equity, social justice and access to resources and power – may be marginalized in order to give precedence to non-humans. Environmental justice movements worldwide, for example, bring to the fore issues of racism, sexism and classism as seen in the differential impacts of environmental degradation. The 'environmentalism of the poor' (Guha and Martinez-Alier 1997), unlike mainstream environmental movements of the West, has articulated a vision of society that gives human survival and issues of self-determination pre-eminence along with the goal of local control over environmental resources. Movements such as the Narmada Bachao Andolan in India have not only exposed the role of the World Bank and the state in promoting environmentally destructive development, but also made the issue of social justice central to their cause. The struggle for empowerment, for freedom from oppressive social structures and domination, and for recognition and respect, go hand in hand with the struggle for ecological goals of sustainability in the Third World.[2]

Fostering an ecologically rational society, therefore, requires enabling some form of an ecological democracy (Dryzek 1998, Plumwood 1998), fundamental to which would be our grappling with the twin problems of 'redistribution' and 'recognition' (Fraser 1997). By redistribution, Fraser refers to the fundamental problem of socioeconomic injustice, 'rooted in the political-economic structure of society' (1997: 13). Juxtaposed against this is the injustice of recognition, namely, discrimination grounded in cultural values and systems – an apt description for what is meted out to the environment in anthropocentric development. Fraser's analysis is useful in understanding how the economic and social injustices that development seeks to address too often get posed antithetically to the problem of environmental protection. As she points out, the distinction between redistribution and recognition is at an analytical level:

> In practice, [economic injustice and cultural injustice] are intertwined. Even the most material economic institutions have a constitutive, irreducible cultural dimension; they are shot through with significations and norms. Conversely, even the most discursive cultural practices have a constitutive, irreducible political-economic dimension; they are underpinned by material supports. Thus, far from occupying two airtight spaces, economic injustice and cultural injustice are usually interimbricated so as to reinforce each other dialectically. (1997: 15)

Environmental destruction, a consequence of a failure of recognition, is fundamentally intertwined with issues of social justice and equality. As a growing literature on environmental racism demonstrates, the poor and the least privileged are likely to face the worst impacts of environmental degradation (see, for example, de Chiro 1996, Bullard 1994). Moving towards an ecologically and socially rational society requires, then, having in place structures, systems, values, ethics and practices that actively undermine those fundamental aspects of modernized societies that allow both oppressive social inequalities and the colonization of an inferiorized nature.

Although the concept of ecological rationality may have 'dubious strategic value ... as a resting point for explanation' (Plumwood 1998: 563), it is unquestionably a sound *starting point* for exploring the implications of technoscience and the place of non-human nature for societies that seek to make good ecologically and socially rational decisions. To what extent are these twin goals of ecological and social justice met when we look at the technoscientific world?

Technoscience and Its Challenges

Many of the environmental problems we confront today may largely be traced to the use of scientific and technological expertise that not only offers new ways of consuming, adapting and transforming nature but also fails in spectacular ways to provide accurate estimates of the impacts of techniques and practices on the biosphere. As Plumwood (1998: 563) points out, 'dominant forms of science have tended systematically to underestimate ... the seriousness and imminence [of environmental problems], and to overestimate the resilience of ecological systems in which we are embedded'.

In the context of the Third World, the impact of science and technology manifests itself in diverse ways. On the one hand, we have the phenomenon of technology transfer that too often translates into the transfer of inappropriate technology creating systems of dependence on the West – for training, spare parts and upgrades. The Green Revolution is just one example of a technology that revolutionized food production while simultaneously undermining subsistence, small-scale agriculture and destroying soil and water quality through excessive use of pesticides and fertilizers. On the other hand, in countries such as India, the state prides itself on its ability to invest in military (including nuclear) science and space science that allow it to claim its place with the 'big boys' of the West. What is evident is that these kinds of investments in science and technology have specific impacts on women, the environment and the development project as a whole (see, for example, Sen and Grown 1987, Shiva 1988, Mies and Shiva 1993).

The issue at the centre of debates and protests in the Third World and elsewhere in recent years is that of genetic engineering (GE), focusing among other things on 'terminator seeds' and cross-species transfer of genetically desirable features. Representing the cross-border movements between nature and the non-natural, genetically engineered products and organisms have aroused more passion, condemnation and activist fervour nationally and inter-nationally than any other issue in recent times. Anti-GE activists and the public have pointed to the range of issues implicated in the business of genetic engineering:

- The privatization of nature through the patenting of life forms.
- The concentration of commercial profit in the hands of an elite private sector.
- The violation of the 'integrity' of life and natural forms.
- The exploitation of the biological commons.
- The increasing dependence of the Third World on the West.
- The rapidly expanding division between the haves and the have-nots, further aggravating discrimination based on gender and race and class.
- The undermining of indigenous and local knowledges and their control over their knowledge bases.
- The destruction of biodiversity as monoculturalization of both mind and biotic organisms takes place.
- The yet-to-be-established health and environmental consequences of 'meddling' with nature.
- The undermining of democratic decision-making with the marginalization of the public from decisions involving only governments, scientists and corporations (see Haraway 1997, Shiva 1998, Rifkin 1998).

Many of these are issues we feel passionately about and, indeed, are in agreement with the activists taking up these causes. Yet we find ourselves caught in a dilemma. Having championed the transgression of boundaries and the need for more porous borders between humans and non-humans, we now are faced with the challenges of a technoscience that has at its heart – in its culture and practice – the breaking down of boundaries. How do we resolve this? Is it possible to align ourselves with the activists on the issues raised above and yet keep open the potential of porous, transgressive bound-aries? Perhaps the problem lies in how we conceptualize the issue. At one level is the actual process of modifying aspects of nature through genetic engineering, which does radically challenge the integrity of the boundaries between species, for example. At another level, it is evident that the genetic engineering business reflects a certain dominant discourse of the biotechno-logy industry – a discourse controlled by scientists and an industry that has appeared impervious to any kind of challenge from civil society. In reaction to this exclusion of the mass public, in the last decade social movements have sprung up reflecting a multitude of resistances to this dominant discourse. As Gottweis comments: 'Images of Nazi eugenics, Third World exploitation and r-BST-tortured cows invaded the biotechnology discourse creating counter-discursive ruptures, blurrings, and mixtures' (1995: 146). Here then is the challenge to a particular boundary-setting attempt by a narrow elite group, which is to be welcomed for its ability in having undermined the 'truthspeak' of the industry.

But what of the actual developments in biotechnology – the cross-species transference of genes, for instance, that undermines a different kind of boundary, one that seeks to maintain in some form the 'integrity' of life forms, as anti-GE advocates argue? We answer this by pointing to the central theme of this chapter: the possibilities and potentials for the creation of an ecologically and socially rational society. Our advocacy of cross-border movements is balanced, indeed shaped, by our fundamental concerns of seeking environmental protection and social justice. In doing so, we acknowledge the concerns that Haraway has voiced about the opposition to genetic engineering:

> I cannot help but hear in the biotechnology debates the unintended tones of fear of the alien and suspicion of the mixed. In the appeal to intrinsic natures, I hear a mystification of kind and purity akin to the doctrines of white racial hegemony and U.S. national integrity and purpose that so permeate North American culture and history. I know that this appeal to sustain other organisms' inviolable, intrinsic natures is intended to affirm their difference from humanity and their claim on lives lived on their terms and not 'man's.' The appeal aims to limit turning all the world into a resource for human appropriation. But it is a problematic argument resting on unconvincing biology ...
>
> [T]he tendency by the political 'left' ... to collapse molecular genetics, biotechnology, profit, and exploitation into one undifferentiated mass is at least as much of a mistake as the mirror image reduction by the 'right' of biological – or informational – complexity to the gene and its avatars, including the dollar. (1997: 61–2)

As Haraway rightly points out, in challenging the many problems with genetic engineering, we need to refrain from using a rhetoric of purity and intrinsic properties that is implicated in the racist discourses and histories of the colonizing First World. There are many other grounds on which to base the challenge, as noted earlier, including especially the accelerating pace of commodification and ownership of genetically engineered products, reflective of 'hypercapitalism', as Rifkin (2000) describes it. The repercussions of the large-scale patenting of genetically modified organisms for Third World countries, in terms of indigenous research, local agricultural practices and economic self-reliance, all of which have specific implications for women, are significant.

Thus, in looking at the various manifestations of genetic engineering and agricultural biotechnology, we need to ask the following questions. What may be the environmental consequences of genetic engineering? What are the implications of agricultural biotechnology for Third World farmers (including rural peasant and tribal women), for existing subsistence agricultural patterns, for local cultures and ways of life, and for the development project as a whole? What are the likely impacts on society of the growing expansion of genetic technologies concentrated in the hands of a few multinational companies?

A persistent claim by proponents of biotechnology is that agricultural biotechnology is needed in order to feed the world – to 'prevent weeds from stealing the sunshine' (Monsanto literature, quoted in Shiva 2000), to stave off blindness in the Third World with the help of genetically engineered rice, and so on. But critics such as Shiva dismiss the claim that without genetic engineering and the 'globalisation of agriculture' the world will starve:

> Take the case of the … 'golden rice' or genetically engineered Vitamin A rice as a cure for blindness. It is assumed that without genetic engineering we cannot remove Vitamin A deficiency. However nature gives us abundant and diverse sources of vitamin A. If rice was not polished, rice itself would provide Vitamin A. If herbicides were not sprayed on our wheat fields, we would have bathua, amaranth, mustard leaves as delicious and nutritious greens that provide Vitamin A. (Shiva 2000: 2)

Shiva argues that the 'monocultures and monopolies' that mark industrial agriculture symbolize 'a masculinisation of agriculture', adding that 'genetic engineering and IPRs [Intellectual Property Rights] will rob Third World women [of] their creativity, innovation, and decision making power in agriculture' (1998: 3–4).

Claims and counter-claims thus mark the debate on biotechnology, but at a minimum what these show is the deep-rooted distrust of 'expert'/scientific discourses called on by dominant political-economic groups to dismiss public concerns as 'irrational' and 'ignorant'. The challenge to Monsanto's crop experiments in India by a growing peasant movement in the late 1990s, for example, may be seen as part of the rejection of 'expert and professional discourses (and the form of rationality they frequently espouse) that underlies the search for an alternative rationality … with which to approach environmental hazards' (Harvey 1998: 345). The danger, of course, lies in the co-optation of the oppositional discourses – their peaceful co-existence with an ongoing scientific and market hegemony.

An ecologically rational society, then, must be one where (a) anthropocentric 'tampering with nature' seen in genetic engineering – a clear example of the 'arrogance of humanism' (Ehrenfeld 1978) – is eschewed at least until more is known about the consequences for nature; and (b) the overwhelming dominance of the technoscientific discourse in determining issues that are ethical at their core gives way to an inclusion of the knowledges of the humanities and local peoples. Testart (2000: 14), for example, points out that the 'knowledge shared by all humankind – intuition, emotion, common sense, aesthetic sense, a sense of how the world works' is crucial to arrive at any understanding of complex phenomena (such as GE) being analysed. A recognition of partial perspectives on all sides, across all actors, is ultimately what could allow concerns for ecological rationality, social justice and science to come together in meaningful ways. Thus, instead of the polarized discourses of technoscientific expertise and public scepticism, an acknowledgement of partial perspectives may give rise to a hybridized discourse where scientific analysis aligns with local, indigenous and popular knowledge with a central focus on ecological and social rationality.

Transforming Deep-rooted Values

These preliminary observations on the consequences of an anthropocentric development project framed by a globalized economy reveal the reality of environmental destruction that has particular impacts on already marginalized, poor women of the rural Third World. An ecologically and socially rational society can become possible only when we actively move to transform deep-rooted cultural values that sanction environmentally destructive development practice – a practice that an extensive literature on WID has demonstrated to be sexist as well. That this must happen in the context of 'globalizing environmentalisms', marked by the convergence of 'environmentalism, the New World Order, global markets' (Sturgeon 1999: 270), underscores the urgency of feminist interventions in such dominant discourses. Only by positioning women as environmental activists, as Sturgeon argues, can activists (such as those working with Third World rural, peasant and tribal women) gain access to critical international political arenas where environmental concerns have acquired currency. In other words, given the hegemonic status of Western-inspired environmentalism that often conjures up neocolonial images of an out-of-control Third World, it may well prove to be in the interests of Third World women to seek control of the environmental agenda by positing a gender–environment linkage.

In examining the implications of anthropocentrism for biospheric actors – human and non-human – we challenge the notion of boundaries as being an unhelpful one, for it too often facilitates destructive practices. But as the study of ecology has demonstrated, boundaries are fundamental: to talk about ecosystems at any level is to acknowledge both the necessity and the artificiality of boundaries. What we call for in this chapter is the importance of preserving some boundaries (as our discussion of genetic engineering showed) while selectively destabilizing others.

The problem with boundaries comes up most significantly in situating ourselves in the context of (political, economic and cultural) globalization. Champions of globalization offer the promise of the borderless world, 'of a unified humanity no longer divided by east and west, North and South, Europe and its Others, the rich and poor … These discourses set in motion the belief that the separate histories, geographies and cultures that have divided humanity are now being brought together by the warm embrace of globalization, understood as a progressive process of planetary integration' (Coronil 2000: 351–2). Yet, as critics have pointed out, the globalized world is one that is not only hopelessly divided between the privileged and the underprivileged, but is also one where dominant, often First World, elites have a lopsided share of the power to shape the world.

Although the concept of democracy is enthusiastically espoused by the champions of globalization, it is never followed in spirit, because, as Gray (1998: 17) says, 'democracy and the free market are rivals, not allies'. Neocolonial institutions such as the World Trade Organization, which see themselves as the epitome of a 'free' market, frame rules for the market which are not open to the scrutiny of any democratic legislature (Gray 1998). These institutions, which idealistically speak of equality for all, actually reinforce what Spivak (1999: 102) calls the 'continuing narrative of shifting imperialist formations', because their norms of functioning adhere to social, cultural and legal frameworks that are predominantly Western.

Neocolonial narratives, despite their egalitarian-sounding slogans of a 'free' market and global 'equity', continue to emphasize, overtly or covertly, the managerial authority of elite groups. These groups talk of transcending borders to allow a multinational flow of capital and enterprise, but retain a clearly marked division between Western or West-trained managers and largely non-Western workers. The dominant managerial core, usually comprising Western 'white males' (Dozier, Grunig and Grunig 1995: 151), formulates policies for the entire workforce, although in numerical terms white male Westerners are only a small minority. In most transnational organizations in the age of globalization, the control of underprivileged groups aligns closely with the control of disempowered employees, who are most likely to be immigrants, women and people of colour (Sassen 1998). This dual control is exercised by core groups of organizational leaders who are thus doubly privileged: by virtue of their ethnicity, and because of their positions in organizational hierarchies.

Such privileged groups are also the ones that build electric fences between humans and nature. 'The conceptual differentiation of "humanity" from that of "nature"' is a socio-cultural construction that helps support the claim that

humans are morally superior to non-humans, thereby justifying the anthropocentric domination of nature' (Purser, Park and Montuori 1995: 1057). An
example of this domination is the indiscriminate exploitation of nature as a
market resource, and the use of advanced technologies not just to discover
natural products but to create new ones, changing nature into what Arturo
Escobar calls 'technonature' (Coronil 2000: 363).

A particular form of culture lies at the core of the discourse of technological mastery over nature, one that privileges humans over non-humans.
Culture is central to the processes of globalization as well. The market plays
a major role in the shaping of cultural identities but, as Firat points out, 'the
power to signify, represent and communicate forcefully what is acceptable,
seductive, attractive and meaningful is not evenly distributed' (1995: 122). It is
these dominant cultural pulls and pushes that marginalize the Other, leading
to a decimation of not only numerous biological species of plants and animals
by the creation of high-yielding hybrid varieties, but also a trampling of
minority cultures and their languages, food habits and ways of doing things
by a universalized T-shirt-jeans-fast-food-digital-television culture.

Conclusion

Destabilizing boundaries takes many forms – writing about the telescoping
categories of culture is perhaps just one. Resolving the tension between
challenging and preserving boundaries means grappling with the ways in
which the WCD approach can transform development studies and projects. It
means conceptualizing and creating development projects which begin to take
seriously the cultural and material aspects of environmental protection that
are the focus of many grassroots environmental justice movements worldwide,
as well as of women's struggles for social justice.

It also means recognizing that the demands placed by the biophysical and
sociocultural environments elicit certain responses from both humans and
non-humans that are often unqueried. In the case of humans, such responses
are shaped by the values of market-driven, capitalist economic systems that
remain invisible in terms of their 'normalcy'. The genetic engineering of
food products is an example of how technologies developed in the first
instance for limited purposes quickly become ubiquitous in their application
and use as their commercial potential becomes evident (see Beck 1995). It is
by identifying, explaining and unravelling these taken-for-granted values and
relationships that we can begin the process of creating a more ecologically
rational society, even in a globalizing world. As Plumwood (1996: 148) notes,
recognizing the significance of nature in non-instrumental ways 'is the ethical
equivalent for nature of desegregating the lunch counter, of giving women
the vote. And as both anticolonial and feminist activists have good reason to

know, this is just the beginning of the journey to liberation, not the end.' From the perspective of those who do policy – where the material in many ways supersedes the 'merely reflexive' turn of late modernity – such an approach helps us actually to begin to do what we say we ought to.

Notes

We thank Robert V. Bartlett, Kum-Kum Bhavnani, John Foran and Stefanie Rixecker for thoughtful and incisive feedback on earlier drafts of this chapter.

1. Harvey (1998: 333) points out that 'It is not fashionable these days, of course, to evoke triumphalist attitudes to nature. But I think it is important to understand this is what we do, whether we care to acknowledge it or not, whenever we let loose the circulation of capital upon the land.' Indeed, we cannot presume to undo anthropocentric development practice if we do not simultaneously challenge capitalistic transformations of land and nature which in turn create and transform social relations in contradictory ways.

2. It should be noted, of course, that anthropocentric perspectives do surface in some environmental justice movements where the focus on humans often ends up relegating nature/environment to the periphery. Ironically, this pits such movements with the very hegemonic structures they struggle against.

CHAPTER 8

. . . .

Imagining India: Religious Nationalism in the Age of Science and Development

Banu Subramaniam

After Independence, India's hydroelectric dams – erected as they were to a secular faith – came to be known as Nehru's 'new temples'. Such projects were to ensure India's future. Today, many recognize that the wings of modernity were not powerful enough to bear the huge nation aloft ... Traditionalists have countered the modernizers with their own Enlightenment. (Rajni Kothari 1989)

§ ON 7 November 1999, during his visit to India, Pope John Paul II sat down with the leaders of ten other religions. All these religious leaders were men and they met in the capital's Hall of Science (Boudreaux 1999). This image is symbolic of the recent convergence of men, science and religion in India today. Science and religion represent two powerful social institutions, often cast as binary opposites, with different and distinct philosophies, traditions, practices and ideologies. What they share is a history of male domination and hostility towards, and exclusion of, women and feminism, and a legacy of colonialism that has shaped both science and religion and the nature of their intersection within the landscape of contemporary Indian politics.

Fifty years after independence, many share Rajni Kothari's sentiments that India has failed to realize and achieve its potential. The founders of independent India began a project of imagining India, an India that fulfilled the dreams and hopes of an independent nation and a free people. The founders imagined a democratic India, one that was secular in its pluralistic vision and would actively include, support and encourage all religions (as opposed to an American model of a separation of church and state). Yet over the last two decades, the rise of religious nationalism has been steady and unmistakable. What has shifted is the very definition of secularism and democracy. Rather than disavow either, religious nationalists have redefined both – secularism as tolerance and democracy as majoritarianism (Vanaik 1997). Thus, they argue that while the presence of religious minorities should be 'tolerated', it is the majority Hindus who should define and govern India. Religious nationalists imagine a Hindu India for a Hindu people. What is at stake is *who* gets to define and imagine 'India'.

The growth of religious nationalism in India over the last decade has been unmistakable. In 1998, the *Bharatiya Janata Party* (BJP) came to power in India. After 13 months the coalition government was toppled, but the next election brought the BJP (in a coalition government again) back to power. The political success of the BJP draws on two other Hindu nationalist movements – the *Vishwa Hindu Parishad* (VHP), an organization of religious leaders, and the *Rashtriya Swayamsevak Sangh* (RSS), a militant youth organization (van der Veer 1994). The Hindu nationalist programme stresses *Hindutva*, or Hindu-ness. Hindu nationalists have successfully tapped into the overall discontent of Indians (economic, social and cultural), and transformed it into a problem about religion and the brand of secularism and democracy that India's founders had envisioned.

In this chapter, I explore how women, culture and development have shaped and been shaped by the rise of religious nationalism in contemporary India. Here is a reinvention of India's past, in the orientalist traditions of invoking a grand and ancient Hindu past. It is this Hindu past, religious nationalists argue, that must shape the dreams and imagination of a future India. But it is the interpretation of this Hindu 'past' that is centrally at stake. The traditionalists, as Rajni Kothari suggests, have countered the modernist project with their own enlightenment, one that reinvokes the grand Vedic tradition. Ironically, this tradition is one that is scientifically and technologically advanced – a tradition that anticipated the development of modern science, and is thus in harmony with modern-day science. As a result, the past melds into the present, religion with science, and tradition with modernity. This new imaginary homeland is used to develop a blueprint for the home and the world, public and private culture, the nation and the individual. The co-construction of the public and private spheres through the common ideology of *Hindutva* is a particular form of the reinvention of India. The secular inclusive ideals that many of us grew up with have been recast, remade anew.

What is particularly significant is that India did not exist before its creation in 1947. The Indian subcontinent has been home to a multitude of religions for centuries, many emerging on its own soil. Yet Hindu nationalists claim for India an 'authentic' past that is exclusively a Hindu past. Such reconstructions mean that what was once made can now be remade; one history can be replaced by a revisionist history. This interpretative nature of history and nation building notwithstanding, what is evident in these recent reconstructions of the past is a deliberate and unscrupulous manipulation of data to arrive at convenient conclusions that serve a particular (political, religious and social) agenda.

The project of nation building that the religious nationalists have under-

taken is deliberate and intentional. It is a creation of a new vision for India –
one that is ancient, modern, scientifically and technologically proficient, Hindu
and Indian at once. As I will explore below, by bringing together the archaic
and the modern, the religious nationalists have created what I have called an
'archaic modernity' (Subramaniam 2000). I begin with a brief analysis of the
rise of religious nationalism and a description of the ideology the nationalists
have put forth. Next, I explore the symbolic and ideological role women play
in the nationalist reinterpretation of Indian culture. Finally, I examine religious
nationalism's use of science, technology and development. What characterizes
this archaic modernity, I argue, is a confluence of masculinity, science, technology, development and militarization. Despite the rhetoric of angry, vengeful
goddesses, women are relegated to the private sphere as vehicles for the
development of masculine agency and a generation of Hindu men who will
work for the recovery of a Hindu India (Pant 1997). To underscore how
archaic modernities work in the nationalist imagination, I examine Vaastushastra, the ancient Indian 'Material Science', as a case study of the merging
of the archaic and the modern. In exploring the repackaging of this ancient
tradition as a 'modern material science', I illustrate how archaic modernities
function. The confluence of the archaic and the modern works as a metaphor
for the home and the individual, and also as a larger metaphor for nations and
nationhood.

The Archaic and the Modern

> For who among us, after all – white or nonwhite, Western or not – is not
> always caught precisely in the space between 'inherited traditions' and 'modern-
> ization projects'? And where else, how else, do 'cultural interpretations' come
> from – 'theirs' or 'ours', local or global, resistant or complicit as the case may
> be – other than from the spaces between the two? (Fred Pfeil 1994: 119)

What, then, is the nature of the modern encounter of science and religion
in India and how are the lives of women and the constructions of gender
shaped by these intersections? At its independence in 1947, India embarked on
a modernization project – a Nehruvian[1] industrial model of development
based on the conviction that the future of India lay in the promise of science,
technology and development. Western science has been a central and powerful
force in the visions, dreams and hopes of a post-independent, post-colonial
India. Indeed, science has been adopted as 'the reason of the state'. As Nandy
explains:

> This expectation partly explains why science is advertised and sold in India the
> way consumer products are sold in any market economy, and why it is sought
> to be sold by the Indian élites as a cure-all for the ills of Indian society. Such a

public consciousness moves from one euphoria to another. In the 1950s and 1960s it was Atom for Peace, supposedly the final solution of all energy problems of India; in the 60s and 70s it was the Green Revolution, reportedly the patented cure for food shortage in the country; in the 70s and 80s it is Operation Flood, the talisman for malnutrition through the easy availability of milk for every poor household in the country. (Nandy 1988: 7–8)

Development – like science – has been central to the modernizing mission of India. The development of India through large-scale industrial growth, hydroelectric dams, agricultural development and militarization is central to the policies of previous secular governments as well as to the current nationalist imagination. India has been pluralistic about religion, but science and development have been untouched by it. Critics and protesters about development have enumerated the profound, often irreversible, consequences of development through the disenfranchisement and dislocation of peoples and the costs to the environment. Religious nationalists condemn the critics, questioning their patriotism and love of country (Rawat 2000). Similarly, while post-colonial critics have questioned the effectiveness and appropriateness of the particular forms of science and development institutionalized in India, these critiques have largely been ignored by past secular governments, and more recently, as I will argue, by the religious nationalists.

At first glance, religious nationalists seem to have a critique of the harsh impact of colonialism. Seeking to erase and overcome centuries of colonialism, they present the glorious aura of a grand civilization forgotten by its own people. Such a move promises the possibility of decolonization by returning to the progressive possibilities of India's rich and diverse history and traditions. However, on closer examination, it appears that religious nationalists embrace some of the more regressive elements of both science and religion, a selective record of history and a promise of a future that serves only the Hindu elite. Religious nationalists in contemporary India have selectively, and strategically, used rhetoric from both science and Hinduism, modernity and orthodoxy, Western and Eastern thought to build a powerful but potentially dangerous vision of a Hindu nation. Rather than characterize Hinduism as ancient, non-modern or traditional, the Hindu nationalists have embraced capitalism, Western science and technology as elements for a modern Hindu nation. However, these ideals of a modern Hindu nation exist alongside contradictory visions of a glorious pre-colonial Hindu past, drawing on the scientific, technological and philosophical scriptures of ancient Hindu India. Religious nationalists thus bring together a *modern* vision with an *archaic* vision, that is, an *archaic modernity* (Subramaniam 2000). By strategically employing elements of science and religion, orthodoxy and modernity, the Hindu right is attempting to create a 'modern Hinduism' for a Hindu India.

Women, Culture, Nation

The move to a modern/scientific Hinduism began with thinkers such as Swami Vivekananda (1863–1902), a central figure in Hinduism. He set out to 'modernize' Hinduism by organizing a disparate set of traditions through a systematic and scientific interpretation of the Vedanta (the Upanishads and the tradition of their interpretation) (van der Veer 1994: 69–70). As India's first modern Swami and missionary to the West (Nandy 1995: 46–7), he created a nationalist discourse that is central to Hindu nationalism in all its versions, including the RSS/BJP/VHP brand of Hindu nationalism (Chatterjee 1989). Through nationalism and the creation of the 'modern' Hindu, there began a campaign to 'recast' women (Sangari and Vaid 1989). Hindu nationalism turned women into a national symbol to create the motif of female power or 'Shakti'. The myth of Shakti was invoked again and again. The nation, now female and a 'motherland', came to symbolize both the powerlessness of the colonial subject as well as 'the awakening conscience of her humiliated (Hindu) sons' (Bagchi 1994: 3). The invocation of the Devi – the goddess with her garland of skulls standing on a supine male Shiva – represented both the protectress and the sacred domain to be protected from alien violation (Bagchi 1990). Yet against this image of female power, Hindu leaders relegated women to the domestic while men were the wage earners. For example, Vivekananda believed that women should not be educated in the modern sciences, but achieve fulfilment within the family (Jayawardena 1988); Dayananda endorsed women's education for a more disciplined child-rearing process (Sarkar 1994); and Gandhi espoused the 'complementarity' of women and men – women in the home and men as wage earners (Joshi 1988). Through these essentialized differences between men and women emerged distinct public and private spheres. The recasting of women as 'authentic' was seen as one of the surest signs of the superiority of the East, trapping women to participate in the nation-building process in particular ways (Bagchi 1994: 5). Women are at once mythologized and empowered, yet subjugated and disciplined. In this archaic modernity, there is a renewed Hindu masculinity, a rhetoric of symbolic female power that in reality perpetuates the redomestication of women.

As others have argued, this resurgence of Hindu nationalism today is a resurgence of Hindu masculinity, a reaction to the 'effeminization' that was the strategy of Western colonialism and orientalism (see, for example, Jeffery and Basu 1994). Science and religion have proved to be two powerful tools through which religious nationalists have imagined and engaged with this project of 'masculinization'. Like most nationalisms, Hindu nationalism seeks inspiration from an imaginary past. Both science and religion have been implicated in this process. The religious nationalists' vision of religion and Hinduism parallels its science policy, and is decidedly militaristic and violent. Indeed, this has been a driving force since the freedom struggle, when Hindu nationalists departed from the pluralistic vision of the founders of India.[2] They disagreed with the founders' vision of secularism and their inclusiveness, and believed that the majority community of Hindus should dominate. They feared that Gandhi's 'effeminacy' would bring about the further 'emasculation' of Hindu men, and this fear culminated in a Hindu nationalist assassinating Gandhi in 1948. Since the rise of Hindu nationalism, there has been an increase in violence against religious minorities through campaigns that target minorities and have led to the destruction and demolition of churches and mosques. Violence, dominance and an increasingly militaristic policy through their vision of science and religion have marked religious nationalists' quest for a Hindu nation.

Religious nationalism breeds sectarian and communal politics and, inevitably, women become markers of the community and synonymous with culture (Butalia 1999). Like other nationalisms, Hindu nationalism implicates women. Contemporary religious nationalism reinvokes Shakti and the power of women, albeit in strategic ways. Primarily anti-minority, especially anti-Muslim in their stance, women leaders herald the great power of women in traditional Hinduism. The president of the all-India BJP women's organization, *Mahila Morcha* (Women's Front), claims that 'In the Vedic era, the status of women used to be much higher than it is today ... After the Muslim invasion all of this changed: Hindus were forced to marry off their daughters at much younger ages, they adopted seclusion, and women's role in public life declined' (quoted in Basu 1998a: 172). During the rise of the BJP and before they came to power, women such as Sadvi Rithambara and Uma Bharati were among the most violent of leaders, 'projecting themselves as victims of Muslim men'. By displacing male violence onto Islam and Muslim men, they claim their 'motherland was being raped by lascivious Muslim men' and they goaded Hindu men to regain their masculinity by violence against Muslims (Basu and Basu 1999). For example, during the Ramjanmabhumi movement, which sought to break down an ancient mosque, the Babri Masjid, and build a Hindu temple in its place because it was *claimed* as the actual place of birth of the Hindu god, Ram, Uma Bharati is quoted as saying:

> The one who can console our crying motherland, and kill the traitors with bullets, we want light and direction from such a martyr, we want a Patel or a Subhash[3] for our nation ...
>
> When ten Bajrangbalis[4] will sit on the chest of every Ali, then only will one know whether this is the birthplace of Ram or the Babri Masjid, then only will one know that this country belongs to Lord Ram. (quoted in Nandy et al. 1995: 53)

What has been significant is that once in power, the BJP has sidelined these women and assumed a more moderate stance and 'channeled their militancy' by sending 'women back to their homes' (Basu 1995).[5] In October 1998, the BJP unsuccessfully introduced a *Hindutva* plank for the national education conference, which included compulsory housekeeping classes for girls. Again, this 'domestic science' invokes the traditions of domesticity with the modernism of science. The rewriting of Indian history (Panikkar 2001) and the 'saffronising' of Indian education (see 'BJP saffronising education' and Bhushan 2000) are actively in process. Consider the Vidya Bharati paper at the State Ministers' Conference on Education in September 1998. The texts mentioned glorified motherhood and named the woman's primary responsibility as the home and the 'turning out of good Hindu citizens'. Stressing images of Sita and Savitri,[6] the paper advocates obedience and the selflessness of women in order to take care of their husbands and family. *Sati*, child marriage and notions of caste and purity of blood are justified and shown as proud elements of Indian culture (Taneja 2000). The redomestication of women through the power of religion and science is at the heart of this archaic modernity. Amrita Basu's analysis of the Hindu right's rhetoric on the role of Hindu women suggests that its central message is the importance of devotion to their families and the dangers that await those who refuse to conform. Juxtaposing Indian values with Western values, they emphasize the links between women's reproductive and social roles (Basu 1998a). In this archaic modernity, the past is glorified and selectively reinvoked to current political purposes. While the top ranks of leadership in the Hindu nationalist movement are filled by men, women have played a significant role in its rise. Furthermore, the religious nationalists embrace consumerism, globalization and capitalism. As Tanika Sarkar argues, contemporary religious nationalism does not deny the privileges of consumerist individualism to its women. She persuasively argues that it 'simultaneously constructs a revitalised moral vision of domestic and sexual norms that promises to restore the comforts of old sociabilities and familial solidarities without tampering either with women's public role or with consumerist individualism ... Patriarchal discipline is reinforced by anticipating and accommodating consumerist aspirations' (Sarkar 1994: 104).

Science, Masculinism and the Bomb

> It had to be done, we had to prove that we are not eunuchs. (Balasaheb Thackeray, outspoken Hindu Nationalist Leader after the nuclear tests in Pokhran, quoted in Dasgupta 1998: 8)

Leaving aside the advocacy of 'domestic science', a more violent nuclear science has been invoked by the ruling BJP to bring about a resurgence of Hindu masculinity that further marginalizes women as sustainers and reproducers of Hindu families. Nowhere was this more apparent than in the euphoria that followed the testing of the nuclear fission bomb in Pokhran in 1998, allowing nationalists to celebrate India's revived masculinity. Swapan Dasgupta of *India Today* writes:

> Vajpayee has released a flood of pent-up energy, generated a mood of heady triumphalism. He has kick-started India's revival of faith in itself. To the west, the five explosions are evidence of *Hindu nationalism on a viagra high*. To Indians, it is evidence that there is nothing to fear but fear itself. Pokhran is only tangentially about security. *Its significance is emotional.* The target isn't China and Pakistan. *It is the soul of India* ... The mood is euphoric. (Dasgupta 1998, emphases mine)

This so-called triumph came at the cost of a military budget of $10 billion, an increase of 14 per cent, twice the amount spent on education, health and social services combined, a female literacy rate of 36 per cent, with women earning 26 per cent of men's earnings, and with 927 women for every 1,000 men in the population (Basu and Basu 1999). After Pokhran, it was estimated that the cost of the nuclear-weaponization programme was equivalent to the cost of primary education for all Indian children of school age (Raman 2000). Such is the price of military nationalism.

While continuing most of the science policies begun under secular governments, what marks the BJP science policy is its nuclear policy. There have been systematic shifts in budgetary allocations to favour military and nuclear research at the expense of agriculture, health, medicine and a general science education (Taneja 2000). It is not accidental that despite India's nuclear capabilities for the last 25 years of secular governments, it was the Hindu nationalists who defied the world to test the ultimate destructive weapon of Western science, the fission bomb in 1998. Indian nuclear scientists and policy-makers form an all-male club. These scientists have been co-opted by the nationalist spirit and become India's new heroes. As Balasaheb Thackeray eloquently summarizes, for the Hindu nationalists, the bomb has proved India's masculinity.

In this 'archaic modernity', tradition and religion, women and woman power embrace and come ironically to symbolize what is allegedly a triumph of 'masculinity'. The bomb, this ultimate destructive weapon, was christened 'Shakti' after the goddess of power and strength. After the testing of the bomb, the VHP began plans to construct a temple at Pokhran to commemorate the tests and dedicated to the goddess Shakti; the temple was christened 'Shakti Peeth' (altar of Shakti). The VHP general secretary invoked women again in suggesting that this was an ideal location for Shaktipeeth as 'Baba Ramdev[7] is worshipped here for the reforms he brought about in the society, especially for waging a movement for the protection of women' ('VHP firm on Pokharan temple, BJP silent', 1998). Some nationalists also proposed that the sacred soil of Pokhran be carried in sanctified vessels across the country in a set of jubilant *yatras*[8] (Singh 1998).

The first anniversary of the Pokhran tests was declared 'Technology Day', and the human resources and development minister, Murli Manohar Joshi, while laying the foundation for a new technology forecasting centre, stated that 'Pokhran and all our scientific endeavors have brought glory to India' (CNN 1999). The nuclear tests have come to symbolize the success of religious nationalism by proving Indian power and might, its strength and scientific capabilities. Central to this model of industrial science and development is a resurgence of Hindu masculinity and the increasing marginalization of women into the cultural role of the sustainers and reproducers of Hindu families. This is the archaic modernity that is to bring glory to Hinduism and India.

'Development Nationalism'

A second example of masculinist rhetoric invoking science, development and nationalism is evident in the rejoicing that met the Supreme Court decision in 2000 to allow construction of the Narmada dam. On 30 October 2000, L. K. Advani, influential nationalist leader and Home Minister, remote control in hand, poured a ton of concrete to resume the Narmada dam construction. This construction had been put on hold by anti-development activists who challenged it in the Supreme Court. Women have been key players in the activist struggles against the dam's construction. When asked about what he considered the great triumphs of the BJP government, Advani named three: the Pokhran tests in 1998, the Kargil war with Pakistan in 1999 and the Supreme Court verdict resuming the Narmada dam construction in 2000 (Rawat 2000). He saw the last as a victory of the development process and a triumph of 'development nationalism'. The nuclear bomb, a military war and a big dam are unarguably the triumphs of science, technology and development. As feminist and post-colonial critiques of science predict, the inevitable connections between science, masculinity and violence emerge (Cohn 1987, Nandy 1988). In the speech, Advani severely criticized the anti-dam protesters who have spent years fighting the mega-dam project and its displacement of millions of people as well as its ecological consequences. He questioned their patriotic credentials and wondered if they were being funded by 'outside' sources. Thus 'development' and the construction of the dam are positioned as a nationalist project, while the critique becomes a 'foreign' and un-Indian response.

During the same speech Advani saw the Narmada dam as a 'victory of development nationalism', highlighting the proposition that religious nationalism is developmental nationalism.[9] The recent events in India are a strong reminder of the colonized Indian psyche, and the primacy of colonialism within post-colonial, independent India. Despite the rhetoric of decolonization, it is Western science that extends its hegemonic hand to stabilize the Hindu nation. The legacy of Western science lives on as the reason of the state. The revival of the ancient scriptures, the Vedas of the rich history of India, is not an attempt to decolonize the Indian psyche, but to reinstate Hindu culture and history as the hub around which the scientific progress of the future is anticipated. There is no epistemological critique of Western science – indeed an embrace of it, whereby its exaltation is simultaneously an exaltation of the scientific Vedas and the Vedic sciences, and the exaltation of development is an exaltation of Hinduism.

Science, Technology and Development

While religious traditions and practices have always been an important part of the Indian psyche, I want to argue that 'science' has also been inscribed deeply within that psyche. Since India's independence in 1947, the country has embarked on a model of scientific and industrial development. A series of secular governments over the decades have continued a similar national programme. Although religious nationalists have available a rich set of postcolonial critiques of Western science and development, these have been ignored, and we now have a seamless continuation of previous governments' policies of industrial and scientific development. There is no move to critique modernity or science or to develop indigenous systems of knowledge. Far from rejecting Western science, medicine and technology as one might expect, Hindu nationalists instead embrace it. Nandy and his collaborators suggest that:

> Hindu nationalism not only accepted modern science and technology and their Baconian social philosophy, it also developed a totally uncritical attitude towards any western knowledge system that seems to contribute to the development and sustenance of state power and which promised to homogenize the Indian population. There is no critique of modern science and technology in *Hindutva*, except for a vague commitment to some selected indigenous systems that are relatively more Brahmanic and happen to be peripheral to the pursuit of power. (Nandy et al. 1995: 62)

When religious nationalists invoke the Vedas or other ancient scriptures in the name of Hindu pride, their vision does not supplant Western science, but instead melds it with appropriating Western science within the rubric of Vedic sciences. Rather than claiming a separate and different past and future for Indian knowledge, the nationalists embrace Western science as Indian knowledge. For example, some argue that many developments in modern science were discovered or anticipated in the Vedas. Scholars have interpreted ancient literary texts to argue that ancient Hindu ancestors have discovered or invented the atom, the bomb, the aeroplane, the evolution of various species, the missing link, the Pythagorean theorem and various technologies (see, for example, Patel 1984). Others use the ancient scriptures as a source of pride in the ancient development of literatures, philosophies and scientific knowledge in ancient India (see, for example, Vivekananda 1992). I want to illustrate this with a few examples of the marketing of Vaastushastra, the ancient Indian Material Science.

Vaastushastra: A Case Study

Vaastushastra, commonly seen as the 'science of architecture' (Babu 1998), is believed to have been developed 4,000–5,000 years ago in Vedic Indian culture and codified in the Atharva Vedas. *Vaastu* is derived from the word *vas*, which means 'to live'. Vaastushastra teaches us about 'living life in accordance with both desire and actuality' (Chawla 1997: 1). Like the Chinese feng shui popular in the USA these days, Vaastushastra has become immensely popular in India. While *feng shui* and Vaastushastra have similarities in the existence of positive and negative forces, there are also differences in the principles that guide their arrangement of space. In fact, my interest in the topic came from being astonished at watching relatives and friends in India remodelling their houses using Vaastu principles, often at great financial and physical hardship. One rich family with an immense grand house, cooked in the living room for eight months on a tiny electric stove while the rest of the house was closed off for renovations in accordance with Vaastu principles. Another family who bought a newly constructed apartment took it apart down to the tiles on the floor to renovate it in accordance with Vaastu principles. Living rooms were converted into bedrooms, bathrooms into *pooja* (prayer) rooms or bedrooms into kitchens.

While individuals undoubtedly renovate homes for many reasons, and while there is a long tradition of religious ceremonies to bless new houses, the recent trend of renovations in order to create Vaastu-friendly homes is an entirely new phenomenon in urban India. What propelled these individuals to refashion their homes causing so much hardship, I wondered? This rage for Vaastu shapes not only the private homes but the public sphere as well. There are now many firms and architects who construct houses, government and office buildings using these principles. Whether they believe in it or not, architects develop an expertise in Vaastu to satisfy the wishes of their clients. The principles of Vaastu are claimed to be described in classical texts and are expected to work in any person's house, irrespective of religion or place. 'Vaastu's concern is not only material property, but also mental peace and happiness and harmony in the family, office etc.' (Babu 1998: 3). My project began as an attempt to understand this phenomenon.

The philosophy behind the practice seemed to me at one level practical and at another level ethereal. Vaastushastra considers the interplay of the five elements – earth, water, air, fire and space – and maintains equilibrium among them. These elements are believed to influence, guide and change the living styles of not only human beings but also every living being on earth. It is ethereal because there is no articulation in the literature on exactly how these elements might bring about health, wealth and wisdom. Over the last decade, this practice has caught on within middle- and upper-class India. As I explored the phenomenon, I went through books that teach in a straightforward and accessible way the various steps to building or creating a house according to Vaastu principles. There are numerous such publications, with varying degrees of detail. Second, there are advertisements in newspapers and magazines where experts offer their services. Ultimately, I found Internet websites promoting and explaining Vaastushastra to be the most useful and engaging source. They combined the best qualities of the other two – like the advertisements, they were concise and short and engaging, and like the books they gave more information and background. I used these websites to analyse the claims and practices of Vaastushastra experts.[10]

Consider Mr Manoj Kumar who owns the vastushastra.com site. He describes himself as:

> an electrical engineer, who has worked with engineering and marketing companies. These experiences gave him the opportunity to observe the functional success of various types of units. In time, he began to assess these premises from Vaastu's viewpoint. His study has included over 3500 industrial, commercial and residential premises ... This formed the basis of 'cause and effect' relationship in today's context, involving Vaastu principles. Synergizing his engineering skills and four years association with reputed architects to understand the logistics of modern architecture, he is today recognized as Vaastu Consultant of repute. (see http://www.vastushastra.com/)

While his training exclusively heralds his scientific skills, that is, he is an engineer and has worked with many architects, his web page begins with greater claims: entitled 'Worries, Woes, Wannabes, Winners and VAASTU', the page lists the conditions that Vaastu can help:

If you are disappointed with the ways things are turning out ...

If you are depressed about the idiosyncrasies of life ...

If your career graph is plummeting ...

If your profits are spiraling, but only downwards...

If your contemporaries repeatedly hog kudos while you do the lion's share of work ...

If you find walking on the cutting edge of technology too sharp a going despite your up-to-date training ...

If your productivity is sub-optimal, and you score only double bogeys in cor-
porate performance when your actual handicap should be under par ...
If your marriage was made in heaven, but is functional in hell ...
If you just don't have that 'Feel Good' aura about you ...

The site lists a long list of problems, all of which the expert claims Vaastu can
help alleviate. In a section, 'What is Vaastu and What Can it Do for Me?' the
site further explains:

Vaastu is a complete understanding of direction, geography, topography, environment and physics. It is a study that dictates the form, size, and orientation
of a building, in relation to the plot, soil, surroundings, and the personality of
the owner/dweller. *There is no room for rituals and superstitions.* Impulsive planning and unorganized architectural methods, have led to the primary malady
mankind faces today – DISHARMONY. Today more and more architects are
turning to Vaastushastra, to undo this. In short, an eco-imbalance is prevented
by synchronising all the Vaastu elements.

While the advertisement begins with claims of improving everything in one's
life – happiness, health, wealth, career plans, marriage and even one's golf
game – the rest of the description consistently underscores how non-super-
stitious and non-ritualistic the practice is. It does not invoke God, or religion,
as a way to promise health, wealth and happiness. Instead, it is the promise of
science. Ultimately, the consultant directly confronts the scientific evidence. In
a section entitled, 'The Truth About Vaastu', he elaborates:

There is nothing metaphysical about Vaastu. It is just that the hidden harmony
of Nature and the environs around have been defied. Mr. Manoj Kumar in his
practice, does not attempt to compare the incomparable or even try to explain
it on the basis of magnetic waves, ultra-violet rays, cosmic rays and so forth, as
these are but the tips of unknown, unexplored icebergs. The truth is that it
works and probably the lower common denominator of any such venture is its
repetitive success, as many conglomerates and inhabitants of Vaastu designed
premises vouch for. Maybe somewhere, sometime in the future, there will be
an explanation for the mechanisms of Vaastu, but to dissect it today is a futile
exercise.

Indeed, practitioners cite scriptures and ancient records, testimonials from
kings, commoners, artists, saints and traders – all of whom have reaped great
benefits from the practice. In this last section, the consultant admits that he
cannot provide 'scientific' evidence to support his case, but instead suggests
that it will one day be found, because Vaastu 'works', it can be reproduced
and those are grounds of profound proof.

Another website (http://www.andhraonline.com/vasthu/WHAT.htm)

takes up the scientific nature of Vaastushastra and argues that: 'Vaastu is considered rational (based on cause and effect), practical, normative (codified and governed by principle), utilitarian and universal.' Two other websites further consolidate the scientific basis of Vaastushastra. The first (http://www.allindian.com/vans2.htm) dismisses the religious overtones by arguing:

> Vaastushastra is a science – it has nothing to do with religion. It is true that over the years, Vaastushastra has imbibed religious overtones, but that does not seem to have been the original idea. The religious implications were probably inculcated by the proponents of the science, when they realized that the society of that times was a God fearing one, which would not accept norms that seemed like rituals performed to appease the God.

The second, and the more interesting (Vaastushastra Home Page through http://www.geocities.com/PicketFence/Street/4700/index.htm), takes the offensive and argues that Western science is much too young to be able to evaluate or appreciate the ancient Vaastushastra:

> But, the key issue here is, can the modern western science developed over last 300 years ... be used as the only yardstick for assessing super sciences like Vastushastra formulated over 5000 years ago? A time has come when a broader perspective is needed to study the ancient Indian sciences including Vaastu-shastra ... In [the] modern era, [the] concept of mass-energy equivalence is identified with [the] great scientist, Albert Einstein. But the same concept, in a different format, has served as a foundation of Vastushastra analysis and prac-tice for almost 5000 years.

Constructing the Home and the World

So what is different about Vaastushastra? After all, different belief systems have always been rampant. Auspicious times have been calculated for jobs, exams and travel. Indians in all walks of life have consulted astrologers, numerologists, palmists and so on. Isn't Vaastushastra an extension of those beliefs, like the priest who blesses the house once it is built? At some level I do believe that it is an extension of a belief system that has long existed in India, but what seems to me to be a departure are the practitioners of Vaastushastra. They are not priests, astrologers or individuals claiming divine inspiration, nor are they individuals on street corners or in the recesses of dark, dilapidated homes. Instead, they are engineers and architects, practitioners trained in the sciences. I have heard anecdotal information that many architectural firms and architects have had to learn about Vaastushastra because of a demand from their clients. For example, an architect is quoted as saying: 'I don't believe in Vaastu. My own house and office do not comply with Vaastu principles. But I am well-versed in the basic parameters of Vaastu Shastra because my clients ask for their building to be Vaastu-compliant' (see Vaastu-Expert Comments in http://hinduism.about.com/r@on/hinduism/library/weekly).

Reflecting the broader pattern of the influence of religious nationalism and other aspects of archaic modernity in present-day India, Vaastushastra is literally and figuratively shaping both public and private spaces, the home and the world. It is especially marketed to women, along with beauty and home decoration tips. Vaastu is directed at women through websites such as 'smartbahu.com' (the smart daughter-in-law) as ways in which to fulfil their roles as good Indian/Hindu wives, mothers and women. Numerous websites aimed at Indian women contain instructions and information on rectifying architectural errors (for example, see women/indiaserver/com/smartbahu/ homedecorr; astrospeak.indiatimes.com/women-beauty-html; women.excel. com/homesinside; lifestylz.indya.com/lifestylz/homefront; zeenext.com/ lifestyle/womensworld; www.womannova.com). By removing the obstacles of bad luck and spirits through Vaastushastra, women are encouraged to take good care of their families and to fulfil their roles as good mothers and wives. Some practitioners argue that Vaastushastra principles themselves are gendered, where the angular placing of plots can have differential impacts on men and women. Certain configurations are argued to make male members of the family into rogues, turn them to bad habits or earn money in unrighteous ways, while other designs can gain women respect in all spheres, cause mental instability or trouble from court litigation (http://www.archriti.com/vaastu/ vaastup1.htm). Many architectural firms actively advertise Vaastu-informed designs and renovations in newspapers and women's magazines, as well as on websites.

Vaastushastra has also shaped public space by its visible presence in the public life of Indian politicians. During the inaugural ceremony of the prime minister, 18 scholars of Vaastushastra from all over India were consulted about the presence of a lone neem tree in the compound of the main entrance of the BJP headquarters. BJP sources reveal: 'Since it was not possible to cut the decade-old tree within an hour, we decided to close the main gate and re-quested visitors to use the other one. We had no time to get permission from the Union ministry of environment and the directorate of estate to cut down the tree' (Bhosle 1998). N. T. Rama Rao, former chief minister of Andhra Pradesh, refused to function from the state secretariat in Hyderabad till changes were made to correct its Vaastu. Tamil Nadu Governor M. Channa Reddy has gone on record that he orders changes every time he moves to a new official residence. B. N. Reddy, former MP and architect, exhorts state governments to correct the Vaastu of sick industries to turn them around (Chopra 1995). All these renovations have been completed at the expense of taxpayers.

Thus, Vaastushastra epitomizes this 'archaic modernity'. It is the practice that adds 'soul' to the architectural sciences, whereby tradition infuses science with depth, meaning and history. This is analogous to the nuclear bomb touted to add 'soul' to India, where science infuses a once-colonized nation with pride, power and strength. Within the imagination of science and religion lies the power of this archaic modernity. Science, technology, religion and capitalism have brought Vaastushastra into the market economy of contemporary India. Vaastushastra emerges as another site of rabid consumerism, and a middle- and upper-class status symbol in urban India today. My use of Vaastushastra as a case study of an archaic modernity is not to determine whether it is scientific or not, religious or not, or whether the Vedas do indeed contain all that modern practitioners claim. Instead, I use the case study to illustrate the ways in which Vaastushastra is marketed and consumed as the best merger of the ancient and the modern – a science with soul and tradition! Vaastushastra is a symptom of a visible shift in the social fabric of India, a masculinist vision of India as Hindu and as a nation celebrating its ancient wisdom and its new technological breakthroughs.

It is frightening to see this Hindu science emerging from nationalism. This is a science that on the one hand purports to be anti-colonial, culturally situated, de-colonizing India by unearthing old cultural practices eroded by colonialism (Nanda 1997). Yet in reality, the nationalists are seeking to create an India that is a 'Hindu' nation. By finding Western scientific innovations anticipated in the Vedic sciences, the nationalists give India's past an aura of Hindu supremacy. Therefore, in order to look to future progress, they say we must delve into India's glorious Hindu past. This archaic modernity will take us away neither from the problems of religion and science, nor from tradition and modernity. We remain deeply implicated in them all. Ultimately, archaic modernity proves to be much too facile a vision, securing the roots and privileges of the upper-class Brahminic elite. Nothing is threatened except the rights of minorities and women.

Imagining India

Archaic modernities invite new interventions in our theories and practices, new alternatives that wrestle with this oxymoronic imagery. The challenge of these developments in contemporary India is in creating new frameworks in which to think about science and religion. Most responses to these recent developments have tended to glorify pre-scientific utopias and revive our dreams of a glorious history and our nostalgia for the simple days of yesteryear, for a world bereft of scientific and technological innovations, where humanity and technology don't begin to fuse dangerously. Alternately, secular activists have invoked a defence of science, scientific objectivity and rationality. These critics have historically fought and continue to fight religious nationalism with the rhetoric of science and scientific nationalism. For them, science is our only saviour from the superstition and irrationality of religion. At the heart of many of these critiques is the juxtaposing of science and religion as oppositional and mutually exclusive practices.

Perhaps the question is not whether the two are related or whether they share the same space, but rather how. How have science and religion worked together to create a masculinist vision of an archaic modernity? To explore this, we must address at least three sets of issues:

1. Social and especially feminist studies of science must develop frameworks on science, development and religion. How can we get beyond the binaries of superstitious religion and progressive science? Indeed, our critiques are rich. How can we engage the contentious histories of these two traditions without using one against the other – science to save religion or religion to save science? We must build on the analyses of feminist science scholars such as Donna Haraway, Sandra Harding and Nancy Tuana, who have traced the roots of Western science back to the Christian clerical tradition (Noble 1992) and explored the ensuing relationships among women, gender, science and religion in the development of Western science. We need to understand better how gender and religion have shaped the progress of science and development.

2. We must find ways to bring the field of science studies and post-colonial studies into conversations with one another. How do science and religion feed our growing understanding of secularism, modernity and democracy? Science, it would seem, has become the central driving force of our economies, imaginations and lives. It has proved to be a powerful political, social and intellectual institution that drives national, global and transnational circuits in this age of globalization. Tracing the global circulations of science through definitions of development, national identity and nationalism, migrations of people and products across national boundaries, the movement and transfer of scientific ideas, products and patents is crucial to our feminist goals.

3. We must use feminist and post-colonial critiques to interrogate the confluence of science and religious nationalism in contemporary India. Feminists have a long history of pointing to the dangers of nationalism as well as tracing the increasing presence of Hindu nationalism in India (Jeffery and Basu 1994). What I hope we will add to this discussion is attention to the new configuration of science and religion. We need to understand how religious nationalism appropriates science and religion for a particularly dangerous and oppressive worldview. Contrary to their claims, religious nationalists are not decolonizing India or Indian history, but merely overlaying Western science with a Hindu agenda. But feminist and post-colonial studies have developed rich frameworks in which we can begin to think

about decolonization. We need to use these theories to create alternatives to the visions of the archaic and the modern.

In this archaic modernity we get to imagine only within the bounded myth of a Hindu India, within a rewritten past, a constructed present and an impoverished vision of the future. However, for centuries India has been a diverse land with multiple religions and the birthplace of several new ones. These centuries of diversity cannot be erased today for a contested mythical version of Hindu India. If we are to imagine India, it must be in its diversity, its contested histories, contradictory pasts and boundless future. The project of decolonization in this age of globalization means taking up the project of rethinking 'development' and its deployment in the archaic and the modern, the religious and the scientific. We can imagine India in all its rich and diverse traditions – Western science, alternate sciences, the rich philosophies and traditions of the country's religions, its indigenous knowledge systems – to re-envision the progressive possibilities of science and religion. We can imagine a new future in an unbounded imagination beyond the worlds of the archaic and the modern.

Notes

1. Jawaharlal Nehru was India's first Prime Minister. In addition to secularism, Nehru was deeply committed to science and to an industrial model of development.

2. Over the last two decades, religion has become a powerful tool in Indian politics. In fairness to the Hindu nationalists, it must be said that secular governments of the past have politicized religion (certainly from Indira Gandhi onwards) and also played the 'Hindu' card.

3. Patel refers to Sardar Vallabbhai Patel and Subhash refers to Subhash Chandra Bose, both well-known figures in the Indian freedom struggle.

4. Bajrangbali refers to followers of Hanuman, the monkey god in the Hindu Pantheon.

5. Although Uma Bharati was given a cabinet position, it was as Minister of Sports.

6. Both Sita and Savitri are women from Hindu mythology especially renowned for their devotion to their husbands, and have come to symbolize the ideals of the 'good' Hindu wife.

7. Baba Ramdev was a Tanwar Rajput and saint in the early fifteenth century. Worshipped by Hindus and Muslims, he is believed to have advocated the equality of all human beings. Ramdevra village lies twelve miles from Pokhran.

8. *Yatra* is a spiritual journey usually undertaken as a voyage of discovery or celebration of a significant event, primarily in the role of a witness. However, in its colloquial use, *yatra* simply means trip or journey.

9. It should be noted that the rhetoric of 'development nationalism' is not new. Since at least 1987 the patriotism of protesters has been questioned.

10. The quotes below contain grammatical and spelling errors – all present in the original. The liberal use of colloquial English in India in these websites is interesting.

. . . .

Conversations Towards Feminist Futures

Arturo Escobar and Wendy Harcourt

Arturo: Let us start by asking how 'visions of the future' in the Women, Culture and Development field are being crafted? By what groups of people? With what combinations of theoretical and practical action? What are the potential implications of these visions for how power is exercised to maintain exploitation over poor women and men and domination over specific groups or nature itself? What configurations of place, space and culture – what networks – might make of such visions a real turn of events in, say, the first half of the century? Does this way of posing the question of 'visions of the future' make sense to you?

Wendy: My visions are grounded in what I see emerging among people's movements, specifically women's groups, who are responding to and shaping resistances to dominant neoliberal capitalist discourses. Such visions are centred on the concept we have been exploring together of 'the politics of place' (Escobar and Harcourt 1998).[1] I am looking with hope at the new cultural permutations that are emerging. I think there is a destabilization of power happening and a strong need for a renewal of thinking about what institutions, what forms of governance, what forms of democracy are needed, based on the knowledge people's groups are building up about how to negotiate (gender, racial, economic, cultural) differences and the sense of the Other. We are restructuring cultural meanings incredibly rapidly, so that our sense of the Other changes with each encounter. In terms of a feminist concern for gender equality and equity and women's empowerment, even in stating those concerns we are layering what are distinct cultural positionings in diverse cultures with a new sense of what it means to be a gendered being. And at the same time these encounters change our own sense of what being a feminist means. We can no longer talk of 'cultural' feminism, as predominantly white women did in the 1980s; there are now historically and politically strong black women's movements, which have been in fact taking a lead in many international settings in the late 1990s.

Envisaging the future becomes much more problematic, because we are evolving new forms of politics along what you call lines of localized power; at the same time, due to the new information and communication technologies (ICTs) and other global links, local networks are connected to what were once far-flung places. So we are now in terms of time and space much closer to the Other.

Just to take one example of a site of political organizing – the struggle for the autonomy and self-determination of women over their bodies. Highly difficult issues such as violence against women in peace and war, the fight against rape, sexual abuse, female genital mutilation, sex workers' rights, women's security and sexual orientation and life choice are no longer silent 'private' issues, but are at the centre of women's rights debates in various cultural and economic contexts. Women's strategies of resistance and struggles for self-autonomy are sometimes carried out in direct support of women who share similar experiences even when living in different geo-political spaces. Without universalizing issues of violence, it is clear that women work in strong solidarity across geographic, ethnic and political divides, creating a type of politics that is a very powerful emotive force. It holds out a promise for the future of security that women's groups are negotiating despite the backdrop for many of severe economic crisis, dire need and violent conflict.

This politics is place-based – with the body being the first site or place for women's struggles. Women's varied resistance to violence at all levels has created very innovative and important changes in women's lives, changing social, medical, health and demographic scientific discourse and practices. To imagine a future where women are truly secure is something I work towards. But I see multiple paths. I do not entertain the idea of one blueprint for the achievement of women's security, as I see the paths to that achievement as extremely complex, tied to both horizontal and vertical power structures and being propelled by local realities and issues that cannot be explained in any universal way. In fact, transformative pathways are emerging out of the resistance to universal, essentialist discourses blind to all the differences among women. Yet it is through solidarity and working with the resistances that I see the future taking place. You are right to pose the question of whether visions of the future make sense. I have a strong sense that we need visions that embrace the possibility that choice, integrity and security for all women in whatever culture can be found. Are such visions just utopian? I think not. However, I do not think that diverse women's groups acting in solidarity and in alliance with other civil society groups are, just like that, going to be able to find solutions to the power imbalances that lead to the violations of their bodily integrity and right to choose. The economic inequities compounded by the vacuum of governance we see today require profound challenges and changes.

Arturo: You mentioned networking and connections through the ICTs.

Taking up the impact of the ICTs on gender and cultural difference, how do you see the engagement with culture among women's groups on the global level?

Wendy: I am very interested in the ICTs as political tools for women's empowerment. If we were to unpack that jargon a bit, what I would say is that ICTs allow political women (feminists of varying shades) around the world access to diverse knowledge, speed of communication and new ways of networking and of knowing one another that has pushed us into new and powerful types of political discourses. We are still wondering where all the interconnectivity could lead us. We are trying to understand what barriers (of time, distance, educational level, language and identity) we are changing or creating, including the very real concern of the majority of women being totally excluded. Another concern is about the issues feminists are just not able to tackle economically and politically, because feminists are not present when the power decisions over technology are being made. This leads to another strong concern about with whom and with what we are colluding.

Nevertheless, there is the sense in which this is a medium that can give many different women tremendous scope to go far beyond traditional cultural experiences, allowing for new types of gender relations and new types of development. Of course, we have to use the barbarian English language mostly and there are hugely varying degrees of access, but once able to navigate there is no bureaucratic red tape, and a great deal of knowledge and groups to tap. We are still trying to work out what works and what doesn't, what type of cultures we are creating and what type of new politics, even new languages across cultures and generations, new structures of feeling (to take up Raymond Williams's definition of culture) we are evolving. The web can allow for safe spaces and new forms of creativity and knowledge and connection. I don't want to celebrate all the hype that is around; clearly ICTs are also producing and creating negative spaces for women (pornography, cyberstalking etc.). But from my experience feminists are finding that the Internet does provide a lot of support and puts them in touch with knowledge networks, and women they would not otherwise meet, on issues that a few years ago would not have been discussed or acted upon beyond their own immediate small groups.

To throw in some examples from other conversations I've had (Harcourt 2000): Arab women are setting up safe cyberspaces where they can converse across geopolitical divides in Arabic about religion, rights, body politics – subjects they would not talk about in public. Or in Rajasthan, India, Bal Rashmi, an NGO based in Jaipur working on violence against women, actively used the Web to squash false charges brought against them. Shirkat Gah, another women's human rights NGO based in Lahore, Pakistan, uses trusted international websites to mobilize around the prosecution of honour killings.

Women working on trade converge first in cyberspace and then in political events at historic moments such as Seattle, Davos, Porto Alegre.

What is interesting in these stories (and I could give many examples) is how in the process of mobilizing support through the ICTs, women's groups have created a series of networks that quickly and strategically link women's local concerns with the global movement. The ability to speak out and act on violence committed against women in a timely way for me is very important. It shows how feminists are adapting the medium and making it a powerful tool, stretching our experiences and our political terrain in ways that are global, though very closely local. My interest is in how these strategies around the body that are so critical to women's movements are connected and linked to other political strategies that engage political women both locally and globally around, for example, consumer and workers' rights, fair trade and equity and health. By way of comparison, do you see the Internet as a useful tool for environmentalists in Latin America where you mainly work? How are the two arenas of feminism and ecology supporting and working together in alternatives to development and towards a vision of social justice? How do you see ICTs and gender in your political and analytical experience?

Arturo: The ICTs have certainly worked in a similar way in the realm of the environment as you have described for women. I could mention, for instance, the case of the U'wa, a small indigenous group in Colombia that has mounted a transnational struggle against the Colombian government and Occidental Petroleum to oppose oil exploration in their ancestral territory. Electronic networks of various kinds have been instrumental to the relative success of this struggle. As you rightly caution, however, in these cases one also senses the unevenness and inequalities in terms of connectivity, interactivity and language. This is why Gustavo Lins Ribeiro (1998), for instance, and I have spoken of the need to consider the relation between social movements and ICTs in terms of two parallel struggles: over the character and democratization of the ICTs themselves, on the one hand; and on the other, over the current restructuring of social and economic conditions fuelled in many ways by these same technologies. It is no secret that globalization and contemporary capitalism are enacted and made possible by new ICTs. This is the main argument Manuel Castells has made in his already famous trilogy on the information or network society, and I think he is essentially correct, despite the fact that his view is strictly globalocentric and does not bring in a perspective of place.

But I am also thinking, in what ways does the unprecedented projection and complexities of environmental and women's struggles by and through ICTs differ from, say, the use that right-wing and reactionary groups make of the same ICTs? In the United States, for instance, we have the case of racial supremacy groups, for which ICTs have also become essential. This question poses a challenge to our arguments about the politics of place in relation to ICTs, which it seems to me we are just beginning to face. Marxist geographers are in many ways correct in suspecting a politics of place and identity that they see as unable to ground a larger spatial politics in terms of, say, broad coalitions of class-based and other social movements. For me, all thinking about place has to tackle immediately the question of flows and networks. And what unites place, flows and networks is power. It is in relation to the powers they oppose, or are able to create, that we can differentiate between various uses of the ICTs that, at many levels (even in their attachment to places, that as we well know from both feminist and ecological concerns can be very reactionary) might look quite similar. Which forms of power do these uses oppose, or which struggles do they contribute to initiate? It may seem paradoxical to use ICTs for a defence of place-based practices. But the fact is that people rooted in local cultures are finding ways to have a stake in national and global society precisely as they engage with the conditions of trans-nationalism in defence of local cultures and ecologies (Escobar 2001). Power, finally, brings to the fore the issue of theory and practice, because it is in their theoretical and practical action – that is, in the production of alternative discourses – that social struggles form networks.

Theoretical and practical action create a system of relays within a larger space – as Foucault and Deleuze (1977) put it long ago – that destabilizes dominant forms of power. As we have suggested elsewhere (Escobar and Harcourt 1998), the result of this process could be described as the creation of 'glocalities' – alternative configurations of culture-nature that also have the potential to be differently gendered. I borrowed this term from geographer Erik Swyngedouw (1997), although I modify it somewhat. In connecting with each other, environmental-ethnic social movements, for instance, circulate identities, visions of the world and practices that result in these parallel networks. I am thinking, for instance, about the growing indigenous networks in South America, the struggles of grassroots black communities in the Americas, or rainforest social movements in many parts of the world. As Dianne Rocheleau (Rocheleau, Thomas-Slater and Wangari 1996) would argue, rightly so in my mind, many of these struggles have to be seen from the perspective of, and in terms of their effect on gendered rights, responsibilities and activism.

But we should not make the mistake of assuming that these networks will necessarily lead to the 'overthrow' of the older or newer forms of power in terms of capitalism and patriarchy. This would mean returning to the older model of the political. But if not an 'overthrow', then what? Perhaps we can now tackle this question in relation to the difficulties we face in imagining 'visions' of the future. First of all, it seems to me that we need to avoid engaging in an exercise of vision-making that consists in providing recipes or grand narratives in the manner of, say, 'sustainable development'.[2] We know from our analyses of development that this grand theorizing is part of the problem, at least at the present moment. (Even if this does not mean giving up the attempt at getting as broad a view of the situation as possible, since at some levels power does indeed effect multiple links among various forms of domination.) We also know, as Donna Haraway (1989) put it in analysing oppositional politics, that 'reversals won't work'. Envisioning a world where women are equal but the same as men, or Third World people equal and the same as, or even superior, to those from the rich countries, would not mean much in terms of creating a plural world with a measure of social justice and ecological sustainability.

Wendy: I agree we need to challenge grand narratives and yet not romanticize place. How do we situate the strategies of the World Bank, for example, with all its recognition of poverty, and knowledge networks, and capability of people and women's groups, and its continued collusion with the major proponents of neoliberal capitalism? All the excitement generated by 'knowledge networks' and the sense of possibility to change does not replace the need to challenge politics with a big 'P' and the need to change radically very powerful dominating vertical power structures. You have spoken usefully to me about the asymmetry of globalization. Can the theoretical and practical action you describe change those asymmetries in your 'visions for the future'?

Arturo: Our awareness of the growing complexity of any situation we might be involved in has led to a more nuanced understanding of power and of how reality is shaped asymmetrically, generally speaking. This complexity should not lead to a paralysis of thought and action, but rather to their continued re-evaluation. And it is here that I want to bring back the sense of utopia in order to build a tension with the more localized and historicized view of political practice we were just discussing. This idea came to me upon rethinking some of the consequences that the new theories of complexity might suggest for a view of the political. From these theories I would highlight the sense of randomness and irreversibility of historical processes (in contrast to the Newtonian deterministic view of a simple world governed by time-reversible laws); the fact that biological and social history are non-linear processes characterized by instabilities, fluctuations and unexpected bifurcations towards unprecedented macro structures that might be radically different from those they evolved from. Complexity theorists highlight the openness of social and biological processes and the dynamics of self-organization that is one of their most constitutive features. This view is quite the opposite of the conventional scientific paradigms of classical mechanics, and of any view of history in terms of stages of development with the concomitant recipes for how to achieve them, whether through technology and economic growth or through revolutionary praxis. It was upon reading a book by the Mexican artist and scholar Manuel de Landa (1997) that the question again came to my mind of the possibility of a radically different world than the one we live in at present.

Julie Graham and Katherine Gibson (Gibson-Graham 1996) argue that capitalocentrism has hampered our best attempts at imagining different worlds from a feminist analysis of capital. But what if we were to think that, through complex and unpredictable dynamics, the conditions were to be established for the creation – through fluctuations, autocatalytic processes and non-linear self-organization dynamics – of a different way of organizing markets and the economy, that is, for the formation of what Prigogine and Stengers (1984) call a 'dissipative structure', one characterized by a different order and higher level of energy? De Landa shows how the formation of markets and the economy took place over the past 300 years in the West, and how, little by little, through superior autocatalytic processes, hierarchies of homogeneous elements gained ascendancy over self-organizing, non-hierarchical 'meshworks' of heterogeneous elements brought together in terms of their functional complementarity. Meshworks, however, were essential to the formation of markets and cities.

In historical terms, and even if meshworks are not necessarily 'morally superior' to hierarchies, it is necessary to foster again their formation. And in many ways this is what I see as happening when we speak of networks and glocalities – what we describe as the hybridity of the global and the local (and without implying the existence of 'pure' or distinct strands of local and global, or traditional and modern). These glocalities would be formed through a double dynamic: strategies of localization that decrease the heterogeneity of each locality (giving localities greater internal consistency) while increasing the heterogeneity between localities; and strategies of interweaving, that tend to increase the heterogeneity of localities while decreasing it between localities (less internal consistency of localities by greater similarities across sites). I am interested in particular in those strategies of localization and interweaving that are set into motion by social movements.

I found an intuitive expression of this idea in the remarks of a Russian ecologist at a convergence of social movements against globalization sponsored by the IGGRI (International Group for Grassroots Initiatives) in Helsinki in 1998, when he said: 'If you want to see a place where globalization is collapsing, come to Russia.' And then he spoke of the rebuilding of economies along relations of barter, reciprocity and the like (what Julie Graham and Katherine Gibson might call practices of economic difference, including women's work in the caring economy). And also in a quite equivalent way by a Sudanese writer, Abu Gassim Goor, who said: 'In Africa, nothing works, but everything is possible.' This phrase always seemed to me a fantastic reversal of the common image of Africa in the development literature as a basket case and a lost cause.

What he meant is that Africa might be in a better position to make do with the remnants of traditions and the rubble of modernities to construct a different path and future.

And what if everything were to be possible, but in a very different sense than when we thought about utopias in earlier decades? If, through other types of dynamics, markets were to start functioning differently, not only along capitalist lines, and economies were to respond to other demands, and culture and nature and gender equality came to be interwoven along plural, ecological principles? Then perhaps the resulting meshworks would be in the position of holding the big financial and development institutions more accountable for the hierarchies they continue to support. So that a measure of diversity could be reintroduced at the very heart of the processes that are most influential in creating socionatural worlds today, so that, in turn, a measure of symmetry could be restored socially and conceptually in the debates about the state of the world. Would we be too foolish in thinking that the social movements meshworks that are being created today (some of which could be seen as creating self-stimulating loops among themselves and with sympathetic NGOs and non-human actors like ICTs and ecosystems), in their strategies of localization and interweaving of heterogeneous elements interlocked in functional complementarity – as complexity theorists would have it – could result in visible alternative orders ('self-consistent aggregates' of a different kind)? If this is the case, we could finally say, 'Development is dead, let it rest in peace', while culture, nature and the economy would be again alive and freer to be articulated with other dreams, such as gender and social equality, material justice and sustainability. Perhaps you can address briefly this way of bringing the need for development to its final effacement in order to conclude our conversation.

Wendy: I find the concept of meshwork intriguing as a metaphor, the sense of strength and purposefulness it conjures up and the room for diverse weavings and connections among groups. I wanted to conclude our conversation by reflecting on two very different observations of social movement meshworks' interactions with power – even if I would hesitate to call it the death of development. I would see it more positively as a hope for new pluralisms that women's movements and social movements are positing in the defence of place against what you have called 'the economic and cultural avalanches of recent decades'. The fact that a growing number of people and groups demand the right to their own cultures, ecologies and economies as part of the modern social world can no longer be easily accommodated into any liberal or neoliberal doctrine (Escobar 2001: 169–70).

One observation is the vision of Sir Brian Urquhart, the well-known high-level UN policy-maker, writing in the *New York Review of Books* on the UN's role to fight evil (his words) – the ethnic conflicts, genocides, wars and tyrannies of the nation-states. He sees civil society 'through the Internet strengthening the influence of activists and concerned citizens throughout the world', to reinforce what he describes as the lonely call of UN Secretary General Kofi Annan to achieve 'changes in behaviour and attitude of people and nations' to ensure international and human security, with the rights of the human individual as paramount (Urquhart 2000: 22). The UN, in short, would play God's police, stepping in where the nation-state failed or is itself perpetrating evil with a cyber-charged civil society at its side. Such a vision depicts the UN as the phoenix rising from the ashes of the crumbling states. It is the death of the nation-state, development transformed into an even greater morally charged project with global citizens and global government. It is a worrying vision, where place-based concerns about globalization are absent, and forcibly reminded me of the limited number of people with whom we can have this conversation.

The other reference is to someone with whom we have both enjoyed conversations: Marisa Belausteguigoitia and her rescuing of the voices of the Chiapas women in her research activities. She shows why we need to look at the intersection of culture, women and development in her narrative on the silencing of Chiapan women's demands within the revolutionary movement. She argues that Chiapan women's call for their rights, poignantly expressed in the women's demand for 'the right to rest', as well as the rights to bodily security, freedom from rape, from exploitation, from beating in the home, from forced marriage – is subsumed in the need for Chiapan male leaders to see women as the repositories of their struggle and of indigenous culture (Belausteguigoitia 2000). Women are the mourners, the mothers, the care-takers and the food providers. Only the demands that reflect those roles (for crèches, schools, bakeries) are given public voice, in article 29 among the 34 demands of the official communiqués. The right to be themselves, to have time and space to think, to have freedom from rape, to 'be' independent of national and communal identities, is silenced. Their voices are replaced by pictures of women mourning the dead or confronting the soldiers. Their demands as autonomous women are not recognized as part of the revolution or as what the Zapatistas want to share with their supporters around the world. In the formation of one of the most celebrated cyber-connected glocalities of indigenous peoples that has challenged the capitalist state, women, culture and development interconnect in such a way that women are relegated to representations of their culture and the violence and oppression they experience as women is sidelined.

The question remains: why is women's marginalization inside and outside their communities not considered an element of the interconnectedness of oppressions and of the relational asymmetries of power interactions? The leaders of the Chiapas rebellion defy both the state and the development project. In the process they reach out to groups around the world, inspiring many to see in their activities the creation of new sites of power. But we need to heed the warning that patriarchal relations, the confining of women to the private realm and to the representations of culture, have to be tackled in social movement meshworks as we release ourselves from the development project.

Notes

1. The Society for International Development is currently working on a project entitled 'Women and the Politics of Place'. Its premise is that it is misleading to see globalization as all-encompassing, or that concrete places are disappearing or being rendered inconsequential for women's lives. Instead, it argues that political struggles around place are a source for strategic vision that provides us with clues about the meaning of politics and development in the global age.

2. The SID journal *Development* has explored this concern in some detail; see, for example, Sachs (1997).

VISIONS 3

. . . .

Knitting a Net of Knowledge: Engendering Cybertechnology for Disempowered Communities

Debashish Munshi and Priya A. Kurian

§ ONE hot, dry, April afternoon in the mid-1990s, we saw what no camera can ever capture – the expressive joy of Ganga, a young tribal woman in the village of Manatalai in Dungarpur district of India's largely arid state of Rajasthan. She had just managed to activate a pump in the village's only well and guide a torrent of water down a freshly made canal to her vegetable patch. Manatalai is so chronically drought-prone that village elders like to indulge in a bit of wishful thinking by naming children after India's mighty rivers.

Like Narmada, Jamuna and two dozen other women in the village, Ganga was very enthusiastic about attending a literacy camp. 'Literacy has taught us how to manage our water resources,' she told us when we met her. But more than that, she went on, 'it has given us the power to take decisions about our own lives'. Literacy had quite literally transformed the lives of the women in the village. For example, the rate of child marriage, the scourge of Rajasthan, was down in the newly literate district. A young mother of two we met told us with quiet confidence that she would never force her children into matrimony at a tender age. She was determined to educate them till they found their feet in the world. This young mother was barely eleven years old herself when she was 'married off' by her parents. She had not only lost her childhood, but was chained to a back-breaking existence of hard labour.

The key to Manatalai's success lay not so much in technology as in a community spirit. Volunteers called *akhardoots* (messengers of literacy) gave their time and energy to teach the village women how to read and write. And it was literacy that allowed these women to take charge of their own lives, assert their own identities and escape from an endless spiral of marriage and childbearing that a patriarchal world had trapped them into.

Literacy is central to our vision of development. But for us, literacy is not merely the knowledge of the alphabet and numerals of one (or more) dominant language(s). Our definition of literacy encompasses the ability to decode messages and access knowledge resources without necessarily being able to write. Such a literacy includes the use of the new media of the Internet and the World Wide Web. The computer is, as Dale Spender points out,

> the site of wealth, power, and influence, now and in the future. Women – and indigenous people, and those with few resources – cannot afford to be marginalized or excluded from this new medium. To do so will be to risk becoming the information-poor. It will be to not count; to be locked out of full participation in society in the same way that illiterate people have been disenfranchised in a print world. (1995: xvi)

Demystifying Technology

It is not the technological aspect of computers and the Net that is crucial to the empowerment of women and other developmentally disenfranchised groups. It is the community spirit of sharing information and solving problems on the Net that can give impoverished women a chance to take decisions and shape policy in the Western male-dominated knowledge economies of the twenty-first century. Just as the *akhardoots* of Rajasthan took the male elite-inspired mystery out of education to spread literacy among the village women, it will take messengers of the Net to demystify technology and usher rural and poor women in the Third World into a less intimidating world of interactive and shared knowledge.

Some alternative women-led projects in South Asia have already made an impressive start. A cluster of 'information villages' in southern India are run by village women, who maintain databases and disseminate information through an indigenously developed cyber network, on locally relevant subjects such as health, commodity prices, inter-village transport and statutory entitlements. A similar community-driven communications revolution is underway in the remote mountainous village of Kothamalee in Sri Lanka, where a community radio station answers listeners' queries by logging on to the Internet and digging up relevant information (Mehta 2000). In another community-oriented project in the Tangail district of Bangladesh, Grameen Communications, an affiliate of the Grameen Bank, pioneers of the poverty-alleviating microloans concept, has launched a village-based computer and Internet programme which aims to provide an information database for the villagers (Grameen 2000).

Resisting (E)male Technolust

These stories of connection and connectivity are routinely underplayed in the mainstream discourse of cybertechnology. The dominant discourse so far has been obsessed with the so-called 'advances' and 'upgrades' in technology for furthering electronic commerce. This discourse is shaped by a 'technolust' for fancy little gadgets like one that 'computes like a piece of pig iron, spits out DVDs like toast, and turns on when your hand enters its electric field' (Wired Tools 2000). It is a discourse in which the dominant voice is that of a 'virtual class' of techno-savvy people and its 'predatory commercial interests' (Ribeiro 1998: 333). Indeed, (e-)commercial exploitation of the Internet is likely to continue in the future (May 2000). In the cut-throat world of electronic business, information sharing for the common good is hardly the norm. On the contrary, the world of e-business is busy erecting 'firewalls' that allow 'security administrators to restrict enterprise users' access to the outside world, as well as fending off inbound attacks' (May 2000: 210). This world of cybertechnology, steeped as it is in the intrigues of hacking, counter-hacking and power play, is overwhelmingly dominated by a culture of masculine aggression. A common symptom of such aggression is the phenomenon of 'flame wars' or the trading of electronic insults.

That this obsession for aggressive territory-staking and territory-protecting smacks of militaristic machismo is hardly surprising, as the Internet, first developed by the US Department of Defense, was built on the foundations of military values (Abbate 1999). This 'march ahead' nature of the Net is, in many ways, responsible for the digital divide between the information-rich and the information-poor. While the English-speaking Western world spends its energy in constantly upgrading software to pursue its goal of conducting *Business @ the speed of thought* (Gates 1999), much of the Third World falls behind in its dream of achieving basic needs like potable water and affordable health care. Statistics available in the UNDP's Human Development Report (1999) capture this divide eloquently: 'English prevails in almost 80 percent of all websites, yet less than one in 10 people worldwide speaks it'; 'To purchase a computer would cost the average Bangladeshi more than eight years' income, the average American, just one month's wage'. This disparity in access to information technologies, the report points out, is 'creating parallel worlds' in which 'those with income, education and – literally – connections have cheap and instantaneous access to information', while 'the rest are left with un-certain, slow and costly access' (UNDP 1999: 6). What is more, the report adds, men overwhelmingly dominate cyberspace. Indeed, as Wajcman points out, 'male dominance of technology has largely been secured by the active exclusion of women from areas of technological work and it is fundamental to the way in which the gender division of labor is still being reproduced today' (1995: 192).

The overarching emphasis on technology as an entity separate from the social and cultural needs of society has not served the interests of women or other disempowered groups. The accent on technology for technology's sake is part of a masculinist worldview epitomized by the association of technical competence with male gender identity (Wajcman 1995). Instead, a feminist approach to technology could look at ways of dealing with core developmental issues of food, clothing, shelter, education and, indeed, survival itself. Such an approach could help marginalized groups to use technology in a manner that makes their lives more meaningful. As Arizpe says, 'women should be active agents in ensuring that the star-like potential of information technologies is directed towards enhancing human well-being rather than strengthening existing power monopolies' (1999: xv).

A feminist approach to technology is one that recognizes that technology can never be neutral. Given the enormous potential of technology to shape social relations, power equations and the fundamental structures of society, a feminist approach would seek the development of appropriate technology with the broader aim of women's empowerment and community empowerment in general. Thus, the Internet and other technologies may be used at the grassroots by women to gather critical information on a range of issues of interest to them and their communities, such as health, transportation, statutory entitlements and collective endeavours.

Cybertechnology is already being used in meaningful ways in some parts of the developing world. In one 'information village' of southern India, for instance, rural women are using weather forecasting data from the Internet to warn the fisherfolk about impending dangers at sea. Complex weather forecasting data, received on one of the two Internet-linked computer terminals at an information centre based in the village temple complex, is processed and relayed to the milling crowds by a woman volunteer through a simple voice-amplifying device. The whole exercise effortlessly plugs together communication devices from the Middle Ages and the twenty-first century and creatively adapts global technology to suit local needs. It is this innovativeness that has the potential to bridge the seemingly insurmountable digital divide.

Such use of technology can be directed towards ensuring well-being, a meaningful life and even a challenge to existing power structures. This approach can, therefore, effectively counter the explicitly masculinist approach of today's mainstream cyberspace discourse, which attempts to mystify the information superhighway as a bevy of microprocessors, fibre-optic sensors and weight-watching chips dancing to get their size down to minuscule fractions of a micron. Such mystification bolsters the myth about cyberspace being the realm of a (usually male) elite. Yet, as many women cyber-entrepreneurs have shown, technology can be engendered. Instead of 'writing programming codes that only computers and other programmers can understand', these entrepreneurs concentrate on creating content that is easily accessible (Schuyler 1996: 38). The focus in such endeavours is clearly on design skills rather than technical wizardry.

Decolonizing (Web)sites of Western Culture

On the Internet, design-based communication, in fact, has the potential of being far more egalitarian than the usual text-based form of information exchange. In Australia, for instance, design-based web communication has been very popular among some remote Aboriginal communities who have been using communication technologies as a means of cultural maintenance. Significant research by Eric Michaels (1994) has shown that the Warlpiri people, an isolated community of the central desert region of Australia, found electronic media much more accessible and attractive than conventional print-based literacy. In fact, the project emphatically asserts that the so-called 'non-modern may actually find the postmodern world of virtuality more compatible than its creators' (Schech and Haggis 2000: 215).

In India, a study undertaken by the National Institute of Information Technology (NIIT) proved conclusively that children who were illiterate and came from non-English backgrounds could intuitively pick up computer concepts through incidental learning and some minimal (human) guidance (Bytesforall 2000). Some alternative computer-link groups in India have, in fact, been trying to reach out to the masses through computer networks that place an emphasis on graphics and images. To break the stranglehold of English, these groups have also been developing Indian-language websites. One among many such sites is 'Web Dunia' (Webdunia 2000) which features information in Hindi relating to current affairs, politics, sport, films, agriculture and business, allowing those who access it to resist the ubiquitous cultural imperialism propagated by the English-language Net.

The success of alternative non-English and indeed non-language sites is, in many ways, what Michaels calls a challenge to the 'fallacy of unilineal evolution of culture' (1994: 81). Protagonists of unilineal cultural evolution built up the colonial idea that those who were far removed from the Victorian English norm were culturally less evolved. As Michaels points out:

> Evidence of the persistence of unilinealism is everywhere, from popular thinking about 'primitives' (aided and abetted by the etymology of the very word), to Third World development agendas, to a remarkable variety of humanist scholarship. It matters not whether the value-loading is Rousseauesque romanticism, or native advancement, or simple garden variety racism. The point is that very few people believe what anthropology teaches: that indigenous, small scale traditional societies are not earlier (or degenerate) versions of our own. They are rather differing solutions to historical circumstances and environmental particulars that testify to the breadth of human intellectual creativity and its capacity for symbolization. (1994: 81–2)

Nurturing a Virtual Community – Byte by Byte

Human intellectual creativity lies at the heart of the Internet and new media technologies. And it is this creativity, rather than technical capability, that can bridge the digital divide of the world. Engendering cybertechnology can play a major role in this.

The problem of a digital divide is indeed far-reaching, but it cannot be solved by shunning or denigrating the Internet. Instead, we need to turn the medium into a contested territory where dominant ideologies of culture and development can be challenged by women and other disempowered groups. As others have argued, 'women can and do actively participate in defining the meaning and purposes of technologies' (Wajcman 1995: 200). Our vision for the future would be to see small- and large-scale ventures empowering disadvantaged groups. Among such ventures would be a Net society that would link Ganga and her fellow villagers from Manatalai to a network of informed 'netizens' (a term coined by Hauben and Hauben, 1997) who could exchange information and ideas about water management, crop sustenance, reproductive health, child immunization and drought management, instead of concentrating on gigabytes of information about the lifestyles of glamorous drivers on information superhighways.

We would like empowered women 'netizens' to reshape the demography of the Net and align it more closely to the demographic profile of the world. Thus, we would like to see women (and other minority groups) break the stranglehold of Western and West-trained men on cyberspace and, in the process, knit a community-oriented net of knowledge.

Seeing the Complexity: Observations and Optimism from a Costa Rican Tourist Town

Darcie Vandegrift

§ LIKE many women in rural Costa Rica, Veronica (with her husband) supports her family from a patchwork of income sources. Living in a tourist town on the Caribbean coast, Veronica usually holds at least one low-paying, service sector job that makes tourist facilities look cleaner and brighter. She rents a small room behind her house to tourists, providing her a chance to 'meet new people' and work 'independently', without a supervisor. In some weeks Veronica sells clothes and shoes to other Afro-Caribbean women living in town. Besides earning money, this work fills an important gap, catering to low-income women's tastes and budgets normally overlooked in a tourist economy. Finally, she occasionally supplements her income by cooking Afro-Caribbean cuisine for tourists or crocheting decorations for neighbours who request them. Together with her husband's less time-consuming but also multiple-earning strategies, Veronica supports her family.

Veronica, like anyone, is a unique and complex person. She stands apart from many women in Puerto Viejo in her community activism and devout Christian faith.[1] She also shares visions of the future and economic goals with other women in the community and, perhaps, in other parts of what is called the Third World. She is one of dozens of women I talked with during fieldwork on the South Caribbean coast of Costa Rica.[2] The region was formerly home to primarily Afro-Caribbean residents, but has changed as mestizo/a Nicaraguans, Europeans and North Americans, as well as non-black Costa Ricans, have relocated to the alluring coast next to the Caribbean Sea. In the course of my research, I examined how people define categories of social difference such as race, class, gender and nation as well as how these definitions shape the course of economic development for this tourist town.

Veronica and her black, white, indigenous and Ladino neighbours are enmeshed in globalization and development processes originating beyond the boundaries of the former cocoa farms and fishing waters. Structural adjustment policies instigated by the IMF (International Monetary Fund) for Costa

Rica partially explain why, as prices escalated and the colon lost value weekly, women in the province suffered 60 per cent higher levels of underemployment than men (and the highest for either sex in any region of the country), leading to the long hours and crazy-quilt income sources (Area de estadística 1998).

In telling Veronica's story, particularly in combination with a larger story about social inequality in a growing tourist economy (which is in turn shaped by Costa Rica's histories of race relations, economic development and position in the world system), how do I proceed in a way that acknowledges what is important? The story of the South Caribbean's development trajectory, and of women's struggles, successes and positionalities within it, becomes more accurate and more useful when I focus on culture. Only through highlighting lived experiences and interpretations of everyday events can we understand how women in the Third World make their way in local economies – and how planners, be they the tourist board or the World Bank, often fail them.

Why does Veronica choose to sell clothes and shoes or crochet slipcovers when she could work another shift at a local restaurant washing dishes? What are the meanings she places on her labour? How does this work contribute to her and her neighbours' sense of the enduring presence of an Afro-Caribbean people in Costa Rica? What do the material and discursive interactions between 'local' and 'tourist' mean when the 'local' is a woman like Veronica who owns her own room to rent?

A Women, Culture and Development (WCD) approach potentially brings forward these types of questions, leading us to a more nuanced understanding of the connections between categories of social difference and economic processes. We can draw the connections between racism (the displacement of Afro-Caribbean women's preferences and public spaces in a town filled with products and opportunities for white foreign consumers and workers), the economy (a regional development strategy that offers mostly low-paid formal sector employment for women, necessitating multiple income strategies) and culture (how women interpret these conditions and strategize to find satisfaction and survival within them). Without these questions, economic planning designed to empower women in the Third World at an internal, domestic and collective level (see Rowlands 1994) actually patronizes and falsely simplifies.

A WCD approach creates the theoretical orientation to imagine another future for the Third World, where people and places thrive in their complexity, where power is distributed more equitably and where women wield greater control over their economic, domestic and creative lives. An imagination of this magnitude develops partially through theoretical attention to social inequalities on the basis of gender, race, class, age, nationality, ability, familial status, sexuality and the complicated interactions among these differences (of course, this imagination is also born through action, and that old notion of praxis).

The Future of the South Caribbean and Points Beyond

Perhaps because I am the parent of a small child, I embrace the expectation of forthcoming social justice. I have to believe in the possibility of a desirable future world, as I spend so much of my emotional and physical labour preparing to send someone into that future. An implicit understanding within such a statement is that their destinies are connected, those of my child and those of Veronica's four children. Simultaneously, I am aware, through my own experience and study in the first three decades of my life, of the caution required in making such a statement, given differences across people based on social categories with obstinate power to shape and define. A careful optimism, then, pushes academics and activists working in the First World to think about using our power (however limited), as well as *our own everyday experiences and interpretations* towards creating the kind of new politics the editors of this volume propose in their introduction.

The trick, of course, is to specify what exactly we hope for. In my short list offered here, I continue with what I identify as a key strength of a WCD paradigm: the feminist synthesis of political economy and discursive approaches to focus on microprocesses and the interconnections between everyday practices and larger economic and political structures. Believing in the importance of local contexts, I offer here topics for reflection for the future, focusing on the part of the Third World I know best: Costa Rica.

Economic transformations allowing diverse groups of women to work fewer hours, labour more autonomously and earn a living wage In indigenous Bribri communities in Costa Rica, for example, when counting domestic labour, women work on average nine hours more a day than men in the same household (Vandegrift 1993). As in most of the First World, employers at my field sites define work typically performed by women as requiring less skill and, therefore, deserving of less pay. Women of all nationalities and racialized groups also earn less than men for performing the same work. Finally, women in the communities where I work often express frustration that others define the nature of women's work, particularly poor and low-status women's work.

Many of these problems are well documented within gender and development literatures. Yet a WCD approach fills many gaps that have made solutions elusive, paying attention to *process* as well as outcome. In the Costa Rican context, a WCD framework examines how women create a host of ingenious individual and collective responses to low pay, the double- and triple-shift day and the desire to define the nature of their work. For example, Bribri women lobbied the government for subsidized community child care, and demanded that development projects redefine how income-generating projects distributed work within villages.

A WCD approach pays attention to the differences across women living in the same town and even claiming the same identities. This focus uncovers, for example, that planners seeking to support microenterprise in south-eastern Costa Rica often fund only individuals or heterosexual couples. This ignores the powerful connections of women across extended families and the differential access to community resources of various extended kin networks. The results can exacerbate local hostilities or fortify patriarchal structures when funding for a nuclear family is paid directly to the 'male head of household'.

Increased democratic participation – and continued discussion about the meanings of these words Costa Ricans living in Puerto Viejo and surrounding areas define the region as 'the most abandoned in the country'. What does this mean for women? This question has gone unexamined in literature on Costa Rica; the answer cannot be obtained without theorizing the day-to-day interactions between the state and women of different classes, races and nationalities. Unlike women in the Central Valley, home to the nation's capital and dominant social and political institutions, women in the Talamanca region often refuse to push publicly for gender equity in local political institutions. Demands for more equitable participation in, for example, the Development Association, the canton's highest level of government, seem less useful if the board holds little power and is ignored by the central government.

To achieve truly democratic participation, citizens, scholars and practitioners must analyse power inequalities at all levels. What do different groups of women consider to be the role of the state in their lives and in their communities? New answers emerge through an attention to micro-processes at local levels where people often feel the hand of government (or note its frequent absence). The answers look different in indigenous, Afro-Caribbean and white Costa Rican populations, as well as along other axes of difference.

In the broader Costa Rican public spheres of laws and social norms, I find many hopeful prospects. Costa Rica constitutionally bans employment discrimination based on gender. It guarantees maternity leave and offers women of all social classes access to birth control, public housing, land ownership and primary education. In 1992, the country witnessed a female pre-candidate for a major political party's presidential nomination, beating its larger, louder neighbour to the north by at least a decade. These important steps mark progress towards creating gender equity and cannot be dismissed as merely symbolic. To measure the impacts that these changes have on Costa Rican women, scholars must theorize from the position of how women interpret attempts at gender equity and how their daily work, relationships and political practices shift as a result of state initiatives.

Recognition and support for the meaningful experiences in women's lives In a recent presentation about Puerto Viejo, I discussed the importance of the newly constructed *Casa Cultural*. The Centre, four years in the building, provided a place where the community analysed drug addiction, hosted a recital showcasing Caribbean dances and publicly strategized on security issues. In two of these three examples, women arranged the meetings. Residents spoke enthusiastically of the new Centre and hoped to include training programmes and perhaps women's consciousness-raising meetings as part of the Centre's uses. At the end of my presentation, a well-meaning US woman asked what I would recommend to a major international financial institution for a course of action, dismissing the Centre as not substantial or 'economic'.

Such a comment, I believe, denies the importance of spaces for people to create meaning in their lives. Perhaps we sacrifice discussion of these hopes and dreams in a mistaken belief that only 'real' issues – meaning economic survival issues – deserve mention. Yet how can a community achieve survival without reflection about what is important to them? How can women's equity be envisioned without noting the gendered dimensions of the processes involved in dreaming for the future? Although strategic and practical steps to ameliorate economic inequality remain absolutely essential, I hope that activists, practitioners and academics also recognize the importance of supporting women's struggles involving the things that give life meaning. In Costa Rica, ordinary citizens have embarked on cultural advocacy projects including underground midwifery collectives in Puerto Viejo to provide a dignified childbirth; minority language use in public education fought for by grassroots indigenous NGOs in Talamanca; artists' collectives in San José who try to counter the 'Americanization' of Costa Rican culture; and a queer cultural and legal advocacy group, also in the capital, that attempts to destigmatize lesbian and gay relationships. Other locations will yield different examples, but all point to the necessity of giving women the time, space and resources to celebrate important aspects of their identity and critically to engage the structures, both internal and external, that prevent such celebrations.

A future for women that includes economic justice, democratic participation and purposeful reflection is a tall order. My research in Costa Rica and even, specifically, my friendship and working relationship with Veronica allow for an optimism that general overviews of global capitalism and development discourse cannot perceive. The small – and not-so-small – victories that I could see in the field articulated the possibility of reaching larger goals. I take my cue from Veronica's perseverance. Although she expressed frustration at how tired she felt and how slow she found the process of activism, she refused to quit her struggles for children's education, community welfare and hope for the future:

We have to be conscious in trying to change. We have to start, I have to start, from myself and who want to follow, join with me. If I waiting for you to start and you are not conscious, I to start. Saying something, doing something actively. And if alone I have to do it, if I'm convinced, I stay alone doing it until someone [joins with me].

Notes

1. Veronica has worked in the town's child advocacy organization as well as in an organization dedicated to combating the growing damage of crack cocaine addiction which accompanies the increased use of the region as a stop for drug traffickers.

2. The fieldwork, conducted in the region in 1991–93 and more intensively for twelve months from August 1997, created the basis for my dissertation, entitled 'Paradise under Development: Social Inequality and Memory in a Costa Rican Caribbean Tourist Economy'.

VISIONS 3

. . . .

Dreams and Process in Development Theory and Practice

Light Carruyo

El derecho de soñar no figura entre los treinta derechos humanos que las Naciones Unidas proclamaron a fines de 1948. Pero si no fuera por él, y por las aguas que da de beber, los demás derechos se morirían de sed. 'The right to dream is not among the thirty human rights that the United Nations proclaimed late in 1948. But if it were not for the right to dream, and for the drinking water it provides, the rest of the rights would die of thirst.' (Eduardo Galeano 1997: 97–8)

§ DEVELOPMENT as a field of research and practice provides a language to talk about the relationships between nations and economies, but continues to struggle with understanding the complicated relationships between people. Understanding these relationships, as well as people's hopes, dreams, visions and the meanings that they give to the process of improving their quality of living, is at the centre of understanding development.[1] This essay is about a vision for the future of development in Latin America, yet it offers no new theory, only a suggestion: put what people think about, care about and dream about first, and work from there.

The Women, Culture and Development approach proposed by the editors of this collection challenges the idea that development looks the same in every corner of the world, and suggests that progress is defined locally. That is not to say that development is agreed on by every member of any given community, for within communities there exist differences of power – such as those based on hierarchies of wealth, sex/gender and race. The emphasis on agency and culture provides not only a way to understand what people think about, care about and dream about, but also a way to analyse these differences in power. Importantly, this approach also proposes a critique of development that is not founded in 'Third World victim status'. In other words, the critique is not that development is something that is 'done to' the Third World; instead, there is an acknowledgement that Third World actors, elite and non-elite, male and female, organized and not organized, contribute to the construction of the discourse and practice of development. An integration of these lines of inquiry on women, culture and development challenges conventional understandings of development, because it permits a careful analysis of local level processes without losing sight of their constitutive role in relationships between nations and economies and vice versa.

Case Study: La Ciénaga de Manabao

When I began my research on women organizing for basic needs in La Ciénaga de Manabao, in the Dominican Republic, I was told very few development projects were underway in the area. La Ciénaga is small, about 400 habitations spread across seven small groupings of houses in the Cordillera Central of the Dominican Republic. The local economy relies primarily on the sale of tayota, a consistent squash-like crop, and tourism to Armando Bermudez National Park. The direct recipients of cash in these two areas are men. There are many interests present in La Ciénaga, not only because of the park, but because it is the closest community to the Cuenca Alta del Yaque, the source of water for both the northern and southern regions of the Dominican Republic. As one local farmer and guide explained to me, 'Everyone depends on this water, even if you buy a plantain from the truck that was grown in the south, you can buy the plantain because *we* are taking care of this water.'

Given the importance of both the Cuenca and the park as a tourist attraction, the region is eligible for support from national and international nongovernmental organizations (NGOs) and has attracted projects directed at small-scale agricultural production, eco-tourism, the arts, reforestation, organic agriculture, soil conservation and park and trail management, to name a few. Yet, when I first arrived and asked local people about the projects that were present in the community, the most frequent responses were 'none', 'very few' and, most commonly, *aquí nunca llega nada* – 'nothing ever comes here'. In my interviews I heard this many times and I believed it. In fact, it is true that much of the funding that is channelled to the Cuenca and surrounding communities radically diminishes, or even disappears in the hands of mediating organizations and local individuals. Nevertheless, *aquí nunca llega nada* has at least two meanings depending on whom one asks. It is used as a way to create and manipulate victim status in order to receive assistance, especially in response to government officials or visitors who are perceived as potentially offering donations or projects. In interviews, when I probed the frequent complaint that 'nothing ever comes here', its other meanings began to emerge. For instance:

Light: Pero a mi me hablaron de un proyecto de café para las mujeres. 'But I've been told about a coffee project for the women.'

Isabella: Si, llego. Pero como que no le dimos importancia. 'Yes, it came. But we didn't really place much importance on it.'

So although projects, such as the coffee project I inquired about, did in fact arrive, it was 'not given importance'. Therefore, 'nothing ever comes here' can also mean, 'It came but we did not value it, give it importance.' The project was proposed, but did not fit into local women's routine, or their vision of what could be worthwhile, enjoyable, profitable.

Development NGOs, the government and even individuals pass through La Ciénaga and want to make a difference, want the community to 'develop'. They feel that a community that is poor – where not every family has a latrine, where babies do not drink milk, where the first thing they notice are children's bare feet, bare bottoms and bloated stomachs – would be thrilled to partake in any project that comes their way. That is the expectation, and if people do not want to participate they are lazy or ungrateful or ignorant. Several people have said this to me about Ciénaguero/as. In my eight months of fieldwork I have seen a series of projects arrive. Most recently, a Spanish NGO has begun to build a greenhouse to grow vegetables.

The greenhouse project has been facilitated by a Dominican NGO that has been working in the community for several years. During planning meetings with the Dominican NGO, I mentioned that I felt we – the residents of La Ciénaga and myself – did not clearly understand the project. However, in the meetings community members said they were in favour of building the greenhouse. When I asked outside the meetings, several said *que lo hagan*, 'sure *they* should build it' (emphasis mine), and told me it was a way to protect crops from the sun and rain. However, not one person spoke of why it would be beneficial. When the women's association leadership checked with the local agronomist he said he saw no need for a greenhouse in the area. Upon the arrival of the Spanish NGO there was a brief meeting in which the Dominican NGO introduced the crew to the association and reminded people that this greenhouse was *de la comunidad* 'of the community'. Therefore, all association members should work with the Spaniards who had come such a long way to support them.

In the second week of work, there was only a handful of community members participating in the building of the greenhouse. When I asked other residents about the project, they said they thought it was 'very important'. The general understanding of the uses of the greenhouse was the same.

So while there was funding and labour available from outside the community, the community was not 'giving importance' to the project even though, when asked, they spoke of its importance. Money and supplies seem only a part of what a development project means. Communities have hopes about the future of their communities; it is necessary to talk about them, to talk about how and why and whether the project of a greenhouse might be a part of those dreams. The reaction of the local agronomist regarding the greenhouse is also bound to influence how Ciénagueras/os feel about the greenhouse and to impact directly the level of participation.

In an effort to support development in the community the Dominican NGO took the greenhouse project on. But there was no talk about the community's needs, desires, visions for the future, just the assumption that once the project began it was the responsibility of all to rally support. Several times I heard both the Spanish and Dominican NGOs remind community members – 'Remember this is yours, this is for you.' The merits of a greenhouse aside, how and by what process is it of the community? It was neither born nor bred in La Ciénaga; it was handed over full-grown and the community was asked to sacrifice itself to bathe, clothe and love it as its own.

I tell this story partly to get it off my chest – it is frustrating to watch this in a community that I have grown to care about – but there are also lessons to be learned. I believe in alliances as a way to work towards development. The Dominican NGO and the Spanish NGO share a vision for the future of the community. In La Ciénaga, most people share basic ideas of what they want for the future of La Ciénaga. In fact, what they wish for and dream of is consistent with what many envision – from USAID to Peace Corps and grassroots organizers: education, health care and plenty to eat. In interviews with community members, many people mentioned working with people from outside the community to improve the quality of life in La Ciénaga. For instance:

Light: ¿Cual es el deseo suyo para el futuro de La Ciénaga? 'What is your wish for the future of La Ciénaga?'

Estella: Esta gente están medio fríos, por eso, porque creen que ya todo el mundo se olvido de ellos … El deseo mío es que La Ciénaga eche pa'lante. Que La Ciénaga eche pa'lante, que La Ciénaga crezca en dinero en sensia (sic). *Que sepan mucho la gente, y que en el futuro algo se vea porque si uno vive todo el tiempo en la misma, todo el tiempo aplastado, aplastado y nunca se ve nada nunca hay nada.* 'These folks are cooling off, because they think the world has forgotten them. My wish is that La Ciénaga move forward. That La Ciénaga move forward and that it grow in wealth and knowledge. That people know a lot and that in the future we see something because if one lives this way, always squashed, squashed and you never see anything you never have anything.'

Light: ¿Y como se haría eso? Que crezca así [la Ciénaga]. 'How can this be done? That it grow like that?'

Estella: Adio! La gente luchando. Si la gente no lucha no crece nada. 'Adio! People fighting. If people don't fight then nothing grows.'

Light: ¿Cual es el deseo suyo para el futuro de La Ciénaga? 'What is your wish for the future of La Ciénaga?'

Josefina: Bueno que se halle donde trabajar, que manden que manden algo de comida porque imagínese uno vive flojo, luchando es por la comida es que uno vive. Y siempre que se acuerden de uno que le traigan algo a uno. Y que lo traiga para todos. Yo tampoco quiero que me lo traigan a mi, porque como uno necesita otro necesita también. 'Well, that we be able to find work here, that they send something, that they send food because we live broke, you see – we live struggling to eat. That people remember to bring something for us. I don't just want stuff for myself, as much as one needs it, so do the others.'

Both of these responses suggest that community members want to work with non-community members to improve the quality of life in the area. The first suggests a more active role for the community members and the second a more passive one. Yet both indicate that working in alliance with organizations such as the Dominican and Spanish NGOs is desirable. To develop an alliance model of development requires knowing, or listening to, what people place importance on and why. A pedagogy of development could provide a way to work towards a mutual understanding of goals and processes for accomplishing them. For instance, it is not that Ciénagueros don't understand why it is important to use organic fertilizers and pesticides to protect the river, it is that they are afraid it is not viable. It is too risky. *La tierra está cansada y hay que usar química.* 'The land is tired and requires chemicals.' Government and private funds that could be invested in minimizing the risks are used for talks on the importance of protecting natural resources. Development is not only about the rural community effort, but about urban citizens, nations and international trade. Farmers depend on markets, consumers and policies that are far removed from their day-to-day experiences. At the same time, their day-to-day experiences are embedded in a complicated web of interests.

In my research on development I am concerned with the ways in which women navigate these webs of interest in their community that make demands on their time. That is to say, the process by which women are working for well-being in their lives and community involves constant negotiation with NGOs, tourists, husbands, mothers and their own sense of what are necessary or appropriate courses of action for them to take as women. It is through this process that women in La Ciénaga become co-creators of what development means in their community, of their daily practices and visions for the future.

In interviews with both men and women in La Ciénaga I took the opportunity to ask about their visions for the future – education, work and health were all priorities, along with not having to worry so much about where the next meal would be coming from. Many wanted the opportunity to have schooling beyond sixth grade available locally should they opt for it. Visions and dreams for the future are shared by many, but it is the 'how', the process, that should be of concern to us. It is 'how' and 'what' one is willing to give up that is not always agreed upon. Why are students in the United States unwilling to give up shopping at Gap and why are Ciénagueras/os unwilling to give up control over their own time schedule, for instance, even when it is the 'sensible' thing to do?

A while ago I saw the Cuban film *Lista de Espera* (directed by Juan Carlos Tabío and Tomás Gutiérrez Alea, based on a story by Arturo Arango). The premise is that a group of people gets stuck waiting for a bus in a run-down terminal in rural Cuba and falls asleep. In a collective dream, the group creates a communal living situation. They transform the terminal into a beautiful home, with gardens, libraries, plenty to eat – a place where every member of the group is valued, where gay men, black women, mechanics, engineers and bohemians, the old and the young, become family. When all wake up at the end of the film, each person remembers the dream and values its beauty, but none stick around the terminal to make it a reality; understandably they all have places to go, families to see, jobs to do.

The sensible thing for Cienaguéras/os to do in the case of the greenhouse project may be to work collectively to build it in order to generate food for local consumption and cash income. But on the other hand, there are the issues of competing projects, unsupportive husbands, rain (which makes it prime time to clean up the tayota crops) scepticism, mistrust among community members, lack of interest in vegetables. Additionally, the dream of a tourist-based economy has been ingrained into local sense-making in an attempt both to encourage reforestation and make up for the lack of markets for small agricultural producers. My dream for the future of development in Latin America is that we stick around; that we dream of the future and that we commit to the process; that we develop strategies to understand and negotiate what is sensible to whom and why.

Note

1. I undertake a project in the field of development with many hesitations. I've considered expelling the word development from my vocabulary for being too loaded. Loaded with the implication of a linear process that, once accomplished, lets First World nations off the hook and leaves the rest of the world faced with the no-win task of progressing to that level. Loaded like an index finger used to point at the 'underdeveloped', either to reprimand or paternalistically offer assistance. Perhaps development could be replaced with something like sustainable well-being. The 'well-being' defined locally, and the 'sustainable' defined locally and globally. In this model the United States would not be off the hook, because patterns of consumption on which well-being are based are not sustainable. And moreover, well-being in the United States is directly linked to the lack of well-being in most of the rest of the world.

PART THREE

The Cultural Politics of Representation

CHAPTER 9

· ·

Of Rural Mothers, Urban Whores and Working Daughters: Women and the Critique of Neocolonial Development in Taiwan's Nativist Literature

Ming-yan Lai

§ TAIWAN'S success in achieving economic growth has become legendary in development studies, contributing to the proposition of an 'East Asian Development Model' that supposedly launched the four 'little dragons' of Singapore, Hong Kong, South Korea and Taiwan into the orbit of newly industrialized stars (Berger and Hsiao 1988). Much has been written about the policies, strategies and role of an authoritarian state that contributed to the island's economic success. Yet, reflecting the general economistic orientation of development studies, local cultural intervention in the course of Taiwan's development has been scarcely mentioned. In so far as culture is taken into consideration, it is in the form of a reified notion of Confucianism (or 'post-Confucianism' according to some) as the common cultural tradition that enables East Asian societies to maintain a competitive edge in the global capitalist market (see, for example, Tai 1989, Bond and Hofstede 1990, Rozman 1991 and Vogel 1991; for critiques of this argument, see Clegg, Higgins and Spybey 1990, and Dirlik 1995).

Aside from controversies over the identification of a common Confucian culture underlying diverse business practices and its putative salutary effects on economic development, this equation of culture with tradition is clearly inadequate to address the dynamic role that culture plays in critiquing, en-visioning and shaping the meaning, goals and process of development. In so far as the political economy of development impacts directly and indirectly on people's daily lives, it informs and even becomes substantive material for cultural production and analysis. In the representation of everyday life, in other words, such cultural productions as fictional writing engage the issues of development and probe the meaning of particular development policies and strategies for different social groups and classes. While such engagement may be subtle and subterranean, it can also be deliberate, calling attention to the effects of political economic changes on the lives of particular individuals, and bringing the aspirations and struggles of these individuals to bear on the national debate about the goals and desirable courses of development. To reduce this dynamic cultural interpretation and interrogation to the influence of traditional values and practices on economic activities, then, is tantamount to dismissing the cultural agency of diverse social groups, especially those subordinated in the dominant tradition. By the same token, it obscures the importance of women in cultural discourses and debates on development.

To highlight the critical interrogation of development in cultural practices and explore the significance of women to such a project, this chapter examines the practice of nativist literature in Taiwan during the period of rapid economic growth from the mid-1960s to the late 1970s. As a deliberate cultural intervention in Taiwan's course of development, nativist literature of this period advances a nationalist discourse to expose and protest about the neocolonial nature of a development oriented towards the needs and demands of foreign capitalist powers. Unpacking this nationalist discourse, my analysis shows how its oppositionality depends on problematic representations of women that undergird patriarchal traditions. A focus on female figures in major works of nativist literature thus enables us to unveil the ideological construction of its nationalist opposition to neocolonial development. In counterpoint, a consideration of the material reality for women under Taiwan's development, and women's own representation of their everyday experiences, casts a different light on the role of women to development and cultural resistance to neocolonial exploitation.

Capitalist Development and the Rise of Nationalist Discourse

The rise of nationalist discourse in Taiwan in the 1970s is arguably an ideological response on the part of male intellectuals to the country's increasing involvement in global capitalism in pursuit of economic development. Adapting to the global restructuring of capitalism with the introduction of offshore production by multinational corporations, a process which, as Harvey (1989) among others has argued, instituted the system of flexible production that has come to characterize the mode of production in postmodernity, Taiwan adopted an export-oriented industrial development policy in the 1960s and set up its first export processing zone in Gaoxiong in 1966. This policy turned Taiwan essentially into a supplier of cheap labour for the offshore production of foreign companies, which retained control of capital flow, technology and markets while increasing their profit margins with overseas operations. Through such arrangements, Taiwan's economy became heavily dominated by foreign capital interests, with the United States and Japan effectively controlling the bulk of Taiwan's industrial development and foreign trade by the early 1970s.[1]

The domination of American and Japanese capital in Taiwan created a situation in which capital–labour contradictions easily corresponded to a foreign-Chinese opposition. This made possible a displacement and super-imposition of social class consciousness onto a desire for national autonomy and independence that remained legitimate and socially sanctioned under the repressive state. The displacement, in turn, allowed a critical reading of Taiwan's development in terms of neocolonialism, with the 'nation' as a whole being exploited and oppressed by Japan and the United States. Such a view became particularly relevant and persuasive in Taiwan's intellectual circles in the early 1970s, when a series of political events starkly exposed Taiwan's subordinate position in the international power structure and its dependency on the United States for political survival as a nation-state. Taiwan's forced departure from the United Nations upon the American withdrawal of support for its representation of China in 1971, and further erosion of its international support after the USA's *de facto* recognition of the Beijing regime at the time of Nixon's presidential visit, and Japan's severance of diplomatic ties with Taiwan in 1972, generated a sense of national subjugation among intellectuals that reinforced their perception of Taiwan's economic development as a case of neocolonial domination.

It is against this sense of national subjugation and neocolonial domination by foreign capitalist powers that a nationalist discourse found articulation in nativist literature. Featuring a 'realist' mode and focusing on the daily struggles of the 'nobodies' as they eke out a living in impoverished environments, particularly in the countryside or small provincial towns, this nativist literature was explicitly critical of the effects of state-directed importation of Western (capitalist) modernity on the native land and its inhabitants. In the represen-tation of concrete lives, the fictional works bring together issues of national dependence, social disintegration, cultural contamination, moral degeneration and social injustice arising from a Western-oriented capitalist modernity. In particular, some prominent nativist writers sought to resolve these issues in a nationalist discourse that projects the native place grounded in the rural village and its erstwhile traditions as a site of opposition. The link between national-ism and the rural village as the remaining base of traditional culture in modernity is spelt out as follows by Wang Tuo, a leading theorist and writer of the literature:

> Bombarded by foreign capital and foreign culture, cities in Taiwan have already been westernised to such an extent that they are not much different from the metropolises of Europe and the United States. This is the case with regard not only to the plainly visible physical constructions, but to human thoughts, values and ideas, as well as attitudes towards life. By comparison, villages have retained

more of traditional cultural characteristics and simple lifestyles, even though they have also undergone tremendous changes upon the penetration of industry and commerce. At the same time, village people often constitute a sacrificed and neglected group in a society changing rapidly under a policy that vigorously promotes industrial and commercial development. Their incomes are low, standard of living poor and work strenuous. It is, therefore, easy for the public to find fulfilment of both their nationalist sentiments and social conscience in fictions that make rural societies and village people their subject matter. (Wang Tuo 1978 [1977]: 116)

This extensive statement makes clear that whether the particular literary text focuses directly on the rural village or not, a hierarchical opposition between the urban and the rural underlies the nationalist discourse of nativist literature. At the same time, this urban–rural hierarchy is mapped onto a Western–native opposition. That is, if the Western-imported hegemonic discourse of modernity valorizes the urban space and the Western values it embraces, the nationalist discourse of nativist literature asserts its oppositionality by reversing the order of valuation and privileging the rural space and its native values. More importantly, in line with the patriarchal nature of both the rural traditions that the nationalist discourse seeks to reclaim and the urban Westernized values that it denounces, the rural–urban opposition is maintained and signified by diametrically different representations of the gendered bodies of women.

Urban Whores, Rural Mothers and the Moral Order of Nationalist Discourse

Feminist analyses of nationalisms around the world have shown the near ubiquity of the symbolic construction of the nation as Woman. In particular, women are typically figured as the biological and cultural reproducers of the nation, whose purity and chastity are thus vital to the nation's survival and identity, and who therefore need protection by their native sons (see, for example, Yuval-Davis and Anthias 1989, Chatterjee 1993, Katrak 1992, Kandiyoti 1991, Marecek 2000, Moran 2000). Central to nationalist discourses, then, are the double moves of valorizing women as mothers and disciplining the female body and sexuality. The nationalist discourse of Taiwan's nativist literature is no exception to this general pattern. As a critique of neocolonial development, however, it interestingly separates the two gender moves and maps them onto the rural–urban divide. In other words, it grounds its critique on bifurcated representations of women and their gendered bodies in the urban and rural symbolic spaces.

Symbolizing the urban space is the Westernized woman associated with foreign institutions and cultures, whose sexualized body becomes the signifier of corruption, decadence and immorality under Western materialism. A paradigmatic figure from a well-known piece of nativist fiction by the writer Wang Zhenhe serves as a good illustration. Mrs Wang is one of the main characters in the 1973 story 'Xiaolin came to Taipei' (1975), which offers a snapshot of urbanites working in an airline office in the capital city from the viewpoint of a recent rural migrant worker who still retains the value system of the native place. As a section chief in charge of the customer counter in the airline office, Mrs Wang is nevertheless not portrayed in her capacity as a worker, even though the workplace is the main scene in the story. Rather, she is graphically depicted as a sexualized body and, as such, an unfit mother totally lacking in moral values. Throughout the story, her very demeanour displays an aversion to maternal virtues: 'Though in her forties, Mrs. Wang sounds like a teenager. ... She speaks with an unnatural countenance and an affected manner ... "Ka-ji-ka-ji," [she] laughs with her whole body trembling so much that she seems to have more than two breasts' (Wang Zhenhe 1975: 224). Instead of a matronly figure that the story implies to befit her maternal status, Mrs Wang here features an over-sexualized body, with her seductive laughs and trembling breasts signifying loose morals and a misuse of the female body that prefigures her utter failure as a mother.[2] More specifically, her sexualization and attendant maternal failure are unequivocally attributed to her adoring submission to Western culture and the unruly materialism and compulsory consumption it cultivates.

In this configuration of Mrs Wang, then, Wang Zhenhe's story not only reveals a fear of social and moral disruption in the form of uncontrollable feminine sexuality that Wilson (1992) has shown to pervade (male) representations of urban life as a marker of modernity – a fear underlined by the story's perverse gaze on the indecently clad female bodies and sexually charged postures of the airline employees. It also establishes a concrete tie between such a fear and the ideological investment in native patriarchal motherhood, of which Mrs Wang's failure to command the obedience of her daughter serves as a negative reminder. In the nationalist rhetoric of the story, Westernization has turned Mrs Wang into a mindless slave of fashion and made her an undesirable model to her teenage daughter, who, like her, lusts after the latest imported fashion and throws a tantrum when she does not get her way. In fact, every woman working in the airline office features such a blind following of Western fashion, which reduces her to little more than a sexualized body to be gazed at and, at times, even groped. In this way, the sexualized bodies of women under Westernized culture serve as a primary sign of decadence, spiritual corruption and moral degeneration, with which the nation, especially its urban sector, is supposed to have become infested under a modernity directed and dominated by foreign interests.

The rural counterpart to this gendered representation of the urban space in the nationalist discourse of Taiwan's nativist literature is the overworked, sacrificing mother whose exhausted body is worn beyond her age by the demands made on her to support urban, Westernized lives under neocolonial development. In contrast to the consumption-driven, over-sexualized body of the Westernized woman inhabiting the urban space, this rural-based sacrificing mother is thoroughly desexualized and figured into a body of endless toil. Jinshuishen, the title character of an acclaimed 1975 nativist fiction by Wang Tuo (1979), illustrates this figure well. Married to a poor fisherman in a remote village, Jinshuishen is distinguished by her maternal achievement, as she carries out an unfailing daily run around the village peddling household odds and ends. By means of this back-breaking job, she has single-handedly raised and put through higher education six sons, who are now successful professionals and administrators enjoying well-to-do lives in the city. She herself, however, has to remain in her primitive, broken shed and continue the daily routine she has kept for almost two decades to support her family. Despite their well-paid jobs and comfortable lives, her sons continue to rely on her to raise money for their sumptuous weddings and business ventures. In the end, all her labours and sacrifices remain unreciprocated and unappreciated. With all her sons abandoning her to face, alone, the debts she has incurred on their behalf, Jinshuishen has to leave the village and become a migrant, temporary worker in the capital city.[3] Thus this sacrificing mother in the rural homeland remains an exploited working body even after she has supported her sons through 'progress' and development into modern living. With such a gendered figure, Wang Tuo's story gives the rural homeland a symbolic meaning of the exploited motherland urgently needing conscientious salvation from its native sons.

The figure of Jinshuishen is particularly telling of the gender politics of nationalist discourse, because her role as the family's primary breadwinner seems to defy the domestication of women that bespeaks the patriarchal underpinnings of most nationalist discourses. Like the story's implicit indictment of irresponsible fathers and unfilial sons, however, this unusual role for a mother serves precisely to underscore the abnormality of the current state of affairs and the need for men to resume their proper duties and relieve their mothers (and motherland) of undue burdens.[4] The story's affirmation of her ability and resilience notwithstanding, Jinshuishen is a paragon of maternal virtues who supports the traditional patriarchal order, rather than an example of female independence and personal development. Her positive portrayal may easily be read as advancing the feminist cause of valuing and affirming women's contribution to society and development. A renowned male writer and critic in Taiwan, Chen Yingzhen, exemplifies this position in his praise for the story's decentring of the dominant Chinese patriarchal order (1979: 11–2).

Against the misogynist tendency of nativist writers such as Wang Zhenhe in blaming women for the woes of the nation, the affirmative representation of Jinshuishen certainly deserves critical appreciation. Yet it must be pointed out that the enduring maternal sacrifices embodied by Jinshuishen are simply the flipside of Chinese patriarchy. Indeed, Jinshuishen's exemplary compliance with the demands of the patriarchal order on female bodies is precisely what makes her a venerable mother in the text:

> In this small remote fishing village, Badouzi, there are two names which no one will find unfamiliar when spoken of. One is the Sacred Mother Mazu in the Temple of Heaven Access, the other is the peddler Jinshuishen. Jinshuishen is so famous in Badouzi for two reasons. First … because of [her] occupational convenience, she naturally has a thorough knowledge of family matters, big or small, in every single home of Badouzi … So, imperceptibly, her position appears to be extremely important. Second, she has become a subject of respect and envy among most of the parents in Badouzi, not only because her belly gave her credit, having borne altogether six sons, but also because her sons are good achievers … That is why whenever Jinshuishen is mentioned, people in Badouzi invariably put their thumbs up and praise her from the bottom of their hearts. (Wang Tuo 1979: 190–91)

The metaphoric association of Jinshuishen with the Sacred Mother Mazu here and elsewhere in the text highlights and affirms her primary identity as an exemplary mother sacrificing herself to meet the demands of the patriarchal order. Her maternal support of traditional patriarchy is further crystallized in her persistence to justify her existence in relation to her sons and absolve them from blame for her exploited and oppressed life:

> Every time she suffered from her husband's irrational kicking and beatings, it was always this son who consoled her, giving her infinite hope, even in the midst of pain, for the future and for her sons, as well as the courage to live on in times when she contemplated suicide or running away from the family. … But now … she thought [about her son's neglect] over and over again, and still could not understand. How come such a filial son suddenly changed in this way? If it weren't for someone constantly abetting him close by, how could he become like this? While she was thinking this, the quietly smiling countenance of Axiu [her daughter-in-law] crossed her mind and doubts rose in her heart. (Wang Tuo 1979: 221–2)

With this displacement of unfilial behaviour from native sons to urbanized women like Jinshuishen's daughters-in-law, who value materialistic pleasures over moral responsibilities and filial duties, Wang Tuo's story simultaneously represents the nation as an overdrawn mother in need of the care of her sons and absolves the native sons from any wrongdoing except for listening to women corrupted by the consumer orientation of modern urban life. This, in effect, constitutes a double call for men to resume their patriarchal duty of controlling women in the name of protecting the mother-nation.

Between the sexualized body of the urban Westernized woman and the overworked body of the rural sacrificing mother, then, Taiwan's nativist literature depicts an immoral social order under neocolonial development that is organized around materialistic values. Against this immoral order, it inscribes a nationalist alternative of returning to native moral traditions that will reverse the hierarchy of value under neocolonial development and restore the national order. In sum, the bifurcated representation of women under neocolonial development enables nativist writers of nationalist persuasions to figure the problem of neocolonial development in terms of the erosion of traditional values, especially familial ethics, and thereby to imagine and articulate an oppositional position in the advancement of a national order that restores the place and power of filial sons and compassionate patriarchs who will look after the exhausted mother (and motherland), as well as control the urban excess of Westernized, sexualized bodies.

Women and the Ideological Representation of Neocolonial Development

Based on a gendered figuration of the problem of neocolonial development, this nationalist discourse constitutes an ideological representation and resolution of neocolonial development in two significant ways. First, it is obviously ideological in its feminization of materialistic consumption as a major sign of national malaise under neocolonial development. As feminist scholars such as Felski (1995) have shown, the feminization of consumption has been a common cultural response to the rapid changes of modernity even in the West, encompassing in it the fear of emasculation and weakening of men's traditional authority over women because of pervasive commodification. In the present case, such a representation has the additional effect of displacing what is essentially a political-economic issue, the loss of national control over the means and ends of production, onto a cultural-moral realm of patriarchal control over the conduct of women. This means that by ideologically representing their sense of loss of national control under neocolonial development in terms of the abrogation of patriarchal authority and responsibility, nationalist intellectuals can find solace in a cultural resolution of the political economic issue of control over the national economy. The ideological representation allows them to imagine that, once the traditional patriarchal order is restored and men resume their rightful place as benevolent fathers, powerful husbands and filial sons, the nation will also regain control of its own destiny and put up resistance against neocolonial domination from foreign capitalist powers.

In pointing out this ideological nature of the nationalist critique, I do not mean to suggest that the cultural constitution of national identity is a secondary issue to political economy. Rather, it is a reminder that nationalist sentiments and cultural concerns can be mobilized for ideological resolution of political economic issues over which intellectuals do not have control, leading to a consolidation of oppressive gender traditions. The relation between women, culture and development, then, can be better understood if the ideological construction of the nationalist critique is carefully unpacked.

Because of the nationalist subtext motivating its representation of women's relation to neocolonial development, Taiwan's nativist literature also renders an ideological representation of the problem of neocolonial development for women. In particular, its bifurcated representation of women under neocolonial development as Westernized urban whores and hard-working rural mothers elides both the significance of women as industrial waged labourers and the specifically gendered exploitation that female workers experience. Especially notable here are the large number of young women drawn from rural villages to work in foreign-operated factories because of their supposed docility and nimbleness, and the urban housewives working under the state-sponsored programme of 'living room factories' that sought to exploit family and neighbourhood female labour by bringing factory work to the family living rooms (Hsiung 1996). With the elision of their significance in the production and reproduction of neocolonial development, the complex interaction between gender ideology and women's exploitation under neocolonial development is grossly simplified and neglected in nativist literature's nationalist discourse.[5]

Furthermore, the location of the problem of sexualization in urban Westernized women also obscures the nature of women's sexual commodification under neocolonial development. The moral order the nationalist discourse inscribes through this representation leaves no room for confronting the issue of women's reduction to sexualized bodies under neocolonial development as a political economic problem of prostitution, rather than a moral problem of the erosion of traditional values. Hence, although the phenomenon of prostitution is thematized in some nativist fictional works, it is invariably presented as a sign of moral degeneration and national subjugation under neocolonial development. That it constitutes a specific form of female labour intimately tied to the global political economy, and particularly symptomatic of neocolonial development, finds little articulation in the moral rhetoric of the nationalist discourse. In more concrete terms, any critical reflection on the state's implicit endorsement of the sex trade to enhance local tourist attraction in response to efforts of the United States and international financial organizations to promote tourism as a development strategy for the Third World is eclipsed by the moral orientation of this nationalist discourse (Truong 1990).

The ideological limitation of such a moral orientation is particularly apparent in its blindness to the compatibility of an emphasis on cultural traditions and the sexual commodification of women under neocolonial development. As feminists in Taiwan have pointed out, Chinese cultural traditions have been actively mobilized to facilitate the development of the sex trade in Taiwan. For instance, promotional campaigns endorsed by government agencies and tourist industries to widen the market of visitors have emphasized the traditional virtues of Chinese women, such as female submissiveness, caring and nurturing, in addition to sexual temptation (Cheng and Hsiung 1992: 246). At the same time, the traditional normatization of feminine self-sacrifice and submissiveness enhances the supply of labour to the sex trade, as dutiful daughters are compelled or forced into prostitution to support the family or finance the education of their brothers. Where women are concerned, then, a continuation of traditional culture and the patriarchal order it legitimizes by no means constitutes an effective opposition to neocolonial development, however strongly the nationalist discourse of Taiwan's nativist literature asserts otherwise.

The inherently phallocentric orientation of this nationalist critique, and its consequent mystification of the material condition and subjective experience of women's sexual commodification under neocolonial development, can be seen clearly in a story about prostitution by Huang Chunming, one of Taiwan's foremost nativist writers. Arguably Huang's most noted work, 'Shayonala, zaijian' (1973; the title gives the Japanese and Chinese words for 'good-bye') gives a first-person narration of the moral dilemma of a professed nationalist whose boss has ordered him to take a group of Japanese businessmen to visit local whorehouses in his hometown. To fulfil his duty as the provider and protector of his wife and child, this nationalist rationalizes, he has no choice but to do as his boss bids. However, he remains torn over the assignment and the story follows his mental and emotional struggle as he negotiates his way through the role of a reluctant but complicitous comprador in the trading of his female compatriots' bodies. Given the story's exclusive focus on the male nationalist's consciousness, little is said about the young women working in the brothel, and is anyway filtered through the mind of the male nationalist. Thus, in a story that places the sex trade at the heart of Taiwan's problematic commerce with global capitalism, prostitution is primarily a metaphor for the predicament of the male nationalist caught in the battle of survival. The young women are once again reduced to sexual bodies over which the male nationalist inscribes his own resistance to mental prostitution.

However compulsory the male narrator in 'Shayonala' considers his selling of himself to global capitalism, he manages to maintain the self-identity of a nationalist and neutralize the power of the Japanese through a surreptitious use of nationalist discourse. Under the pretext of interpreting between a Taiwanese university student and the Japanese businessmen, he interrogates the Japanese about their participation in Japan's imperialist war against China and challenges them to confront their shameful history. While this does not take away his guilt as a national pimp, it affords him a sense of power and moral victory over the Japanese that is totally denied the female prostitutes. Indeed, if his nationalism enables the male narrator to claim an oppositional subjectivity, it does so partly by usurping the voices of the female prostitutes, appropriating their experiences and representing them as defenceless victims of neocolonial development and symbols of a morally superior nation dominated by the power of economic wealth (see Lai 1998: 45–6 for a more detailed discussion). This is particularly clear in the following scene: when one of the prostitutes jokingly repeats a line from a popular local opera to ward off the groping hands of a Japanese who is not her main client, the narrator turns this clever self-defence of a savvy professional into an unconscious display of national cultural superiority: 'Of course, Xiaowen said "A friend's wife is not to be taken advantage of" only casually, allowing none but Ochiai to touch her. Still, I thought, Xiaowen is a Chinese after all. Though she is a prostitute, she is superior to this group of Japanese when it comes to civilization of some sort' (Huang 1973: 244). Thus the nationalist discourse of the male narrator elides Xiaowen and the other young women's subjective understanding of their situation and resistance to sexual objectification and commodification, claiming their experiences for its own purpose.

Working Daughters and the Critique of Sexual Commodification

Given such elision of women's subjective experiences and usurpation of their voices in the nationalist critique of neocolonial development, a recentring of women's experiences and voices is necessary for and suggestive of a more inclusive and enabling challenge to neocolonial development. Tellingly, there are no women among the writers commonly identified with Taiwan's nativist literature. One who associated closely with nativist writers and was sympathetic to their nationalist sentiments is Zeng Xinyi. Based on her personal experiences and observations of friends and acquaintances, Zeng's short stories focus on the plights, sacrifices and consciousness of young women struggling to make a living in the harshly competitive urban environment of a country under capitalist development. As working daughters, the protagonists in many of her stories were compelled by circumstances into various forms of the sex trade to support themselves and their families. The most representative of these stories is 'Yige shijiusui shaonu de gushi' ('The story of a nineteen year-old girl', 1977), which describes the life of a teenager who quits school to work in a dance club. It details the dire poverty and familial pressure that push the young girl onto this path, the exploitation and indignity she suffers at work and the almost insurmountable obstacles against her wish to leave the sex trade and resume a normal life. In an authorial statement, Zeng reveals that the theme of the story has preoccupied her for ten years and she was driven to it by an 'imminent fact':

> For years, I have seen too many teenage girls around me resolutely give up pursuing their personal happiness to enter the sex trade in order to relieve their family destitution. Based on my understanding of the life of a sex worker, I firmly believe that their sacrifice is a cruel tragedy. It can only alleviate the emergency at hand, but cannot solve the fundamental problem. The price they pay for their sacrifice is so tremendous that I have to say: it is not worth it! I absolutely oppose making such a choice because of economic problems. ... Through publication, I hope to let more teenage girls facing the same problem read this story, and also let people see a horrible fact through fictional writing. (1977a: 12)

Zeng's motivation and approach to the theme of prostitution are thus firmly grounded in the reality and standpoint of struggling young women. Notably absent from her handling of the theme is the moralistic nationalist rhetoric that characterizes (male) nativist writers' treatment, though Zeng clearly disapproves of the women's choices. Instead, her stories on sex workers focus on the exploitation and oppression these women suffer on and off the job, as do her other stories on women working as salesgirls and other petty commercial jobs. Thus, her stories in effect situate the problem of prostitution in the pervasive commodification and exploitation of women under capitalist modernity.

That prostitution is but the crystallization of a rampant sexual exploitation and commodification of women in a profit-oriented and money-driven economy is made explicit in one of Zeng's most noted stories, 'Caifeng de xinyuan' ('Caifeng's wish', 1978). Caifeng, the title character of the story, is a salesgirl in a department store which seeks to promote sales by organizing an open beauty-cum-singing contest where customers convert their sales receipts into votes for the contestants. Chosen to represent the store in the contest, Caifeng is ambivalent about her chance of becoming a 'future star', vacillating between hope for fulfilling her wish to escape poverty and support her parents and dread of the predatory attention that dogs her as she 'works' to muster votes for herself. With rumours that some contestants are willing to exchange sexual favours for votes, she feels pressured at least to go out with some senior managers and big customers who obviously have designs on her. Dining with one such customer tempts her to become his mistress, in exchange for the luxurious living and material comforts that he presents. Another customer, the owner of a 'restaurant', offers her an in-house singer position. Naïvely taking this to be an opportunity to embark on a singing career, she accepts the offer and goes to work after a runner-up finish in the contest. What she finds is a covert prostitution ring and a first assignment of spending the night with a Japanese businessman. The story ends on an anti-imperialist note, with Caifeng facing the Japanese as an old picture flashes across her eyes: 'roadside execution ground / a kneeling Chinese with hands bound behind the back / a leveled neck with head chopped off / Japanese military wielding a crescent shiny sword / head by the sword, hanging in the air / what a painful, silent countenance, that head hanging in the air' (1978: 42).

This plot scheme allows Zeng to show both the female body's multiple levels of exploitation under capitalist development and the struggle of a working daughter to negotiate her way through the traps of sexual commodification, while suggesting a neocolonial dimension to the plight of women in Taiwan. If nativist literature's nationalist critique of neocolonial development relies on a culturalism that constructs the problem in terms of a feminine disorder of materialistic consumption as discussed above, 'Caifeng de xinyuan' implicitly returns the problem to a fundamental issue of power and control over (re)productive bodies. Rather than insatiable consumers, it presents women as exploited workers whose bodies are constantly under surveillance and often sexualized by men in a profit-oriented economy to sell products and spur consumption. To highlight the materiality of women's exploitation, the narrative begins with a description of the gruelling working conditions of Caifeng and her fellow salesgirls:

After punching the time-cards, [the salesgirls] happily put the cards back and are anxious to rush out of the store; but there is still another hurdle. The uniformed male guards are still patiently checking the bags and clothes of each salesgirl ...

Who would ever think about stealing goods from the store! We are checked everyday going in and out. How lowly they see us! The supervisors keep strict control on the merchandise, checking stocks every month. If anything is missing or broken in any way, we have to pay. Is that not supervision enough? ...

Huh, we come to work early everyday. The streets are still quiet when we arrive. We stand in the store the whole day, not being allowed to go out or look out even for a minute. We don't even know if it is sunny or rainy. Soon, we will forget even what the sun looks like. By the time we leave work, it is already so late that people have finished all their goings and bustlings. (1978: 1–4)

From the points of view of Caifeng and her colleagues, then, women are indeed intimately caught up in the web of consumption in the capitalist economy – but as workers, not leisured consumers. The indignity and objectification they experience in their strictly regimented work of seducing customers to the glamorous goods offered by capitalism, furthermore suggest that the difference between 'proper' employment for women and prostitution may well be a matter of degree rather than substance. In the face of such a reality for women, the moral approach of the nationalist critique of neo-colonial development appears lame and ineffectual. A faithful representation of this reality, such as Zeng's story is, in comparison, a far more powerful and effective critique of the exploitative and oppressive nature of development under capitalism.

Conclusion

In the 20 or so years since the height of nativist fiction and its nationalist sentiment much has changed in Taiwan. By transforming itself from a struggling developing country to an export powerhouse and importer of foreign workers, Taiwan has achieved the once almost unthinkable in terms of development. With the changing tides, the nationalist outcry against neo-colonial development has faded into distant memory. Yet it may be argued that the issues raised here about women, culture and development *vis-à-vis* the nationalist rhetoric of nativist fiction are no less relevant today in Taiwan, albeit in something of an inversion. Women, once again, are at the centre of cultural imaginings and representations, as the 'nation' of Taiwan wrestles with the problem and anxiety of its identity and its relation to mainland China, where the bulk of its investment has gone in pursuit of capitalist profit. This is epitomized in media construction in the mid-1990s of the figure of *dalumei* ('mainland sister'), who is typically a mainland woman employed in various forms of sex trade in Taiwan, sometimes in disguise as a native (Shih 1998). The threat of mainland China to the national identity and survival of Taiwan, the moral unease generated by the monetary and materialistic obsession of capitalist development, and Taiwan's insecurity over its newfound capital and industrial power, all find cultural expressions in this representation of mainland women. With such a familiar displacement, the material reality and subjective experiences of mainland Chinese women in the crossroads of the economic development of Taiwan and China are rendered invisible and inaudible.

Similarly elided are the experiences of Taiwanese women, whose desires and struggles for equality are thwarted by the sexual exploits of Taiwanese men with mainland women. This double elision and the opposing interests involved pose a particular challenge to feminist critique of the exploitation and oppression of women under Taiwan's current phase of development. Confronting the problem, feminists in Taiwan have yet to find a satisfactory way of championing the cause of native sisters *and* challenging the media representations of mainland women. At issue is a problem of (re)configuring global–local relations that feminists will perhaps increasingly face, as global capitalism races furiously along a multicultural track.

While an effective strategy to deal with such a problem will no doubt be context-specific, our consideration of Taiwan's experiences affords a useful lesson. To uncover the intricate complexity of the commonly linked, but apparently opposing, interests of women located across national boundaries under global capitalism, feminists need to go beyond, but remain cognizant of, the territorial and discursive boundaries encoded in the idea of the nation. For feminists in Taiwan, it means that they have to suspend their primary identification with Taiwanese women, and accord equal attention and importance to the experiences of mainland women under Taiwan's economic advancement into their homeland. Only then can they untangle the web of nationalism and see the structural exploitation and oppression of both Taiwanese and mainland women under the dominant mode of economic development. Without such a transnational vision, which enables a critique of the simultaneous systemic erosion and clever manipulation of national boundaries that facilitate the far-reaching exploitation and commodification of female bodies under global capitalism, feminists may have a hard time building coalitions which can effectively check the divide-and-conquer momentum of the patriarchal capitalist machine.

Notes

1. As of 1970, US and Japanese capital accounted for 85 per cent of Taiwan's investment. See Gold (1986: 76–87) for a summary of the role of foreign capital in Taiwan's post-war economic development, and Hsiung (1981: 179–87) on the domination of the USA and Japan in foreign trade.

2. It is noteworthy that Mrs Wang's last name in Chinese signifies a body of water; and with familiar phrases like *shuixing yanghua* (literally, 'having the characteristics of water and flowers swaying in the wind'), water when associated with woman often carries the negative connotation of infidelity and promiscuity.

3. Persistent in its rural focus, the story gives no direct description of Jinshuishen's life in the city. The information about her working as a domestic help to repay the family debts before returning to the village is related through a villager, who chanced upon her praying in a temple in the city for the well-being of her sons in an inauspicious year. This brief description suggests that she basically continues in the city the old pattern of her life as an overworked and sacrificing mother. Her representation as the quintessential mother(land) in the story is thus reinforced.

4. Whether the unfilial sons of Jinshuishen are up to such duties is another matter. The point of the story, according to this reading, is to call the attention of readers, especially the native sons of Taiwan, to the plight of their mother(land) and their responsibilities towards her. The real hope lies with the readers rather than Jinshuishen's sons. In this light, how readers view the sons and respond to the call is particularly interesting. Unfortunately, such information is not readily available.

5. The plight of female factory workers is not totally neglected in Taiwan's nativist literature. Yang Qingchu, a nativist writer who once worked in a factory himself, has written a series of short stories on 'the circle of factory girls' (1978), describing the problems of the lack of compensation for work injury, the violation of sick leave

benefits, sexual discrimination in employment and promotion, and sexual harassment in the workplace. Notably, however, Yang's stories do not extend the level of engagement to questions of neocolonial development and nationalist resistance. Thus, they fall outside the framework of nationalist discourse and critique under consideration in this chapter. Without the trappings of a nationalist discourse, the class-based critique of capitalist development that simultaneously informs Taiwan's nativist literature in the 1970s becomes rather evident in Yang's stories about factory workers, for which he was particularly known and from which the series on factory girls was a spinoff. Rather than a nationalist attribution of all the 'evils' of capitalist development to foreigners and Western(ized) culture, Yang's stories focus on 'native' factory owners and the local management of foreign-owned factories as the immediate culprits in the exploitation and mistreatment of workers. While most of the stories do not go beyond a phenomenological description of the workers' experiences and the problems they face, some betray an implicit socialist persuasion, articulating hope for a better future with the establishment of independent unions and even worker-owned factories. As reflected in this focus on class, however, the stories about female factory workers tend to overlook the gender ideology underlying the employment and working conditions of women, and treat gender-specific problems such as sexual harassment as secondary issues that are subordinate to the larger problem of economic exploitation. For this reason, though Yang's factory girl stories are noteworthy for their exceptional attention to a neglected group and sensitivity to the gender-specific problems that female workers face, they still obscure the complexity of women's relation to development.

CHAPTER 10

The Representation of the Mostaz'af/ 'the Disempowered' in Revolutionary and Post-revolutionary Iran

Minoo Moallem

Ideologies 'work' by constructing for their subjects (individual and collective) positions of identification and knowledge which allow them to 'utter' ideological truths as if they were their authentic and unified experience, not because they emanate from our innermost, authentic and unified experience, but because we find ourselves mirrored in the positions at the center of the discourses from which the statements we formulate 'make sense.' Thus the same 'subjects' (e.g., economic classes or ethnic groups) can be differently constructed in different ideologies. (Stuart Hall 1995: 19)

Zainab: Brother, you were never like this,
Never so alarmed and concerned as this ...

(from the *Ta'ziyeh* [a religious performance referring to the tragic battle of Karbala in AD 680] of the martyrdom of Ali Akbar)

They cut my roots off; I am growing from the stem. (Tahmineh Milani, 2001)

§ THE Iranian revolution of 1979 exemplified the importance of visual media for postmodern social revolutions.[1] Fifteen years before the extensive application of information technologies by the Zapatistas in Chiapas, the 'cassette revolution' (to use Foucault's phrase) in Iran played a key role in 'putting into meaning', in Stuart Hall's terms, the revolution as a unified event. It was able to do so by creating an oppositional collective will and by calling upon various groups of people to take part in the revolutionary process – a process which led to the production of a revolutionary discourse that became antecedent to its agents and actors, defining the temporality of the revolution – its pre-, during and post phases. In other words, particular meanings inhered in the events of the revolution. It also enabled the production of the revolution both as the possession of all its participants and as the charge of 'true revolutionaries' in the post-revolutionary era.

In his reflections on culture and social revolutions, John Foran (1997) has noted that scholarship on social revolutions and movements of resistance can benefit from the theoretical contributions of cultural studies, Foucauldian post-structualism and post-colonial studies by tracing the importance of culture in shaping political action, contributing to what he calls Third World cultural studies. Foran's proposal is productive in breaking with both the more conventional sociological theories of revolution and the new social movement frameworks, because it attempts to grapple with issues of power, discourse and subject formation. However, it still leaves out the significant contribution of feminist transnational and post-colonial studies and the importance of gender and sexuality in understanding revolution both as a social event and as a discourse. I agree with Grewal and Kaplan (1994: 9) when they argue that 'it is impossible to analyze postmodernity without an understanding of geopolitics, it is difficult to make sense of the theories of culture emanating from economics and political theory without a clear connection to theories of the postmodern'. Building on feminist scholarship that writes women into the history of modern revolutions has been crucial for understanding what Emma Perez (1999: 55) calls 'a feminism-in-nationalism'. In addition, women's entry in revolutionary and decolonization movements has been essential in unsettling gender constructions (Lazreg 1994, Moallem 1999, 1999a). By focusing on the question of social resistance and women's agency in the context of feminist studies, cultural studies and Third World development studies, the editors of this volume have provided a fertile ground for discussions of gender and social revolutions.

Modern revolutions as discourse, fashion and cultural spectacles as well as historical events have been an important part of modernity and postmodernity. While the modern narratological frame of revolutions, with its temporal reliance on 'progress', requires a radical break with the premodern past and the birth of the nation-state and citizenship under the leadership of a revolutionary avant-garde, postmodern revolutions have thrown into crisis – both spatially and temporally – the linear narrative of revolutions by their capacity to engage with the new material and cultural conditions of a global world. The compression of time and space via information technologies has created new spaces for revolutionary subject formation and the circulation of 'revolutions' in the world of media and markets.

The twentieth century is marked by Third World revolutions, launched both by modernizing governments from above and by masses of people from below. These revolutions are particular in their pro-/anti-colonial, pro-/anti-imperialist and pro-/anti-West components.[2] In this chapter, I will investigate:

- The notion of *mostaz'af* (the 'disempowered') which came into the political discourse in the context of the Iranian revolution of 1979 and provided space for the emergence of an Islamic subject.
- Its capacity to unify various groups of people in a gender-divided community of brothers and sisters.
- Its potential to address both the local and the global.
- The ways in which *mostaz'af* has been thrown into crisis in the context of post-revolutionary cinema.

I am interested in this concept, first, because of its relationship to the pluralized moment of the revolution and second, its importance as an emblem of the new sign system, which changed a religious system into a militant system. By a pluralized moment of revolution I intend to draw attention to the temporality of revolution as an event with multiple points of entry. I omit any discussion here of revolution from above, specifically the Shah's 'White Revolution' and the Islamic Republic's cultural revolution. I would like to emphasize not only the important role of the media in the exercise of revolutionary hegemony, in unifying masses of people regardless of their gender, class, ethnic, rural or urban locations, but also the ways in which the media are implicated in the production of reduced or even oppositional readings of hegemonic discourses.[3]

While the revolutionary period was characterized by the intensive negotiation of contesting political forces, certain notions such as *mostaz'af* enabled the renegotiation of hegemony by reconstructing a central consensus through which the revolutionary reality could be disciplined. It was in the name of the *mostaz'af* that Khomeini led the revolution. The power of *mostaz'af* is not only in its polysemy and its capacity to bring together both different experiences and identities, as well as popular and high culture, but also in the ways in which it could bring the local and the global into the same frame of reference. On a number of occasions, Ayatollah Khomeini (1984) called for the breakdown of idolatry in the world and unity of all Muslims of the world with the disempowered *mostaz'afan* of the world.

Not a Class War but a War of Position: The *Mostaz'af* and the *Mostakbar*/'the Powerful'

> Hail, Muslims of the world, and the *mostaz'afan* under the rule of the oppressors, rise and unite and defend Islam and your destinies, and don't be afraid of the tumult of those in power because with the will of god, this century is the century of the victory of the *mostaz'afan* over the *mostakbaran* and justice over falsehood. (Ayatollah Khomeini 1984: 116)

The *mostaz'af* provided space for the formation of a unified, religious, nationalist, oppositional subject. This concept unifies all those who had been disempowered both nationally and internationally. It also bridges the public and the private spheres, since *mostaz'af* incorporates the notion of *za'if* which refers to somebody who is weak. Traditionally, the word *zaifeh*, which derives from *zaif*, was coded as feminine, referring to a woman who lives under the protection of a man. *Mostaz'af* as a concept has the power of mobilizing both protectors and protected under the banner of Islam. In the case of men, the word has the power of mobilizing men who have been emasculated in the process of colonization and modernization. In the case of women, it refers to the disempowerment and objectification of women by consumer capitalism, and their need for mobilization, under the sign of the *mostaz'af*. Thus, *mostaz'af* brought together various classes and ethnic groups to create a religious nationalist community, an Islamic *ummat*, the invocation of which created space for a revolutionary position that addresses the deterritorialization of the nation-state and refers to subalternity as located both with/in and with/out the nation.[4] The concept imbricates power relations in cultural, political and economic spheres; it has the potential, therefore, to speak for those subjects who are being put in a position of powerlessness in multiple ways.[5] So the religious meanings found linguistic expression for the militancy of the *mostaz'af* in their opposition to the *mostakbar*. Both positions were seen as illegitimate, since they represented either a surplus or a deficit of power, wealth and privilege. However, the cultural religious nationalist effort to give the *mostaz'af* a voice, and the voice of the *mostaz'af* being constructed as the voice of authenticity, was central in what Foucault calls the 'authentification of the revolution' (1994: 759).

It should be noted that *mostaz'af* functioned as an indigenous concept, to be distinguished from the modern and imported concepts of the left – such as proletariat, *ranjbaran* ('labourers') *karegaran* ('workers'), *dehaghanan* ('peasants') which referred rather to the exploitative nature of the Shah's regime. Ayatollah Khomeini used the concept of *mostaz'af* to marginalize competing nationalist, Marxist and socialist groups. Far from being an avant-garde group, the *mostaz'af* included all those who were disempowered, both locally and globally. *Mostaz'af* as a concept and as a signifier linked the local and the global, not in a class war but in a war of position.[6] The concept created linkages between the local and the global by its identification of power as both temporal and spatial relations. In this process, culture became the main locus of power, and the cultural nationalist framework of an Islamic vision placed the *mostaz'af* at once in a polar and oppositional relation with *mostakbar*. It was used to undermine the diversity and particularities of revolutionary struggles – from the general strike of oil workers to the mass participation of women, from the demands of ethnic and religious minorities to peasant revolts. It also blurred differences between urban and rural classes.

While multiple contestations were the order of the day during the revolution, the work of hegemony made it possible for the discourse of revolution to invest power in particular values and concepts by winning the consent of those who participated in the revolution for varied and sometimes antagonistic reasons. In this context, the discourse of revolution engages with particular images and signifiers, enabling the unification of multiplicity and easing the transmission of power from one state elite to another. Such unification was an important tool in bringing together the contradictory demands of the various groups participating in the revolution, by creating an oppositional framework that worked effectively to put an end to the Shah's reign. The unification enabled a positioning beyond the modernist categories of worker, labourer or proletariat to create space for fluidity and multiplicity, including various classes and groups. In addition, this category was able to address the disempowered not as an abstract category, but as those located in particular cultural and religious traditions. As a result, it was able to distinguish itself from the humanist subject of modernist revolutionary discourses both of secular nationalists and various groups on the left. Ayatollah Khomeini challenges the idea of the 'classless human' proposed by a student (*talabeh*) of Islam. He states:

> These groups of people, who have emerged and are from a religious background, are likeable but they are mistaken ... They think Islam has come to make a classless human ... meaning that they all have to live in the same way in this world and there should be one state that would support them. They all have to pay taxes to the state and serve it at the same time. (1994: 12)

The idea of a 'classless' society entered Iranian revolutionary discourse via the Marxist-Leninist left and was transcoded by Islamist groups as 'classless monotheistic society'. Khomeini, in his attempt to claim an indigenous discursive space – *na sharghi, na gharbi, jomhouri-yi eslami* ('neither west nor east, but an Islamic Republic') – interrupted such discursive continuity. In the post-revolutionary era, numerous groups who participated in the revolution – from the oil workers whose strike immobilized the machinery of the Shah's economy, through peasant land claims to women's movements of resistance – were suppressed and rendered abject in the name of the revolution. Those who gained power through hegemony then became the protectors of revolutionary values, containing conflict and contradiction. For example, the massive participation of women in demonstrations against imposed veiling in Tehran was condemned by various fractions of the revolutionary movement, both secular and religious, as an act of collaboration of women both with the Westernized elite of the *ancien régime* and its ignorant victims, such as entertainers and prostitutes. The participation of some of the prostitutes and women entertainers in demonstrations was used to condemn the misbehaviour of 'good revolutionary' women in keeping with the oppositional models of femininity.[7] Women were blamed for betraying the revolutionary ideals by their intentional and unintentional collaboration with the counter-revolutionary forces that were distracting the revolution from its primary concerns.

By blurring the boundaries of 'respectability' separating pure from impure women, and by transgressing the revolutionary/counter-revolutionary border, women became the first to need disciplining and containment within the terms of revolutionary discourse. The epithets *mostakbar* and *mostaz'af* were applied as markers of boundaries between those who had access to representational power (even though their power was illegitimate, since it belonged to the contaminated spheres of the *ancien régime* and the West) and those who did not have power. As a result of a particular system of signs, which emphasized a constant antagonism between the *mostakbar* and the *mostaz'af* as signifiers of revolutionary and counter-revolutionary subjectivities, militant religious and cultural meanings became the main focus of regulatory forces of the new state elite in a post-revolutionary era. Through the production of both gendered bodies and Muslim bodies as the surface on which an Islamic nation could be inscribed, inclusive of the *mostaz'af* in opposition to the *mostakbar*, the cultural and religious nationalists were able to write their meanings onto the events of the revolution. However, in the context of the post-revolutionary cinema, *mostaz'af* as a category has been thrown into crisis because of the narration of the Islamic nation in the territorial space of the nation-state, which is divided by gender, sexuality, class and ethnicity.[8]

Cinema and Post-coloniality

The emergence of a vital and internationally competitive Iranian cinema, characterized by its representation of women and youth, marks the active participation of a Third World country in the fabrication of a global media reality. Third World cinema, in general, is challenging the stereotype of the Third World as passive consumer of First World cultural productions. As Shohat and Stam argue, while 'Third worldist filmmakers see themselves as part of a national project, the concept of national is contradictory, the site of competing discourses' (1994a: 285). The post-colonial reality is marked by mimicry and the global circulation of images that are reinscribed and reinvented in the context of particular localities. Also, the consumer capacity of a transnational audience, located in both the First and Third Worlds, influences such filmic production. Themes emerging in the Iranian cinema appeal not only to domestic audiences but to Iranians in the diaspora, engaging them not as political subjects in Iran but as cultural subjects *vis-à-vis* Iranian cultural productions. One could make the claim that non-mainstream films are beneficiaries of the fluid exchanges between the domestic cinema and diasporic audiences.

Iranian cinema emerged in the pre-revolutionary period with a high level of domestic production and a regular international film festival. In the early 1970s, with the appearance of the Iranian 'new wave', Iranian intellectuals began to use film as a medium to reach a mass audience and to communicate their critiques of Iranian society. As noted by Akrami (1987: 132), while large doses of violence and sex were permitted, harsh censorship was imposed in both the domestic and export market on films dealing with political topics. The state was supportive of non-threatening films and those glorifying the Pahlavi regime, and the private sector continued to invest in cheap and safe melodramas called 'film Farsi'.

In the aftermath of the revolution, the state embarked on a project of nationalization and Islamization of Iranian cinema. It began banning and blocking both foreign films and the mainstream 'film Farsi'. Paradoxically, this allowed space for the politicized new wave cinema. The Islamic Republic, which came out of an image-based revolution, took numerous measures to 'decontaminate' the media from the pro-West Pahlavi culture industry. With the elimination of the 'film Farsi' and state investment in the production of the media that matched revolutionary ideals, cinema gradually became a most desirable space for active participation.[9]

While the history of post-revolutionary Iranian cinema is beyond the scope of this chapter, it is worth noting that its filmmakers have focused extensively on the themes of children and women, not only as objects, but as subjects and agents both in the making and unmaking of the nation. While in many cases women and children are represented as the markers of national boundaries and the uniqueness of the Iranian Islamic nation, some films have used both women and children as subversive models of subjectivity. They are portrayed as fragmented and unintegrated subjects, signifying the impossibility of the completion of the cultural nationalist project. The representation of children necessarily deals with the period of subject formation, of 'one's becoming' as a gendered, sexualized, classed and nationalized subject.

In a recent film, *The Day I Became a Woman*, a triptych of connected stories directed by Marzieh Meshkini, Hava's transition into adulthood at the age of nine is marked by her sexualization and genderization – she is asked not to play with the boys any more and to recognize and conform to dominant models of femininity. At the same time she undergoes her 'nationalization'; she is asked to wear the veil as a marker of her citizenship in an Islamic nation. However, the protagonists in all three stories – a young girl (Hava), a married woman (Ahoo) and an older woman (Houra) – refuse to be unitary and complicit subjects because of the need to fulfil their own desires. Representing three passages in a woman's life, they fail to comply with the pressures of gender and national forms of subjectivity and respectability. Hava takes pleasure in sexual transgression by sharing the oral pleasure of sucking the same lollipop with her male friend Hassan in the last hours before she becomes a woman.' Ahoo, a young woman, escapes her marriage and family pressures to conform by taking a competitive bicycle ride along the coast with other young women. Houra, an older woman, uses an inherited legacy to buy all the domestic goods she has coveted in her lifetime, and takes them along with her on a seaside adventure. She fulfils Hava's childhood desire for a forbidden boat ride. Children encounter the culture and politics as 'subjects in formation', and therefore undermine the taken-for-granted realm in various forms of nationalism.

Mostaz'af in the Post-revolutionary Cinema

Modern information technologies – from cassettes to cinema and TV – not only played an important role in the success of the Iranian revolution, but also remain a crucial site of cultural and political negotiations in Iran. With the dominance of visual over written culture and the expansion of civil society to the transnational realm, cinema has become an important space for national transgressions and transnational encounters. The boundaries of the nation are blurred by visual media and cyberspace, where cultural products target audiences both within and beyond the borders of the nation-state. While the nation-state is still the main regulatory agent of what can or cannot be produced or circulated, the demands of both local and diasporic audiences have been equally important in media production. The transnational market of consumers and their taste for the Iranian cinema has pressured the Islamic state to relax its censorship. While 'banned in Iran' seems to be a good marketing strategy, rather than representing necessarily the limits and problems of state-controlled film, Iranian film production, located at the intersection of the national and the transnational, has forced civil society to include Iranian-diasporic communities in various parts of the world and to reach out to larger audiences worldwide, thereby being exposed to critiques and the possibility of cross-cultural exchange.

The post-revolutionary reorganization of national media production both in terms of the application of a politics of de-Westernization as well as promotion of indigenous media production, has created space for participation of a new generation of filmmakers, producers and performers who are less concerned about the mimicking of Western narratives and filmic representations and are focusing more on national and local cultural negotiations. By looking 'in' rather than 'out', the Iranian film industry has been able to respond creatively to the demands of the national market without needing to compete with Western films. At the same time, as national product it has been able to enter international film festivals and markets. In its obligation to 'do the nation', Iranian cinema has also participated in the 'undoing of the nation' by challenging the notion of an Islamic *ummat*/community as unified or homogeneous, thereby disturbing the revolutionary harmony of the nation of *mostaz'afan* in its war against the *estekbar-i jahani* ('world powers'). A number of Iranian films, especially those concerned with issues of gender and poverty, have been the main sites of such a challenge to the notion of *mostaz'af*.

Through a reading of two recent Iranian movies, *Do Zan (Two Women)* by Tahmineh Milani and *Bacheha-ye Aseman (Children of Heaven)* by Majid Majidi, I will illustrate the parallel process of doing and undoing the nation. I will argue that while doing the nation is a result of market needs and national production, undoing the nation involves the very impossibility of the nation in its fragmentation, displacement and disjunction. Both are important case studies, because of the ways in which they challenge the notion of a homogeneous *ummat* by engaging with issues of class and gender differences. Both have been produced within the last few years and have gained popularity in national and international markets. Each works with the revolutionary notion of *mostaz'af* by portraying disempowered subjects as resourceful agents. However, they break with *mostaz'af* by unsettling its homogeneity via an investigation of class and gender hierarchies.

Children of Heaven and Postmodern Consumer Capitalism

Children of Heaven depicts the story of Ali, a young boy who loses his sneakers on the way to the cobbler for repair. He arranges with his sister Zahra to share her sneakers, so that he can continue to go to school. Ali and Zahra are able to share a single pair of shoes because the school has two shifts a day, one for girls and the other for boys.[10] In this way they manage to avoid shaming the family in its daily struggle for survival. Ali feels responsibility for the family's financial difficulties; his sick mother needs expensive medication and his father, like masses of migrant workers in south Tehran, has to search for seasonal jobs. The sharing of the home/room by Ali, Zahra and their parents makes impossible the separation of modern middle-class notions of domestic space (home/house/room), as well as spheres of responsibility and the very idea of childhood and adulthood. Everyone in the family is exposed to the daily struggle for survival and the need to take an active role in it. Sleeping, eating, talking, homework – all take place within the boundaries of a home/room. The audience, like Zahra and Ali, witness the conversations of the parents as they strategize survival. The film radically challenges mainstream and homogenizing notions of youth in Iran as consumers of MTV and Western fashion. The filmmaker Majid Majidi (1999), who was himself raised in a working-class family, has spoken about a generation of Iranian youth that has not become the consumers of a service-based society but participants in its economic survival, a generation which on account of their material conditions, rather than their belonging to the imagined community of the *ummat*, is able to experience life in the process of becoming.

The film opens in south Tehran, where there is a concentration of rural immigrants and seasonal workers, and moves to north Tehran where the middle and upper classes live. The poverty of Ali's family and their struggle for survival is portrayed neither as loss of dignity and solidarity nor as moral decadence. Class hierarchy is not depicted as the antagonistic encounter of rich and poor. Rather, in its representation of poverty and class differences the film evades modernist notions of poverty as lack of nobility or moral judgement, by showing a rich culture of family and community care and support. However, it avoids sentimentality by its frank depiction of the spatial segregation of class and the gap between rich and poor. By this means it challenges any ideologically inclusive notion of *mostaz'af*. In addition, the 'sneaker' is an object which stands for the whole adult world of consumer capitalism, in which the child is initiated regardless of his need or desire.

A foot-race organized by the school becomes a potential solution for Ali because the third place prize is a new pair of sneakers. The first two prizes – attendance at a modern youth camp on the Caspian sea, offering activities from swimming to painting to sports – are of no interest to him. The staging of the race and the participation of children from various classes, some with fancy clothing and some barely equipped for the race, is a spectacular representation of children's formation as consumer subjects. Ali's desire for the new sneakers is ironically thwarted, thanks to his victory in the race; the audience is thus left to contemplate the capacity of consumer capitalism to produce in its subjects desires beyond their needs. The reality of class differences and the dismantling of the triumphant narrative of cultural nationalism in its capacity to resist consumer capitalism for the sake of an Islamic economy undermines a cultural nationalist construal of *mostaz'af*.

Do Zan and the Revolution that Did Not Take Place

I believe that to be able to lead a healthy social life, we have to be able to criticize ourselves by looking at our past. Once I said we have to plow our past to see what happened and I was ridiculed in the media. In the history of the last twenty-two years there has been a horrible silence and generally history and the revolution have been distorted and defined one-sidedly. It is important for us to look back and see what happened to us. When the revolution took place, my generation was eighteen years old. We were like a traveler who boarded a ship that was struck by a storm or blown up and destroyed. Consider my generation: they are either refugees, or died in prison, or were executed, or died in the war, since the war started one year after the revolution. They lost their lives in the war, or got stuck at home. They are all my generation and this generation was judged very harshly, they were treated with cruelty, bad decisions were made about them. In other words, none of the ideals that we imagined materialized. (Tahmineh Milani 2001: 6)

Do Zan is another challenge to the cultural nationalist narrative of the revolution, since it brings up the differences of gender and class. The film is about the ways in which the revolution dismissed women and gender issues by marginalizing them to the sphere of family and community. *Do Zan* makes the point that where women's issues were relegated to the private domain of patriarchal relations, class position made a difference in enabling women to negotiate their gender position. Again, the notion of *mostaz'af* and the revolt of the disempowered against the powerful is thrown into crisis in the re-narrativization of the revolution and its deromanticization as bringing change for women.

The film focuses on a brilliant and energetic student of architecture, Fereshteh, who develops a friendship with Roya, a mediocre student who needs tutoring to get through the university. The events take place during and after the revolution of 1979, yet the worlds of Fereshteh and Roya are filled with anxieties and concerns that are lived in parallel with the unfolding revolution. No matter what the revolutionary ideals are, the revolution as an event becomes incidental to the lives of the two women since they continue to deal with the same issues both during and after revolution. The two come from different class backgrounds; Roya is from an upper-middle-class Tehrani family and Fereshteh is from a lower-class family from the countryside. While the events of the revolution are taking place, Fereshteh has to deal with Hassan, an obsessive young man who has fallen in love with her and expects her to love and marry him; otherwise he is going to throw acid in her face.[11] With the support of Roya, Fereshteh manages to cope with the man and his advances, until one day the stalker throws a bottle of acid at Fereshteh's cousin, mistaking him for a boyfriend. Blaming her for bringing disgrace upon the family, Fereshteh's father forces her to return home after the student strikes and the shutdown of the universities. But the stalker follows Fereshteh to her home-town and confronts her as she sneaks away from her house to make a phone call to Roya. Fereshteh rushes back to her car, while Hassan hysterically follows her on his motorcycle. He shouts that he will find her wherever she goes. Fereshteh turns into a narrow street where a couple of kids are playing. She hits one of them with her car. Hassan follows her on the motorcycle and hits another kid. Both Fereshteh and Hassan are arrested and sent to jail.

In the Islamic court of justice, the stalker, accused of child homicide and harassment of Fereshteh, is sentenced to 13 years in prison and payment of blood money. Fereshteh is accused of breaking the highway code and injuring a child. While Hassan is sent to jail, Fereshteh is given the possibility of release from jail on the consent of the child's parents and payment of blood money. Fereshteh's family feels frustration and anger because of her imprisonment and the dishonour she has brought upon them. While Fereshteh's father is unable to pay the blood money to free her from prison, Ahmad, a family friend who is interested in Fereshteh, settles the payment and saves the family reputation. While Tehran burns in the fires of revolution, Fereshteh is forced to save her family's honour by marrying Ahmad.

Roya's trajectory is different; she manages to finish school, marry the man she chooses and find a job as an architect. A number of issues central to the discourse of cultural nationalists – including Islamic identity, veiling and anti-West opposition – seem to be irrelevant to both Fereshteh's and Roya's lives. The pressure of patriarchal relations and the criminalization of women resisting normative regimes of respectability is at the centre of both Fereshteh's and Roya's preoccupations at the time of the revolution. Fereshteh continues to be harassed by the stalker after his release from prison. While she tries to keep alive her intellectual interest in reading, the husband becomes obsessed about her developing an identity that might threaten her role as a 'loyal wife'. Disempowered by the stalker, her family and her husband, Fereshteh is not portrayed as a passive victim but as actively resisting her circumstances. She continues to acquire and read books, secretly manages to keep her friendship with Roya, and maintains the hope of being able to reconcile her desires with the material conditions of her life. She becomes a prisoner of her husband once he discovers her secret life. In the absence of any public institutions to support Fereshteh in resisting the stalker, taking refuge in the family forces her into a new web of oppressive relations. After the dramatic death of her husband, who attacks the stalker at the moment where he is about to kill Fereshteh, she is left with the responsibility of raising two children as a single mother. She faces a life of struggle untouched by the events of the revolution or its outcome. The film ends with Fereshteh's anxious statement of how much is left for her to do and how she is going to cope with it all.

The film looks away from the political and urban tensions of the revolution and deals with the complexity of what the revolution might have meant for the protagonist, who is subjected to the crimes of passion of an obsessive man, the pressures of the family and the gendered norms of respectability, and the criminalization of women who resist gender oppression. Because the film turns away from the drama of revolutionary events and from the unified agency of the *mostaz'af*, it opens up the narrative of the revolution to gender conflict where no alliance is possible between the aggressor and the aggressed. The renarrativization of revolution as an absence in the life of the two women reveals the untenability of *mostaz'af* as a unitary category.

An examination of the stalker's life and his masculinity seems to be pertinent, no matter how involved he became in the events of the revolution and who he became after the revolution. While he is portrayed as an unemployed young man with a motorcycle who turns to an obsessive love object as a way of dealing with unemployment and lack of education, the film cannot avoid evoking both the young men who found a place for themselves in the *Basiji* organization and the revolutionary guards who were also charged with disciplining women.[12] The post-revolutionary state legitimized, channelled and institutionalized violence against women by transforming women from singular love objects to the love object of a whole nation of men. While revolutionary models of femininity broke with the notion of family honour by transgressing the boundaries of gender respectability for revolutionary causes, the tragic compromises of Fereshteh reveal the unfulfilment of the revolution, that is, a revolution that did not take place.

Conclusion

Mostaz'af as a revolutionary oppositional concept is therefore put in crisis by the representation of class and gender antagonisms in the new Iranian cinema. This key concept in the construction of a transnational Islamic nation is being worked out in a contradictory way that exposes the fragmented realities of Iranian society. The writing of women, as well as of various ethnicities and classes into the nation via visual media and film where the national history is reimagined, creates space for the opening of the nation and its narrativizing. Furthermore, the circulation of Iranian films in the global market makes possible the participation of the Iranian diaspora in this process. The diasporic audiences – the 'nation' that has left its territorial boundaries – view the depiction of this contradiction and find different meanings in these representational practices. These audiences write their own meanings into the films, which escape the intentions of the filmmaker. The 'undoing of the nation' in Iran as portrayed in these films paradoxically may serve to 'do the nation' among diasporic communities. This parallel but inverted process of undoing and doing the nation is well suited to the postmodern moment of an image-based consumer capitalism.

Notes

1. For an illuminating analysis of the impact of the media in the Iranian revolution of 1979, see Fischer and Abedi (1990).

2. 'Revolution' is used in two major senses, one describing change 'from above' and the other an eruption 'from below'. In both cases there is the implication of radical social change, which may in turn provoke what is called 'counter-revolution'. It is 'in the name of revolution' that the discourses of modernity and modernization

have been circulated and have legitimized social transformations of various kinds. In the context of postmodernity, the convergence of revolution with the commercial culture of capitalism has defused the idea of social revolt by reducing the sense of revolution to novelty and the world of commodities – the Revlon revolution (femininity), Che Guevara T-shirts (avant-garde masculinity) or Zapatista dolls (progressive life-style).

3. By hegemony I mean both the competing social and ideological forces as well as those forms of representation that are major sources of hegemony. Gramsci (1971) and Foucault (1980) are guides to the circulation of power in the context of representation, and in particular the ability, both through coercion and seduction, to gain consent in establishing leadership and authority.

4. As argued by John Beverly (1999: 141–2) the function of the nation is not only to articulate to itself elements of other class or group projects as the embodiment of the nation, but to articulate the nation as a necessary signifier for hegemonic articulation.

5. There is not much engagement between post-colonial and subaltern studies and Middle Eastern Studies with regard to the formation of subaltern consciousness and subjectivity in the context of Middle Eastern societies. *Mostaz'af* can be referred to as the subject position of the subaltern as a social category.

6. In the war of position, in the Gramscian sense, the Islamic movement achieved hegemony over the other oppositional movements by referring to a revolutionary agency that was not uniquely defined by class relations. It also distinguished itself from the secular nationalist movements and their primordial notions of the nation by calling for a transnational nation of disempowered Muslims 'in becoming', in an alliance with all the wretched of the earth.

7. See Moallem (1999a) for an analysis of oppositional models of femininity in the context of the 1979 revolution.

8. I am not able in this discussion to elaborate on the representation of ethnicity in Iranian cinema. It should, however, be noted that the post-revolutionary cinema has included a representation of various ethno-linguistic groups. For the first time, Persian subtitles were used when Turkish, Kurdish and other minority languages and dialects were spoken. For example, *Bashu, the Little Stranger*, by filmmaker Bahram Baizai, depicts ethnic and regional differences. The representation of religious minorities, however, is still missing from Iranian films.

9. In a fascinating semi-documentary entitled *Salaam Cinema*, by the Iranian filmmaker Mohsen Makhmalbaf, hundreds of people from all classes, genders, ages and ethnicities show up for an audition for new actors and actresses.

10. Two shifts a day are a way of dealing with the increased demographic pressure on the school system.

11. Throwing acid is a common form of violence against women in Iran.

12. The *Basiji* and revolutionary guards were volunteer forces composed mainly of young men, who took part in nation building in the post-revolutionary era. Among their tasks was the disciplining of women to conform to Islamic rules and regulations.

. . . .

CHAPTER 11

Mariama Bâ's So Long a Letter: Women, Culture and Development from a Francophone/ Post-colonial Perspective

Anjali Prabhu

The discipline is a principle of control over the production of discourse.
(Michel Foucault 1981: 61)

§ THE main argument put forth in favour of the WCD paradigm is the urgency to move away from economistic analyses, specifically in the context of Third World women, in order to understand women's lives and agency in all their complexity. In this chapter, I begin by explaining the position from which I consider this proposal, and further clarify how this position articulates with the triad proposed. I actively engage with the proposals put forth by Chua, Bhavnani and Foran (2000). My reading of the now canonical Francophone text, *Une si longue lettre* (*So Long a Letter*), by the Senegalese author Mariama Bâ, is preceded by a consideration of the position of literature within the proposed paradigm.

Francophone studies – loosely defined as the study of literature and culture (in/through the French language) outside of hexagonal France and within France's post-colonial communities – is, in the US academic world, linked closely to the larger field of post-colonial studies, which is in an eternal struggle to generate and define itself with and against, most notably, post-structuralism and postmodernism (see, for example, Appiah 1991, Kadir 1995 and Shohat and Stam 1994). The departure from 'pure' literary studies (departments are more and more using the term French studies, as opposed to French literature) has the field bound up with cultural studies, a field or sub-field under constant redefinition (for a recent questioning of this field, see Schwartz 2000).

It is from this position that I come to understand the terms Women, Culture and Development. If 'women' is retained over 'gender' to focus on women rather than on men (Chua, Bhavnani and Foran 2000: 824), I would, in addition, insist that the 'gendered' articulation of this category of 'women' is what becomes important within the current project: gendered in the sense of socially constructed with and against the signifying practices at a specific location.[1] Therefore, opting to study 'gendered women' implies that 'women' act from, define and defy positions that are recognizably those of women in the culture in question, and that significantly affect their daily lives and their relations to individuals and aspects of society in immediate as well as not so immediate ways. On that account, the idea of the 'feminine' – mostly suggested from the domain of the literary – as resistant, defying definition, the uncontainable and the physical becomes ostensibly of less significance – because the 'feminine' is not necessarily tied to 'women'.[2]

Since the 'Third World' is largely the context whence the paradigm is proposed, I should clarify that my engagement with the Third World is specifically invested in the 'national' and the 'post-colonial' as they relate to nations formerly colonized by France.[3] The purely chronological signification of the latter term (referring to the period following official independence or the dismantling of colonial administration), as well as the more complex concerns involving differential sources and forces of power and resistance that it has come to encompass, become important in this study, which is built around the rhetoric of independence.[4] Moreover, and perhaps more pertinently, the recognition in the field (and in the term) of the 'post-colonial' is that the colonial encounter can only account for part of the structuring force, because newer external pressures, as well as older societal and historical realities, figure alongside colonial legacies in very real ways, in the daily deployment of agency in the lives of the peoples of these geographical regions.

Development is therefore tied very specifically to the idea of (new) nation, with the nationalist rhetoric of development being clearly linked to catching up with the 'mother' country, and to modernization. While the WCD paradigm quite judiciously calls for a retreat from these simplistic definitions of development, which have to do with modernization and measurable economic progress, such definitions must be actively engaged, if only to subvert them, precisely because it is the resulting policies, procedures, laws and practices in the new nation that in part structure – and perhaps often hinder – women's practices of everyday life. If literature is easily seen as belonging to the realm of the cultural, then the location from which I write, and the texts that I consider, vitiate the force of privileging the 'cultural' over the 'economic'. In fact – and location aside here – any extrication of the cultural from the economic, quite simply, gives renewed pertinence to the old base–superstructure metaphor and – specifically here – precludes the understanding of the literary text in its material reality. One of the definitions of the cultural engaged by feminist analysts, namely, as the 'non-economic' (Chua, Bhavnani and Foran 2000: 820, 826), proves to be less theoretically productive from the disciplinary location that this chapter is written. The approach taken to 'culture' delineates the framework within which 'being' (and thus agency and resistance) can be theorized and understood. It is useful, for this reason, to consider Homi Bhabha's notion of culture as 'enunciation' rather than as epistemology, where the 'enunciative is a more dialogic process that attempts to track displacements and realignments that are the effects of cultural antagonisms and articulations – subverting the rationale of the hegemonic moment and relocating alternative, hybrid sites of cultural negotiation' (Bhabha 1992: 443). We could read this process of generating culture as one that is anchored in the specific social context, but tied closely to disruptions of static ideas of culture and tradition within it. The consideration of these disruptions that are enabled by oppositions and ongoing practices within the circumscribed space upsets an understanding of culture as a given that pre-exists action. Such an understanding would then provide the means for questioning purely 'economistic' understandings and open up possibilities for reading development that can take into account multiple areas, especially those inhabited and generated by 'women' and unconventional types of action, with, for example, a new understanding of 'production'.

In the Francophone context, the voices of nationalist movements have been largely male and masculinist. The privileging of 'women's' writing, therefore, immediately complicates these discourses, since, as is known, women's concerns were seen as too 'narrow' to be addressed in the urgency of independence movements. These nationalist voices have also stemmed from extremely elite locations, in the language (in the specific Francophone context: in French, but also in the most encompassing sense of language that Bourdieu gives it, for example) of the elite: in the language of the (ex-)colonizer.[5] Class and, or rather with, gender (specifically women here), then, enter this idea of development when seen through literature, not as entities which have been privileged in previous analyses and need to be done away with, but rather as problematizing and questioning the unitary nature of the elite nationalist discourses. Yet – and this is of utmost importance – the category of writing 'women' hardly fits *a priori* as a counter-discourse producing entity: women (authors and their texts) can reinforce and advance masculinist nationalist causes with efficacy, even if not necessarily with intention, and this is because all writers are 'significantly situated even before [they] come to write' (Williams 1989: 258). If these points call for a slightly different set of tactics, the overall strategy remains the same: to reach a more complete, nuanced understanding of women in the context of development, which engages their creative resistance to various hegemonic forces.[6]

Culture is by far the most problematic of the terms implicated. My understanding of its definition is filtered through the battles waged over it in the arena of cultural studies. The borrowing of Williams's term, 'structures of feelings', by WCD as an antidote to the vulgar Marxist and economically determining trends in the previous approaches, brings with it, however, first, the debate over what the cultural is; and second, how other terms such as economic, material, gender, class, race or ethnicity, for example, articulate themselves within this definition. This warrants some attention, since any understanding of agency or resistance within particular cultures must necessarily relate to how exactly this notion of culture is defined.

The development of the idea of culture from Raymond Williams and those who followed has always been closely tied to the idea of class – in particular, working class. For Williams, 'there is a distinct working-class way of life', which he goes on to propose as a model for English society as a whole, based on 'its emphases of neighbourhood, mutual obligation and common betterment, as expressed in the great working-class political and industrial institutions' (Williams 1989a: 8). The type of working through proposed by the WCD project is, then, similar to the one that took place in 'cultural studies' and continues to do so. As Stuart Hall has summarized its dominant paradigm:

> It stands opposed to the residual and merely-reflective role assigned to 'the cultural'. In its different ways, it conceptualizes culture as interwoven with all social practices and those practices, in turn, as a common form of human activity: sensuous human praxis, the activity through which men and women make history. It is opposed to the base–superstructure way of formulating the relationship between ideal and material forces, especially where the 'base' is defined as the determination by 'the economic' in any simple sense ... It defines 'culture' as *both* the meanings and values which arise amongst distinctive social groups and classes, on the basis of their given historical conditions and relationships, through which they 'handle' and respond to the conditions of existence; *and* as the lived traditions and practices through which those 'understandings' are expressed and in which they are embodied. (Hall 1986: 39, emphases in original)

Thus, how people live and experience structures of relations is what is privileged, and the emphasis is on creative and historical agency. But as Hall continues, in his understanding of Thompson (1963): 'every mode of production *is also a culture*, and every struggle between classes *is also a struggle between cultural modalities*; and which, for [Raymond] Williams, is what a "cultural analysis", in the final instance, should deliver' (Hall 1986: 39, my emphases).

If we invoke Williams's term, 'structures of feelings' (Chua, Bhavnani and Foran 2000: 821), then we are also obliged to account for how feelings are structured: feelings of happiness, sadness, competence, powerlessness, ambiguity, fitting in, standing out, complacency, enthusiasm, independence, dependency, desire, repugnance, attraction, love, are all experienced within and around, in resistance to and complicity with, forces of (most pertinently here) patriarchy, and dominant and accepted ways of being, which are in turn reinforced by laws and supported by relations that cannot be adequately understood outside their economic figuring. The sanctioning of feelings through these forces cannot be discounted. In other words, approaching the problem through structures of feelings still requires some accounting of the structuring of these feelings. Experience and culture thus serve as overarching unities within which specific struggles, feelings, lives and agencies, can be figured: 'This sense of cultural totality – of *the* whole historical process – over-rides any effort to keep the instances and elements distinct. Their real interconnection, under given historical conditions, must be matched by a *totalising movement* "in thought" in the analysis' (Hall 1986: 39). This type of analysis recalls Fredric Jameson's conception of the dialectical method, where everything, as it were, must be figured at once: 'The peculiar difficulty of dialectical writing lies indeed in its *holistic, "totalizing" character*: as though you could not say any one thing until you had first said everything; as though with each new idea you were bound to recapitulate the entire system' (Jameson 1971: 306, emphases in both quotations mine). The impossibility of this task, from the point of view of systematic study, clearly calls for practical measures. The first of these, in my view, is interdisciplinary dialogue, which can provide far more complexity than academic disciplinarity generally permits, and in which this volume participates. Another, suggested elsewhere by Jameson himself, is specific to literary criticism. It has to do with criticism being able to 'transform' statements about aesthetics or form 'into genuinely historical ones' (Jameson 1988: 120). Still in the context of such formal analysis, he is interested in pursuing them 'all the way' until they re-emerge in or as history. Such 'momentary contact with the real' can emerge when 'literary criticism abolishes itself as such and yields a glimpse of consciousness momentarily at one with its social ground' (1988: 120). I will consider the literary text from a new perspective and therefore be obliged to rethink its functioning. My textual analyses will constantly seek out such momentary contact with the real.

Francophone literary production, framed in the ways described, must be understood in its elite and representational (of the nation, of the people) complexity. Many of the early figures in Francophone writing were also implicated politically on the national scene, whether or not they were endorsed by the 'official' nation: Aimé Césaire (mayor of Fort-de-France, Martinique until as recently as March 2001); Léopold Sédar Senghor (first president of Senegal for 21 years); Frantz Fanon (radical Martinican, involved in the struggle of the National Liberation Front in Algeria and later associated with the Black Panther movement in the USA). All of them went through the French school system and went to university in Paris. Most of the figures – and this is more so with the early writers such as Mariama Bâ (in her own way) and the men named above – were involved in the dual processes of representation: as artists and political representatives.

Literature and WCD

> Every act of criticism is always literally tied to a set of social and historical circumstances; the problem is in specifying or characterizing the relationship, not merely in asserting that it exists. (Said 1984: 956)

My next task is to understand and, what seems even more formidable, to explain, what it means to read a literary text in the context of a WCD project. How does an ostensibly fictional text become pertinent to the working out of women's experience in the Third World? First, I have obviously chosen to read a text by a woman that largely concerns women's struggles – and therefore implicates authorial position (the biographical). Can we then assume that *a* woman writing automatically remedies the masculinist tendencies of nationalist discourse?

The author, as the point at which various forces come together to generate the text, is but one point of juncture between the fictional textuality and the other texts/discourses with which it connects.[7] The literary text, or at least its reading, is a practice that exploits the ideas of 'contiguity, metonymy, the touching of spatial boundaries at a tangent' (Bhabha 1992: 452). Is the subject (content) of the text, in that case, to be revealing of the corresponding realities? For Williams, a 'correspondence of content between a writer and his [*sic*] world is less significant than his correspondence of organization, of structure' (quoted in Hall 1986: 37). In the following reading, I engage the contiguity of the literary text with its outside reality in terms of both the shared content and the significance of its narrative organization. In fact, the societal structures that are subverted in the story of the text are also inscribed 'narratively'. I suggest, in this piece, a greater scope for the literary text might be generally conceded. 'Allegorical' readings – notwithstanding the furore this suggestion has caused with regard to the 'national'; see Jameson 1986; then Ahmad (1994) and Bensmaïa (1999), for example – provide another effective mode of linking the literary text to its larger reality for the paradigm in question. In making a choice of what can be done here, I will not pursue such a reading, even though the text certainly invites it.[8]

I should clarify, then, that my interest in Mariama Bâ's text is specifically in identifying 'moment[s] in which the *system as a whole* [specifically the post-colonial national],[9] or *some limit of it*, is being touched' (Jameson in Stephanson 1998: 27, my emphasis). In any case, the reading, while revelatory of certain specificities of Senegalese society as presented by the text, does not consequently become a study of the women in Senegalese society (for a descriptive study that discusses WID and GAD approaches to 'social service' interventions in Senegal, see Sarr, Bâ and Sourang 1997). Following Lucien Goldmann, Williams suggested the importance of the use of common 'categories' between a fictional text and the 'outside' world (see Hall 1986: 37). Just as the author provides one of the connections between text and world, the common categories between these two realms provide a conceptual fulcrum for our articulation of one with the other. I actively pursue, through Bâ's text, such an articulation.

Articulating Mariama Bâ's *Une si longue lettre* in Women, Culture, Development

This entire novel takes the form of a 'letter' (from Ramatoulaye to her childhood friend Aïssatou) in which the writer of the letter reminisces about her life and that of her friend: shared childhood, meeting and falling in love with their respective spouses, marriage, polygamy, the heartache of the first wives and the very different ways in which the two women manage this situation. Published in 1979, this novel, which received the Nouma prize in 1980, remains one of the benchmark texts of Francophone literature and is taught in virtually every programme. One of the early texts by a woman, its ideas about progress, feminism and modernity are very nicely, up to a point, recuperated into Western understanding of these issues (see Champagne 1996: 22–30, and for a discussion of how the 'feminist' side adequately explains only part of the text, Guèye 1994). The text is also short, and makes relatively easy reading for introductory courses in Francophone literature.

While Ramatoulaye's narrative censures nationalist discourse in various ways, there is not, in fact, such a radical departure from nationalist views of development and progress, thus debunking any unproblematically radical ascription to women's writing. The practice of writing by women in this period, of which Bâ's text is an instance, while in itself radical due to the restricted entry of women into French schools in Senegal at the time, must thus first be seen in the conditions that reproduce it. This reproduction (of the practice of women's writing) is inseparable from the reproduction of the social relations in which access to writing (here in French) is restricted to those who have the possibility of a high level of literacy in French. This latter possibility is in turn tied to the structural positioning of such individuals and groups in the period just preceding independence in French colonies.[10]

Still, the return of the familiar nationalist rhetoric concerning development and modernity, couched in terms borrowed from the colonizer, is destabilized through the uprooting procedure by which the female narrator appropriates it. The discussion of such issues from the perspective of a woman, and a mother, and the weighing of these consequences at the level of the personal and the familial, effectively wrenches their significance away from 'objective' large-scale measurement processes, while reinstating them as having consequences at the micro-level. As Mariama Bâ has indicated in an interview, there was not much space for women's voices in official spheres, and she herself preferred to work through non-governmental agencies to promote change (Dia 1979). Ramatoulaye's fictional engagement with this sphere of education and progress effectively uproots this discourse from its possession by precisely such figures as Léopold Sédar Senghor, then President of Senegal. For example: 'Did these interminable discussions [around the political career of Ramatoulaye's husband Modou], during which points of view concurred or clashed, complemented each other or were vanquished, determine the aspect of the New Africa?' (Bâ 1981: 24). Ramatoulaye and her friend Aïssatou are clearly in this new 'we' that has the 'privilege … to be the link between two periods in our history, one of domination, the other of independence … With independence achieved, we witnessed the birth of a republic, the birth of an anthem and the implantation of a flag' (25). As the above passages indicate, the concerns of the larger context of the nation and its society are not just present, but become the preoccupations of the personal voice of autobiography (of the character).

Writing of the idealism of their youth and of the two couples, Ramatoulaye notes that they 'were full of nostalgia but were resolutely progressive' (19). The young women were formed by the French school, where the aims of the 'admirable headmistress' were, in the words of the narrator: 'To lift us out of the bog of tradition, superstition and custom, to make us appreciate a multitude of civilizations without renouncing our own … to develop universal moral values in us' (15). Along with the standard, dominant nationalist ideas of Western universalism, the idea that tradition lives unquestioned as long as it is outside the influence of the colonizer is further suggested by Aunty Nabou, Aïssatou's mother-in-law: 'You have to come away from Dakar to be convinced of the survival of traditions' (27). This is similar to the suggestion that vices were brought from the outside, while in tradition lay virtues: 'Now our society is shaken to its very foundations, torn between the attraction of imported vices and the fierce resistance of old virtues' (73). Here, Ramatoulaye struggles in her parental role with her twelve children, especially her girls, three of whom have not only taken to wearing trousers, but also smoke cigarettes.

As Williams has argued (1960: 320–21) and subsequently Hall (1981, especially 227–8), among others, tradition is born of a process of selection and reworking. Bâ's text, while overtly subscribing to a rather static understanding of 'tradition', does provide for a more nuanced view. In describing the rituals that follow Modou's death, Ramatoulaye remarks on the annoying presence of her co-wife, Binetou, who 'has been installed in [Ramatoulaye's] house for the funeral, in accordance with tradition' (Bâ 1981: 3). Then comes the 'moment dreaded by every Senegalese woman, the moment when she sacrifices her possessions as gifts to her family-in-law', finally 'becoming a thing in the service of the man who has married her, his grandfather, his grandmother, his father, his mother' (4). In this painful recollection there is now a sharp observation on the functioning of this tradition: '[The woman's] behaviour is conditioned: no sister-in-law will touch the head of any wife who has been stingy, unfaithful or inhospitable' (4). Without a doubt, this 'conditioning' is to be read in Ramatoulaye's 'tolerance' narrated in a different chapter: 'I tolerated his sisters, who too often would desert their own homes to encumber my own ... I tolerated their spitting, the phlegm expertly secreted under my carpets ... I would receive [Modou's mother] with all the respect due to a queen, and she would leave satisfied, especially if her hand closed over the banknote I had carefully placed there' (19). There is a clear suggestion of the structuring of the woman's propensity for tolerance, her respect for her in-laws, her regard for tradition, as it were.

'Woman' becomes the site for the playing out of 'tradition'. If behaviour is conditioned, as seen above, her reputation brings her recognition from society at large: 'I receive the greater share of money and many envelopes ... The regard shown me raises me in the eyes of others' (Bâ 1981: 6). Yet this recognition is followed by the wives being stripped of it all. The family-in-law leaves them 'utterly destitute' (7) after the ritual of the 'dreaded moment' discussed in the above paragraph. This is a propitious moment for reconsidering the useful concepts of injustices of distribution and recognition that Nancy Fraser presents in her response to Judith Butler's statement that new social movements have been viewed in recent theoretical discussions as 'merely cultural' (Butler 1997). For Fraser, 'misrecognition' is 'analytically distinct from, and conceptually irreducible to, the injustice of maldistribution, although it *may* be accompanied by the latter' (Fraser 1997: 280). It also includes 'the *material* construction through the institutionalization of cultural norms of a class of devalued persons who are impeded from participatory parity' (Fraser 1997: 283, all emphases in original).

The complexity of the situation described by Ramatoulaye arises from the fact that it is through a recognition of her supposed value that the visitors hand out money to the widow. This recognition is then reaffirmed in the paradoxical way in which her possessions are transferred to the dead man's family, sanctioning and materially constructing the destitution of widows. That is, even if the outcome is negative and deplorable for the woman, the recognition, as process, continues and is accredited in that 'dreaded moment'. None of the above (traditions) would be possible, however, without the injustice of maldistribution (related to laws against women's inheritance of property, for example) *to begin with*. In the situation described, I suggest that the injustice of maldistribution functions as an enabling condition of the specific ritual of 'recognition' (in the 'regard shown for [her]'), which actually accomplishes *mis*recognition (as it is an institutionally accomplished devalu-ation of this widow and contributes to creating a group of destitute widows) and results in further maldistribution (because she is forced to sacrifice her belongings to her family-in-law). One is not merely accompanied by the other, and even if they are mutually irreducible, misrecognition and maldistribution become cyclical processes that endlessly reinstate each other.

Clearly, Ramatoulaye writes from an elite perspective of French education, available only to a few. The Rufisque boarding school (with the enlightened headmistress) served all of West Africa – it is also the school Mariama Bâ herself attended. Modou's death, from the perspective of the 'scavenging' old woman who is seen at the funeral, is therefore beyond her appreciation:

> My horizon is lightened, I see an old woman. Who is she? Where is she from? Bent over, the ends of her *boubou* tied behind her, she empties into a plastic bag the left-overs of red rice …
>
> Standing upright, her eyes meeting my disapproving look, she mutters between teeth reddened by cola nuts 'Lady, death is just as beautiful as life has been'. (Bâ 1981: 7–8)

The meaning of the two questions (Who is she? Where is she from?) requires more than a cursory examination. The narrator cannot know her nor understand where she is from, even if she indicates she might be from the poor outskirts of Dakar – 'Ouakam, Thiaroye or Pikine' (Bâ 1981: 8). This short intervention could be a significant moment immediately following the widows becoming 'utterly destitute' in the consideration of incommensurable spaces within post-colonial locations. It forces into deliberation spaces within post-colonial worlds that do not share the same 'language' in the senses I alluded to in the introduction following Bourdieu. It is a moment that problematizes Francophone writing because 'the area of a culture … is usually proportionate to the area of a language rather than to the area of a class' (Williams 1960: 320). The text's silence here and elsewhere, even on the question of language, for example, when education is critically evaluated (see Bâ 1981: 17–9), becomes a reason for productive interrogation beyond the scope of this piece.[11]

Nevertheless, the most radical proposal in Bâ's text is the narration of the friendship between Ramatoulaye and Aïssatou, because it challenges the structural stability of heterosexual polygamy (for men) that is held in place by the forces of colonialism *as well as* older patriarchal forces, operating in tandem. Using the form of a letter for the intimate account of the lives of Ramatoulaye and Aïssatou creates a space for critical discourse (as I have shown earlier) between (and by extension among) women that excludes from her text the male as either producer or receiver. It creates 'narratively' (rather than *in* the narrative), a female–female couple in the form of a new discursive practice within the 'national', even if the text is silent about sexual intimacy for these two women after the break with their husbands. At first, Ramatoulaye establishes the endurance of friendship between women over the 'love' in the heterosexual couple: 'If over the years, and passing through the realities of life, dreams die, I still keep intact my memories, the salt of remembrance [of friendship]' (Bâ 1981: 1). And later: 'Friendship has splendours that love knows not. It grows stronger when crossed, whereas obstacles kill love. Friendship resists time, which wearies and severs couples. It has heights unknown to love' (54).

This latter quotation is from the chapter where Aïssatou purchases a car for her friend, after learning how difficult it is for her to get about with the children using public transportation. It is impossible to ignore how this couple of Ramatoulaye–Aïssatou replaces the heterosexual one. She recounts elsewhere her refusal of offers of marriage from various suitors (appropriate according to 'tradition') because she is still true to her one love, Modou, but also due to a reticence to reproduce a 'co-wife'. The above quotation is preceded, in the same chapter, by Ramatoulaye's admission that she begins to wait for 'another man', even if she knows that 'It would not be easy to get [her] children to accept a new masculine presence' (53). I believe that the suggestion becomes stronger and is rendered radical, perhaps paradoxically, by Ramatoulaye's admission that she 'ha[d] never conceived of happiness outside marriage' (56). What I am proposing is that it is the structuring of this feeling of the necessity of the couple – through the repeatedly sanctioned polygamous practice of the husband in which the first wife 'accepts' her role as secondary for the purposes of financial support, as well as through the Western and romantic notion of one true love for one man, to which Ramatoulaye wholly subscribes – that prevents what is otherwise logical, effectively real and materially actualized: that of the female–female couple.

One of the categories that Bâ's text shares with larger society is that of heterosexuality. Following the above proposal, one might ask if 'it [is] not possible to maintain and pursue heterosexual identifications and aims within homosexual practice, and homosexual identifications and aims within heterosexual practices' (Butler 1991: 17)? In fact, the division here between aims and practices becomes blurred. This friendship, as it is constructed, could be seen as the accomplishment of an aim (homosexual interdependency, as in the example of the car, and emotional intimacy, as the entire letter testifies), accomplished in heterosexual practice (both women are in heterosexual relationships and subsequently deal with separation from their respective spouses, without any explicit reference to homosexual practice). Or it can be seen as a homosexual practice (in the forming of a couple, whether or not the physical sexual is implicated) which maintains heterosexual identifications and aims (by not changing the structural relations between men and women, even if polygamy is contested). It is perhaps in this way that the 'feminine', which I more or less excluded from this study in the introduction, could productively re-enter the discussion of women's agency: the feminine as that which is not contained by practices and which can accomplish aims that are contrary to those suggested by a specific practice, for example.

If the masculinist *négritude* writing and the movement in general were able to propose a new radical understanding and functioning of the 'Black' man, even through the feminine (see, for example, Smith's 1994 study on the feminine in Césaire's poetry), various new material practices through the innovative strategies of individuals and collectivities in the Francophone world demand a reassessment of the understanding of the active being/becoming of women.[12] I ask, then, that we consider this writing as a means of producing this woman, outside heterosexual married polygamy, and not quite, as Jameson writes (of Sartre's understanding of Flaubert), as a resolution 'in the imaginary, [of] what is socially irreconcilable' (Jameson: 1971: 383). I also ask that we go beyond 'remember[ing] the fact of successful revolutions as well, and mak[ing] a place for an art which might be prophetic rather than fantasy-oriented, one which might portend genuine solutions underway rather than projecting formal substitutes for impossible ones' (1971: 385). I urge, indeed, that we credit this discursive forging of a female subjectivity as one which *is* (part of) a solution to women's oppression in polygamous, patriarchal (here) Senegalese society, as well as an articulation of a social resolution to women's participation in forging (a) national culture. I suggest we think of the literary text as the material from which we work towards that 'totalizing' moment in thought and materially inscribe it in language, as we seek to approach what, as Hall put it, 'for Williams ... a "cultural analysis", in the final instance, should deliver'. I hope, before these ideas are seen as over-extensions of the scope of the 'literary', that the intervention of the concept of 'languaging' with which I conclude this piece, helps in arguing for them.

There is no doubt that through a gradual changing of a structurally supported feeling, by changing the practice, Ramatoulaye alters the supportive structure. For example, she begins going to the cinema on her own:

> I overcame my shyness at going alone to cinemas; I would take a seat with less and less embarrassment as the months went by. People stared at the middle-aged lady without a partner. I would feign indifference, while anger hammered against my nerves and the tears I held back welled up behind my eyes.
>
> From the surprised looks, I gauged the slender liberty granted to women. (Bâ 1981: 51)

Yet it is clear that Ramatoulaye extends the limits of this liberty through her persistent practice. I suggest that the writing of this letter is ultimately the larger extension of liberty that one must both appreciate as agency and problematize with regard to the question of language, as indicated earlier. It is the creation of a discourse (about the future of the nation and of the women in it) that disrupts the properly political field as being that of men; it is an appropriation of this discourse and its injection into the sphere of autobiography and women's lives at the level of 'story', and into women's and men's personal lives through readership. Both the act of going to the cinema on her own, as well as the larger act of (this) writing itself, can be read as acts that effectively question social practices and redefine the aims of the character. Ramatoulaye ends her letter with: 'I shall go out in search of [happiness]. Too bad for me if once again I have to write you so long a letter ...' (Bâ 1981: 89), thus clearly inscribing any quest for happiness in this discursive search, in-between aims and practices as it were, anchored between herself and her friend. Given the wide readership this text enjoys, I believe its readings in the context of WCD are significant because their framing through this paradigm opens the exploration of new practices, or at very least, the exploration of the same practices in new terms.

Yet, the instability of categories such as those of aims and practices, or misrecognition and maldistribution, must be invited into the field of assessment with much caution. It is one thing to show that categories are not as fixed as we would like, and quite another to reject completely their possibility as tools for research. Also, before the 'cultural' shift, one might more rigorously scrutinize the investment in individual agency or, rather, the pursuit to tell the story of individual agency.[13] In other terms, our narrative and the assessment towards which it strives are deeply situated in Western academic discourse. Are we certain that it is from this vantage point that the story of individual agency in Third World contexts can, and should, be most appropriately theorized? Alternatively, how does the telling of individual agency alter the research agenda and methods, and what types of outcomes could one anticipate for the understanding of development?[14]

Conclusions: Literature and 'Languaging'[15]

Taking culture, as proposed through WCD, in its most dynamic and complex conception for the analyses of women's practices in the context of what is seen as development, would consequently require a radical restructuring of these very categories. From this perspective, therefore, how would considerations of 'development' in the 'Third World' alter the constituent of 'woman' as proposed? Evidently, the definition for woman will be inadequately achieved from the older paradigms through which development has been studied. For example, would we find useful Judith Butler's call for the understanding of gender as performative, as 'a kind of imitation for which there is no original' (1997: 21)? It would follow from this that there is no essential quality or basis for the category of 'woman', which would be generated in its entirety by performances that create an image (of woman) for which the 'original' is never attainable. We would understand 'gender [as] performative in the sense that it constitutes as an effect the very subject it appears to express' (Butler 1997: 24). How ready and equipped are we, really, to attend to how 'woman' is created through processes of performance, by series of individual acts by women in our societies, even as the role in development of the provisional group these acts posit is studied? Butler's proposal, that 'those ontologically consolidated phantasms of "man" and "woman" are theatrically produced effects that posture as grounds, origins, the normative measure of the real' (1997: 21), would require us to forgo the category of woman as a given from which we can easily analyse its role in development. We would, moreover, be obliged to seek out the conditions that enable such a category to exist, and to exist as such, in particular situations. This would create huge problems for any kind of measurement, and preclude, for example, numerous generalizations. The WCD concern with resistance and agency would also have to be re-evaluated.[16]

Further, the linking of women to production, reproduction and (making visible of) agency that is central to the WCD paradigm also becomes implicated in this 'cultural' shift.[17] From here, reproduction can be understood in terms of making a copy from an original as well as making a new organism of the same species (see Williams 1995: 185). Are we interested, from a WCD perspective, in using these valences of the terms to understand women's agency? What would be the consequences of considering women's production to be innovation in practices by women, as they constantly and conditionally define themselves; and the consequences of including in reproduction the idea of the reproduction of practices as well as the relations that condition them? Even (especially) giving birth will be seen as a practice which reproduces not just the species, but the relations for this practice – in most cases heterosexual male–female relations, sanctioned and maintained through a complex set of other practices, indubitably tied to relations of production in the economic sense.

Walter Mignolo explains that: 'The very concept of literature presupposes the major or official languages of a nation and the transmissions of the cultural literacy built into them' (1996: 188). Its relevance to any study involving spaces demarcated 'nationally', or with reference to the 'nation', thus become important, especially in those instances where the idea of a shared culture is of consequence. Mignolo submits that the concept of literature should move towards 'the idea of languaging as a cultural practice' (1996: 189), where 'languaging' suggests a 'moving away from the idea that language is a fact (e.g. a system of syntactic, semantic and phonetic rules) toward the idea that speaking and writing are moves that *orient* and *manipulate* social domains of interaction' (1996: 188, my emphasis). I have tried to attend to the dual actions of 'orientation' and 'manipulation' that the text effects through its work on specific categories.

It is only by privileging cultural analyses (in the sense discussed earlier) in the context of development that literature can make any contribution to our understanding of specific issues within development. Still, the idea of culture suggested by Stuart Hall – as the meanings and values shared by groups and arising from their historical conditions, relationships and dynamic relation to their existence, along with the practices that can be read as contingent inscriptions of these different relations – demands that cultural analyses 'deliver' an understanding that matches this totalized conception of culture through a similar movement in 'thought'.

Cultural analyses and dialectical thought, accomplished through areas that have too often eschewed the logic of the economic within them, must necessarily move in that direction, while analyses achieved through domains that have reductively considered economic structures outside of experiential and innovative figuring, which is difficult to quantify, for example, must necessarily learn to articulate these areas of what generates the 'culture' in question. For WCD both directions become consequential, because a more complete understanding of women's lives would mean not just making the very important (but measured, as I have suggested above) cultural shift in analyses relating to areas already considered in development studies, but rather, would involve a parallel enlargement of the field of inquiry itself, which would require a legitimization of other bases of information on, and insight regarding, its central questions.

Notes

I gratefully acknowledge Dominic Thomas for his useful comments, particularly those regarding Francophone literature; Tim Watson for his thoughtfully suggested readings on/in cultural studies for a different project, many of which inform this piece or have led to readings used here; Sarah Karim for her excellent research assistance; and the editors of this volume, whose patience and generosity in engaging with my arguments are appreciated and have greatly improved this chapter.

1. The term 'gender' 'suggests that relations between the sexes are a primary aspect of social organization (rather than following from, say, economic or demographic pressures); that the terms of male and female identities are in large part culturally determined (not produced by individuals or collectivities entirely on their own); and that differences between the sexes constitute and are constituted by hierarchical social structures' (Scott 1988: 10). Although it does not attend specifically to differences between gendered women, Scott's definition does move away from an emphasis on the purely economic.

2. Drawing from Cixous or Irigaray, for example; and in general from psychoanalysis, especially following Lacan.

3. While it is clearly impossible to understand the 'Third World' in terms of geographical divisions alone, for the purposes of this chapter the nation of Senegal implicated in the text under consideration as an area of post-coloniality is of significance.

4. See McClintock (1992) regarding the pitfalls of the terminology associated with the 'post-colonial', and McClintock (1992), Bahri (1995), Michel (1995) and Li (1995) for considerations of the field.

5. Bourdieu (1994) convincingly shows how language (different languages, but also differently accented or otherwise marked versions of a single language) is both a marker of social and economic class and also a symbol of status, and thus an important factor in the access to material and discursive power.

6. For a discussion of 'tactics' and 'strategies' see de Certeau (1984: xii–xix). Simplified here for my purposes, tactics are provisional and time-bound, while strategies visualize a more easily identifiable opposition. So, if my tactics differ from those proposed (for example by engaging more actively the economic or by emphasizing structuring processes rather than those that allow their disruption) due to what is more commonly examined in the discipline from which I write, the overall strategy that aims to reach a more complete understanding of women's actions in the context of development is shared.

7. 'The author is what gives the disturbing language of fiction its unities, its nodes of coherence, its insertion in the real' (Foucault 1981: 58).

8. Such a reading is suggestive of the literary text as a space in which to imaginatively and in imagination deal with realities external to it. I believe strongly that they indeed accomplish this, and that this is a valuable and important process. In this discussion, however, I want to engage with a different articulation of the literary text.

9. To be sure, the specific national space would itself be too reductive for Jameson's conception of the 'system as a whole'. Yet, to invoke the post-colonial national space necessarily forces into consideration the larger systems that validate and oppose it.

10. For a discussion of this sense of 'reproduction', see Williams's essay on 'Reproduction' in *Sociology of Culture* (1995: 181–205). I return to this understanding of 'reproduction' in my conclusion below.

11. For a forceful argument regarding the place of indigenous (specifically African) languages, see Barber (1995). See also Alexander, Bamgbose, Obanya, Rabenoro, Rassool and Wolff in the special issue of *Social Dynamics* (1999) regarding this question of languages in the more recent African post-colonial context.

12. To be sure, the disciplinary demarcation of 'Francophonie' (and, for example, its separation from other areas of post-coloniality, its connections to other spaces of post-coloniality in the same areas) also becomes problematized in such a consideration.

13. Clearly, I believe that individual agency and a recognition of this agency by individuals is crucial to any kind of positive self-image; it is essential to survival in many instances. I also see the effect of telling these stories: to combat the essentializing, generalizing theories that label Third World women as victims in need to be rescued. I still think, however, that there is room for further discussion of the investment in the narrative of individual agency.

14. My use of 'we' here and elsewhere in this chapter relates specifically to this WCD project and book and the debates and questions it summons. The questions my chapter raises are the result of my thinking through the new WCD proposal, and I therefore participate in this collective project of evaluating how best to figure women's lives in the Third World while analysing development.

15. The term is from Walter Mignolo (1996).

16. See, for example, Seyla Benhabib's objection to this idea of performativity:

First, what kind of empirical social research paradigms is Butler privileging in her views of gender constitution as performativity? Are these adequate for the explanation of ontogenetic processes of development? Second, what normative vision of agency follows from, or is implied by this theory of performativity? Can the theory account for the capacities of agency and resignification it wants to attribute to individuals, thus explaining not only the constitution of the self but also the resistance that this very self is capable of in the face of power/discourse regimes? (1995: 111)

See also Butler's response regarding agency. She argues: 'To the extent that a performative act appears to "express" a prior intention, a doer *behind* the deed, that prior agency is only legible as the effect of that utterance' (1995: 134), underscoring the need to reconsider the consequences of the cultural shift proposed.

17. Note the frequent return of these (linked) terms in Chua, Bhavnani and Foran (2000). Early in their essay, they propose the fruitfulness of viewing culture 'as the relationship between production and reproduction in women's lives, and when women's agency is made explicit' (2000: 821).

VISIONS 4

· ·

The Subjective Side of Development: Sources of Well-being, Resources for Struggle

Linda Klouzal

§ THE problem of development contains an existential question: how do people deal with suffering? In every life there is suffering, yet regions that have enormous material problems are characterized by hardship on an everyday basis that is often difficult to imagine. A development focus on suffering privileges a humanitarian agenda, because its implicit concern is the immediate well-being of people.

The issue of suffering adds to scholarship by broadening the category of development. To address suffering, the scholar must ask both about material conditions and the experience of hardship, countering a tendency in development research to ignore subjectivity. One important issue raised by this approach is whether scholars can study women's suffering without contributing to the depiction of women as victims in public discourse. The problem, however, is not that current scholarship and the media pay too much attention to women's pain, but how they characterize that pain.

Attending to emotional pain can heighten awareness of women's agency. Subjective responses tap into human agency and reflect the complexity and depth of people, a process that involves confronting personalities, values, emotions and relationships as well as the ways psychological needs go unmet. A woman's experience contains her definition of the situation. Narratives about suffering are stories about women struggling against conditions that threaten their dignity; gaining insight into actors' internal lives allows audiences to develop a complex and empathic understanding of women's suffering. Such an approach also prompts scholars to examine the conditions and relations that threaten women's dignity, attachments, autonomy and self-fulfilment. By looking at what women's experiences mean to them, scholars gain insight into under-represented perspectives. This approach broadens the definition of resources to include non-material responses such as avenues of self-expression and relationships of trust. It foregrounds the problems of women in a way that facilitates creative solutions.

In this essay I reflect on the potential of a Women, Culture and Development paradigm to address subjective issues relevant to development, by drawing on preliminary impressions from research I conducted in 1999 on women who fought in Cuba's revolutionary insurrection during the 1950s. These women's struggle, as defined by them, targeted social problems such as poverty, health care and access to education. An impressive aspect of these interviews is the sense of vitality, self-fulfilment and pride the women conveyed in telling their stories. This comes across although more than 40 years have passed. More than moving tales, their recollections are occasions of, and insights into, something that helped nurture and strengthen the women during the fight – memories that still sustain them.

Studying women revolutionaries allows one to examine the relationship between politics and development not just at the structural level, but also through an analysis of the experiences of people who pursued a particular vision of development. I treat development here as not merely a set of programmes, policies or a series of historical events, but also as about the preservation of a person's integrity – material, emotional and physical. It is a lifelong issue for every citizen, for every woman. The issue of what constitutes development thus revolves at least partly around such questions as:

- What sustains women at the local level *during* their struggles for a better life?
- What gives one a sense of vitality and self-fulfilment over the long run?
- What sustains a person's sense of self, pride, creativity and humour – evidence of psychological well-being – under conditions of hardship and change?
- What enables women as women and as members of specific communities within diverse cultural milieus to confront suffering and to survive and grow?

As scholars, we need to address explicitly the non-material aspects of women's lives, their psychological, relational and emotional well-being. There are two general questions I would like to see Women, Culture and Development scholars address. First, what forms of suffering are the women we study experiencing, and why? Second, how are women sustaining themselves and what types of changes would contribute to their continued well-being?

This essay targets a specific subjective problem that is one aspect of the larger issue of suffering: how women deal with trauma. A trauma refers to the combined affective, physiological and cognitive response to a serious external threat to one's physical and emotional well-being.[1] Trauma is a central issue of psychology. It was a subject of Freud's early studies. Trauma is currently understood in diverse ways by different schools of psychology; here I use the term trauma in a general, not clinical, sense.[2]

The ubiquity of traumatic experience in much of the world makes it an important subject for development studies. Trauma in a woman's life exacerbates her material problems by adding another layer of trouble on top of a precarious situation. A woman who can confront her internal pain is able to seek creative solutions to her considerable external difficulties and take action.[3] Studying trauma is consistent with an emphasis on culture in the Women, Culture and Development approach as trauma research highlights women's subjectivity, lived experience and their means of overcoming the harmful impact of traumatic events. Here, I offer some preliminary observations about resources that appear to sustain women despite externally stressful experiences.

The women I interviewed in Cuba, because of the political nature of their struggle, are a valuable source for preliminary discussion about this issue. Virtually all of these women suffer visibly from the loss of people close to them. Their own lives had been in danger at times and they lived with the constant threat of loss of loved ones during the insurrection. Some were on the run for extended lengths of time. A few had been seriously physically hurt or tortured as a result of their participation. What is striking about these women is that although they clearly suffer from trauma, they also appear vital, have a strong sense of self-efficacy and express positive feelings about their actions and the future.[4] In assessing the current situation in Cuba, many expressed continued conviction in the importance of their work and the future of the revolution. For example, when asked about the longevity of the achievements of the revolution in the face of Cuba's current hardships, one woman replied: 'I have a great deal of hope. This is what we fight for and we are not discouraged because we have seen the outcome among the students, the youth ... we have seen how they have bettered themselves' (interview with the author, 1999).

Another woman ties her work in the literacy campaign to her confidence in the future.

> I'm going to give you the example of my own work. We launched the literacy campaign with the government, and all the work associated with this campaign is being continued today, nothing has been lost. We launched the literacy campaign – this is just an example, but it applies to everything else – and we keep on working on that, we won't go back to illiteracy. We keep on advancing and maintaining our gains. And these are precisely the aspirations you find everywhere else in Latin America, aspirations that have not been achieved yet. (interview with the author, 1999)

Despite their advancing years, these women maintain a keen interest in the well-being of their communities. Their demeanour, tone and stories reflect pride in their achievements and the achievements of their revolution. So, what specifically about their struggle and activism has this therapeutic, life-sustaining quality? I will suggest three ways the women sustained themselves in the face of considerable trauma, all connected to insurrectionary activism.[5] The first is a sense of one's place in history, and awareness of a legacy of struggle and suffering similar to one's own. The second is the importance of community and secure relational ties. The third is the memory, through stories, of empowering acts.

There appears to be a positive psychological aspect to trauma victims having a sense of place in some larger history of suffering. Terr's research (1990, 1994) on trauma documents that the young people she studied experienced improvement by reading histories, news stories or biographies containing incidents in which others experienced similar difficulties. She also observes that when people keep abreast of current events, locally or around the world, they feel more comfortable about what has happened to them, even when their trauma is the result of a random act of violence or parental abuse.

Insurrection is an instance in which people are aware of a history of struggle involving suffering in the past and present. Revolutionaries learn this history and often feel personally connected to past revolutionaries and martyrs. Several of the women I interviewed, especially those who were most active, had close ties to other revolutionaries in the movement and expressed a vivid awareness of a continuous history of struggle for freedom and social justice in their country. They also had a keen appreciation for the role of women in this history.

Community is a key theme in the women's stories. Relationship ties may be important to reducing trauma in a number of ways. Communities of activists reinforce the fact that one's feelings of oppression have external causes, shifting the trouble from the internal problems of the person to external conditions in the world. Unlike many instances of trauma in which the individual has no outlet upon which to vent, revolutions involve a clear enemy, which allows a target for negative feelings like rage. Yet, feelings of vulnerability and terror have a paralysing effect on people and are often seen as unacceptable or shameful to the person experiencing them (Scheff and Retzinger 1991, Scheff 1994).[6] Feeling and expressing these states require a sense of safety from the immediate external threat and a compassionate listener with whom one has bonds of trust.

Uncomfortable affective states such as shame, terror and rage are made bearable by having supportive people whom one trusts. Communities, large or small, which provide caring witnesses to members' suffering, enable people to feel their pain. Awareness of another's genuine empathy may alleviate the destructiveness of the traumatic event, reiterating that one's own emotions are legitimate and that one is acceptable and valued. Miller (1982 and other works) has written extensively about the healing effect of a caring witness in the life of traumatized children. The question is, do women who struggle with humiliating abuse or violence have access to people whom they trust enough to express to and work through with the paralysing emotions of shame, vulnerability and terror?

To the extent that communities facilitate the expression of such emotions, they free people from affective states which may otherwise be channelled into depression and anxiety. Scheff and Retzinger have documented that expressing shame can actually have the effect of improving bonds between people (Retzinger 1991, Scheff and Retzinger 1991, Scheff 1994). Thus, transforming the external conditions of one's life may hinge, in part, on an internal transformation involving the expression of negative affective states. Communities empower women not only cognitively, by allowing them to understand their problems better, but emotionally and psychologically by building inner reservoirs of strength.

One striking aspect of the interviews I conducted in Cuba was that my interviewees often spoke at length about specific incidents of resistance. I decided to resist treating these stories as anecdotal and instead treated them as insights into something subjectively meaningful to these women. Many of the stories were about incidents in which people whom they knew, usually women, stood up to the military either as individuals or as a group to help others in danger. In one story, a woman describes the scene of a burial procession for a fallen revolutionary in which she marched with a group of women:

> That same afternoon we participated in Frank's burial.[7] There were some rumours saying that the police were waiting for us at the cemetery with machine guns and all that ... but nobody turned a hair. The burial ceremony was majestic. I remember that we were walking at the front of the burial procession and people at their balconies were throwing flowers to us. The people from Santiago had a revolutionary spirit ... you could communicate with no words at all. (interview with the author, July 1999)

Memories of successful resistance were often told with great emotion, eliciting expressions of pride and awe. What do these stories mean to the women? I believe they serve in part as sources of empowerment in the face of mortal danger, even retrospectively. Confronting a more powerful enemy and feeling shame, vulnerability and terror is traumatizing not just in the moment, but also when remembered years later. Thus, incidents of strength may be relived to remind the person that she is empowered, and to counter the horrible experience of being a victim, in whatever sense that may have occurred (loss of loved ones, torture, repression of expression).

To be empowered means to have allies who are strong (brave, crafty, resilient, successful) and who share one's struggle. The women selected incidents from their past that reveal both the intensity of their experiences and how they manage to confront that past. The issue of representation is important to the long-term psychological well-being of people who exhibit the effects of trauma. What counts to the person one studies is how she is represented in her own mind, and how she imagines herself represented in the minds of those whom she loves and respects.

As development scholars, we need to take a close look at the people we study, their internal needs and resources as individuals and their roles as members of communities. The women I interviewed provided me with insights into how they sustained a sense of well-being in the face of trauma. Community is a momentous component of this: to feel one is part of some larger community of people, living or past, who have experienced similar suffering; to have an intelligent, trustworthy, compassionate witness to one's pain; and to have a sense of self as empowered through one's connection to allies who are strong and brave in the face of external threat.

A Women, Culture and Development approach seeks to address spheres that impact women's lives, but are often not defined as part of development. Material well-being is tied to, affected by and affects, psychological well-being. Understanding how material problems have an impact on women's subjective states and how women sustain a sense of well-being during hardship, enables scholars to identify the priorities of women in their communities as well as the resources – subjective, cultural and material – they have at their disposal. Many such resources have been overlooked in economistic development studies. The approach advocated here encourages thinking more broadly about development problems and development resources.

Notes

1. Events frequently associated in psychology with trauma and traumatic symptoms include one-time life-threatening experiences such as accidents, natural disasters and assaults, as well as chronic forms of deprivation and abuse, including repeated beatings, molestation, rape and poverty.

2. Many of the ideas in this essay come from the work of Miller (1982, 1984, 1990, 1990a) and Terr (1990, 1994).

3. In a specific discussion of therapeutic responses to trauma, Miller advocates Stettbacher's approach (1990) which consists of: '(1) describing the situation and one's sensations; (2) experiencing and expressing emotions; (3) querying the situation; and (4) articulating needs' (1990a: 179).

4. The existence of trauma is indicated by the nature of the women's experiences, the expression of intense feelings of grief and loss and vivid memories of long past events. These are present alongside pride, humour, a strong sense of having contributed to history and to their communities, and a positive outlook for the future of Cuba (the latter are usually absent in trauma victims).

5. These could apply to other types of activism, such as community development.

6. It is important to note that how emotions are interpreted (that is, whether they are considered shameful) will vary by culture.

7. Frank País was the organizer of the urban arm of the M-26-7, Fidel Castro's insurrectionary organization, in the eastern province of Oriente. His assassination in 1957 sparked spontaneous protests throughout the island.

VISIONS 4
· ·

Culture and Resistance: A Feminist Analysis of Revolution and 'Development'

Julia D. Shayne

§ ONE thing academics, policy-makers and activists seem to agree on is that the term 'development' is loaded. Intellectually it is replete with problems, perpetual imbalances in power and enhanced divisions between the rich and the poor. However, from my travels, informal discussions and research in Latin America it became clear to me that development is a goal on the minds of most of the women I spoke with. The women I met in the smaller towns of Guatemala, or the sprawling urban centre of Santiago de Chile, certainly did not conceive of development as a United States Agency for International Development (USAID) package to arrive on the executive branch's desk, complete with orders of deeper debt and stranglehold structural adjustment policies. Nor did development mean neoliberalism or privatization. It did not equal free trade or export processing zones, but rather started with what many of us have grown to consider basic: removal of the rubbish from the source of water, education for boys *and* girls, health care, nutritious meals and decent housing. This is not to say that the women of Latin America were arguing only for 'basic needs'. However, my feminist sensibilities indicate that it is safe to assume that if needs as basic as sanitation, potable water, literacy, housing and education are addressed, a sense of empowerment rooted in well-being is fostered, allowing women to use their creative capacities to expand the academic meaning of development (see Sen 1995).

My vision of the Third World is one that eliminates the omnipotence of First World–Third World power imbalances. It would be a place where 'traditional dress' was worn for culture's sake, not as an 'exotic' photo opportunity for the Western tourist, and where the woman wearing it also has access to shoes, vaccinations and education in her first language. The roads would be lined with cultivated agricultural fields, harvested both for export and internal consumption. The debt would be eaten by the irresponsible lender nations and, most significantly, the future of the Third World would be directed by its citizens. The government members of the World Trade Organization (WTO),

International Monetary Fund (IMF) and World Bank might be forced to take some vacations (which their salaries could certainly accommodate) or re-formulate their programmes to address labour and environmental laws. Were the profit motive eliminated, the inequities between First and Third Worlds would eventually flatten as well. This vision is idealistic, to be sure, but the women with whom I spoke reminded me that small victories are often the beginning of larger ones.

When researching Latin American revolutions and feminism, I have found that we can move closer to the reasons why people rebel and risk their lives, their families and their homes, often in opposition to military regimes which have been established or supported by the West. Revolutions offer a glimpse of the causes of nationalism and all its masculine tendencies, including the simultaneous responsibility, and thus subjugation, that fall to women in order to protect 'the nation'. Similarly, violent revolutions illuminate patterns of exile, immigration and thus race relations in the First World. In my latest project, '"The Revolution Question": Feminism in Cuba, Chile, and El Salvador Compared (1952–1999)', I sought to understand the complex interplay between gender, revolution and feminism through the use of an original concept called 'gendered revolutionary bridges'. Gendered revolutionary bridges (GRBs) are a three-tiered way of understanding and interpreting the roles women play in revolutionary movements, how gender relations shift through such participation and the attendant feminist consciousness and/or movements that grow from revolutionary mobilization. First, GRBs are instrumental, in that revolutionary movements use femininity as a way to gain access to dangerous or hostile political environments. Second, they are strategic, where women (as opposed to male leadership) consciously decide to exploit society's social construction of gender in order to perform revolutionary tasks. And third, GRBs are feminist, as long-term gender relations may be altered by women in public positions, thus laying the groundwork for the reconstruction of masculinity and femininity in post-revolutionary situations. In short, both men and women subvert femininity into a revolutionary tool, in some cases leading to long-term transformations in gender roles in the post-revolutionary period.

This book helps to demonstrate that a Women, Culture and Development (WCD) analysis is the fusion of much exemplary scholarship from the past 20 years, minus the disciplinary boundaries. Such a paradigm has allowed me to pursue rigorously questions of gender, revolution and feminism. As always, it is imperative that we are clear on our definitions. In this case, we may understand culture as the praxis of agency. That is, a cultural analysis allows us to ask *how* women rebelled, not just what structural causes lead to resistance. The causes of revolution, after all, do not illuminate women's presence, let alone the methods of women's resistance. A WCD lens facilitates the uncovering of women's revolutionary agency that was previously cloaked behind the rigid and misleading façade of femininity. This paradigmatic expansion leads to the reinvestigation and rewriting of history, which inevitably elaborates the roles of women and gender in our understanding of any and every social pattern in the Third, and by extension First, World.

Reconciling the contradictions of academia and beyond is one of the most difficult challenges that many of us confront. Picking our battles strategically – in both the discursive and political spheres – is often a path interrupted by frustration and inner intellectual turmoil. In my own work I have always attempted to meet several goals, all of which are closely related to Women, Culture and Development and the challenge of reconciling the academic with the activist. Understanding First World–Third World dynamics is of great significance in understanding power dynamics at many levels. If the world is indeed 'shrinking', this suggests that social problems are crossing borders as quickly as Nike plants. To stay abreast of such changes I have found that studying revolutions and, more precisely, the women who make them, is a path to a partial understanding of First World–Third World dynamics.

Related to this, I would argue that it is imperative that we step beyond analysis of secondary sources about revolution in order to move towards the above goals. Historical archives, as many of us are often reminded, tend to elide women's participation. Interview-centred fieldwork is thus fundamental to the systematic documentation and creation of historical narratives from and about the feminine side of revolution. While in Latin America I was privileged to interview over 60 revolutionary and / or feminist women leaders from Cuba, Chile and El Salvador. I spoke with women who struggled alongside Fidel Castro and Salvador Allende; women who fought on the frontlines in El Salvador's guerrilla war; women who stared down the military governments of Pinochet's Chile, Batista's Cuba and wartime El Salvador with only their maternal wardrobes, headscarves and bullhorns to protect them. Eighty-year-old María Antonia Figueroa, former treasurer with the July 26th Guerrilla Movement led by Fidel Castro (M-26-7), explained that:

> Many women thought that their husbands and their sons would get killed and that it was more difficult for women to get killed … My mother was an organizer of the mothers' demonstration; it was all women. That was in … 1958. It was a beautiful demonstration: they came out of a church and they exited as if they were coming out of mass. But they were not in mass and they all marched like that through all of the main streets; thousands of women in Santiago de Cuba … The main sign said 'we mothers demand an end to the assassination of our sons'. (personal interview, 1999)

Figueroa goes on to explain how these women, led in part by her mother, confronted the military using their feminine persuasion and position to diffuse the potential violence of a revolutionary street demonstration in the midst of a dictatorial climate.

I met younger and older women in all three nations who experienced various degrees of personal and political marginalization as a result of dialoguing and organizing for feminism and gender equity in sociopolitical contexts that were often less than friendly to such debate. I met elected officials attempting to merge their feminist and leftist convictions into platforms advantageous to their often disparate constituencies. I also met women with the less glamorous jobs, such as revolutionary 'logistics'. Logistics, as I was reminded, is not a simple matter of pushing paper, but of transporting weapons, for example. Women were often assigned these tasks as they had skirts in which to hide the otherwise conspicuous tools of revolution. As tends to be the case in transnational fieldwork, it is important to remain attentive to one's preconceived categories. Indeed, a seemingly politically neutral and unideological concept like 'logistics' is imbued with the beholder's own worldview. The challenge to discursive patterns is something with which feminists (and academics) have long been experimenting. The women revolutionaries in Latin America provided one of many parallel examples for such debate, where the long-term results provide aftershocks beyond the ivory towers and into the walls of the state. In other words, if First World academics have identified the need to challenge categories, then Latin American feminists and revolutionaries have shown us how. As Aracely López, a former member of the Salvadoran guerrillas (FMLN), then of the Committee of Mothers of Political Prisoners, the Disappeared and the Assassinated of El Salvador (CO-MADRES) and currently part of the feminist movement, explained:

> I, for example, worked on health care when we went clandestine. Then I incorporated myself as a guerrilla, and then I came here [San Salvador]. But I do consider that *any activity* one engages in as a force for revolutionary change, that transforms the living conditions of people, I believe that in that sense I have been doing many [revolutionary] things in the spaces in which I have participated. In each space I have seen myself as working [towards] allowing people to express what they don't like and not to remain silent. When it is not possible at an individual level, [we] work to do it in a group or collectively. (personal interview, 1998, emphasis added)

López, then, is urging us to rethink what we mean by revolution and revolutionary.

Reflecting for a moment on the histories intertwined with the visions of the women I met, I am left inspired and encouraged by their words. Incarceration, failed revolution, disappearances of loved ones, physical and psychological resistance from male partners, misogynist laws and tensions in the left (among other things) were/are real obstacles to organizing in the three cases I looked at. One could easily walk away defeated. In my many interviews with Latin American feminists and/or revolutionaries, however, I am always left inspired. Indeed, the sorrow, grief and pain of deep physical and emotional scars have touched me as well. But alongside that is the perseverance to redress old questions, rethink new ones and offer transnational models of feminism from which our 'shrinking globe' could certainly benefit. In other words, the Latin American revolutionary feminists whom I met offered a grassroots model of a Women, Culture and Development paradigm. Women's revolutionary contributions are not always explicitly such, but when sifting through the lesser-known stories we come to see that women did far more than support 'their men' in struggle, but rather orchestrated and offered exemplary models of resistance. It is the task of WCD scholars to assist in the excavation and archiving of these provocative tales.

The Latin American revolutionary feminists I met provide more than an academic model for research. As critical scholars, activists and women in the Third World themselves know, development programmes devoid of input from local populations and/or not directed in significant ways by women tend to exacerbate already difficult situations. Many Western policy-makers seem set on believing that Third World women are ill-equipped to manage the massive tasks that comprise the development regime. What the revolutionary feminists of Latin America remind planners who are stuck in this way of thinking is that women have been organizing, shaping and redirecting projects as national in scope as revolutions for decades: why should we assume that such courage and foresight cannot also be applied to the revolutionary development projects that WCD advocates?

VISIONS 4

. . . .

Alternatives to Development: Of Love, Dreams and Revolution

John Foran

The true revolutionary is guided by a great feeling of love. (Che Guevara)

To make love means that you have to love and understand love. And that's what the basis of revolution is about. Who ever said that love ain't part of the revolution? (stic, rapper, in *Blu #8*)

§ THIS essay evokes and pays homage to several beautiful films which have always inspired me to keep going in the struggle: *Love, Women, and Flowers*; *Chile: Obstinate Memory*; *Maria's Story* (see further the essay by Maria Navarrete in this book) and *Jonah who will be 25 in the year 2000*, some of which I will discuss later. I've spent most of my scholarly life studying various aspects of revolutions – their causes, who makes them (and why), what role culture plays in them and, finally, what difference do they make? In this essay, I'd like to offer a few thoughts on what they might teach us about alternatives to development, and how we might draw on a Women, Culture and Development understanding to think about how revolutions might achieve better outcomes in the future – a rather large and speculative topic.

First of all, I would say that revolutions and development go together: that is, there is something about the inequalities and dependency entailed by Third World development that contributes significantly to revolutions where they have occurred. My own understanding draws on the notion of dependent development, taken from the groundbreaking work of Fernando Henrique Cardoso and Enzo Faletto (1979). The concept denotes a decidedly double-edged process: economic growth (as conventionally measured in terms of GNP, trade, industrialization and so forth), accentuated by severe limitations (growing inequality, substandard housing, lack of educational opportunities and health care, inflation, unemployment and more). This combination fuels grievances across class, ethnic and gender lines and is found in the structural background of the revolutions I have studied, in Mexico 1910, China 1949, Cuba 1959, Iran 1979 and Nicaragua 1979, among others.

Revolutions everywhere have attempted to put in place new forms of development – usually socialist – to solve some of these problems, typically with mixed results. Revolutions have many times improved people's lives, including women's, yet everywhere fallen short of the dreams of those who made them. This can be attributed to many things: outside pressures from governments, such as my own country's unspeakably shameful record of intervention in the Third World; the limits of poverty and dependency which continue to exist in revolutionary societies that lack the resources and time to overcome them; and differences among revolutionaries about how to construct a better society – that is, their inevitable flaws as people, and their enmeshment in structures of patriarchy and racism.

Let us recall briefly a few of the twentieth century's revolutionary moments:

- In Russia, in 1917, the feminist Alexandra Kollontai was one of the Bolshevik leaders, calling for 'free love', in the sense that one should be able to love whom one chose; that marriage should be both harder to contract and divorce easier to obtain; and that men should take on their share of the emotional work of the family – ideas that were not adopted and for which she suffered great personal and political loss during her long life (see Kollontai 1977).

- In revolutionary Cuba in the 1970s, legislation was in fact passed that men do 50 per cent of the housework – perhaps showing the influence of Kollontai? This too was something which proved unenforceable, given prevailing cultural attitudes about gender roles – but it points to the willingness of the Cuban revolutionaries to confront their own contradictions (the film *Strawberry and Chocolate* affords a poignant glimpse of how this worked out in the realm of sexuality, another vexed issue in Cuba) (see Randall 1993).

- In Iran, women stood in the front ranks of the demonstrations which faced down the Shah's army in 1978 and 1979, only to be hemmed in afterwards by the Islamic regime's rigid views of gender roles (it is noteworthy that Iranian women have continued to struggle creatively in many ways for their rights, with some success of late) (see Afary 1997).

- In the revolutions of the 1980s in Central America, women participated in growing numbers – most scholars put this at one-third of the guerrilla forces – and took on ever greater responsibilities, yet still suffered so much sexism at the hands of their male comrades that after the revolutions they started their own feminist movements for autonomy in Nicaragua and El Salvador (two superb works on this topic are Shayne 2000 and Kampwirth 2002).

What these experiences seem to share is vigorous activism by women; a degree of success for both women and people generally; and a rollback of gains, a falling short of promise, that stands as a revealing measure of the limited outcomes of all revolutions to this day.

Of Love and Dreams

What does love have to do with it? H. L. Mencken famously claimed that 'Revolution is the sex of politics.' By this he meant that in revolution lay excitement and drama, and the potential for change. Women have long realized this. As Paula Allen and Eve Ensler write in *The Feminist Memoir Project*: 'Being an activist means owning your desire' (Allen and Ensler 1998: 425). And for Alice Walker, in the aptly named *Anything We Love Can Be Saved: A Writer's Activism*:

> There is always a moment in any kind of struggle when one feels in full bloom. Vivid. Alive. One might be blown to bits in such a moment and still be at peace. Martin Luther King, Jr., at the mountaintop. Gandhi dying with the name of God on his lips. Sojourner Truth bearing her breasts at a women's rights convention in 1851. Harriet Tubman exposing her revolver to some of the slaves she had freed, who, fearing an unknown freedom, looked longingly backward to their captivity, thereby endangering the freedom of all ... During my years of being close to people engaged in changing the world I have seen fear turn into courage. Sorrow into joy. Funerals into celebrations. Because whatever the consequences, people, standing side by side, have expressed who they really are, and that ultimately they believe in the love of the world and each other enough *to be that* – which is the foundation of activism. (1997: xxiii)

Latin American women revolutionaries also speak to this vision of love and passion as the basis of revolutionary feminist activism. For Vilma Vázquez, president of Madres Demandientes in El Salvador:

> Feminism is a struggle that has to see itself with the other struggles ... It should have a foundation of love of people. ... I do have the critique that feminism becomes elitist, it becomes for those at the top, and it has to have a foundation of love, hope, and freedom, as well as a search for dignity, of human dignity and in this case for women and men. ... Changes happen with negotiation, debate, and disputes always struggling with men and women. (as interviewed and quoted in Shayne 2000: 256–7)

Love, then, is arguably the emotion that most strongly underlies the vital force that impels many ordinary people into extraordinary acts, across time and place. Expressing hope and optimism, it provides a constructive counterpoint to those other powerful animating emotions, hatred and anger. It is something that the revolutionaries of the future will need to learn to nurture and build upon.

Dreams, too, can feed revolutions. In Patricio Guzmán's remarkable, powerful film, *Chile: Obstinate Memory*, the former director of public relations for Salvador Allende's Popular Unity (UP) government, ex-professor Ernesto Malbran, says:

> The UP was a ship of dreamers propelled by a collective dream, which ran aground. The dream was to carry along and unite the entire country. It was a dream of justice: the right to an education, good health, and shelter. Dreams that don't come true confirm the saying: 'Don't believe in dreams as they are not nourishing.' That's wrong. It was a noble dream. The failure of a dream is hard to take. Especially knowing you can't progress without dreams. Because dreaming is part of the way we apprehend life. (Guzmán 1997, translation from the subtitles)

The film is a powerful meditation on the meanings of remembering such dreams and desires and transmitting them, despite censorship and repression, to a new generation. This process of recalling and teaching memories has profound effects both on those who recall the events they lived through, and those too young to have experienced them. When Guzmán shows his earlier epic documentary, *The Battle of Chile*, to a group of teenage schoolchildren, many at first try to justify the coup that killed the UP's dreams, but eventually some weep openly at the dawning knowledge of a historical opportunity missed and of their parents' world of locked-up secrets. That this dream is still alive, that it did not fail, is suggested by the detention of Pinochet in England and his political eclipse in Chile. As Ariel Dorfman notes of these recent events: 'It's only a dream ... yet ... The Pinochet case will remain a fundamental step in this search for a better humanity, a better mind for a different sort of mankind and womankind, the arduous construction of a universal consciousness' (Dorfman 2000: 50). The power of love, and of magic, and their connection to dreams of breaking the chain of violence, is underlined fictionally as well in *The House of the Spirits* (1985), Isabel Allende's moving account of Chilean history.

Of Visions

If love and dreams lie at the emotional roots of struggles for 'real development' (for the word 'development' must be reappropriated and revalued), what forms might they take in the future? I would suggest considering this question under the following aspects.

Love of social justice Mercedes Cañas, a Salvadoran sociologist and president of the *Centro de Estudios Feministas*, a small co-operative, renders their goals in these terms:

We have two fundamental axes though we don't always put them into practice: one is the struggle against violence and for tenderness, we say for relationships filled with tenderness, and second is the struggle against neo-liberalism, and the right for everyone to have a happy life. (as interviewed and quoted in Shayne 2000: 260)

Revolutionaries in many places have articulated this goal in terms of social justice, always culturally defined yet remarkably consistent in their insistence that this involves the meeting of basic needs for everyone – a notion embraced of late by the World Bank in a patronizing, if well-intentioned way – increasingly coupled with the realization, in North and South, that this entails ecological sustainability as well. As Gandhi put it long ago: 'Development is a moral force that does not accept poverty, does not accept the widening disparities between the rich and the poor and does not accept the over-exploitation of natural resources' (paraphrased by Chowdhry 1989: 145). Or as 'Old Antonio', the mythical Chiapan character embodied in many of Subcomandante Marcos's communiqués, puts it:

Antonio dreams that the land he works belongs to him. He dreams that his sweat earns him justice and truth; he dreams of schools that cure ignorance and medicines that frighten death. He dreams that his house has light and his table is full; he dreams that the land is free, and that his people govern themselves reasonably. He dreams that he is at peace with himself and with the world ...

A wind comes up and everything stirs. Antonio rises, and walks to meet the others. He has heard that his desire is the desire of many, and he goes to look for them ...

In this country everyone dreams. Now it is time to wake up. (Marcos 1995: 50)

Dreams of inclusion This leads into a second key to revolutionary development: what Amartya Sen has termed 'the freedom to develop our human capabilities', or 'development as freedom' (Sen 2000). For Lorena Peña, FMLN deputy in El Salvador and president of the prominent women's organization MAM, this would mean cultivation of a broad vision of inclusiveness:

Feminism is ... a political current that proposes a different society, from women, but not only for women. It's a women's proposal for a different kind of society for men and women and I believe it's of great value for this reason ... For me this is what feminism is and it has at its center to break all forms of oppression and exploitation between men and women, between rich and poor, between old and young, between races. (as interviewed and quoted in Shayne 2000: 258)

This resonates closely with her comrades Vilma Vázquez and Mercedes Cañas quoted above. Elsewhere, Peña has said: 'A proposal of the left that doesn't integrate the elements of class, gender and race, is not viable or objective, and it doesn't go to the root of our problems' (quoted in Polakoff 1996: 22). And, it might be added, a strategy that doesn't rely on a radical deepening of freedom and democracy into participation across these lines, whatever the difficulties, will fall short.

Of Hows and Mights: The Power and Magic of Love

A large question remains, of course: if there are to be revolutions in the future – and I do believe that the era of revolution has not closed with the end of the Cold War; indeed, I believe that the down- and undersides of 'globalization' will spark struggles of all kinds in the future – how might they have better outcomes? (I take up this question in more detail in Foran 2002.)

One of the most touching filmic depictions of the revolutionary life is offered by John Berger and Alain Tanner's *Jonah who will be 25 in the year 2000/ Jonas qui aura 25 ans en l'an 2000*, a 1976 look at the aftermath of May 1968 in France. In the film's final scene, the worker-intellectual Mathieu drives to work in the dreary gloom of winter on his moped, and delivers a moving monologue to his friends and wife, and to his newborn son, Jonah:

> I want to try to weave the threads of your desires together so that they won't scatter. I'm returning to work. I'll be exploited. I'll try to tie all this together, to unify the field of your desires so that they'll function as levers. I'm cold.
>
> I am the twentieth century, Jonah. All they ask is simply that I accept everything quietly. I can't touch the goods they pay me for. I'm manual labor, manual labor on my bike …
>
> Jonah, the game's not up. Let's take it from the moment when you learn to walk.
>
> Right to the one when the police and the army fire on thousands like you. From your first reading lesson right up to the final democratic decision: to yield nothing more whatever the danger.
>
> Will it be better for you? The better is systematically set aside.
>
> I'll say: no one's going to make decisions for us anymore. The first time maybe nothing will happen, the tenth there'll be a committee, the hundredth time a strike and the hundred and first time, another reading lesson for you, Jonah. As many times as I'll get on my bike to go to work. No, more: as many times as the days of my life. (Berger and Tanner 1983: 159–60, translation slightly modified by me)

In an earlier scene, set in a greenhouse which Mathieu and the local children have turned into a school, we find him asking them questions concerning the attribution of consciousness to things and to objects:

> Does the wind feel the clouds? Does the bicycle know it's moving?
> Can water feel anything?
> And what if it's boiling?
> Where does the sun's name come from?
> Does it know we call it 'sun'?
> When we move does the moon move with us?
> And if we stop? And if we start out again in the other direction?
>
> (Berger and Tanner 1983: 120–22)

The metaphor-image of stopping the path we are all on and setting out on another is the recurrent dream of revolutions, and a profoundly poignant one.

Finally, we might seek concrete answers in the ongoing events in Chiapas, where indigenous women have been struggling to claim the right to define the movement alongside men from the beginning. This is an incredibly creative and dynamic movement, with a real chance of leading to a more democratic, less racist and sexist, and more egalitarian society in Mexico. Love of life, love of people, love of justice, all play a role in its core values. These have been expressed in marvellously poetic ways and strikingly beautiful symbolic acts, as well as in courageous organizing against state violence and for alternative forms of development in the communities of the Lacandón jungle and the Mayan highlands of Mexico (see Foran 2002).

I close with the most famous of the many wonderful slogans of the May 1968 student and worker movement in France: 'Power to the imagination!' I believe that it is imagination, coupled with the courage to dream and love, and to transmit these, in many ways, that may yet change the world for the better.

Bibliography

Abad, A., M. Briones, T. Cordero, R. Manzo and M. Marchán (1998) 'The Association of Autonomous Women Workers, Ecuador, "22nd June"', in K. Kempadoo and J. Doezema (eds) *Global Sex Workers: Rights, Resistance and Redefinition*, London: Routledge, pp. 172–7.

Abbate, J. (1999) *Inventing the Internet*, Cambridge, MA: MIT Press.

Abrahamson, V., M. Meehan and L. Samuel (1998) *The Future ain't What it Used To Be: The 40 Cultural Trends Transforming Your Job, Your Life, Your World*, New York: Riverhead Books.

Afary, J. (1997) 'The war against feminism in the name of the almighty: making sense of gender and Muslim fundamentalism', *New Left Review* 224 (July–August): 89–110.

Agarwal, B. (1988) 'Patriarchy and the "modernising" state: an introduction', in B. Agarwal (ed.) *Structures of Patriarchy: The State, the Community and the Household*, London: Zed Books and New Delhi: Kali for Women, pp. 1–28.

— (1992) 'The gender and environment debate: lessons from India', *Feminist Studies* 18: 119–58.

— (1995) 'Gender, property and the land: bridging a critical gap in economic analysis and policy', in E. Kuiper and J. Sap (eds) *Out of the Margin: Feminist Perspectives on Economics*, London: Routledge, pp. 264–94.

— (1998) 'Environmental action, equity and ecofeminism: debating India's experience', *Journal of Peasant Studies* 25 (4): 55–95.

Agnihotri, I. and V. Mazumdar (1995) 'Changing terms of political discourse: women's movement in India, 1970–1990s', *Economic and Political Weekly* (22 July): 1869–78.

Ahmad, A. (1994) 'Jameson's rhetoric of otherness and the "national allegory"', in A. Ahmad, *In Theory: Classes, Nations, Literatures*, London: Verso, pp. 95–122.

Akrami, J. (1987) 'The blighted spring: Iranian political cinema in the 1970s', in J. D. H. Downing (ed.) *Film and Politics in the Third World*, New York: Praeger, pp. 131–44.

Alexander, M. J. (1991) 'Redrafting morality: the postcolonial state and the sexual offenses bill of Trinidad and Tobago', in C. T. Mohanty, A. Russo and L. Torres (eds) *Third World Women and the Politics of Feminism*, Bloomington and Indianapolis: Indiana University Press, pp. 133–52.

Alexander, N. (1999) 'An African renaissance without African languages?' *Social Dynamics* 25: 11–12.

Allen, P. and E. Ensler (1998) 'An activist love story', in R. Blau DuPlessis and A. Snitow (eds) *The Feminist Memoir Project: Voices from Women's Liberation*, New York: Three Rivers Press, pp. 413–25.

Allende, Isabel (1985) *The House of the Spirits*, translated by Magda Bogin, New York: Bantam.

Alternative Survey Group (1997) *Alternative Economic Survey 1996–97*, New Delhi: Delhi Science Forum.

Alvarez, S. (1999) 'Advocating feminism: the Latin American Feminist NGO boom', *International Feminist Journal of Politics* 1 (2): 181–209.

Alvarez, S., E. Dagnino and A. Escobar (1998) 'Introduction: the cultural and the political in Latin American social movements', in S. Alvarez, E. Dagnino and A. Escobar (eds) *Cultures of Politics/Politics of Cultures: Re-visioning Latin American Social Movements*, Boulder, CO: Westview Press, pp. 1–29.

Amadiume, I. (1987) *Male Daughters, Female Husbands: Gender and Sex in an African Society*, London and New Jersey: Zed Books.

— (1997) 'Part one: Re-writing history', in I. Amadiume, *Reinventing Africa: Matriarchy, Religion and Culture*, London and New York: Zed Books, pp. 29–158.

— (1998) 'Religion, sexuality and women's empowerment in Nwapa's *The Lake Goddess*', in M. Umeh (ed.) *Emerging Perspectives on Flora Nwapa: Critical and Theoretical Essays*, Trenton, NJ: Africa World Press, pp. 515–29.

— (2000) *Daughters of the Goddess, Daughters of Imperialism: African Women, Culture, Power and Democracy*, London and New Jersey: Zed Books.

Anita (1996) 'Reproductive health care strategy – a gender-sensitive approach to family welfare', *Health for the Millions* (May/June): 5–7.

Appiah, K. A. (1991) 'Is the post- in postmodernism the post- in postcolonial?' *Critical Inquiry* 17: 336–57.

Area de estadística y censos y ministério de economia indústria y comércio et al. (1998) *Encuesta de hogares de propósitos múltiples módulo de empleo, julio 1997*, San José, Costa Rica.

Arizpe, L. (1999) 'Freedom to create: women's agenda for cyberspace', in W. Harcourt (ed.) *Women @ Internet: Creating New Cultures in Cyberspace*, London: Zed Books, pp. xii–xvi.

Armitt, L. (ed.) (1991) *Where No Man Has Gone Before: Women and Science Fiction*, London: Routledge.

Athanasiou, T. (1996) *Divided Planet: The Ecology of Rich and Poor*, Boston, MA: Little, Brown & Co.

Bâ, M. (1981) *So Long a Letter*, translated by M. Bodé-Thomas, London: Heinemann.

Babb, F. (2001) *After Revolution: Mapping Gender and Cultural Politics in Nicaragua*, Austin: University of Texas Press.

Babu, B. N. (1998) *Handbook of Vastu*, New Delhi: UBS Publishers' Distributors Ltd.

Baden, S. and A. M. Goetz (1997) 'Who needs [sex] when you can have [gender]? Conflicting discourses on gender at Beijing', *Feminist Review* 56: 3–25.

Bagchi, J. (1990) 'Representing nationalism: ideology of motherhood in colonial Bengal', *Economic and Political Weekly* (20–27 October): 20–27.

— (1994) *Indian Women: Myth and Reality*, Hyderabad: Sangam Books.

Bahri, D. (1995) 'Once more with feeling: what is postcolonialism?' *Ariel* 26 (1): 51–82.

Bakker, I. (1994). 'Introduction: engendering macro-economic policy reform in the era of global restructuring and adjustment', in I. Bakker (ed.) *The Strategic Silence: Gender and Economic Policy*, London: Zed Books/North–South Institute, pp. 1–29.

Balderston, D. and D. J. Guy (eds) (1997) *Sex and Sexuality in Latin America*, New York: New York University Press.

— (1997a) 'Introduction' in D. Balderston and D. J. Guy (eds) *Sex and Sexuality in Latin America*, New York: New York University Press, pp. 1–6.

Bamgbose, A. (1999) 'African language development and language planning', *Social Dynamics* 25 (1): 13–30.

Bandarage, A. (1984) 'Women in development: liberalism, marxism and marxist-feminism', *Development and Change* 15 (4): 495–515.

Bang, A. and R. Bang (1989) 'WCH rather than MCH', *Lancet* 2 (8672) (11 November): 1158.

Barber, K. (1995) 'African language, literature and postcolonial criticism', *Research in African Literatures* 26 (4): 3–30.

Barnett, T. E. (1992) 'Legal and administrative problems of forestry in Papua New Guinea', in S. Henningham and R. J. May (eds) *Resources, Development and Politics in the Pacific Islands*, Bathurst: Crawford House Press, pp. 90–118.

Barroso, C. and C. Bruschini (1991) 'Building politics from personal lives: discussions on sexuality among poor women in Brazil', in C. T. Mohanty, A. Russo and L. Torres (eds) *Third World Women and the Politics of Feminism*, Bloomington: Indiana University Press, pp. 153–72.

Bartlett, R. V. (1986) 'Ecological rationality: reason and environmental policy', *Environmental Ethics* 8: 221–39.

Bartlett, R. V. and P. A. Kurian (1999) 'The theory of environmental impact assessment: implicit models of policy making', *Policy & Politics* 27 (4): 415–33.

Basu, A. (1995) 'Introduction', in A. Basu (ed.) *Women's Movements in Global Feminism*, Boulder, CO: Westview Press, pp. 1–18.

— (1998) 'Appropriating gender', in P. Jeffrey and A. Basu (eds) *Appropriating Gender: Women's Activism and Politicized Religion in South Asia*, London: Routledge, pp. 3–14.

— (1998a) 'Hindu women's activism in India and the questions it raises', in P. Jeffery and A. Basu (eds) *Appropriating Gender: Women's Activism and Politicized Religion in South Asia*, London: Routledge, pp. 167–84.

Basu, A and R. Basu (1999) 'Of men, women, and bombs: engendering India's nuclear explosions', *Dissent* 46 (1) (Winter), at http://www.igc.org/dissent

Bay, M. (director) (1998) *Armageddon* [videocassette], USA: Touchstone Pictures.

Beall, J. (1997) 'In sickness and in health: gender issues in health policy and their implications for development in the 1990s', in I. Baud and I. Smyth (eds) *Searching for Security: Women's Responses to Economic Transformation*, London and New York: Routledge, pp. 67–95.

Beck, U. (1992) *Risk Society: Towards a New Modernity*, London: Sage Publications.

— (1995) *Ecological Politics in an Age of Risk*, Cambridge: Polity Press.

Beck, U., A. Giddens and S. Lash (1994) *Reflexive Modernization: Politics, Tradition and Aesthetics in the Modern Social Order*, Cambridge: Polity Press.

Bekic, Z. and B. Forté (1993) 'Crime in time and space', *Mean Streets* 10 (October): 31–3.

Belausteguigoitia, M. (2000) 'The right to rest: women's struggle to be heard in the Zapatistas' movement', *Development* 43 (3): 81–7.

Benería, L. (1996) 'The foreign debt crisis and the social costs of adjustment in Latin America', in J. Friedmann et al., *Emergences: Women's Struggles for Livelihood in Latin America*, Los Angeles, CA: UCLA Latin American Center, pp. 11–27.

Benería, L. and G. Sen (1981) 'Accumulation, reproduction, and women's role in economic development: Boserup revisited', *Signs* 7 (3): 279–98.

— 1982) 'Class and gender inequalities and women's role in economic development: theoretical and practical implications', *Feminist Studies* 8 (1): 157–76.

Benhabib, S. (1995) 'Subjectivity, historiography, and politics: reflections on the "feminism/postmodernism" exchange', in S. Benhabib, *Feminist Contentions: A Philosophical Exchange*, New York: Routledge, pp. 17–34.

Bensmaïa, R. (1999) 'Postcolonial nations: political or poetic allegories? (On Tahar Djaout's "L'invention du désert")', *Research in African Literatures* 30 (2): 151–63.

Berger, J. and A. Tanner (1983) *Jonah who will be 25 in the year 2000/Jonas qui aura 25 ans en l'an 2000*, translated by Michael Palmer, Berkeley, CA: North Atlantic Books.

Berger, P. and H. Hsiao (1988) *In Search of An East Asian Development Model*, New Brunswick: Transaction Books.

Bergeron, S. (2001) 'Political economy discourses of globalization and feminist politics', *Signs* 26 (1) (Summer): 983–1006.

Beverly, J. (1999) *Subalternity and Representation: Arguments in Cultural Theory*, Durham and London: Duke University Press.

Bhabha, H. (1992) 'Postcolonial criticism', in S. Greenblatt and G. Gunn (eds) *Redrawing the Boundaries: English and American Studies*, New York: MLA, pp. 437–65.

Bhavnani, K.-K. (1997) 'Women's studies and its interconnections with "race", ethnicity and sexuality', in V. Robinson and D. Richardson (eds) *Introducing Women's Studies: Feminist Theory and Practice*, London: Macmillan, pp. 27–53.

Bhavnani, K.-K., J. Foran and P. Kurian (2000) 'Notes for book project on *Feminist Futures*'.

Bhosle, V. (1998) 'Thirteen at the Table', *Rediff on the Net* (19 March).

Bhowmik, S. and R. Jhabvala (1996) 'Rural women manage their own producer co-operatives: Self Employed Women's Association (SEWA)/Banaskantha Women's Indian Association in Western India', in M. Carr, M. Chen and R. Jhabvala (eds) *Speaking Out: Women's Economic Empowerment in South Asia*, London: Intermediate Technology Publications, pp. 105–41.

Bhushan, R. (2000) 'Joshi's class of 2000', *Outlook* (27 November).

'BJP saffronising education, say Cong, CPM' (2000) *The Times of India* (18 November).

Bond, M. and G. Hofstede (1990) 'The cash value of Confucian values', in S. Glegg and S. Redding (eds) *Capitalism in Contrasting Cultures*, New York: De Gruyter, pp. 383–90.

Bornstein, K. (1998) *My Gender Workbook*, London: Routledge.

Borren, S. (1988) 'Lesbians in Nairobi', in *Second ILGA Pink Book: A Global View of Lesbian and Gay Liberation and Oppression*, Utrecht: Interfacultaire Werkgroep Homostudies, pp. 59–66.

Boserup, E. (1970) *Women's Role in Economic Development*, New York: St Martin's Press.

Bottomore, T., L. Harris, V. G. Kiernan and R. Miliband (1983) *A Dictionary of Marxist Thought*, Cambridge, MA: Harvard University Press.

Boudreaux, R. (1999) 'India religious leaders trade ideas with Pope', *Los Angeles Times* (8 November).

Bourdieu, P. (1994) *Language and Symbolic Power*, translated by G. Raymond and M. Adamson, Cambridge, MA: Harvard University Press.

Braidotti, R., E. Charkiewicz, S. Häusler and S. Wieringa (1994) *Women, the Environment and Sustainable Development: Towards a Theoretical Synthesis*, London: Zed Books.

Brodie, J. (1994) 'Shifting the boundaries: gender and the politics of restructuring', in I. Bakker (ed.) *The Strategic Silence: Gender and Economic Policy*, London: Zed Books /North–South Institute, pp. 46–60.

Bullard, R. (ed.) (1994) *Unequal Protection: Environmental Justice and Communities of Color*, San Francisco, CA: Sierra Club Books.

Bunster-Borroto, X. (1986) 'Surviving beyond fear: women and torture in Latin America', in J. Nash and H. Safa (eds) *Women and Change in Latin America*, Massachusetts: Bergin and Garvey, pp. 297–325.

Butalia, U. (1999) 'Soft target', *Himal South Asian* 12 (2) (February), at www.himalmag. com

Butler, J. (1990) *Gender Trouble: Feminism and the Subversion of Identity*, London: Routledge.

— (1991) 'Imitation and gender insubordination', in Diana Fuss (ed.) *Inside/Out: Lesbian Theories; Gay Theories*, New York: Routledge, pp. 13–31.

— (1995) 'For a careful reading', in S. Benhabib, J. Butler, N. Fraser and D. Cornell, *Feminist Contentions: A Philosophical Exchange*, New York: Routledge, pp. 127–43.

— (1997) 'Merely cultural', *Social Text* 15 (3–4): 265–77.

— (1997a) *Excitable Speech: A Politics of the Performative Speech*, New York: Routledge.

Byres, T. (1998) 'State, class and development planning in India', in T. Byres (ed.) *The State, Development Planning and Liberalization in India*, New Delhi: Oxford India Paperback, pp. 1–35.

Bytesforall [on-line] (2000) Available: http://www.bytesforall.org Issue 7 (March).

Califia, P. (1997) *Sex Changes: The Politics of Transgenderism*, San Francisco, CA: Cleis Press.

Campbell, C. (1995) 'Out on the front lines but still struggling for voice: women in the rubber tappers' defense of the forest in Xapuri, Acre, Brazil', in D. Rocheleau, B. Thomas-Slayter and E. Wangari (eds) *Feminist Political Ecology: Global Issues and Local Experiences*, London: Routledge, pp. 27–61.

Canadian Council for International Co-Operation (1991) *Two Halves Make a Whole: Balancing Gender Relations in Development*, Ottawa: CCIC.

Cardoso, F. H. and E. Faletto (1979 [1969]) *Dependency and Development in Latin America*, translated by M. M. Urquidi, Berkeley and Los Angeles: University of California Press.

Champagne, J. (1996) '"A feminist just like us?" Teaching Mariama Bâ's "So Long a Letter"', *College English* 58 (1): 22–89.

Chang, K. and L. H. M. Ling (1996) 'Globalization and its intimate Other: Filipina domestic workers in Hong Kong', paper presented at the annual meeting of the International Studies Association, San Diego, CA (16–21 April).

Chatterjee, M. (1996) 'Addressing gender and poverty concerns in a reproductive health program', in A. R. Measham and R. A. Heaver (eds) *Supplement to India's Family*

Welfare Program: Moving to a Reproductive and Child Health Approach, Washington, DC: The World Bank, pp. 30–45.

Chatterjee, P. (1989) 'The nationalist resolution of the women's question', in K. Sangari and S. Vaid (eds) *Recasting Women: Essays in Colonial History*, Delhi: Kali for Women, pp. 233–53.

— (1993) *The Nation and its Fragments: Colonial and Postcolonial Histories*, Princeton, NJ: Princeton University Press.

Chaudhuri, M. (1995) 'Citizens, workers and emblems of culture: an analysis of the First Plan document on women', *Contributions to Indian Sociology* 29 (1–2): 211–35.

Chawla, R. (1997) *The Pocket Book of Vaastu*, New Delhi: Full Circle.

Chen Yingzhen (Xu Nancun) (1979) 'Shiping "Jinshuishen"' [a preliminary review of 'Jinshuishen'], in Wang Tuo, *Jinshuishen*, Taipei: Xiangcaoshan chubanshe, pp. 11–12.

Cheng, L. and P. Hsiung (1992) 'Women, export-oriented growth, and the state: the case of Taiwan', in R. Appelbaum and J. Henderson (eds) *State and Development in the Asian Pacific Rim*, Beverley Hills: Sage Publications, pp. 233–66.

Chopra, P. (1995) 'The south is Yama's direction', *The Pioneer* (20 October).

Chowdhry, K. (1989) 'Poverty, environment, development', *Daedalus* 118 (1): 141–54.

Chua, P. (2001) 'Condom Matters and Social Inequalities: Inquiries into Commodity Production, Exchange and Advocacy Practices', PhD dissertation, Department of Sociology, Santa Barbara: University of California.

Chua, P., K.-K. Bhavnani and J. Foran (2000) 'Women, culture, development: a new paradigm for development studies', *Ethnic and Racial Studies* 23 (5) (September): 820–41.

Clegg, S., W. Higgins and T. Spybey (1990) '"Post-Confucianism", social democracy, and economic culture', in S. Glegg and S. Redding (eds) *Capitalism in Contrasting Cultures*, New York: De Gruyter, pp. 31–78.

CNN (1999) 'A year on, India's leaders cheer its nuclear tests', 11 May.

Cohn, C. (1987) 'Sex and death in the rational world of defense intellectuals', *Signs* 12 (4): 687–718.

Connell, R. W. (1990) 'The state, gender and sexual politics: theory and appraisal', *Theory and Society* 19: 507–44.

Cook, R. (1993) 'International human rights and women's reproductive health', *Studies in Family Planning* 24 (2) (March/April): 73–86.

— (1995) 'Gender, health and human rights', *Health and Human Rights: An International Quarterly Journal* 1 (4): 309–12.

Coronil, F. (2000) 'Towards a critique of globalcentrism: speculations on capitalism's nature', *Public Culture* 12 (2): 351–74.

Correa, S. (1994) *Population and Reproductive Rights: Feminist Perspectives from the South*, New Delhi: Zed Books.

Correa, S. and R. Petchesky (1994) 'Reproductive and sexual rights: a feminist perspective', in G. Sen, A. Germaine and L. C. Chen (eds) *Population Policies Reconsidered: Health, Empowerment, and Rights*, Cambridge, MA: Harvard Center for Population and Development, pp. 107–23.

Dankelman, I. and Davidson, J. (1988) *Women and Environment in the Third World: Alliance for the Future*, London: Earthscan Publications/International Union for Conservation of Nature and Natural Resources.

Dasgupta, S. (1998) *India Today* (25 May).

Davies, C. B. (1998) 'Carnivalised Caribbean female bodies: taking space/making space', *Thamyris, Mythmaking from Past to Present* 5 (2) (Autumn): 333–46.

Davis-Floyd, R. (1998) 'Storying corporate futures: the Shell scenarios', in G. E. Marcus (ed.) *Corporate Futures: The Diffusion of the Culturally Sensitive Corporate Form*, Chicago, IL: University of Chicago, pp. 141–76.

de Certeau, M. (1984) *Practice of Everyday Life*, translated by S. Rendall, Berkeley: University of California Press.

de Chiro, G. (1996) 'Nature as community: the convergence of environmental and social justice,' in W. Cronon (ed.) *Uncommon Ground: Rethinking the Human Place in Nature*, New York: W. W. Norton, pp. 298–320.

de Landa, M. (1997) *A Thousand Years of Nonlinear History*, New York: Zone Books.

de Manila, Quijano [Nick Joaquin] (1980) *Manila, Sin City? And Other Chronicles*, Manila: National Book Store.

Desai, N. (1986) 'From articulation to accommodation: women's movement in India', in L. Dube, E. Leacock and S. Ardener (eds) *Visibility and Power: Essays on Women in Society and Development*, Delhi: Oxford University Press, pp. 287–99.

Dev Sen, N. (1999) 'Sisters in sorrow: contemporary Indian women's re-telling of the Rama tales', in B. Ray and A. Basu (eds) *From Independence Towards Freedom: Indian Women Since 1947*, Delhi: Oxford University Press, pp. 201–20.

Dia, A. T. (1979) 'Succès littéraire de Mariama Bâ pour son livre *Une si longue lettre*', *Amina* 84: 12–14.

Dibdin, M. (1990) *Rynosseros*, Adelaide: Aphelion Publications.

— (1992) *Blue Tyson*, Adelaide: Aphelion Publications.

— (ed.) (1993) *The Picador Book of Crime Writing*, London: Picador.

Dirlik, A. (1995) 'Confucius in the borderlands: global capitalism and the reinvention of Confucianism', *boundary 2*, 22: 229–73.

Doorbenoo, E. (1994) *Cutting the Rose: Female Genital Mutilation: The Practice and its Prevention*, London: Minority Rights Group.

Dore, E. and M. Molyneux (eds) (2000) *Hidden Histories of Gender and the State in Latin America*, Durham, NC: Duke University Press.

Dorfman, A. (2000) 'Pinochet's mind', *NACLA Report on the Americas* XXXIII (5) (March/April): 4, 50.

Dowling, T. (1990) *Rynosseros*, Adelaide: Aphelion Publications.

— (1992) *Blue Tyson*, Adelaide: Aphelion Publications.

— (1993) *Twilight Beach*, Adelaide: Aphelion Publications.

Dozier, D., L. Grunig and J. Grunig (1995) *Manager's Guide to Excellence in Public Relations and Communication Management*, Mahwah: Lawrence Erlbaum.

Drake, F. and D. Sobel (1994) *Is Anyone Out There? The Scientific Search for Extraterrestrial Intelligence*, New York: Delta.

Drewal, H. J. (1988) 'Mermaids, mirrors and snake charmers: Igbo Mami Wata shrines', *African Arts* 21 (2): 38–45, 96.

— (1988a) 'Performing the other: Mami Wata worship in Africa', *The Drama Review* 32 (2): 160–85.

— (1996) 'Mami Wata shrines: exotica and the construction of self', in M. J. Arnoldi,

C. M. Geary and K. L. Hardin (eds) *African Material Culture*, Bloomington and Indianapolis: Indiana University Press, pp. 308–33.

Dryzek, J. (1987) *Rational Ecology: Environment and Political Ecology*, New York: Basil Blackwell.

Eckersley, R. (1992) *Environmentalism and Political Theory: Toward an Ecocentric Approach*, Albany: State University of New York Press.

Ehrenfeld, D. (1978) *The Arrogance of Humanism*, New York: Oxford University Press.

Elson, D. (1992) 'Gender analysis and development economics', paper for the ESRC Development Economics Group annual conference, Manchester.

Emmerich, R. (director) (1996) *Independence Day* [videocassette], USA: Twentieth Century-Fox.

Engineer, A. (1987) (ed.) *The Shah Bano Controversy*, Hyderabad, India : Orient Longman.

Enloe, C. (1990) *Bananas, Beaches and Bases: Making Feminist Sense of International Politics*, Berkeley: University of California Press.

— (2000) *Maneuvers: The International Politics of Militarizing Women's Lives*, Berkeley: University of California Press.

Escobar, A. (1995) *Encountering Development: The Making and Unmaking of the Third World*, Princeton, NJ: Princeton University Press.

— (2001) 'Culture sits in places: reflections on globalism and subaltern strategies of globalization', *Political Geography* 20: 139–74.

Escobar, A. and W. Harcourt (1998) 'Editorial: creating glocality', *Development* 41 (3): 3–5.

Evans, P. (1996) 'Introduction: development strategies across the public–private divide', *World Development* 24 (6): 1033–7.

Fagan, G. H., R. Munck and K. Nadasen (1997) 'Gender, culture and development: a South African Experience', in V. Tucker (ed.) *Cultural Perspectives on Development* (London: Frank Cass, 1997), pp. 93–109.

Farmer, P. (1992) *AIDS and Accusation: Haiti and the Geography of Blame*, Berkeley: University of California Press.

Felski, R. (1995) *The Gender of Modernity*, Cambridge, MA: Harvard University Press.

Fernández-Alemany, M. (2000) 'Negotiating gay identities: the neoliberalization of sexual politics in Honduras', paper presented at the Congress of the Latin American Studies Association, Miami, FL (March).

Filer, C. (ed.) (1997) *The Political Economy of Forest Management in Papua New Guinea*, Port Moresby: The National Research Institute and London: International Institute for Environment and Development.

Firat, A. (1995) 'Consumer culture or culture consumed?', in J. Costa and J. Bamossy (eds) *Marketing in a Multicultural World*, Thousand Oaks, CA: Sage, pp. 105–25.

Fischer, M. M. J. and M. Abedi (1990) *Debating Muslims: Cultural Dialogues in Postmodernity and Tradition*, Madison: University of Wisconsin Press.

Foran, J. (1993) *Fragile Resistance: Social Transformation in Iran from 1500 to the Revolution*, Boulder, CO: Westview Press.

— (1997) 'The comparative-historical sociology of Third World social revolutions: why a few succeed, why most fail', in J. Foran (ed.) *Theorizing Revolutions*, London: Routledge, pp. 227–67.

— (1997a) 'Discourses and social forces: the role of culture and cultural studies in understanding revolutions', in J. Foran (ed.) *Theorizing Revolutions*, London: Routledge, pp. 203–26.

— (2000) 'Discursive subversions: *Time* magazine, the CIA overthrow of Mussadiq, and the installation of the Shah', in C. G. Appy (ed.) *Cold War Constructions: The Political Culture of United States Imperialism, 1945–1966*, Amherst: University of Massachusetts Press, pp. 157–82.

— (2001) 'Studying revolutions through the prism of race, gender, and class: notes toward a framework', *Race, Gender & Class* 8 (2): 117–41.

— (2002) 'Magical realism: how might the revolutions of the future have better end(ing)s?' in John Foran (ed.) *The Future of Revolutions: Re-thinking Radical Change in an Age of Globalization*, London: Zed Books.

Foster, D. W. (1997) *Sexual Textualities: Essays On Queer-ing Latin American Writing*, Austin: University of Texas Press.

Foucault, M. (1981) 'Order of the discourse', in R. Young (ed.) *Untying the Text: A Poststructuralist Reader*, Boston and New York: Routledge, pp. 47–78.

— (1994) *Dits et Ecrits. 1954–1988*, Vol. III, D. Defert and F. Ewald (eds) Paris: Gallimard.

Foucault, M. and G. Deleuze (1977) 'Intellectuals and power' in M. Foucault, *Language, Counter-Memory, Practice*, Ithaca, NY: Cornell University Press, pp. 205–17.

Franco, J. (1996) 'The gender wars', *NACLA Report on the Americas* XXIX (4) (January–February): 6–9.

Franzway, S., D. Court and R. W. Connell (1989) *Staking a Claim: Feminism, Bureaucracy and the State*, Cambridge: Polity Press.

Fraser, N. (1997) 'Heterosexism, misrecognition, and capitalism: a response to Judith Butler', *Social Text* 15 (3–4): 279–89.

— (1997a) *Justice Interruptus: Critical Reflections on the 'Postsocialist' Condition*, New York: Routledge.

Freeman, C. (2001) 'Is local : global as feminine : masculine? Rethinking the gender of globalization', *Signs* 26 (1) (Summer): 1007–38.

Fuss, D. (1996) 'Introduction: human, all too human', in D. Fuss (ed.) *Human, All Too Human*, New York: Routledge.

Galeano, E. (1997) 'El derecho de soñar', *Apuntes para el fin del siglo 97–98*, Santiago: Lom Ediciones.

Gardner, K. and D. Lewis (1996) *Anthropology, Development and the Post-Modern Challenge*, London: Pluto Press.

Gates, B., with C. Hemingway (1999) *Business @ the Speed of Thought: Using a Digital Nervous System*, Harmondsworth: Viking.

Gibson-Graham, J. K. (1996) *The End of Capitalism (As We Knew It): A Feminist Critique of Political Economy*, Oxford: Blackwell.

Gilliam, A. (1991) 'Women's equality and national liberation', in C. T. Mohanty, A. Russo and L. Torres (eds) *Third World Women and the Politics of Feminism*, Bloomington and Indianapolis: Indiana University Press, pp. 215–36.

Gold, T. (1986) *State and Society in the Taiwan Miracle*, Armonk, NY: M. E. Sharpe.

Gore, C. and J. Nevadomsky (1997) 'Practice and agency in Mammy Wata worship in southern Nigeria', *African Arts* 30 (2) (Spring): 60–69, 95.

Gottweis, H. (1995) 'Genetic engineering, democracy, and the politics of identity', *Social Text* 13 (1): 127–52.

Government of India (1997) *Reproductive and Child Health Programme: Schemes for Implementation*, Ministry of Health and Family Welfare, New Delhi.

— (1997a) Report of Financial Status under RCH marked official No. M. 15012/3/96 - UIP (B&A), Ministry of Health and Family Welfare, New Delhi.

— (1997b) Memo from Deputy Director of MoHFW officially marked as No. M. 14015/7/97 -RCH (DC), Ministry of Health and Family Welfare, New Delhi.

Grameen Communications [on-line] (2000) Available: http://www.grameen-info.org/vcip/index.html/ (12 December).

Gramsci, A. (1971) *Selections from Prison Notebooks of Antonio Gramsci*, Q. Hoare and G. N. Smith (eds and translators) New York: International Publishers.

Gray, J. (1998) *False Dawn: The Delusions of Global Capitalism*, London: Granta.

Green, J. (2000) *Beyond Carnival: Male Homosexuality in Twentieth-Century Brazil*, Chicago, IL: University of Chicago Press.

Grewal, I. and C. Kaplan (eds) (1994) *Scattered Hegemonies: Postmodernity and Transnational Feminist Practices*, Minneapolis: University of Minnesota Press.

Grossman, K. (1994) 'The people of color environmental summit', in R. Bullard (ed.) *Unequal Protection: Environmental Justice and Communities of Color*, San Francisco, CA: Sierra Club Books, pp. 272–97.

Guèye, M. (1994) 'La politique du roman féminin au Sénégal', PhD dissertation, University of Cincinnati, OH.

Guha, R. and J. Martinez-Alier (1997) *Varieties of Environmentalism: Essays North and South*, London: Earthscan.

Guzmán, P. (1997) *Chile: Obstinate Memory*, Les Films d'Ici and National Film Board of Canada.

Halberstam, J. (1998) *Female Masculinity*, Durham, NC: Duke University Press.

Hall, S. (1981) 'Notes on deconstructing the popular', in R. Samuel (ed.) *People's History and Socialist Theory*, London and Boston: Routledge & Kegan Paul, pp. 227–40.

— (1986) 'Cultural studies: two paradigms', in R. Collins (ed.) *Media, Culture, and Society: A Critical Reader*, London: Sage Publications, pp. 33–48.

— (1995) 'The whites of their eyes: racist ideologies and the media', in G. Dines and J. M. Humez (eds) *Gender, Race and Class in Media*, Thousand Oaks, CA, London and New Delhi: Sage Publications, pp. 18–22.

Hall, S., D. Hobson, A. Lowe and P. Willis (eds) (1980) *Culture, Media, Language: Working Papers in Cultural Studies 1972–1979*, London: Hutchinson.

Hammond, A. L. (1998) *Which World? Scenarios for the 21ˢᵗ Century*, Washington, DC: Island Press.

Haraway, D. J. (1989) *Primate Visions*, New York: Routledge.

— (1991) *Simians, Cyborgs, and Women: The Reinvention of Nature*, London: Routledge.

— (1992) 'The promises of monsters: a regenerative politics for inappropriate/d Others' in L. Grossberg, C. Nelson and P. Treichler (eds) *Cultural Studies*, New York: Routledge, pp. 295–337.

— (1997) *Modest_Witness@Second_Millennium. FemaleMan_Meets_OncoMouse: Feminism and Technoscience*, New York: Routledge.

Harcourt, W. (2000) 'Women's empowerment through the internet', *Asian Women* 10 (6): 19–31.

Hartmann, B. (1995) *Reproductive Rights and Wrongs: The Global Politics of Population Control*, Boston, MA: South End Press.

Harvey, D. (1989) *The Condition of Postmodernity: An Inquiry into the Origins of Cultural Change*, Oxford: Basil Blackwell.

— (1998) 'What's green and makes the environment go round?', in F. Jameson and M. Miyoshi (eds) *The Cultures of Globalization*, Durham, NC: Duke University Press, pp. 327–55.

Hasan, Z. (ed.) (1994) *Forging Identities: Gender, Communities and the State*, Kali for Women: New Delhi.

Hauben, M. and R. Hauben (1997) *Netizens: On the History and Impact of Usenet and the Internet*, Los Alamitos, CA: IEEE Computer Society Press.

Hau'ofa, E. (1993) 'Our sea of islands', in E. Waddell, V. Naidu and E. Hau'ofa (eds) *A New Oceania: Rediscovering Our Sea of Islands*, Suva: University of the South Pacific, pp. 2–16.

Head, B. (1974) *A Question of Power*, London: Heinemann.

Hindu, The (2000) (9 March, 25 December, 29 December).

Hoogvelt, A. (1997) *Globalization and the Post-Colonial World: The New Political Economy of Development*, Baltimore, MD: Johns Hopkins University Press.

Hospital, J. T. (1992) *The Last Magician*, Brisbane: University of Queensland Press.

Howard, R. (1995) 'Women's rights and the right to development', in J. Peters and A. Wolper (eds) *Women's Rights, Human Rights*, New York: Routledge, pp. 301–13.

Howe, A. C. (2000) 'Undressing the university queer subject: Nicaraguan activists and transnational identities', paper presented at the Congress of the Latin American Studies Association, Miami, FL (March).

Howitt, R. (1998) 'Scale as relation: musical metaphors of geographical scale', *Area* (30): 49–58.

Hsiung, J. C. et al. (eds) (1981) *The Taiwan Experience, 1950–1980: Contemporary Republic of China*, New York: Praeger/American Association for Chinese Studies.

Hsiung, P. (1996) *Living Rooms as Factories: Class, Gender, and the Satellite Factory System in Taiwan*, Philadelphia, PA: Temple University Press.

Huang Chunming (1973) 'Shayonala, zaijian', in *Xiazi Amu: Huang Chunming xuanji* [The Blind Amu: Selected Works of Huang Chunming], Hong Kong: Wenyifeng, pp. 227–69.

India Today International (1998) (25 May).

Ingraham, C. (1999) *White Weddings: Romancing Heterosexuality in Popular Culture*, London: Routledge.

Instituto Femenino para la Formación Integral (IFFI) (1999), personal interview with two members, April 16.

International Gay and Lesbian Human Rights Commission (IGLHRC) (1996), 'Hundreds detained in raids on gay discos in Peru', Action alert (March).

— (2001) 'Police officers attack gay men, lesbians and transvestites in Monterrey, Nuevo Leon, Mexico', Action alert (May).

— (2001a) 'Historical progress at the United Nations: IGLHRC applauds UN move to address human rights violations against sexual minorities', press release (5 June).

Jackson, C. (1993) 'Doing what comes naturally? Women and environment in development', *World Development* 21 (12) (December): 1947–63.

Jackson, C. and R. Pearson (eds) (1998) *Feminist Visions of Development: Gender Analysis and Policy*, London: Routledge.

Jagtenberg, T. and D. McKie (1997) *Eco-Impacts and the Greening of Postmodernity: New Maps for Communication Studies, Cultural Studies and Sociology*, Thousand Oaks, CA: Sage Publications.

James, W. (1999) 'Empowering ambiguities', in A. Cheater (ed.) *The Anthropology of Power: Empowerment and Disempowerment in Changing Structures*, London: Routledge, pp. 13–27.

Jameson, F. (1971) 'Towards dialectical criticism', in F. Jameson, *Marxism and Form: Twentieth Century Dialectical Theories of Literature*, Princeton, NJ: Princeton University Press, pp. 306–416.

— (1986) 'Third-world literature in the era of multinational capitalism', *Social Text* 15: 65–88.

— (1988) 'Criticism in history', in F. Jameson, *The Ideologies of Theory: Essays 1971–1986*, Vol. 1, Minneapolis: University of Minnesota Press, pp. 119–37.

— (2000) 'Globalization and political strategy', *New Left Review*, new series, 4 (July/August): 49–68.

Jaquette, J. S. (1990) 'Gender and justice in economic development', in I. Tinker (ed.) *Persistent Inequalities: Women and World Development*, Oxford: Oxford University Press, pp. 54–69.

— (ed.) (1994) *The Women's Movement in Latin America: Participation and Democracy*, second edition, Boulder, CO: Westview Press.

Jayal, N. G. (1994) 'The gentle Leviathan: welfare and the Indian state', *Social Scientist* 22 (9–12): 18–26.

Jayawardena, K. (1988) *Feminism and Nationalism in the Third World*, London: Zed Books.

Jeffery, P. and A. Basu (eds) (1994) *Appropriating Gender: Women's Activism and Politicized Religion in South Asia*, London: Routledge.

Jell-Bahlsen, S. (1997) 'Eze Mmiri di Egwu, the water monarch is awesome: reconsidering the Mammy Water myths', in F. Kaplan (ed.) *Queens, Queen Mothers, Priestesses and Power: Case Studies in African Gender*, New York: New York Academy of Sciences, pp. 103–34.

John, M. (1996) 'Gender and development in India – 1970s–1990s: some reflections on the constitutive role of contexts', *Economic and Political Weekly* (23 November): 3071–7.

Joshi, P. (1988) *Gandhi on Women*, Delhi: Centre for Development Studies.

Kabeer, N. (1994) *Reversed Realities: Gender Hierarchies in Development Thought*, London: Verso.

Kabeer N. and R. Subramanian (1999) *Institutions, Relations and Outcomes*, New Delhi: Kali.

Kadir, D. (1995) 'Postmodernism/postcolonialism: what are we after?', *World Literature Today* 69 (1): 17–21.

Kainer, K. and M. Duryea (1992) 'Tapping women's knowledge: plant resource use in extractive reserves, Acre, Brazil', *Economic Botany* 46 (4): 408–25.

Kampwirth, K. (2002) *Women and Guerrilla Movements: Nicaragua, El Salvador, Chiapas, Cuba*, University Park: Penn State University Press.

Kandiyoti, D. (1998) 'Gender, power, contestation: rethinking bargaining with patriarchy', in C. Jackson and R. Pearson (eds) *Feminist Visions of Development*, London: Routledge, pp. 135–51.

— (ed.) (1991) *Women, Islam, and the State*, London: Macmillan.

Kassindja, F. and L. M. Bashir (1998) *Do They Hear You When You Cry?*, New York: Delacorte Press.

Kasturi, L. (1996) 'Development, patriarchy and politics: Indian women in the political process', in V. M. Moghadam (ed.) *Patriarchy and Development: Women's Positions at the End of the 20th Century*, Oxford: Clarendon Press, pp. 99–144.

Katrak, K. (1992) 'Indian Nationalism, Gandhian "satyagraha", and representation of female sexuality', in A. Parker, M. Russo, D. Sommer and P. Yaeger (eds) *National-isms and Sexualities*, London: Routledge, pp. 395–406.

Kelkar, G. (1987) 'Violence against women: an understanding of responsibility for their lives', in M. Davies (compiler) *Third World, Second Sex*, London: Zed Books, pp. 179–89.

Kempadoo, K. and J. Doezema (eds) (1998) *Global Sex Workers: Rights, Resistance and Redefinition*, London: Routledge.

Khomeini, R. (1984) *Kungrah-i 'ibadi-yi siyasi-yi hajj : majmu'ahi sukhanan va payamha-yi Imam Khumayni* [A Collection of Lectures and Sayings],Tehran: Markaz-i Tahqiqat va Intisharat-i Hajj.

— (1987) *Faryad-i baraat : payam-i Imam Khumayni bih hujjaj-i Bayt Allah al-Haram* [The Message of Imam Khumayni to Mecca pilgrims], Tehran: Vizarat-i Farhang va Irshad-i Islami.

— (1994) *Hikayatha-yi talkh va shirin : 314 khatirah va hikayat az zaban-i Hazrat-i Imam-i Khumayni* [Bittersweet Tales: 314 Reminiscences and Stories Narrated by Hazrat-i Imam Khumayni], Tehran: Muassasah-i Farhangi-i Qadr-i Vilayat.

Knight, C. (1991) *Blood Relations: Menstruation and the Origins of Culture*, New Haven, CT: Yale University Press.

Kollontai, A. (1977) *Love of Worker Bees*, translated by C. Porter, London: Virago.

Kothari, R. (1989) 'The Indian enterprise today', *Daedalus: Journal of American Academy of Arts and Sciences* (Fall): 51–67.

Kuhn, A. (ed) (1990) *Alien Zone: Cultural Theory and Contemporary Science Fiction*, London: Verso.

Kumar, R. (1993) 'Identity politics and the contemporary Indian feminist movement', in V. M. Moghadam (ed.) *Identity Politics and Women: Cultural Reassertions and Femin-isms in International Perspective*, Boulder, CO: Westview Press, pp. 274–92.

Kurian, P. A. (1995) 'Gender and Environmental Policy: A Feminist Evaluation of Environmental Impact Assessment and the World Bank', PhD dissertation, Purdue University, IN.

— (2000) 'Generating power: gender, ethnicity and empowerment in India's Narmada Valley', *Ethnic and Racial Studies* 23 (5): 842–56.

— (2000a) *Engendering the Environment? Gender in the World Bank's Environmental Policies*, Aldershot: Ashgate.

Kurian, P. and D. Munshi (1999) 'Unthinking Anthropocentrism: Scientific Rationality and Economic Development in a Subaltern Biosphere', paper presented at the 20th Annual Conference of the National Women's Studies Association, Albuquerque, New Mexico, USA.

Lai, M. (1998) 'The intellectual's deaf-mute, or (how) can we speak beyond post-coloniality?' *Cultural Critique* 39: 31–58.

Lancaster, R. (1994) *Life is Hard: Machismo, Danger and the Intimacy of Power in Nicaragua*, Berkeley: University of California Press.

Landes, J. (1998) 'Introduction', in J. Landes (ed.) *Feminism, the Public and the Private*, Oxford: Oxford University Press, pp. 1–17.

Langton, M. (1993) '*Well, I Heard it on the Radio and I Saw it on the Television* – ': An Essay for the Australian Film Commission on the Politics and Aesthetics of Filmmaking by and about Aboriginal People and Things, Sydney: Australian Film Commission.

Lazreg, M. (1994) *The Eloquence of Silence: Algerian Women in Question*, New York and London: Routledge.

Leiner, M. (1994) *Sexual Politics in Cuba: Machismo, Homosexuality and AIDS*, Boulder, CO: Westview Press.

Leslie, N. (1993) 'Black and white: photographic imagery and aboriginality', *Australian Journal of Communication* 20 (2): 79–96.

Levine, R., C. Locke, D. Searis and D. Weinberger (2000) *The Cluetrain Manifesto: The End of Business as Usual*, Cambridge, MA: Perseus Books.

Li, V. (1995) 'Towards articulation: postcolonial theory and demotic resistance', *Ariel* 26 (1): 167–89.

Lind, A. (1990) 'Economic crisis, women's work and the reproduction of gender ideology: popular women's organizations in Quito, Ecuador', master's thesis, Cornell University, NY.

— (1997) 'Gay rights: out of the closet and into *la calle*', *NACLA Report on the Americas* XXX (5) (March/April): 6–9.

— (in progress) 'Gendered encounters with development: women's movements and the cultural politics of neoliberalism in the Andes'.

Lister, R. (1997) 'Citizenship: towards a feminist synthesis', *Feminist Review* 57 (3): 28–48.

Mackie, G. (1998) 'A way to end female genital cutting', http://www.fgmnetwork.org/articles/mackie1998.html

MacKinnon, C. A. (1987) 'Sex and violence: a perspective', in C. A. MacKinnon, *Feminism Unmodified: Discourses on Life and Law*, Cambridge, MA: Harvard University Press, pp. 85–92.

Majidi, M. (1999) *Children of Heaven: Script, Interview, Critique*, Tehran: Farhang Kavesh Publication.

Marchand, M. H. (1995) 'Latin American women speak on development: are we listening yet?', in M. Marchand and J. Parpart (eds) *Feminism/Postmodernism/Development*, New York: Routledge, pp. 56–72.

— (1996) 'Reconceptualising "gender and development" in an era of globalisation', *Millennium: Journal of International Studies* 25 (3): 577–603.

Marchand, M. H. and J. Parpart (eds) (1995) *Feminism/Postmodernism/Development*, New York: Routledge.

Marchand, M. H. and A. S. Runyan (eds) (2000) *Gender and Global Restructuring: Sightings, Sites and Resistances*, New York: Routledge.

Marcos, Subcomandante (1995) *Shadows of Tender Fury: The Letters and Communiqués of Subcomandante Marcos and the Zapatista Army of National Liberation*, translated by F. Berdacke, L. López and the Watsonville, CA, Human Rights Committee, New York: Monthly Review Press.

Marecek, J. (2000) '"Am I a woman in these matters?": notes on Sinhala nationalism and gender in Sri Lanka', in T. Mayer (ed.) *Gender Ironies of Nationalism: Sexing the Nation*, London: Routledge, pp. 139–62.

Marston, S. (2000) 'The social construction of scale', *Progress in Human Geography* 24 (2): 243–65.

Martinez-Alier, J. (1991) 'Ecology and the poor: a neglected issue of Latin American history', *Journal of Latin American Studies* 23 (3) (October): 621–39.

Martinussen, J. (1997) *State, Society and Market: A Guide to Competing Theories of Development*, London: Zed Books.

M. A. Singamma Sreenivasan Foundation (1993) 'Integrating women in development planning: the role of traditional wisdom', in J. Massiah (ed.) *Women in Developing Economies: Making Visible the Invisible*, Providence and Paris: Berg/UNESCO, pp. 280–300.

Mathews, A. (2000) *Vienna Blood*, London: Vintage.

May, P. (2000) *The Business of Ecommerce: From Corporate Strategy to Technology*, Cambridge: Cambridge University Press.

Mayo, K. (1936) *Mother India*, London: Jonathan Cape.

McClintock, A. (1992) 'The angels of progress: pitfalls of the term post-colonialism', *Social Text* 10 (3): 84–98.

McCorduck, P. and N. Ramsey (1996) *The Futures of Women: Scenarios for the 21ˢᵗ Century*, Reading, MD: Addison Wesley.

McDowell, L. (1999) *Gender, Identity and Place: Understanding Feminist Geographies*, Cambridge: Polity Press.

Mehta, A. (2000) 'Radio, telephone, internet can be "weapons to fight poverty"', interview to Bytesforall, fifth online issue (March-April). Available: http://www.bytesforall.org/5th/aruninter.htm

Melching, M. (2001) 'What's in a name? (Re)contextualizing female genital mutilation', in S. Perry and C. Schenck (eds) *Eye to Eye: Women Practising Development Across Cultures*, London: Zed Books, pp. 155–70.

Michaels, E. (1994) *Bad Aboriginal Art: Tradition, Media, and Technological Horizons*, Sydney: Allen & Unwin.

Michel, M. (1995) 'Positioning the subject: locating postcolonial studies', *Ariel* 26 (1): 83–9.

Mickler, S. (1992) *Gambling on the First Race: A Comment on Racism and Talk-Back Radio, 6PR, the TAB, and the W.A. Government*, Perth: Murdoch University Centre for Research in Culture and Communication.

Mies, M. and V. Shiva (1993) *Ecofeminism*, London: Zed Books.

Mignolo, W. (1996) 'Linguistic maps, literary geographies, and cultural landscapes: languages, languaging, and (trans)nationalism', *Modern Language Quarterly* 57 (2): 181–96.

Milani, T. (1997) *Do Zan*, Tehran: Tofigh Afarin.

— (2001) 'They cut me from the root, I grow from the stem: a dialogue between Efat Mahbaz and Tahmineh Milani', *Iran Emrooz*, Iranian Political Bulletin, 26 June, http://www.iran-emrooz.de/goftgu/milani0404.html

Miller, A. (1982) *Prisoners of Childhood: The Drama of the Gifted Child*, New York: Basic Books.

— (1984) *For Your Own Good: Hidden Cruelty in Child-Rearing and the Roots of Violence*, New York: Farrar, Straus and Giroux.

— (1990) *The Untouched Key: Tracing Childhood Trauma in Creativity and Destructiveness*, New York: Doubleday.

— (1990a) *Banished Knowledge: Facing Childhood Injuries*, New York: Doubleday.

Miller, C. and S. Razavi (1998) 'Gender analysis: alternative paradigms', url: http://www.undp.org/gender/resource/mono6.html (May).

Misra, K. (1997) 'Indian feminism and the post-colonial state', *Women and Politics* 17 (4): 25–45.

Mitchell, J. (1971) *Woman's Estate*, New York: Pantheon Books.

Moallem, M. (1999) 'Transnationalism, feminism and fundamentalism', in C. Kaplan, N. Alarcon and M. Moallem (eds) *Between Women and Nation: Transnational Feminisms and the State*, Durham, NC, and London: Duke University Press, pp. 320–48.

— (1999a) 'Universalization of particulars: the civic body and gendered citizenship in Iran', *Citizenship Studies* 3 (3) (November): 319–35.

Mogrovejo, N. (2000) *Un amor que se atrevió a decir su nombre: la lucha de las lesbianas y su relación con los movimientos homosexual y feminista en América Latina*, Mexico City: CDAHL/Plaza y Valdes Editores.

Mohanty, C. T. (1991) 'Under Western eyes: feminist scholarship and colonial discourses', in C. T. Mohanty, A. Russo and L. Torres (eds) *Third World Women and the Politics of Feminism*, Bloomington: Indiana University Press, pp. 51–80.

— (1997) 'Women workers and capitalist scripts: ideologies of domination, common interests and the politics of solidarity', in C. T. Mohanty and M. J. Alexander (eds) *Feminist Genealogies, Colonial Legacies, Democratic Futures*, London: Routledge, pp. 3–29.

'Monsanto: A legacy of fraud' at http://www.purefood.org

Monsanto at http://www.monsanto.com/monsanto

Moran, M. (2000) 'Uneasy images: contested representations of gender, modernity and nationalism in pre-war Liberia', in T. Mayer (ed.) *Gender Ironies of Nationalism: Sexing the Nation*, London: Routledge, pp. 113–38.

Moser, C. (1993) *Gender Planning and Development: Theory, Practice and Training*, London: Routledge.

Mott, L. (1996) *Epidemic of Hate: Violations of the Human Rights of Gay Men, Lesbians and Transvestites in Brazil*, San Francisco, CA: IGLHRC.

Munshi, D. (forthcoming) 'Through the subject's eye: situating the Other in discourses of diversity', *Organization Communication: Emerging Perspectives* 7.

Murray, S. and M. Arboleda (1995) 'Stigma transformation and relexification: gay in Latin America', in S. Murray (ed.) *Latin American Male Homosexualities*, Albuquerque: University of New Mexico Press, pp. 138–44.

Naficy, H. (1987) 'Cinema as a political instrument', in M. E. Bonine and N. Keddie (eds) *Continuity and Change in Modern Iran*, Albany: New York, pp. 256–83.

Nanda, M. (1997) 'The science wars in India', *Dissent* (44) (Winter), at http://www.igc.org/dissent

Nandy, A. (ed.) (1988) *Science, Hegemony and Violence: A Requiem for Modernity*, Oxford: Oxford University Press.

— (1995) *Alternative Sciences: Creativity and Authenticity of Two Indian Scientists*, second edition, Oxford: Oxford University Press.

Nandy, A., S. Trivedy, S. Mayaram and A. Yagnik (1995) *Creating a Nationality: The Ramjanmabhumi Movement and the Fear of the Self*, Delhi: Oxford University Press.

Nederveen Pieterse, J. (ed.) (1992) *Emancipations, Modern and Postmodern*, London: Sage Publications.

— (2001) *Development: Deconstructions/Reconstructions*, London: Sage Publications.

Noble, D. (1992) *A World without Women: The Christian Clerical Culture of Western Science*, New York: Knopf.

Nussbaum, M. (2000) 'The "capabilities" advantage to promoting women's human rights', *Human Rights Dialogue* 2 (3): 10–12.

Nussbaum, M. and J. Glover (1995) (eds) *Women, Culture, Development: A Study of Human Capabilities*, Oxford: Clarendon Press.

Nwapa, F. (1995) [1981] *One is Enough*, Trenton: Africa World Press.

— (1997) 'Priestesses and power among the riverine Igbo', in F. Kaplan (ed.) *Queens, Queen Mothers, Priestesses and Power: Case Studies in African Gender*, New York: New York Academy of Sciences, pp. 415–24.

— (forthcoming) *The Lake Goddess*, Trenton: Africa World Press.

Obanya, P. (1999) 'Popular fallacies on the use of African languages in education', *Social Dynamics* 25 (1): 81–100.

Ogunyemi, C. O. (1996) *Africa Wo/Man Palava: The Nigerian Novel by Women*, Chicago, IL: University of Chicago Press.

Ogunyemi, C. O. and M. Umeh (eds) (1995) *Research in African Literature* 26 (2) (Summer).

Ong, A. (1997) 'The gender and labor politics of postmodernity', in L. Lowe and D. Lloyd (eds) *The Politics of Culture in the Shadow of Capital*, Durham, NC: Duke University Press, pp. 61–97.

Onwurah, N. (1993) *Monday's Girls*, California Newsreel.

Ordoñez, J. P. (1995) *No Human Being is Disposable: Social Cleansing, Human Rights and Sexual Orientation in Colombia*, joint report of Colombia Human Rights Committee, IGLHRC and Proyecto Dignidad por los Derechos Humanos en Colombia.

Ordway, F. I. and R. Liebermann (1992) *Blueprint for Space: Science Fiction to Science Fact*, Sydney: Allen & Unwin/Smithsonian Institution.

Oyarzún, K. (2000) 'Engendering democracy in Chile's universities', *NACLA Report on the Americas* 33 (4): 24–9.

Oyewùmí, O. (1997) *The Invention of Women: Making an African Sense of Western Gender Discourses*, Minneapolis: University of Minnesota Press.

Paehlke, R. and D. Torgerson (eds) (1990) *Managing Leviathan: Environmental Politics and the Administrative State*, Lewiston: Broadview Press.

Panikkar, K. N. (2001) 'Outsider as enemy', *Frontline* 18 (1) (6–19 January), at http://www.the-hindu.com/fline

Panikulangara, V. (1986) 'Christian succession: impact of the SC judgement', *Indian Express* (13 March).

Pant, N. (1997) 'Facilitating genocide: women as fascist educators in the Hindutva movement', *Ghadar* 1 (1) (1 May) at http://www.proxsa.org/resources/ghadar/ghadar.html

Paredes, J. and M. Galinda (n.d.) *Sexo, Placer y Sexualidad*, La Paz: Mujeres Creando.

Parreñas, R. S. (2001) *Servants of Globalization: Women, Migration and Domestic Work*, Stanford, CA: Stanford University Press.

Patel, G. (1997) 'Home, homo, hybrid: translating gender', *College Literature* 24 (1) (February): 133–51.

Patel, I. (ed.) (1984) *Science and the Vedas*, Bombay: Somaiya Publications.

Patton, C. (1996) *Fatal Advice: How Safe-Sex Education Went Wrong*, Durham, NC: Duke University Press.

Paulson, S. and P. Calla (2000) 'Gender and ethnicity in Bolivian politics: transformation or paternalism?' *Journal of Latin American Anthropology* 5 (2): 112–49.

Pearson, R. and C. Jackson (eds) (1998) *Feminist Visions of Development: Gender Analysis and Policy*, London: Routledge.

Penley, C. (1997) *NASA/Trek: Popular Science and Sex in America*, New York: Verso.

Perez, E. (1999) *The Decolonial Imaginary: Writing Chicanas into History*, Bloomington: Indiana University Press.

Perry, S. and C. Schenck (2001) *Eye to Eye: Women Practising Development Across Cultures*, London: Zed Books.

Petchesky, R. (1995) 'From population control to reproductive rights: feminist fault lines', *Reproductive Health Matters* 6 (November): 152–61.

Pfeil, F. (1994) 'No basta teorizar: in-difference to solidarity in contemporary fiction, theory and practice', in I. Grewal and C. Kaplan (eds) *Scattered Hegemonies: Postmodernity and Transnational Feminist Practices*, Minneapolis: University of Minnesota Press, pp. 197–230.

Plumwood, V. (1996) 'Androcentrism and anthrocentrism: parallels and politics', *Ethics and the Environment* 1 (2): 119–52.

— (1998) 'Inequality, ecojustice, and ecological rationality', in J. Dryzek and D. Schlossberg (eds) *Debating the Earth: The Environmental Politics Reader*, Oxford: Oxford University Press, pp. 559–83.

Polakoff, E. (1996) 'Gender and the Latin American left', *Z Magazine* (November): 20–23.

Porter, M. and E. Judd (1999) *Feminists Doing Development: A Practical Critique*, London: Zed Books.

Prigogine, I. and I. Stengers (1984) *Order Out of Chaos*, New York: Bantam Books.

Proyas, A. (1998) (director) *Dark City* [videocassette], USA: New Line Cinema.

Purser, R., C. Park and A. Montuori (1995) 'Limits to anthropocentrism: toward an ecocentric organization paradigm?', *Academy of Management Review* 20 (4): 1053–89.

Rabenoro, I. (1999) 'Multilingual developing countries facing globalization', *Social Dynamics* 25 (1): 70–80.

Raheja, G. G. and A. G. Gold (1994) *Listen to the Heron's Words*, Berkeley: University of California Press.

Rai, S. (1996) 'Women and the state in the Third World', in H. Afshar (ed.) *Women and Politics in the Third World*, London and New York: Routledge, pp. 25–39.

— (1996a) 'Women and the state in the Third World: some issues for debate', in S. Rai and G. Lievesley (eds) *Women and the State: International Perspectives*, London: Taylor and Francis, pp. 5–23.

— (2002) *Gender and the Political Economy of Development*, Cambridge: Polity Press.

Raman, J. S. (2000) 'The bomb club', *Hindustan Times* (11 November).

Randall, M. (1993) *Gathering Rage: The Failure of Twentieth Century Revolutions to Develop a Feminist Agenda*, New York: Monthly Review Press.

Ranger, T. O. (1997) 'The invention of tradition in colonial Africa', in R. R. Grinker and C. B. Steiner (eds) *Perspectives on Africa: A Reader in Culture, History, and Representation*, Oxford: Blackwell, pp. 597–612.

Rassool, N. (1999) 'Literacy and social development in the information age: redefining possibilities in sub-Saharan Africa', *Social Dynamics* 25 (1): 130–49.

Rathgeber, E. M. (1990) 'WID, WAD, GAD: trends in research and practice', *Journal of Developing Areas* 24 (4) (July): 489–502.

Rawat, B. (2000) 'Advani tribute in concrete to iron man', *The Telegraph* (31 October).

Razavi, S. and C. Miller (1995) 'From WID to GAD: conceptual shifts in the women and development discourse', *UN Fourth Conference on Women Occasional Paper No. 1*, Geneva: UN Research Institute for Social Development.

Reinfelder, M. (1996) 'Introduction', in M. Reinfelder (ed.) *Amazon to Zami: Towards a Global Lesbian Feminism*, London: Cassell, pp. 1–10.

Retzinger, S. (1991) *Violent Emotions: Shame and Rage in Marital Quarrels*, London: Sage Publications.

Ribeiro, G. L. (1998) 'Cybercultural politics: political activism at a distance in a transnational world', in S. Alvarez, E. Dagnino and A. Escobar (eds) *Cultures of Politics/Politics of Culture: Revisioning Latin American Social Movements*, Boulder, CO: Westview Press, pp. 325–52.

Rich, A. (1986) 'Compulsory heterosexuality and lesbian existence', in A. Rich, *Blood, Bread and Poetry: Selected Prose 1979–1985*, New York: W. W. Norton & Co.

Richards, A. (1992) [1956] *Chisungu: A Girl's Initiation Ceremony among the Bemba of Zambia*, London: Routledge.

Rifkin, J. (1998) *The Biotech Century: Harnessing the Gene and Remaking the World*, New York: Penguin Putnam.

— (2000) *The Age of Access: The New Culture of Hypercapitalism, Where All of Life is a Paid-for Experience*, New York: J. P. Tarcher/Putnam.

Rixecker, S. (2000), personal communication.

Rocheleau, D., B. Thomas-Slater and E. Wangari (eds) (1996) *Feminist Political Ecology*, New York: Routledge.

Rodríguez Pereyra, R. (2001) 'Estereotipos gay en la literature y el cine Argentino', paper presented at the Seminar on the Acquisition of Latin American Library Materials (SALALM), Tempe, AZ (26–29 May).

Rose, K. (1992) *Where Women are Leaders*, London: Zed Books.

Rosenbloom, R. (1995) 'Introduction', in R. Rosenbloom (ed.) *Unspoken Rules: Sexual Orientation and Women's Human Rights*, San Francisco: International Gay and Lesbian Human Rights Commission (IGLHRC), pp. ix–xxvii.

— (ed.) (1995a) *Unspoken Rules: Sexual Orientation and Women's Human Rights*, San Francisco, CA: International Gay and Lesbian Human Rights Commission (IGLHRC).

Ross, J. (2000) *The War Against Oblivion: Zapatista Chronicles 1994–2000*, reprinted as 'Homophobia reignited in PAN-ista Mexico', *Weekly News Update on the Americas* (14 October).

Rost, J. (1993) *Leadership for the Twenty-First Century*, New York: Praeger.

Rowlands, J. (1994) 'Empowerment examined', in D. Eade (series ed.) *Development with*

Women: Selected Essays from Development in Practice, London: Oxfam GB, pp. 141–50.

— (1998) 'A word of the times, but what does it mean? Empowerment in the discourse and practice of development', in H. Afshar (ed.) Women and Empowerment: Illustrations from the Third World, London: Macmillan, pp. 11–34.

Rozman, G. (1991) The East Asian Region: Confucian Heritage and its Modern Adaptation, Princeton, NJ: Princeton University Press.

Rusnak, J. (director) (1999) The Thirteenth Floor [videocassette], USA: Columbia.

Russell, M. D. (1997) The Sparrow, London: Black Swan.

— (1998) Children of God, London: Black Swan.

Sachs, W. (1997) 'Ecology, justice and the end of development', Development 40 (2): 8–15.

Said, E. W. (1984) 'The future of criticism', Modern Language Notes 99 (4): 951–8.

Sangari, K. and S. Vaid (eds) (1989) Recasting Women: Essays in Colonial History, Delhi: Kali for Women.

Sarkar, T. (1994) 'Women, community, and nation: a historical trajectory for Hindu identity politics', in P. Jeffery and A. Basu (eds) Appropriating Gender: Women's Activism and Politicized Religion in South Asia, London: Routledge, pp. 89–104.

Sarkis, M. (1995) 'Female genital mutilation: an introduction', http://www.fgmnetwork.org/intro/fgmintro.html

Sarr, F., H. Ba, and M. Sourang (1997) Genre et intervention sociale: quelle approche dans le contexte sénégalais, Dakar: Editions nord-sud.

Sassen, S. (1998) Globalization and its Discontents, New York: The New Press.

Schech, S. and J. Haggis (2000) Culture and Development: A Critical Introduction, Oxford: Blackwell.

Scheff, T. (1994) Bloody Revenge: Emotions, Nationalism, and War, San Francisco, CA: Westview Press.

Scheff, T. and S. Retzinger (1991) Emotions and Violence: Shame and Rage in Destructive Conflicts, Lexington, MD: Lexington Books.

Schild, V. (1998) 'New subjects of rights? Women's movements and the construction of citizenship in the "new democracies"', in S. Alvarez, E. Dagnino and A. Escobar (eds) Cultures of Politics/Politics of Cultures: Re-visioning Latin American Social Movements, Boulder, CO: Westview Press, pp. 93–117.

Schuyler, N. (1996) 'It's not just e-male', Working Woman 21 (6): 38–43.

Schwartz, P. (1996) The Art of the Long View: Planning for the Future in an Uncertain World, New York: Currency Doubleday.

Schwartz, S. A. (2000) 'Everyman an Übermensch: the culture of cultural studies', Substance 29 (1): 104–38.

Scott, A. (ed.) (1999) The Politics of GM Food: Risk, Science, and Public Trust. Special Briefing No. 5, ESRC Global Environmental Change Programme, Sussex.

Scott, J. W. (1988) Gender and the Politics of Women's History, New York: Columbia University Press.

Sedgwick, E. (1990) Epistemology of the Closet, Berkeley: University of California Press.

— (1993) Tendencies, Durham, NC: Duke University Press.

Sen, A. (1985) Commodities and Capabilities, Oxford: Oxford University Press.

— (1990) 'Gender and co-operative conflicts', in I. Tinker (ed.) Persistent Inequalities: Women and World Development, Oxford: Oxford University Press, pp. 123–49.

— (1992, 1995) *Inequality Re-examined*, Cambridge, MA: Harvard University Press, and Oxford: Clarendon Press.

— (2000) *Development as Freedom*, New York: Alfred A. Knopf.

Sen, G. and C. Grown (1987) *Development, Crisis, and Alternative Visions: Third World Women's Perspectives*, New York: Monthly Review Press.

Shayne, Julie D. (2000) '"The Revolution Question": Feminism in Cuba, Chile, and El Salvador Compared (1952–1999)', PhD dissertation, Department of Sociology, University of California, Santa Barbara.

Shih, S. (1998) 'Gender and a new geopolitics of desire: the seduction of mainland women in Taiwan and Hong Kong media', *Signs* 23 (2): 287–319.

Shiva, V. (1988) *Staying Alive: Women, Ecology, and Survival*, New Delhi: Kali for Women.

— (1998) 'Monocultures, monopolies, myths and the masculinisation of agriculture', statement for the Policy Round Table on 'Women's Knowledge, Biotechnology and International Trade – Fostering a New Dialogue into the Millennium' during the International Conference on Women in Agriculture, Washington (June 28–July 2).

— (2000) 'Poverty and globalisation', BBC Reith Lectures 2000 at http://news.bbc.co.uk/hi/english/static/events/reith_2000/lecture5.stm

Shohat, E. and R. Stam (1994) 'From eurocentrism to polycentrism', in E. Shohat and R. Stam, *Unthinking Eurocentrism: Multiculturalism and the Media*, London: Routledge, pp. 13–54.

— (1994a) *Unthinking Eurocentrism: Multiculturalism and the Media*, London: Routledge.

Singh, T. (1998) 'Beware the nuclear yogis', *India Today* (1 June).

Sinha, M. (2000) 'Refashioning Mother India: feminism and nationalism in late-colonial India', *Feminist Studies* 26 (3): 623–44.

Sittirak, S. (1998) *The Daughters of Development: Women and the Changing Environment*, London: Zed Books.

Skocpol, T. (1979) *States and Social Revolutions: A Comparative Analysis of France, Russia, and China*, Cambridge: Cambridge University Press.

Smith, A. (1994) 'Césaire au féminin: où et comment chercher la femme dans son oeuvre?' *Oeuvres et critiques* 19 (2): 377–87.

Smith, C. (1996) 'What is this thing called queer?' in D. Morton (ed.) *The Material Queer*, Boulder, CO: Westview Press, pp. 277–85.

Snyder, M. C. and M. Tadesse (1995) *African Women and Development: A History*, Johannesburg: Witwatersrand University Press/London: Zed Books.

Spender, D. (1995) *Nattering on the Net: Women, Power and Cyberspace*, Melbourne: Spinifex.

Spivak, G. C. (1999) *A Critique of Postcolonial Reason: Toward a History of the Vanishing Present*, Cambridge, MA: Harvard University Press.

Srinivas, S. (1997) 'Self-Employed Women's Association (SEWA) of India paving the way for women's economic progress', *Women and Money* (June).

Stephanson, A. (1988) 'Regarding postmodernism: a conversation with Fredric Jameson', in A. Ross (ed.) *Universal Abandon? The Politics of Postmodernism*, Twin Cities: University of Minnesota Press, pp. 3–30.

Stettbacher, K. (1990) *Wenn Leiden einen Sinn haben soll* [If Suffering is to Have a Meaning], Hamburg: Hoffmann & Campe.

Sturgeon, N. (1999) 'Ecofeminist appropriations and transnational environmentalisms', *Identities* 6 (2–3): 255–79.

Subramaniam, B. (2000) 'Archaic modernities: science, secularism, and religion in modern India', *Social Text* 18 (3) (Fall): 67–86.

Swaminathan, P. (1991) 'Gender in Indian planning: a critique', in S. L. Raj (ed.) *Quest for Gender Justice*, Madras: Satya Nilayam Publications, pp. 53–68.

Swarup, H., N. Sinha, C. Ghosh and P. Rajput (1994) 'Women's political engagements in India: some critical issues', in B. J. Nelson and N. Chowdhury (eds) *Women and Politics World Wide*, New Haven, CT and London: Yale University Press, pp. 361–79.

Swyngedouw, E. (1997) 'Neither global nor local: glocalisation and the politics of scale', in K. Cox (ed.) *Spaces of Globalization: Reasserting the Power of the Local*, New York: Guilford Press, pp. 137–66.

Tai, H. (1989) *Confucianism and Economic Development*, Washington, DC: The Washington Institute Press.

Taneja, N. (2000) 'Communalisation of education in India: an update', *Akhbàr: A Window on South Asia* 1 (February), at http://wzw.xitami.net/indowindow/akhbar

Taylor, D. (1997) *Disappearing Acts: Spectacles of Gender and Nationalism in Argentina's 'Dirty War'*, Durham, NC: Duke University Press.

Terr, L. (1990) *Too Scared to Cry: Psychic Trauma in Childhood*, New York: HarperCollins.

— (1994) *Unchained Memories: True Stories of Traumatic Memories, Lost and Found*, New York: HarperCollins.

Testart, J. (2000) 'Be careful, take precautions: how to let ordinary people in on the future', translated by Jerry Cook-Radmore, *Le Monde Diplomatique* (September): 14–15, at http://mondediplo-com/2000/09

Thadani, G. (1996) 'Jami or lesbian?' in M. Reinfelder (ed.) *Amazon to Zami: Towards a Global Lesbian Feminism*, London: Cassell, pp. 56–69.

Thayer, M. (1997) 'Identity, revolution and democracy: lesbian movements in Central America', *Social Problems* 44 (3): 386–407.

Thomas, S. (ed.) (2000) *Dark Matter: A Century of Speculative Fiction from the African Diaspora*, New York: Warner Books.

Thompson, E. P. (1963) *The Making of the English Working Class*, New York: Vintage.

Tinker, I. (ed.) (1990) *Persistent Inequalities: Women and World Development*, New York: Oxford University Press.

— (1990a) 'The making of a field: advocates, practitioners and scholars', in I. Tinker (ed.) *Persistent Inequalities: Women and World Development*, New York: Oxford University Press, pp. 27–53.

Truong, T. (1990) *Sex, Money and Morality: Prostitution and Tourism in Southeast Asia*, London: Zed Books.

Tsing, A. L. (1993) *In the Realm of the Diamond Queen: Marginality in an Out-of-the-Way Place*, Princeton, NJ: Princeton University Press.

Turner, G. (1987) *The Sea and Summer*, London: Grafton.

Uberoi, P. (1996) 'Introduction: problematizing social reform, engaging sexuality, interrogating the state', in P. Uberoi (ed.) *Social Reform, Sexuality and the State*, New Delhi: Sage Publications, pp. ix–xxvi.

Umeh, M. (ed.) (1998) *Emerging Perspectives on Flora Nwapa: Critical and Theoretical Essays*, Trenton: Africa World Press.

Underhill-Sem, Y. (2000) '(Not) Speaking of maternities: pregnancy and childbirth in Wanigela, Oro Province, Papua New Guinea', PhD dissertation, Department of Geography, University of Waikato, Hamilton, New Zealand.

Ungar, M. (2000) 'Constitutionalism and LGBT rights in Latin America', paper presented at the Congress of the Latin American Studies Association, Miami, FL (March).

United Nations Development Programme [UNDP] (1999) *Human Development Report*, New York: UNDP and Oxford University Press.

Urquhart, B. (2000) 'In the name of humanity', *New York Review of Books* (April 27): 22–5.

Vanaik, A. (1997) *The Furies of Communalism: Religion, Modernity, and Secularism*, New York: Verso.

Vandegrift, D. (1993) *Perspectivas de la mujer Bribri: su situación actual y su participación organizativa en Talamanca*, San José, Costa Rica: Librería San Pedro.

— (2001) 'Paradise under Development: Social Inequality and Memory in a Costa Rican Caribbean Tourist Economy', PhD dissertation, Department of Sociology, University of California, Santa Barbara.

Van der Heijden, K. (1996) *Scenarios: The Art of Strategic Conversation*, Chichester: John Wiley & Son.

van der Veer, P. (1994) *Religious Nationalisms: Hindus and Muslims in India*, Berkeley: University of California Press.

Vargas, V. (1992) *Cómo cambiar el mundo sin perdernos*, Lima: Centro Flora Tristan.

Verschuur, G. L. (1996) *Impact! The Threat of Comets and Asteroids*, New York: Oxford University Press.

'VHP firm on Pokharan temple, BJP silent' (1998) *Indian Express* (21 May).

Vivekananda, Swami (1992) *The Complete Works of Swami Vivekananda*, twelfth reprint, Calcutta: Advaita Ashrama.

Vogel, E. (1991) *The Four Little Dragons: The Spread of Industrialization in East Asia*, Cambridge, MA: Harvard University Press.

Wachowski, A. and L Wachowski (directors) (1999) *The Matrix* [videocassette], USA: Warner Brothers.

Wajcman, J. (1995) 'Feminist theories of technology', in S. Jasanoff, G. Markle, J. Petersen and T. Pinch (eds) *Handbook of Science and Technology Studies*, Thousand Oaks, CA: Sage Publications, pp. 189–204.

Walker, A. (1997) *Anything We Love Can Be Saved: A Writer's Activism*, New York: Random House.

Wang Tuo (1979) [1975] 'Jinshuishen', in *Jinshuishen*, Taipei: Xiangcaoshan chubanshe, pp. 189–256.

— (1978) [1977] 'Shi "xianshi zhuyi" wenxue, bushi "xiangtu wenxue"' [It is 'realist literature', not 'native place' literature], in T. Yu (ed.) *Xiangtu wenxue taolun ji* [Collection on the Native Place Literature debate], Taipei: Yuanliu Publishers, pp. 100–19.

Wang Zhenhe (1975) [1973] 'Xiaolin lai Taibei' [Xiaolin came to Taipei], in *Jiazhuang yi niuche*, Taipei: Yuanjing chubanshe, pp. 219–49.

Webdunia [On-line] (2000) Available: http://www.webdunia.com (December 12).

Williams, R. (1960) *Culture and Society 1780–1950*, London: Chatto & Windus.

— (1989) 'Culture is ordinary', in R. Williams, *Resources of Hope: Culture, Democracy, Socialism*, R. Gable (ed.), London: Verso, pp. 3–18.

— (1989a) 'Socialism and ecology', in R. Williams, *Resources of Hope: Culture, Democracy, Socialism*, R. Gable (ed.), London: Verso, pp. 210–26.

— (1989b) 'Commitment', in R. Williams, *What I Came to Say*, London: Hutchinson Radius, pp. 256–60.

— (1995) [1981] *Sociology of Culture*, Chicago, IL: University of Chicago Press.

Wilson, E. (1992) *The Sphinx in the City: Urban Life, the Control of Disorder, and Women*, Berkeley: University of California Press.

Wired Magazine at http://www.wired.com/wired/scenarios/build.html

Wired Tools (2000) *Wired* 8 (12 December).

Wolff, H. E. (1999) 'Multilingualism, modernisation, and mother tongue: promoting democracy through indigenous African languages', *Social Dynamics* 25 (1): 31–50.

World Bank (1991) *Gender and Poverty in India: A World Bank Country Study*, Washington, DC: The World Bank.

— (1992) *World Development Report 1992: Development and the Environment*, New York: Oxford University Press.

— (1994) *Enhancing Women's Participation in Economic Development: A Policy Paper*, Washington, DC: The World Bank.

— (2000) *The World Bank Annual Report 1999*, Washington, DC: The World Bank.

Wright, T. (2000) 'Gay organizations, NGOs and the globalization of sexual identity: the case of Bolivia', *Journal of Latin American Anthropology* 5 (2): 89–111.

Yang Qingchu (1978) *Gongchang nu'er quan* [The circle of factory girls], Gaoxiong: Dunli chubanshe.

Young, I. M. (1994) 'Gender as seriality: thinking about women as a social collective', *Signs* 19 (3): 187–215.

— (1997) 'Unruly categories: a critique of Nancy Fraser's dual systems theory', *New Left Review*, 222: 147–60.

Youssef, N. (1995) 'Women's access to productive resources: the need for legal instruments to protect women's development rights', in J. Peters and A. Wolper (eds) *Women's Rights, Human Rights*, New York: Routledge, pp. 279–88.

Yuval-Davis, N. and F. Anthias (eds) (1989) *Woman–Nation–State*, London: Macmillan.

Zaretsky, E. (1976) *Capitalism, the Family and Personal Life*, New York: Harper & Row.

Zeng Xinyi (1977) 'Yige shijiushui shaonu de gushi' [The story of a nineteen year-old girl], in *Wo ai boshi*, Taipei: Yuanjing, pp. 95–156.

— (1977a) 'Wo de xiezuo guocheng' [My writing process], in *Wo ai boshi*, Taipei: Yuanjing, pp. 11–14.

— (1978) 'Caifeng de xinyuan' [Caifeng's wish], in *Caifeng de xinyuan*, Taipei: Yuanjing, pp. 1–42.

Index